MCTS Guide to Microsoft® Windows Server® 2008 Applications Infrastructure Configuration (Exam # 70-643)

MCTS Guide to Microsoft® Windows Server® 2008 Applications Infrastructure Configuration (Exam # 70-643)

John E. Tucker
Darrel Nerove
Greg Tomsho
Matt Tomsho
Jack Hogue

COURSE TECHNOLOGY
CENGAGE Learning·

Australia • Brazil • Japan • Korea • Mexico • Singapore • Spain • United Kingdom • United States

COURSE TECHNOLOGY
CENGAGE Learning

MCTS Guide to Microsoft® Windows Server® 2008 Applications Infrastructure Configuration (Exam # 70-643)

John E. Tucker, Darrel Nerove, Greg Tomsho, Matt Tomsho and Jack Hogue

Vice President, Editorial: Dave Garza

Executive Editor: Stephen Helba

Acquisitions Editor: Nick Lombardi

Managing Editor: Marah Bellegarde

Senior Product Manager:
Michelle Ruelos Cannistraci

Developmental Editor: Deb Kaufmann

Editorial Assistant: Sarah Pickering

Vice President, Marketing: Jennifer Ann Baker

Marketing Director: Deborah Yarnell

Senior Marketing Manager: Mark Linton

Associate Marketing Manager: Erica Ropitzky

Production Director: Wendy Troeger

Production Manager: Andrew Crouth

Senior Content Project Manager: Andrea Majot

Art Director: Jack Pendleton

Technology Project Manager: Joseph Pliss

© 2012 Course Technology, Cengage Learning 2007, 2004, 2002, 2000

ALL RIGHTS RESERVED. No part of this work covered by the copyright herein may be reproduced, transmitted, stored or used in any form or by any means graphic, electronic, or mechanical, including but not limited to photocopying, recording, scanning, digitizing, taping, Web distribution, information networks, or information storage and retrieval systems, except as permitted under Section 107 or 108 of the 1976 United States Copyright Act, without the prior written permission of the publisher.

For product information and technology assistance, contact us at
Cengage Learning Customer & Sales Support, 1-800-354-9706

For permission to use material from this text or product, submit all requests online at **cengage.com/permissions.** Further permissions questions can be e-mailed to **permissionrequest@cengage.com.**

Library of Congress Control Number: 2011933982

ISBN-13: 978-1-4239-0237-9

ISBN-10: 1-4239-0237-8

Course Technology
20 Channel Center Street
Boston, MA 02210
USA

Cengage Learning is a leading provider of customized learning solutions with office locations around the globe, including Singapore, the United Kingdom, Australia, Mexico, Brazil, and Japan. Locate your local office at: **international.cengage.com/region**

Cengage Learning products are represented in Canada by Nelson Education, Ltd.

For your lifelong learning solutions, visit **www.cengage.com/coursetechnology**

Purchase any of our products at your local college store or at our preferred online store **www.cengagebrain.com**

Visit our corporate website at **www.cengage.com**

Notice to the Reader

Some of the product names and company names used in this book have been used for identification purposes only and may be trademarks or registered trademarks of their respective manufacturers and sellers. Microsoft and the Office logo are either registered trademarks or trademarks of Microsoft Corporation in the United States and/or other countries. Course Technology, a part of Cengage Learning, is an independent entity from the Microsoft Corporation, and not affiliated with Microsoft in any manner. Any fictional data related to persons or companies or URLs used throughout this book is intended for instructional purposes only. At the time this book was printed, any such data was fictional and not belonging to any real persons or companies. Course Technology and the Course Technology logo are registered trademarks used under license. Course Technology, a part of Cengage Learning, reserves the right to revise this publication and make changes from time to time in its content without notice. The programs in this book are for instructional purposes only. They have been tested with care, but are not guaranteed for any particular intent beyond educational purposes. The author and the publisher do not offer any warranties or representations, nor do they accept any liabilities with respect to the programs.

Printed in the United States of America
1 2 3 4 5 6 7 14 13 12 11

Dedication

We dedicate this book to our families with deepest thanks for their support.

1 + 2 ⑧⓪

1.1 - 1.4
2.1 - 2.2 ㉒⓪

5

5.1-5.3 (60)

Introduction

MCTS Guide to Microsoft® Windows Server® 2008 Applications Infrastructure Configuration (Exam # 70-643) provides coverage of the 70-643 certification exam objectives and provides the skills needed to properly configure an application infrastructure. Windows Server 2008 offers more server roles, more flexibility, more security, and more manageability than any previous Microsoft server operating system. With this book, you gain an in-depth understanding of Windows Server 2008 application infrastructure configuration.

Each chapter is written for easy understanding and contains numerous hands-on activities to help your learning come to life. *MCTS Guide to Microsoft® Windows Server® 2008 Applications Infrastructure Configuration (Exam # 70-643)* includes an evaluation DVD so that you can install Windows Server 2008 R2 and complete the hands-on activities. The hands-on activities give you the experience you need to truly learn Windows Server 2008 and retain what you have learned.

The goals of this book are to give you the knowledge and confidence to be able to configure a Server 2008 application infrastructure and to provide the foundation for taking Exam 70-643: Windows Server 2008 Applications Infrastructure, Configuring.

Intended Audience

MCTS Guide to Microsoft® Windows Server® 2008 Applications Infrastructure Configuration (Exam # 70-643) is intended for people who want to learn to configure a Server 2008 application infrastructure. The focus is to give new and experienced users alike the opportunity to study in depth the core technologies and features of Windows Server 2008 and those features that relate to configuring and application infrastructure. The book is an excellent text for classroom teaching, but self-paced learners will also find that it is written in clear, easy-to-understand language with a wealth of hands-on activities and case studies for mastery of the topic.

This Book Includes:

- A Windows Server 2008 R2 Standard, Enterprise, and Datacenter evaluation DVD (bundled with the book) which can be installed directly on a computer or installed in a virtual machine, such as in Microsoft Hyper-V, Microsoft Virtual PC 2007, Microsoft Virtual Server, or VMware Server.

- Step-by-step hands-on activities for learning nearly every phase of Windows Server 2008 application infrastructure configuration, with all activities tested by a technical editor, reviewers, and validation experts.

- Best practices listed at the end of each chapter, describing best practices from the practical application and configuration of an application infrastructure.

- Extensive review and end-of-chapter materials to strengthen your learning.

- Coverage of Windows Server 2008 Release 2 (R2) enhancements.

- Abundant screen captures and graphics to visually reinforce the text and hands-on activities.

Chapter Descriptions

The chapters are balanced to provide you with a thorough understanding of Windows Server 2008 application infrastructure configuration along with preparation for Exam 70-643. The first chapter introduces fundamental Server 2008 topics and concepts. The remaining chapters focus on topics specific to configuring a Server 2008 application infrastructure.

- **Chapter 1,** "Introducing Windows Server 2008," covers many of the new features and capabilities within Windows Server 2008, including the Windows Server 2008 editions, hardware requirements, migration considerations, enhancements, roles and features, planning phases, and application infrastructure tools and capabilities. It also gives step-by-step instructions for installing Windows Server 2008 R2.

- **Chapter 2,** "Deploying Windows Servers," shows you how to use the Windows Server 2008 Windows Deployment Services (WDS) to automatically and remotely install supported Windows operating systems over a network. You will also learn how to add boot images and install images to Windows Deployment Services and enable Volume Activation using a Multiple Activation Key (MAK) or Key Management Service (KMS). This approach can save time and money over individual DVD-based installations, and enables servers to be configured and deployed in a consistent manner.

- **Chapter 3,** "Configuring Windows Server 2008 Storage Services," shows you how to use the various storage management tools and utilities in Windows Server 2008 to effectively manage storage requirements in an enterprise network, provide fault-tolerance and data recovery solutions, and provide quality of service solutions giving priority based on application or criticality of the data. You will become familiar with the Disk Management console, create new volumes and partitions, add mirrors to a volume, create mount points, install multipath I/O (MPIO), describe and configure the Microsoft Internet Small Computer System Interface (iSCSI) Software Initiator, and learn about storage area network (SAN) capabilities in Windows Server 2008.

- **Chapter 4,** "Windows Server 2008 Remote Desktop Services, Part 1," shows you how to use the Remote Desktop Services capabilities in Windows Server 2008, including Remote Desktop Connection settings and Desktop Experience enhancements, publishing remote applications, packaging Remote Desktop Services RemoteApp programs, RD Web Access, and the RD Gateway.

- **Chapter 5,** "Windows Server 2008 Remote Desktop Services, Part 2," covers additional Remote Desktop Services concepts and capabilities within Windows Server 2008, including additional tools for managing the Remote Desktop Connection Host, monitoring and terminating processes and user sessions, additional Remote Desktop Gateway configurations, the Remote Desktop Connection Broker, and Remote Desktop Licensing.

- **Chapter 6,** "Configuring Windows Server 2008 Web Services, Part 1," covers creating and configuring Web applications, managing Web sites using IIS7 including publishing, configuring virtual directories and migrating sites, creating and configuring FTP 6 and FTP 7 sites, and configuring SMTP virtual servers.

- **Chapter 7,** "Configuring Windows Server 2008 Web Services, Part 2," shows you how to back up and restore IIS Web site configurations and monitor the performance of an IIS Web site plus configure Web site security including SSL certificates, site authentication, and site and application permissions.

- **Chapter 8,** "Configuring Windows Server 2008 Network Application Services," shows you how to install and configure a Windows Media Server, stream broadcast and on-demand content, and use cache and proxy streaming to maximize performance; in addition you learn to install and use Active Directory Rights Management Service and configure a wide variety of Windows SharePoint options.

- **Chapter 9,** "Configuring Windows Server 2008 Hyper-V Virtualization," covers common virtualization terms and describes the role of virtualization in the datacenter; in addition you install and use the Hyper-V role and create and manage Hyper-V virtual machines and manage the virtual environment including virtual networks and virtual storage options.

- **Chapter 10,** "Configuring Windows Server 2008 for High Availability," describes Windows Server 2008 high availability technologies including round-robin DNS, network load balancing, and failover clusters. You will create and configure an NLB cluster and a server farm using failover clusters.

- **Appendix A,** "70-643 Exam Objectives," lists the objectives for the 70-643 Windows Server 2008 Applications Infrastructure Configuration certification exam and references the chapters and sections in the book that cover each objective.

Features

To help you better understand how Microsoft Windows Server 2008 Application Infrastructure Configuration concepts and techniques are applied in real-world organizations and to help you master information for the 70-643 exam, this book includes the following learning features:

- *Chapter objectives*—Each chapter begins with a detailed list of the concepts to be mastered. This list provides you with a quick reference to the chapter's contents and is a useful study aid.

- *Hands-on activities*—Numerous hands-on activities are incorporated throughout the text, giving you practice in configuring a Server 2008 application infrastructure. The activities give you a strong foundation for carrying out server tasks in the real world.

- *Screen captures, illustrations, and tables*—Numerous reproductions of screens and illustrations of concepts aid you in the visualization of theories, concepts, and how to use tools and features.

- *Chapter summary*—Each chapter's text is followed by a summary of the concepts introduced in the chapter. These summaries provide a helpful way to recap and revisit the ideas covered in each chapter.

- *Best practices*—Each chapter contains a list of best practices for implementing and configuring a Server 2008 application infrastructure.

- *Key terms*—All of the terms within the chapter that were introduced with boldfaced text are gathered together in the Key Terms list at the end of the chapter. This provides you with a method of checking your understanding of all of the terms introduced.

- *Review questions*—The end-of-chapter assessment begins with a set of review questions that reinforce the ideas introduced in each chapter. Answering these questions helps ensure that you have mastered the important concepts.

- *Case projects*—Each chapter closes with several case projects. In realistic case examples, you apply the skills and knowledge gained in the chapter through real-world scenarios.

- *On the DVD*—On the DVD you will find a free 120-day evaluation copy of Microsoft Windows Server 2008.

Text and Graphic Conventions

Additional information and exercises have been added to this book to help you better understand what's being discussed in the chapter. Icons throughout the text alert you to these additional materials. The icons used in this book are described below:

 Tips offer extra information on resources, how to attack problems, and time-saving shortcuts.

 Notes present additional helpful material related to the subject being discussed.

 The Caution icon identifies important information about potential mistakes or hazards.

 Each Hands-on activity in this book is preceded by the Activity icon.

 Case Project icons mark the end-of-chapter case projects, which are scenario-based assignments that ask you to apply what you have learned in the chapter.

CertBlaster Test Prep Resources

MCTS Guide to Microsoft® Windows Server® 2008 Applications Infrastructure Configuration (Exam # 70-643) includes CertBlaster test preparation questions that mirror the look and feel of the CompTIA Security+ certification exam. For additional information on the CertBlaster test preparation questions, go to http://www.dtipublishing.com.

To log in and access the CertBlaster test preparation questions for the MCTS 70-643 Exam, please go to http://www.certblaster.com/cengage.htm.

To install CertBlaster:

1. Click the title of the CertBlaster test prep application you want to download.

2. Save the program (.EXE) file to a folder on your C: drive. (Warning: If you skip this step, your CertBlaster will not install correctly.)

3. Click Start and choose Run.

4. Click Browse and then navigate to the folder that contains the .EXE file. Select the .EXE file and click Open.

5. Click OK and then follow the on-screen instructions.

6. When the installation is complete, click Finish.

7. Click Start, choose All programs, and click CertBlaster.

To register CertBlaster:

1. Open the CertBlaster test you want by double-clicking it.

2. In the menu bar, click File > Register Exam and enter the access code when prompted. Use the access code provided inside the card placed in the back of this book

Instructor Resources

The following supplemental materials are available when this book is used in a classroom setting. All of the supplements available with this book are provided to the instructor on a single CD, called the Instructor's Resource CD (ISBN: 978-1-1111-2995-8).

- *Electronic Instructor's Manual*—The Instructor's Manual that accompanies this book includes additional instructional material to assist in class preparation, including suggestions for classroom activities, discussion topics, and additional activities.

- *Solutions*—The instructor's resources include solutions to all end-of-chapter material, including the review questions, hands-on activities, and case projects.

- *ExamView*—This textbook is accompanied by ExamView, a powerful testing software package that allows instructors to create and administer printed, computer (LAN-based), and Internet exams. ExamView includes hundreds of questions that correspond to the topics covered in this text, enabling students to generate detailed study guides that include page references for further review. The computer-based and Internet testing components allow students to take exams at their computers and to also save the instructor time by grading each exam automatically.

- *PowerPoint presentations*—This book comes with Microsoft PowerPoint slides for each chapter. These are included as a teaching aid for classroom presentation, to make available to students on the network for chapter review, or to be printed for classroom distribution. Instructors, please feel at liberty to add your own slides for additional topics you introduce to the class.

- *Figure files*—All of the figures and tables in the book are reproduced on the Instructor's Resource CD, in bitmap format. Similar to the PowerPoint presentations, these are included as a teaching aid for classroom presentation, to make available to students for review, or to be printed for classroom distribution.

Instructor's Resource CD ISBN: 978-1-1111-2995-8

Please visit **login.cengage.com** and log in to access instructor-specific resources.

To access additional course materials, please visit www.cengagebrain.com. At the CengageBrain.com home page, search for the ISBN of your title (from the back cover of your book) using the search box at the top of the page. This will take you to the product page where these resources can be found.

Additional materials designed especially for you might be available for your course online. Go to www.cengage.com/coursetechnology and search for this book title periodically for more details.

System Requirements

Hardware

- Listed in the Windows Server Catalog of Tested Products or has the Certified for Windows Server 2008 sticker
- 1 GHz CPU or faster for an x86 computer or 1.4 GHz CPU or faster for an x64 computer (2 GHz or faster is recommended)
- 512 MB RAM or more (for x86 and x64 computers), but 2 GB or more is recommended
- 15 GB or more disk space (for x86 and x64 computers)
- DVD-ROM drive
- Super VGA or higher resolution monitor
- Mouse or pointing device
- Keyboard
- Network interface card connected to the classroom, lab, or school network for on-ground students—or Internet access (plus a network interface card installed) for online students

Software

- Windows Server 2008 Standard or Enterprise Edition (included with the DVD in the book)

Acknowledgments

We are very grateful for the outstanding and professional support provided by the Course Technology/Cengage Learning staff in the development of this textbook (Nick Lombardi, the Acquisitions Editor; Michelle Ruelos Cannistraci, the Senior Product Manager; Deb Kaufmann, the Developmental Editor; Andrea Majot, Senior Content Project Manager; Danielle Shaw, Technical Editor and Contributor; and John Bosco, for providing Quality Assurance).

We would also like to thank the following reviewers: Jared Spencer, Marcia Thompson, and Daniel Ziesmer.

We would also like to thank our families for the continued support they provided to us through the development of this textbook.

About the Authors

Darrel Nerove

Darrel Nerove has worked in the IT field for over 20 years in multiple areas of IT, including networking, internetworking, programming, and security. He was the Network Control Manager at the Pentagon and has been a Network Engineer and Systems Engineer on many Microsoft Server 2003 and Microsoft Server 2008 deployments in support of government and Department of Defense contracts. Additionally, Darrel teaches IT courses at the college and university level in the Northern Virginia area and online.

John E. Tucker

John E. Tucker holds graduate and undergraduate degrees from The American University and Strayer University and has more than 34 years of experience in Higher Education, Information Technology, Government, and Business. John has held positions as Provost, Chief Academic Officer, Senior Academic Officer, Chief Architect, Vice President of Information Systems, Director of Systems Engineering, Dean of Curriculum Development, Dean of Academic Technology, Director of Operations, Campus Director, and Campus Dean.

Greg Tomsho

Greg Tomsho has more than 25 years of computer networking experience and has earned the CCNA, MCITP, MCTS, MCSA, A+, Security+, and Linux+ certifications. Greg is the director of the Computer Networking Technology Department and Cisco Academy at Yavapai College in Prescott, Arizona. His other books include *MCTS Guide to Microsoft® Windows Server® 2008 Active Directory Configuration*, *Guide to Networking Essentials*, and *Guide to Network Support and Troubleshooting*.

Matt Tomsho

Matt Tomsho has over 30 years of computer programming and networking experience working with Microsoft Windows®. Currently an independent database consultant specializing in Web-based applications based in Pittsburgh, Pennsylvania, Matt has been IT Director at several Internet companies, managing Web and database servers running both Windows and Linux.

Jack Hogue

Jack Hogue has over 21 years of computing and network experience. He currently specializes in Microsoft Windows® environments and also supports integration of Mac and Linux in those networks. Jack began his first Web hosting business in 1995 and has since hosted streaming media and web applications. He is a Microsoft Certified Professional (MCP) and is also A+ certified. Jack has been the co-owner of his current IT services business (Chordata Technologies located in Pittsburgh, Pennsylvania) for more than 8 years with over 150 clients across the United States and Canada.

MCTS Guide to Microsoft® Windows Server® 2008 Applications Infrastructure Configuration (Exam # 70-643)

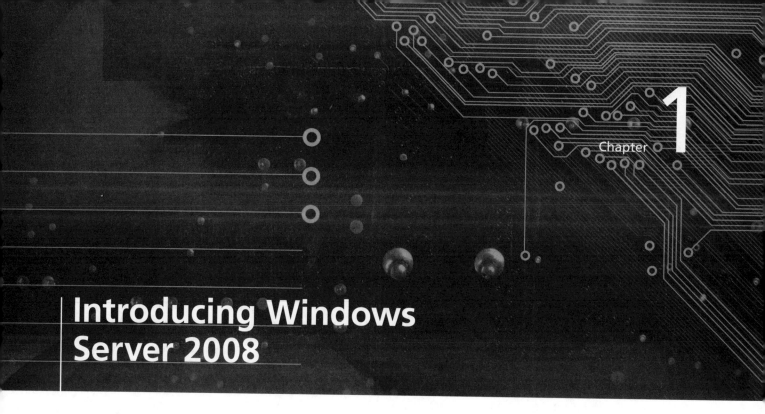

Chapter 1

Introducing Windows Server 2008

After reading this chapter and completing the exercises, you will be able to:

- Distinguish among the different Windows Server 2008 editions based on organizational needs
- Describe Windows Server 2008 hardware requirements
- Discuss reasons for migrating from Windows Server 2003 to Server 2008
- Describe new Windows Server 2008 enhancements
- Describe Windows Server 2008 roles and features
- Describe the basic planning phases for a Windows Server 2008 implementation
- Provide an overview of the primary application infrastructure tools and capabilities of Windows Server 2008

Windows Server 2008 includes many new features designed to elevate organizations from small businesses to enterprise networks. This book covers Microsoft Windows Server 2008 Applications Infrastructure features and concepts. Additionally, this book helps you prepare for the MCTS Exam #70-643: Microsoft Windows Server 2008 Applications Infrastructure Configuration.

This first chapter introduces many of the new features and capabilities within Windows Server 2008, including the Windows Server 2008 editions, hardware requirements, migration considerations, enhancements, roles and features, planning phases, and application infrastructure tools and capabilities. It also gives step-by-step instructions for installing Windows Server 2008.

Windows Server Editions

Windows Server 2008 provides the tools and capabilities needed for all businesses from small companies to large, enterprise-level organizations. Microsoft offers three general editions of Server 2008: Standard, Enterprise, and Datacenter. Web Server and High-Performance Computing (HPC) are two additional editions that are designed for special-purpose server applications.

Each edition, except HPC, is available for 32-bit and 64-bit processors; HPC is only available for 64-bit processors. Installations include full installation, which includes all options and features, and Server Core, which includes a minimal installation that is designed to provide a hardened, secure system. The different editions and Server Core will be discussed in more detail in upcoming sections.

 Windows Server 2008 was released in February, 2009. A second release, Windows Server 2008 R2, was released in July, 2009. This text is based on Windows Server 2008 R2.

Windows Server 2008 Standard Edition

The Standard edition (SE) is designed for smaller networks and for single-purpose installations. It is an entry-level edition that provides the tools and features needed to run your network. The Standard edition can be suitable in small business networks, as well as for special purposes in large business networks. The Standard edition works as a single domain server, which would be suitable for a smaller business network. This edition would also be suitable for a single file/application server in a larger network. Common features supported by the Standard edition include:

- File and Print Services
- Internet Information Services (IIS) 7.0
- Active Directory
- Distributed and Encrypting File Systems
- Management Tools
- Network load balancing (added to the Standard edition in Server 2008)

Windows Server 2008 Enterprise Edition

When deciding between the Standard edition and the Enterprise edition, organizations will typically be deciding between cost and functionality. The Enterprise edition includes more functionality, but has an increased cost; however, the cost is often acceptable given the increased functionality. The Windows Server 2008 Enterprise edition (EE) includes the features available in the Standard edition and the following additional features:

- Increase in maximum allowable memory
- Active Directory Federation Services
- Failover clustering
- Installation of up to four virtual machines per physical host
- Hot-add memory

Windows Server 2008 Datacenter Edition

The Datacenter edition (DE) includes all of the features offered in the Enterprise edition with some additional capabilities. Additional features available in the Datacenter edition include:

- Ability to run up to 32 processors
- Ability to hot-add and replace processors
- Installation of unlimited virtual machines per physical host

Windows Web Server 2008

Windows Web Server 2008 provides an operating system designed as a single-purpose Web server, with the purpose of hosting Web sites and applications. The overall functionality of Windows Web Server 2008 is reduced to better accommodate the functionality of hosting Web sites and applications. Thus, many server roles, including Dynamic Host Configuration Protocol (DHCP), Domain Name System (DNS), and file server, are not available.

Web Server 2008 includes **Internet Information Services (IIS) 7.0, ASP.NET**, and the **.NET Framework** as part of the installation. Unlike other editions, Web Server 2008 does not require client access licenses (CALs) for users. The Web Server 2008 edition is available as a 32-bit and 64-bit operating system in the full version only; Server Core does not support the .NET Framework and ASP.NET.

Windows HPC Server 2008

Windows **High Performance Computing (HPC)** Server 2008 is designed to accommodate numerous processing cores; it is built on the 64-bit architecture. It is designed to support HPC applications.

Windows HPC Server 2008 is designed to support clients ranging from desktop applications to high-performance applications and fault tolerant clusters. Windows HPC Server 2008 provides a rich development environment for parallel programming supported by Visual Studio 2008, **Web Services**, and other third-party libraries.

Additionally, SQL Server is used as the repository for the Job Scheduler. The Job Scheduler queues, schedules, and monitors the status of jobs and their associated tasks. An existing SQL Server installation can be used, or Windows HPC Server 2008 will install SQL Express upon installation for this purpose.

Windows Server 2008 Edition Server Role Comparison

Table 1-1, based on Microsoft's Web site, compares server roles supported in the Enterprise, Datacenter, Standard, Web, and HPC editions of Windows Server 2008.

Table 1-1   Windows Server 2008 server role comparison

Server Role	Enterprise Edition	Datacenter Edition	Standard Edition	Web Edition	HPC Edition
Active Directory Certificate Services	X	X	X [1]		X [1]
Active Directory Domain Services	X	X	X		X
Active Directory Federation Services	X	X			
Active Directory Lightweight Directory Services	X	X	X		
Active Directory Rights Management Services	X	X	X		
Application Server	X	X	X		

(continues)

Table 1-1 Windows Server 2008 server role comparison (*continued*)

Server Role	Enterprise Edition	Datacenter Edition	Standard Edition	Web Edition	HPC Edition
DHCP Server	X	X	X		X
DNS Server	X	X	X	X	X
Fax Server	X	X	X		
File Services	X	X	X [2]		X [2]
Hyper-V	X	X	X		X
Network Policy and Access Services	X	X	X [3]		X [3]
Print and Document Services	X	X	X		
Remote Desktop Services	X	X	X [4]		X [4]
Web Services (IIS)	X	X	X	X	X
Windows Deployment Services	X	X	X		X
Windows Server Update Services (WSUS)	X	X	X		X

(1) Limited to creating Certificate Authorities
(2) Limited to 1 standalone DFS root
(3) Limited to 250 RRAS connections, 50 IAS connections and 2 IAS Server Groups
(4) Limited to 250 Remote Desktop Services connections

Windows Server 2008 Hardware Requirements

Microsoft provides minimum and recommended hardware requirements. For an application server, organizations will typically need at least the recommended hardware requirements, if not more. The minimum hardware requirements will typically support only the basic system and not support many of the resources and services that would typically be required from an application server. Additionally, organizations need to plan for current and future hardware requirements when acquiring their hardware.

Table 1-2 gives the Windows Server 2008 hardware requirements.

Table 1-2 Microsoft hardware requirements for Windows Server 2008

Hardware Component	Minimum Requirements	Recommended Requirements	Maximum Requirements
Processor	1 GHz (x86) or 1.4 GHz (x64)	2 GHz (or faster)	Not specified
Memory	512 MB RAM	2 GB RAM	32-bit systems: 4 GB (Standard) 64 GB (Enterprise) 64 GB (Datacenter) 64-bit systems: 32 GB (Standard) 2 TB (Enterprise) 2 TB (Datacenter)
Available disk space	10 GB	40 GB (or greater)	Not specified
Drive	DVD-ROM	DVD-ROM	DVD-ROM
Display	Super VGA monitor (800 X 600)	Super VGA monitor (800 X 600)	Super VGA monitor (800 X 600)
Peripherals	Keyboard and mouse	Keyboard and mouse	Keyboard and mouse

Activity 1-1: Install Windows Server 2008

Time Required: Approximately 30 minutes
Objective: Learn how to install Windows Server 2008

Description: This activity walks you through the steps of installing Windows Server 2008 using the current version, R2.

1. Insert the Windows Server 2008 R2 DVD in the DVD drive and restart the computer.

The steps performed to begin the Windows Server 2008 R2 installation could change based on the system environment, such as if a virtual machine is being used.

2. If prompted, boot from the DVD. The installation program begins. Confirm that the time, currency format, and keyboard layout is correct (Figure 1-1). Click **Next**.

Figure 1-1 Install Windows – language and other preferences
© Cengage Learning 2012

3. Click **Install now** (Figure 1-2). Enter your product key for activation. Click **Next**.

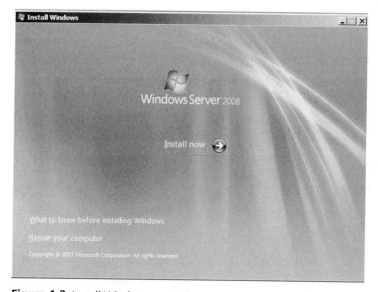

Figure 1-2 Install Windows – Install now
© Cengage Learning 2012

4. If you did not enter a product key, a message appears asking if you want to enter a product key (Figure 1-3). Click **No** if you want to install without a product key.

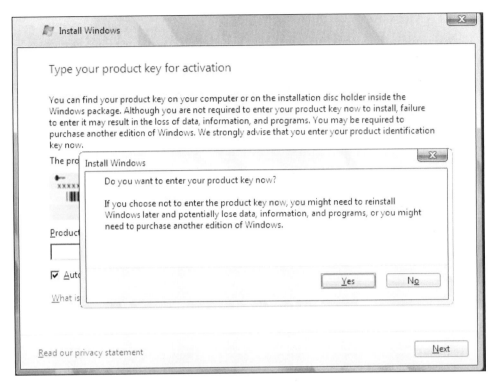

Figure 1-3 Install Windows – product key
© Cengage Learning 2012

5. Select the edition of Windows that you purchased (Figure 1-4). Click **Next.**

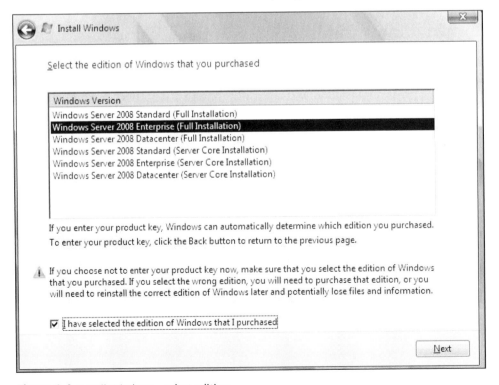

Figure 1-4 Install Windows – select edition
© Cengage Learning 2012

6. Read the Microsoft Software License Terms and check the **I accept the license terms** box (Figure 1-5). Click **Next**.

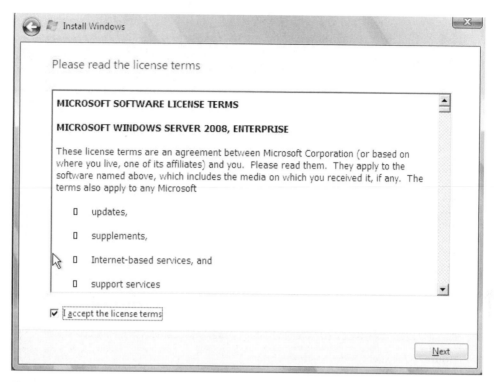

Figure 1-5 Install Windows – license terms
© Cengage Learning 2012

7. Select which type of installation you want (Figure 1-6). Click **Custom (advanced)**.

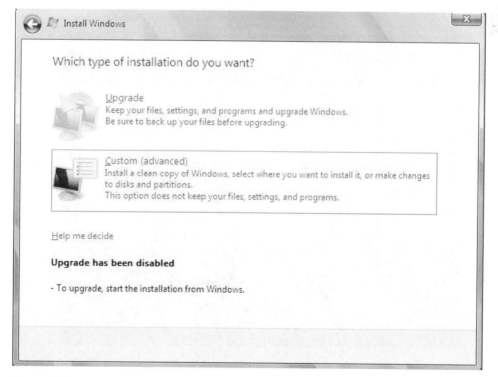

Figure 1-6 Install Windows – installation type
© Cengage Learning 2012

8. Select where you want to install Windows. You can click the Drive options (advanced) link to display partitioning options (Figure 1-7). Click **Next**.

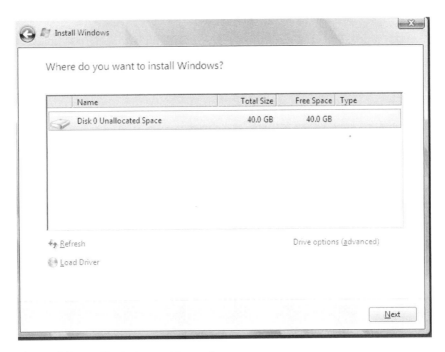

Figure 1-7 Install Windows – drive options
© Cengage Learning 2012

9. Windows begins installing Windows Server 2008. The system will restart one or more times during the installation process. Follow any instructions that appear onscreen.

10. When prompted, enter a password and click the arrow to submit the new password (Figure 1-8). Click **OK** when alerted that the password has changed.

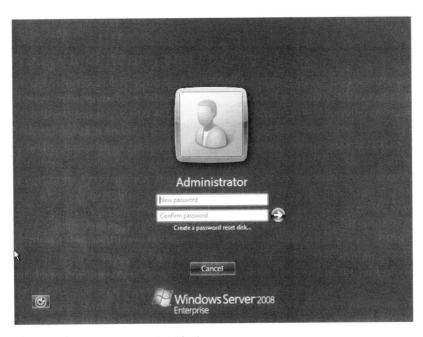

Figure 1-8 Windows Server 2008 login screen
© Cengage Learning 2012

11. When Windows Server 2008 starts for the first time, the Initial Configuration Tasks window displays. The installation process is streamlined in Windows Server 2008; many of the tasks that were required to be entered during the installation process are now available through the Initial Configuration Tasks window (Figure 1-9).

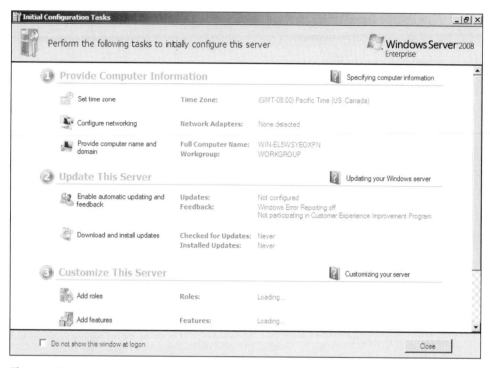

Figure 1-9 Initial Configuration Tasks screen
© Cengage Learning 2012

12. Click the task that you want to configure. If you do not want the Initial Configuration Tasks window to display when Windows Server 2008 starts, check the **Do not show this window at logon** check box.

13. Click **Close** when finished configuring tasks.

Migrating from Server 2003 to Server 2008

The decision to migrate from a previous server version to Windows Server 2008 is based on various factors, such as performance, reliability, and security. Organizations seeking the benefits of an improved applications server will likely be quicker to migrate to Windows Server 2008. Many of the features discussed throughout this text enable organizations to quickly realize the benefits of Windows Server 2008 as an applications server. There are many new features available in Windows Server 2008 that organizations will quickly take advantage of to improve their functionality, reduce operating costs, improve fault tolerance, improve security, and realize other benefits.

Many organizations will replace member servers with Windows Server 2008 as an initial migration path towards eventually upgrading the entire network to Windows Server 2008, including the Windows Server 2008 **Active Directory** infrastructure. Many organizations needing specific application-related services will first migrate their member servers to Windows Server 2008. Services such as **Remote Desktop Services**, **Windows SharePoint Services**, Windows Media Services, Web Services, and **Network Application Services**, which are discussed throughout this text, can realize significant performance enhancements with many of the services and features improved in Windows Server 2008.

Windows Server 2008 Enhancements

Windows Server 2008 provides many enhancements and improved technologies to support network administrators and improve server functionality. These enhancements include application functionality and support. Windows Server 2008 enhancements include:

- Improved installation process
- Hyper-V
- Server Core
- TCP/IP improvements
- Network Access Protection
- Server Manager
- Windows Remote Management
- PowerShell
- Group policy management
- Failover clustering

Improved Installation Process

Windows Server 2008 streamlines the installation process by requiring minimal user input. The installation program does not ask for networking information, regional settings, and other settings that can be provided through the Initial Configuration Tasks window, which will display the first time that you log onto Windows Server 2008. The Initial Configuration Tasks window provides sections for specifying computer information, updating the Windows server, and customizing the server.

Hyper-V

Virtualization is becoming popular because it conserves system resources by enabling one or more separate instances of an operating system to run on a single server system. Without virtualization, an organization might need to operate multiple separate servers; these servers might only be using a small fraction of the total system resources. To conserve system resources, organizations can consolidate multiple systems into a high-powered server. Each operating system that previously ran on a separate platform can now run in its own virtual instance. Microsoft's **Hyper-V** is the server virtualization capability provided in Windows Server 2008.

Server Core

Microsoft provides the **Server Core**, a minimal command-line installation of Windows Server 2008. Server Core is designed to provide a hardened, secure system to minimize exposure and vulnerabilities of a system to security breaches. Server Core provides only a command-line window with the tools needed for administration tasks. As a role, Server Core can be installed on the Standard, Enterprise, and Datacenter editions. The role needs to be selected during the initial installation of the operating system. If you want to change from Server Core to the Full version, you will need to reinstall the operating system.

TCP/IP Improvements

Windows Server 2008 includes improvements to the TCP/IP implementation. Key features of the TCP/IP implementation include the Next-Generation TCP/IP stack and Teredo. The Next-Generation TCP/IP stack supports IP version 4 (**IPv4**) and IP version 6 (**IPv6**). Teredo is an IPv6 technology that encapsulates IPv6 packets as IPv4 packets; this enables IPv6 packets to be sent across IPv4 networks.

Network Access Protection

Network Access Protection (NAP) protects the network from malware. NAP provides a layer of protection by helping to ensure that the corporate security policy, also referred to as the health policy, is enforced within the computers connected to the network. For example, if a user turns off the Windows Firewall on a NAP-compatible client, the local health policy will turn the Windows Firewall back on in order to remain compliant with the network's health policy.

Server Manager

The **Server Manager** console centralizes the server management tools. When you display the Server Manager, the major Server Manager categories include Roles, Features, Diagnostics, Configuration, and Storage. The Server Manager console in Windows Server 2008 consolidates the various administrative management consoles from previous versions, which were provided as separate management consoles, into a single centralized management console.

Windows Remote Management

Windows Remote Management (WinRM) is a new feature in Windows Server 2008. WinRM enables remote administration of the server; administrators can remotely run management scripts and manage data on remote machines. The WS-Management protocol handles connections; this is a public standard for remotely exchanging management data. The WS-Management protocol is not vendor specific. WinRM has many features similar to the features provided through the **Windows Management Instrumentation (WMI)** that was installed on previous versions.

PowerShell

PowerShell is a powerful command-line interface (CLI) and full scripting language for administrative tasks. PowerShell was first introduced in Microsoft Exchange Server 2007 as the Exchange Management Shell (EMS). PowerShell enables you to issue commands and string commands together by passing the results of one command to another command; this process is referred to as **pipelining**. The results are not passed as text; they are passed as .NET objects. PowerShell is built on Microsoft's .NET Framework and provides the capability to perform complex tasks through PowerShell scripting.

Group Policy Management

Group policy management tasks have been enhanced in Windows Server 2008. One enhancement is Group Policy preferences; Group Policy preferences are applied but are not enforced. While settings in the Group Policy are enforced, preventing the user from making changes, Group Policy preferences are not enforced. The Group Policy preferences and the Group Policy together provide enhanced group policy management capabilities. The **Group Policy Editor (gpedit)** and the **Group Policy Management Console (GPMC)** are essentially the same as in Windows Server 2003, although more setting and options are available.

An application security enhancement is the ability for applications to have network location awareness. For example, a policy could allow access to an application from one location, such as the local network, but not allow access to the same content from another network segment, such as a remote segment.

Failover Clustering

Failover clustering enables organizations to provide high-availability for their services and applications. Failover clustering is used for services and applications that organizations cannot afford to have down, such as file and print services, e-mail servers, and enterprise level databases.

Windows Server 2008 Roles and Features

Windows Server 2008 distinguishes between roles and features. A **role** is a major server function or service. A feature is added to enhance or support a role, or it can provide a standalone service.

Roles in Server 2008

Roles are organized into the following categories:

- Active Directory roles
- Network roles
- Infrastructure roles

Active Directory Roles Active Directory roles provide an integrated management of internal and external resources. Active Directory roles include:

- Active Directory Certificate Services (AD CS). This role provides digital certificates for objects in the organization that use the public key infrastructure (PKI).
- Active Directory Domain Services (AD DS). This role manages information about objects within the organization. This enables objects to access resources on the network.
- Active Directory Federation Services (AD FS). This role provides the capability for simplified identity federation and single sign-on services.
- Active Directory Lightweight Directory Services (AD LDS). This role provides the capability to deploy directory-enabled applications in the Windows Server 2008 environment.
- Active Directory Rights Management Services (AD RMS). This role, combined with rights management-aware applications, enables organizations to protect their intellectual property and data.

Network Roles Network roles manage major network protocols and services. Network roles include:

- **Dynamic Host Configuration Protocol (DHCP).** This role is used to dynamically assign IP addresses to clients on the network.
- **Domain Name System (DNS).** This role is used to resolve IP addresses based on host names.
- Network Policy and Access Services. This role provides network capabilities for **virtual private networks (VPNs)**, dial-up services, and 802.11 wireless access. Services include Network Policy Server, Routing and Remote Access Service, Health Registration Authority, and Host Credential Authorization Protocol.

Infrastructure Roles Infrastructure roles provide major services for clients. Infrastructure roles include:

- Remote Desktop Services. This role enables users to access programs installed on a terminal server or to access the Windows desktop.
- Fax Services. This role enables users to send, receive, and manage faxes on the network.
- Print Services. This role enables users to access networked print resources.
- File Services. This role enables the sharing and managing of file resources on the network.
- Hyper-V. This role enables organizations to deploy multiple virtual machines on a single Windows Server 2008; this enables organizations to potentially consolidate resources.
- **Universal Description, Discover, and Integration (UDDI)** Services. This role provides the capability to publish and locate Web services information.
- Web Server / Internet Information Services (IIS) 7.0. This role provides Web services and also provides a platform for Web-based technologies, such as Windows SharePoint Services.
- **Windows Deployment Services (WDS).** This role provides tools for deploying operating systems and applications as a network-based installation.

Additional New Features in Windows Server 2008

- Server features are needed for certain roles to operate properly. New features in Microsoft Server 2008 include the .NET 3.0 Framework. The .NET Framework 3.0 includes Windows Communication Foundation (WCF), Windows CardSpace (WCS), Windows Presentation Foundation (WPF), and Windows Workflow Foundation (WF).
- Windows Desktop Experience. This provides features similar to those experienced in Windows Vista. This is especially useful when used with Remote Desktop Services.

- BitLocker Drive Encryption. This feature increases security by encrypting the entire volume. It checks file integrity of the boot components. This feature protects data on lost or stolen computers.

- **Network load balancing (NLB)** clusters. This capability provides high availability, through load balancing, for Web services and network-based applications.

- Remote Server Administration Tools. This capability enables you to remotely manage Windows Server 2008. You can remotely manage the server from another system running Windows Server 2008 or Windows Vista SP1.

- Windows Server Backup Features. This capability provides a Microsoft Management Console (MMC) for backup and recovery requirements.

- **NTFS** improvements. Windows Server 2008 includes a self-healing NTFS, which makes necessary file system corrections when a corrupted file or directory is detected.

- Hot-swap. Windows Server 2008 includes hot-swappable capabilities built into core hardware components, such as memory, processors, and other adapter cards.

- **Server Message Block 2.0 (SMB2).** Windows Server 2008 includes the SMB2 protocol, which improves the efficiency and speed of transferring files between computers. SMB2 was first introduced in Windows Vista. To gain the efficiency advantage of SMB2 both systems must be Windows Server 2008 or Windows Vista or higher.

- Session Manager Subsystem. The Session Manager Subsystem (smss.exe), in Windows Server 2008, will create a separate instance for each session. The number of possible sessions is dependent on the number of processors in the server.

- User Profiles. Windows Server 2008 includes a User Profile Hive Cleanup Service that removes temporary files and other user profile-related information when the user logs off. This service increases security by ensuring that user sessions and user profile information is completely removed when the user logs off the system.

- Quality Windows Audio Video Experience (qWAVE). This feature enhances Audio Video (AV) streaming and provides network quality-of-service (QoS) for AV applications.

- Subsystem for UNIX-based Applications. This feature provides the capability to run UNIX-based programs and applications in the Windows environment.

- Windows Process Activation Service (WAS). This feature removes the dependency on **HTTP**; features previously available to only HTTP applications are available to applications hosting Windows Communication Foundation (WCF) services that are not reliant on HTTP.

- Security features. Windows Server 2008 includes many security enhancements, such as Authorization Manager improvements, BitLocker Drive Encryption, **Encrypting File System (EFS)** improvements, User Account Control (UAC), and Security Configuration Wizard (SCW).

Planning Windows Server 2008 Networks

Planning and implementing a Windows Server 2008 network typically follows the same, or similar, phases as other projects. Typical phases, or project processes include project initiation, project planning, project execution, project monitoring and control, and project closing.

Project Initiation

Project initiation often begins with the identification of project needs. Organizations need to identify the business goals and objectives, the information technology goals and objectives that support the business goals and objectives, and what services and features need to be implemented in Windows Server 2008 to support those goals and objectives. For example, an organization's business goals might be to decrease downtime or to eliminate wasted system resources. To support these business goals, organizations would configure high-availability in Server 2008 to decrease downtime and configure Hyper-V virtualization to conserve system resources by running one or more separate instances of an operating system on a single high-powered server.

Project Planning

Project planning begins with the development of a project plan that defines the scope of the project, the tasks needed, the resources needed, and the associated timeline for implementing Windows Server 2008. One of the key components in the planning of Windows Server 2008 deployment is defining the personnel that will participate on the design team and the deployment team.

Organizations need to understand the existing environment when determining the resources needed in the new system to better support business goals and objectives. Understanding the existing environment includes the network diagrams, documentation, and configurations of the current systems. Additionally, it includes understanding how the current system supports the business goals and objectives and how the current systems do not fully support the business goals and objectives.

Project Execution

After an implementation plan has been developed, organizations can acquire the hardware, software, and other resources needed. When organizations have those resources available, they should first create a lab environment where they configure and test the implementation plan prior to implementation on the actual network. The results of configuring and testing the implementation plan in a lab environment serve as a validation of the implementation plan's completeness and accuracy. The implementation plan will likely be revised based on the results of configuring and testing the plan in a lab environment.

After the implementation plan has been validated in a lab environment, it can be implemented in the production environment. The intent of this section is not to define the contents of the implementation plan, as that is covered in other texts and exams. Sections of this text will describe configuration tasks and considerations for features and services more specific to Microsoft Windows Server 2008 Applications Infrastructure Configuration.

Among the many tasks involved in implementing Windows Server 2008, organizations need to ensure that applications and services supporting applications have been thoroughly tested. Additionally, organizations need to ensure that a user and administrator training plan has been developed and is implemented during the implementation of Windows Server 2008. Users need to be aware of the system changes and how those changes will affect their daily tasks and operations. For example, if Remote Desktop Services is implemented, users need to know how to use this service.

Project Monitoring and Control

As the project is being implemented, the project must be monitored and controlled. From a project management perspective, the project tasks must be monitored to ensure that the tasks are being conducted, that they are being conducted on schedule, they are being conducted within budget, and that the resources are being utilized as scheduled.

From a technical perspective, the implementation project must be monitored to ensure that Windows Server 2008 is optimally configured and that there are no conflicts with other systems and applications. Performance monitoring needs to be conducted throughout the implementation.

In the event of unexpected problems during the implementation, organizations need to have checkpoints that define when a rollback plan will be executed. If serious problems are encountered, organizations might need to roll back to their previous implementation while researching and resolving problems encountered during the Windows Server 2008 implementation.

Another key aspect of monitoring and controlling the implementation is having checkpoints for user compliance, satisfaction, and training. Training plans will often be revised based on user input and feedback throughout this phase of the project.

Documentation must be maintained throughout each phase of the project. Additionally, organizations must have a change management and documentation plan in place after the implementation is complete; maintaining thorough documentation and having change control procedures are continual processes that must be maintained throughout the life of a system.

Project Closing

Prior to closing a project, organizations need to ensure that the project was implemented as planned. From a project management perspective, organizations need to ensure that the tasks were conducted in the timeframe and budget allocated, and that the resources were utilized efficiently. Deviations from the project plan need to be recorded and analyzed so adjustments can be made to future projects.

From a technical perspective, documentation and test results need to be reanalyzed and verified that the system is performing as expected, that the server is optimally configured, and that the applications are operating as expected in the new environment. Server and application performance measurements and benchmarks must be well documented and issues or deviations from expected performance must be recorded and analyzed to determine corrective actions, if necessary.

From a business perspective, the implementation results need to be compared with the business goals and objectives that the Windows Server 2008 implementation was expected to support. If business goals and objectives are not fully supported, they need to be recorded and reevaluated from a business perspective to determine corrective actions or future upgrades or modifications.

Organizations need to conduct an after-action-review to record the successful aspects of the project and the areas that need improvement. This information can be used to identify areas that need to be enhanced, upgraded, or modified in the future. This information is also used to refine the project plan for future implementations.

Overview of Primary Application Infrastructure Tools and Capabilities

This section provides a brief overview of the tools and capabilities in Windows Server 2008 that support the application infrastructure needs within an organization, and an overview of the remaining chapters of this textbook. Many of these tools and capabilities have been previously mentioned in this chapter as new features and capabilities in Windows Server 2008.

An **application infrastructure** is composed of Windows Server 2008 systems with the Application Server role configured. The Application Server role is installed using the Add Roles Wizard in Server Manager. When the Application Server role is installed, the Application Server Foundation is installed, which is primarily the .NET Framework 3.0. Primary Application Server Foundation components include the Windows Communication Foundation (WCF), Windows Workflow Foundation (WF), and Windows Presentation Foundation (WPF).

Windows Server 2008 Windows Deployment Services (WDS)

The Windows Server 2008 Windows Deployment Services (WDS) combines the tools, features, and functionality of previous versions and new features specific to Windows Server 2008. These new features include support for current operating system images, the capability to deploy images utilizing multicast communications, support for 32-bit and 64-bit deployments, and enhanced functionality for boot and installation image media using the .wim extension.

 Chapter 2 covers Windows Server 2008 Windows Deployment Services.

Windows Server 2008 Storage Services

Windows Server 2008 administrators can define disks as basic or dynamic and as **Master Boot Record (MBR)** or **GUID Partition Table (GPT)**. Additionally, mount points are useful for disk access and make use of many small disks versus one larger disk.

Multiple dynamic disks can be used to create fault-tolerant volumes. Windows Server 2008 supports software-based mirrored volumes and **Redundant Array of Independent Disks (RAID)** Level 5. Mirrored volumes (RAID-1) require two separate disks. RAID-5 requires three or more dynamic disks.

Microsoft capability, combined with **Storage Area Network (SAN)** vendor capability, provides the functionality for diskless servers to boot from SAN disks. This capability enables organizations to recover quickly from server hardware failures.

Windows Server 2008 supports failover clusters and shared storage through **Serial Attached SCSI (SAS)** storage arrays, **Fiber Channel (FC)** storage arrays, and **iSCSI** software initiators.

Chapter 3 covers Windows Server 2008 Storage Services.

Windows Server 2008 Remote Desktop Services

Windows Server 2008 Remote Desktop Services enables clients to remotely connect to a server and remotely run applications, as well as provide the capability for remote administration. Applications and services can be available to clients from any location. Clients can connect through the **Remote Desktop Connection** client.

Chapters 4 and 5 cover Windows Server 2008 Remote Desktop Services.

Windows Server 2008 Web Services

There have been significant enhancements to Internet Information Services (IIS) 7.0 as a Web server and application platform. The Web Server modular service role provides the primary Web server functionality. Among other features, the features that pertain to the support for application infrastructure capabilities include the support for common HTTP functionality and the Application Development role. The Application Development role enables creating and hosting Web applications including support for ASP.NET, .NET extensibility, and programming extensions.

Chapter 6 and 7 cover Windows Server 2008 Web Services.

Windows Server 2008 Network Application Services

Windows Media Services is a free, optional Windows Server 2008 tool that enables digital media streaming, live or on-demand, over an intranet or the Internet. Windows Server 2008 provides the capability to cache digital media content and provides the capability to install the Windows Media Services on a Server Core, which can provide additional security enhancements.

The Active Directory Rights Management Services (AD RMS) provides a **Digital Rights Management** capability by restricting content. Managing, transmitting, and viewing data can be restricted.

Windows SharePoint Services (WSS) 3.0 provides a collaboration and document management capability within Windows Server 2008. The collaboration and document management capabilities include document libraries, various types of lists, the creation of sites and workspaces, Web pages, and site management and administration tools.

Chapter 8 covers Windows Server 2008 Network Application Services.

Windows Server 2008 Hyper-V Virtualization

Windows Server 2008 Hyper-V virtualization, as discussed previously, provides an enhanced virtualization environment. Windows Server 2008 enables the virtualized environment to interact directly with the system's hardware layer. This eliminates many of the system bottlenecks that were previously experienced when the virtualized environment was extremely dependent on the host operating system environment. Virtualization enables an organization to save resources by consolidating multiple system environments on one hardware platform.

Chapter 9 covers Windows Server 2008 Hyper-V virtualization.

Windows Server 2008 for High-Availability

Failover clustering allows services and applications running on a failed node to be taken offline and moved to a node providing the needed functionality and access.

Network load balancing clusters improve network performance and availability by load balancing server requests across multiple servers. In addition, in Windows Server 2008, this capability can be configured in a short period of time.

Chapter 10 covers Windows Server 2008 for high-availability.

Best Practices

1. When planning to implement Windows Server 2008, identify the features and technologies that will provide the most value to the organization. This will help to justify the need for the upgrade or implementation and support the business justification.

2. When planning an implementation or migration, identify the business goals and objectives first and which server features and technologies are needed to support those business goals and objectives.

3. When defining the technical goals, define them from the technical perspective, the business perspective, and the user perspective.

4. Use Windows Deployment Services (WDS) to create client images that can be quickly deployed.

5. Use Remote Desktop Services to enable clients to remotely connect to a server and remotely run applications, especially if client hardware systems are aging or incapable of running new applications that are otherwise needed for the business.

6. Use Hyper-V virtualization to deploy multiple server operating systems or to deploy clustering to increase fault tolerance without having to add additional physical servers.

7. Ensure that a training plan is properly executed throughout the implementation.

8. Maintain accurate documentation during an implementation or upgrade.

9. When resources allow, use the recommended or optimal hardware and software configurations.

10. Windows Server Core installations provide the highest level of security.

Chapter Summary

- This chapter introduced Windows Server 2008, the new features and capabilities in Windows Server 2008, and the capabilities that distinguish Windows Server 2008 in its ability to support an application infrastructure.

- Windows Server 2008 provides the tools and capabilities needed for all businesses from small companies to large, enterprise-level organizations. To support different business needs, Microsoft offers different editions of Server 2008: Enterprise, Datacenter, Standard, Web Server, and High-Performance Computing (HPC) editions.

- Microsoft provides minimum and recommended hardware requirements. The minimum hardware requirements will typically support only the basic system and not support many of the resources and services that would typically be required from an application server. As an application server, organizations will typically need at least the recommended hardware requirements.

- Windows Server 2008 provides many enhancements and improved technologies to support network administrators and improve server functionality. These enhancements include improved installation process, Hyper-V virtualization, Server Core, TCP/IP improvements, Network Access Protection, Server Manager, Windows Remote Management, PowerShell, and Group Policy preferences.

- Windows Server 2008 roles are organized into Active Directory, Network, and Infrastructure roles.

- New features in Microsoft Server 2008 include, but are not limited to the .NET 3.0 Framework, Group Policy Management enhancements, remote server administration tools, Windows PowerShell, NTFS improvements, Hyper-V Virtualization, Windows Process Activation Service, and enhanced security features.

- Typical project phases in planning and implementing a Server 2008 network include project initiation, project planning, project execution, project monitoring and control, and project closing. There are unique considerations for Windows Server 2008 implementations during each phase of the project.

- Windows Server 2008 provides a solid foundation to support the application infrastructure needs within an organization. These tools, features, and capabilities will be covered in upcoming chapters in this textbook, as they pertain to Windows Server 2008 Application Infrastructure Configuration.

Key Terms

.NET Framework A software framework for Windows operating systems provided by Microsoft that includes a code library and other programming tools for managing programs.

Active Directory Microsoft directory services technology providing various network services.

application infrastructure An infrastructure that provides the tools and services for applications to work together and integrate within an enterprise.

ASP.NET Microsoft Web application framework that enables developers to develop Web services and applications.

digital rights management (DRM) Tools and methodologies used to control and limit access to and usage of digital content.

Domain Name System (DNS) TCP/IP application protocol that translates domain names into IP addresses.

Dynamic Host Configuration Protocol (DHCP) Network protocol used for the dynamic assignment of IP address and other configuration information.

Encrypting File System (EFS) Microsoft file system that provides symmetric encryption to preserve data confidentiality.

failover clustering Provides high-availability to services and applications by enabling an application to failover from one server to provide continued service.

Fiber Channel A technology used for high-speed connections, such as storage area networks.

Group Policy Editor (gpedit) Microsoft Windows Server 2008 tool that provides the capability to edit and manage group policies.

group policy management The management and maintenance of group policies.

Group Policy Management Console (GPMC) An MMC (Microsoft Management Console) snap-in for managing group policies.

GUID Partition Table (GPT) Provides a layout of the partition table on the hard disk; used on Windows Vista and later.

High-Performance Computing (HPC)   An edition of Windows Server 2008 for enterprise high-performance computing needs.

Hypertext Transfer Protocol (HTTP)   A TCP/IP protocol used for retrieving hyperlinked documents and information.

Hyper-V   The server virtualization capability provided in Windows Server 2008.

Internet Information Services (IIS)   A Microsoft Windows Server component that provides Web server tools, services, and functionality.

IPv4   Internet Protocol Version 4, the most commonly used version of IP, which provides a 32-bit IP address.

IPv6   Internet Protocol Version 6, the newest version of IP that provides a 128-bit IP address.

Internet Small Computer System Interface (iSCSI)   A storage networking standard for carrying SCSI commands over IP networks.

Master Boot Record (MBR)   The first sector, which is the boot sector, of a storage device.

Network Access Protection (NAP)   Introduced in Windows Server 2008, enables administrators to define system health policies and monitor network and server resources to ensure that these policies are being followed.

network application services   Services that enable network applications, application monitoring, and application performance.

network load balancing (NLB)   A clustering technology available in Windows Server that balances network traffic across multiple devices and is often used for network redundancy.

NTFS   New Technology File System, the standard file system used in Microsoft operating systems.

pipelining   Microprocessors use pipelining to begin executing multiple instructions simultaneously. The microprocessor will begin executing the next instruction before the current instruction has been completed.

PowerShell   A powerful Windows Server 2008 command-line interface (CLI) and full scripting language for administrative tasks.

Redundant Array of Independent Disks (RAID)   A set of standards that defines different storage architectures for increasing storage performance and fault-tolerance.

Remote Desktop Connection   A Windows Server feature used by clients to remotely connect to a server and remotely run applications.

Remote Desktop Services   Windows feature that enables users to access programs installed on a terminal server or to access the Windows desktop.

role   Defines the services and functionality that will be provided by the server operating system.

Serial Attached SCSI (SAS)   A data transfer technology for moving data between storage devices.

Server Core   A minimal, command-line installation of Windows Server 2008 that is designed to provide a hardened, secure system.

Server Manager   Console that centralizes the server management tools including roles, features, diagnostics, configuration, and storage.

Server Message Block 2.0 (SMB2)   Protocol that improves the efficiency and speed of transferring files between computers.

Storage Area Network (SAN)   Grouping of storage devices that includes storage devices connected to the network but typically appear to clients as locally attached storage devices.

Storage Services   Windows Server 2008 storage technologies for providing fault-tolerant storage.

Universal Description, Discover, and Integration (UDDI)   Windows Server feature that provides the capability to publish and locate Web services information.

virtual private network (VPN)   A private network that is like a tunnel through a larger network that enables secure communications between networks.

virtualization   Software that enables one or more separate instances of an operating system to run on a single physical system.

Web Services   Windows Server 2008 feature that provides Web server and application platform tools.

Windows Deployment Services   Services in Windows Server 2008 that provide tools for deploying operating systems and applications as a network-based installation.

Windows Management Instrumentation (WMI)   A Windows Server 2008 feature that provides Web-based management tools and capabilities.

Windows Remote Management (WinRM)   A new feature in Windows Server 2008 that enables remote administration of the server; administrators can remotely run management scripts and manage data on remote machines.

Windows SharePoint Services (WSS)   Windows Server 2008 service that provides a collaboration and document management capability.

Review Questions

1. Which of the following Windows Server 2008 editions is suitable for small business networks and supports network load balancing?

    a. Standard

    b. Enterprise

    c. Datacenter

    d. High-Performance Computing

2. Which of the following is provided in the Enterprise edition, but not in the Standard edition?

    a. File and print services

    b. Active Directory

    c. Network Load Balancing

    d. Installation of up to four virtual machines per physical host

3. Which of the following editions is designed to accommodate numerous processing cores; it is built on the 64-bit architecture?

    a. Standard

    b. Enterprise

    c. Datacenter

    d. High-Performance Computing

4. What is the recommended processor requirement for Windows Server 2008?

    a. 1 GHz

    b. 1.4 GHz

    c. 512 GHz

    d. 2 GHz

5. What is the recommended memory requirement for Windows Server 2008?

    a. 1 MB

    b. 2 GB

    c. 512 MB

    d. 512 GB

6. Which of the following conserves system resources by enabling you to run one or more separate instances of an operating system on a single system?

    a. Hyper-V

    b. Server-V

    c. NLB

    d. Server Core

7. Which of the following will display the first time that you log onto Windows Server 2008 to streamline the installation process by gathering networking information, regional settings, and other settings after installation?

   a. Initial Configuration Tasks

   b. Initial Setting

   c. Server Manager

   d. Server Settings

8. Which of the following simplifies the task of providing a hardened system that minimizes the system's exposure and vulnerabilities to security breaches?

   a. Server Core

   b. Security Core

   c. Network Core

   d. Network Security

9. Which of the following protects the network from malware by providing a layer of protection by helping to ensure that the corporate security policy, also referred to as the health policy, is enforced within the computers in the network?

   a. Network Access Protection

   b. Network Layer Protection

   c. Network Security Protection

   d. Network Security Layer

10. Which of the following is a powerful command-line interface (CLI) and full scripting language for administrative tasks?

    a. Server Core

    b. PowerShell

    c. ScriptShell

    d. PowerCore

11. Which AD role provides digital certificates for objects in the organization that use the public key infrastructure (PKI)?

    a. AD CS

    b. AD DC

    c. AD FS

    d. AD LDS

12. Which AD role provides the capability for simplified identity federation and single sign-on services?

    a. AD CS

    b. AD DC

    c. AD FS

    d. AD LDS

13. Which AD role provides the capability to deploy directory-enabled applications in the Windows Server 2008 environment?

    a. AD CS

    b. AD DC

    c. AD FS

    d. AD LDS

14. Which AD role, when combined with rights management-aware applications, enables organizations to protect their intellectual property and data?

    a. AD CS

    b. AD DC

    c. AD RMS

    d. AD LDS

15. Which of the following features provides high availability, through load balancing, for Web services and network-based applications?

    a. Network load balancing

    b. Group Policy Management

    c. PowerShell

    d. Server Core

16. Which of the following consolidates the various administrative management consoles from previous versions, which were provided as separate management consoles, into a single centralized management console?

    a. Server Manager

    b. Consolidated Manager

    c. Initial Configuration Tasks

    d. Administrative Manager

17. Which of the following enables remote administration of the server; administrators can remotely run management scripts and manage data on remote machines?

    a. WinRM

    b. WinAM

    c. WinDM

    d. WinAD

18. During which project phase should documentation be developed?

    a. Project initiation

    b. Project planning

    c. Project execution

    d. All phases

19. Which of the following roles enables users to access programs installed on a terminal server or to access the Windows desktop?

    a. Remote Desktop Services

    b. File Services

    c. WDS

    d. Print Services

20. Which of the following provides collaboration and document management capability within Windows Server 2008?

    a. Windows SharePoint Services

    b. Microsoft Office 2007

    c. PowerShell

    d. Server Core

Case Projects

The following scenario will be utilized for many Case Projects throughout this textbook.

You are a Network Engineer for Peppin Associates, a solutions provider for Information Technology in the St Louis area. Peppin Associates specializes in solving complex IT systems integration problems for clients in various sectors, including national security, homeland security, civil government, manufacturing, and global health.

Your manager has asked you to work with one of its clients – New Enterprises, a leading independent distributor of specialty construction equipment replacement parts, power transmission components, and other specialty items in the U.S.

New Enterprises has been in business for over 10 years and is currently running a Windows Server 2003 network. They are currently seeking direction for upgrading their Windows Server 2003 with Active Directory network to Windows Server 2008.

New Enterprises has its main office in St Louis, Missouri and they have four branch offices in Portland, Oregon; San Diego, California; Atlanta, Georgia; and Nashville, Tennessee.

Characteristics of the New Enterprises network include:

- They are currently running Windows Server 2003 at their main office and their branch offices

- They must be able to support custom-developed applications on their network

- They must be able to support UNIX-based applications

- They require a high-availability solution to minimize downtime within their network

- They have used virtualization, but want to expand their virtualization solutions to further consolidate resources

- They require a high level of fault tolerance within their network

- They have a centralized help desk and want to be able to administer client changes, upgrades, and help desk support from their centralized help desk

Case Project 1-1: Comparing Windows Server 2003 and Windows Server 2008

The IT department in New Enterprises is certain that they need to upgrade to Windows Server 2008; however, they need your analysis to provide documentation to senior management. They need the analysis results to be articulated in a manner that senior management will understand; they need the justification to be expressed in business terms.

New Enterprises has asked you to take a look at the characteristics of the New Enterprises network and to provide a brief comparison of Server 2003 with Active Directory to Server 2008 Enterprise Edition with Active Directory. They have asked that you identify the features of Windows Server 2008 that will support their characteristics and provide an explanation of the differences between Windows Server 2003 and Windows Server 2008, by filling out a table similar to Table 1-3. Include at least 10 capabilities in the table.

Table 1-3 Comparison of Windows Server 2003 and Server 2008 capabilities

Feature	Server 2003 Capabilities	Server 2008 Capabilities

Case Project 1-2: Features and Benefits of Windows Server 2008

New Enterprises is asking you to provide them with a brief overview of the features and benefits offered in a Windows Server 2008 Enterprise Edition Application Environment.

They have asked that you identify the features of Windows Server 2008 that will support their application infrastructure, provide a technical explanation supporting the upgrade, and provide a business justification supporting the upgrade, as depicted in Table 1-4 (note that some features might not have a significant impact on the decision to upgrade). Include at least 10 features and benefits in the following table.

Table 1-4 Features and benefits of Windows Server 2008

Feature	Technical Explanation	Business Justification

Chapter 2

Deploying Windows Servers

After reading this chapter and completing the exercises, you will be able to:

- Describe Windows Deployment Services (WDS) server, client, and management components
- Install Windows Deployment Services
- Configure Windows Deployment Services
- Add boot images and install images to Windows Deployment Services
- Enable Volume Activation using a Multiple Activation Key (MAK) or Key Management Service (KMS)

This chapter shows you how to use the Windows Server 2008 Windows Deployment Services (WDS) to automatically and remotely install supported Windows operating systems over a network. This service can save time and money over individual DVD-based installations, enables servers to be configured and deployed in a consistent manner, and provides an enormous benefit to those administering the initial deployment or upgrade of a large corporate network. In this chapter, you will first install and configure WDS to deploy boot and install images. Then, you will learn how to use volume activation (VA) to automate the activation process for multiple installations.

Deploying Images Using Windows Deployment Services

Windows Deployment Services (WDS) is a Windows Server 2008 role that provides the capability to install supported Windows operating systems remotely using a network-based installation. Prior to remote installation tools, administrators had to manually configure each system in order to install an operating system or to upgrade an operating system. Thus, remote installation tools, such as WDS, provide many benefits to the organization, including reducing the time spent manually installing systems and enabling administrators to manage multiple installations from a central location. The Windows Server 2008 Windows Deployment Services role is the replacement for **Remote Installation Services (RIS)** that was available in Windows Server 2003.

Deploying operating system images using WDS involves:

- *Verifying that the server meets the necessary prerequisites for WDS installation.* The WDS server must have DHCP and DNS configured, use the NTFS file system, and be a member server in an Active Directory domain.

- *Installing WDS.* After you have verified that the server meets the necessary prerequisites, you will install the WDS role.

- *Configuring WDS.* WDS requires very little configuration; however, you will need to configure some basic options before using WDS.

- *Adding boot and install images.* WDS enables you to customize the images with the desired configurations needed to be deployed within the organization.

New Features and Enhancements of WDS

Previous Windows Server operating systems, such as Windows Server 2003, supported RIS as a remote installation service. Additionally, Windows Deployment Services could be installed on Windows Server 2003. However, there have been significant enhancements to WDS. The following reflects the major changes from RIS:

- Can deploy newer operating systems, such as Vista and Windows Server 2008
- Uses Windows PE as the boot operating system
- Uses Windows image (.wim) files for image-based installations
- Has multicast functionality
- Includes enhancements to the PXE server component
- Has an enhanced client GUI
- Allows WDS management through the WDS MMC snap-in

Benefits of WDS

WDS eliminates the necessity to install the operating system manually on each computer from a DVD, and it provides a cost-effective and efficient method of performing multiple installations from a central location. WDS also provides consistency in the manner in which the operating systems are installed. Windows Deployment Services provides the following installation and deployment benefits:

- Enables network-based Windows operating system installations, which reduces or eliminates the need for manual installations
- Can be configured to support the installation of multiple operating systems, including Windows XP, Windows Server 2003, Microsoft Windows Vista, and Windows Server 2008
- Enables the deployment of operating systems to computers without operating systems
- Reduces installation complexities, which is especially evident for medium and large deployments
- Reduces installation costs associated with excessive man-hours spent on manual installations, if WDS were not utilized
- Provides consistent installation process, which establishes a consistent baseline for the installation of systems within the organization

WDS Server, Client, and Management Components

Windows Deployment Services include server components, client components, and management components that together enable network administrators to effectively and efficiently deploy operating systems within the organization.

The server components are needed to boot the client system and to install the operating system on that client system. Server components include:

- **Pre-Boot Execution Environment (PXE)** server—PXE is an environment to boot computers over a network connection.
- **Trivial File Transfer Protocol (TFTP)** server—TFTP is a protocol used to transfer files, similar to FTP but uses User Datagram Protocol (UDP)
- A shared folder and image repository with the boot and install images and other files needed for network booting
- A multicast and diagnostics component at the network layer

The client components are used by the client system to communicate with the server to ensure that the installation and configuration tasks are performed properly. Client components include:

- A graphical user interface (GUI)
- Client components that communicate with the server components over the network to perform the network-based installation

Management components are used to create the needed images and to manage the server and client system accounts. Management components include:

- Management tools to manage the server
- Tools to manage the operating system images
- Tools to manage the client computer accounts

Installing Windows Deployment Services

WDS must be properly installed and configured, before it can be used. The following sections will cover installing the WDS role, configuring WDS, and installing Install.wim images and Boot. wim images. Installing and configuring Windows Deployment Services involves:

- Installing Windows Deployment Services
- Configuring WDS by adding the Install.wim and Boot.wim (images are available in the \Source folder on the product CD/DVD)
- Installing the operating system

You can install Windows Deployment Services as a Deployment Server or Transport Server.

- A **Deployment Server** provides complete Windows Deployment Services functionality and when you select the Deployment Server option, both the Deployment Server and Transport Server are installed, which includes the WDS image store, support for network boots, multicast, and other options and management tools.

- A **Transport Server** provides the core networking components to transmit data, such as operating system images, from a standalone server, but it does not include the WDS image store. It is used for booting from the network using PXE and TFTP and is often used in environments without AD DS, DNS, or DHCP. The server does not need to have AD, DHCP, or DNS installed.

 During the installation and configuration steps, Windows Server 2008 provides various links with more information about WDS and the associated tasks being performed.

Prerequisites for Installing WDS

Following are the prerequisites for the default WDS installation which includes both the Deployment Server and Transport Server:

 If you are only installing the Transport server, all prerequisites are not required, as stated previously.

- Active Directory Domain Services (AD DS).   A Windows Deployment Services server must be either a member of an AD DS domain or a domain controller for an AD DS domain.

- Dynamic Host Configuration Protocol (DHCP).   WDS relies on DHCP for IP addressing.

- Domain Name System (DNS).   WDS relies on DNS using a static IP for name resolution.

- New Technology File System (NTFS) volume.   The WDS image store requires an NTFS volume.

- Local Administrators Group Credentials.   The server must be a member of the Local Administrators group in order to perform the installation tasks and other server tasks required.

- Windows Server 2008.   It is assumed that Windows Server 2008 is installed.

Following are the prerequisites for installing the Transport Server only:

- Local Administrators Group Credentials.   Must be a member of the Local Administrators group.

- PXE Provider.   You must create a custom PXE provider to network boot. Windows Server 2008 R2 has a PXE Provider.

 This chapter will cover installing the Deployment Server, which installs both the Deployment Server and the Transport Server.

Windows Deployment Services can be installed in three ways:

- From Server Manager.   This chapter focuses on performing tasks using the Server Manager.

- Using the Initial Configuration Wizard.   From the Initial Configuration Wizard, you can select to Add Roles to your server. The process of selecting the desired role to add is very similar to adding roles to your server using the Server Manager.

- From the command line.   This chapter does not focus on performing tasks from the command line. Some commands are indicated in Notes throughout the chapter.

Activity 2-1: Install WDS from Server Manager

Time Required: Approximately 30 minutes
Objective: Learn how to install WDS from Server Manager
Description: This activity walks you through the steps of installing WDS from the Server Manager. This process adds the WDS server role to your server. The time required will vary based on hardware characteristics. This activity assumes that you are already logged on to your server; if not, you must log on first.

1. To display the Server Manager, click **Start,** click **Administrative Tools,** and click **Server Manager,** click **Continue** in the User Account Control dialog box if necessary. Expand the **Roles** node in the left pane to display the server roles or add new roles (Figure 2-1).

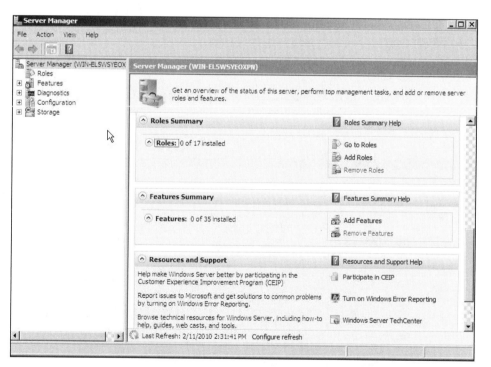

Figure 2-1 Server Manager – Roles
© Cengage Learning 2012

2. Click **Add roles**.

3. Click **Next**.

4. Click **Windows Deployment Services** (Figure 2-2).

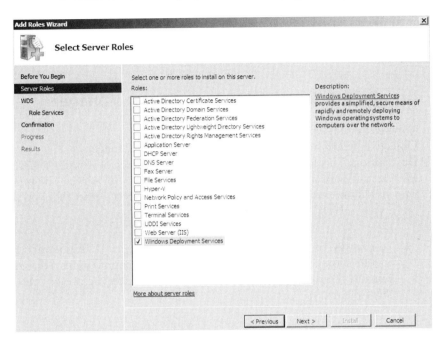

Figure 2-2 Add Roles Wizard – Select Server Roles
© Cengage Learning 2012

5. Click **Next**.

6. The Add Roles Wizard displays information about Windows Deployment Services, including an introduction to WDS, things to note, and additional information (Figure 2-3). Click **Next**.

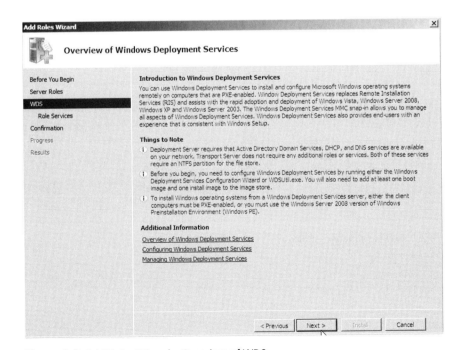

Figure 2-3 Add Roles Wizard – Overview of WDS
© Cengage Learning 2012

7. View the information about the role services and select Deployment Server, Transport Server, or both (Figure 2-4). Click **Next**.

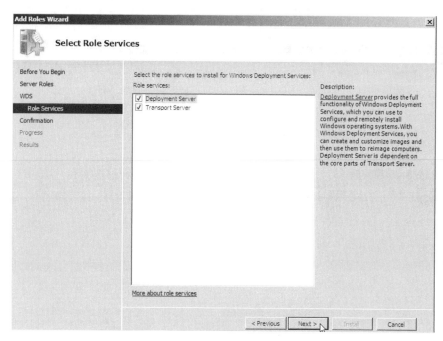

Figure 2-4 Add Roles Wizard – Select Role Services
© Cengage Learning 2012

8. Confirm the installation selections and click **Install** (Figure 2-5).

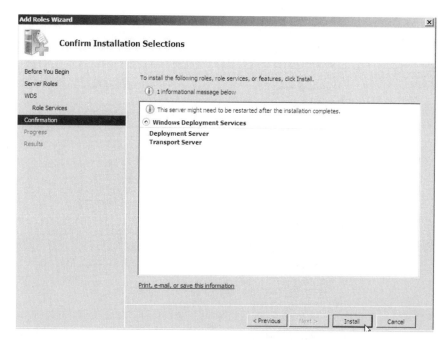

Figure 2-5 Add Roles Wizard – Confirm Installation Selections
© Cengage Learning 2012

9. View the installation results (Figure 2-6) and click **Close**. The wizard will display the services installed, the installation results, and other warnings, as applicable. The Server Manager's Roles Summary displays Windows Deployment Services added to the Roles (Figure 2-7).

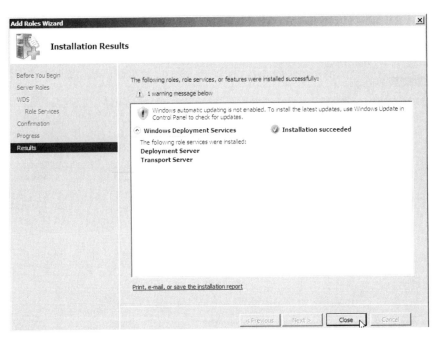

Figure 2-6 Add Roles Wizard – Installation Results

© Cengage Learning 2012

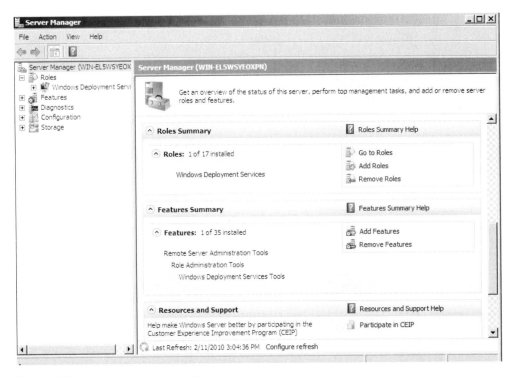

Figure 2-7 Server Manager – Roles Summary

© Cengage Learning 2012

To install WDS from a command line prompt, enter **ServerManagerCmd -install WDS** to install a Deployment Server. Enter **ServerManagerCmd -install WDS-Transport** to install a Transport Server. If the command prompt is not displaying, first click **Start,** click **Run,** enter **cmd,** and click **OK.**

2

Configuring Windows Deployment Services

Once you have installed WDS, you need to configure the Windows Deployment Services role and add images to the server that you want deployed. Since WDS is installed as a role, there is little configuration required after installation before you are ready to begin configuring WDS and adding images.

To configure WDS, you must be a member of the local Administrators group.

Activity 2-2: Configure Windows Deployment Services

Time Required: Approximately 30-60 minutes
Objective: Learn how to add a WDS server to the console and configure the WDS server
Description: This activity adds a WDS server to the console and configures the WDS server using the configuration wizard. The time required to complete this activity will vary based on the prerequisites installed; if prerequisites are not installed, they will be installed as part of the configuration process and the time required could increase. This activity assumes that you are already logged on to your server; if not, you must log on first.

1. Click **Start,** click **Administrative Tools,** then click **Windows Deployment Services** (click **Continue** in the User Account Control dialog box). Information displays about Windows Deployment Services, including instructions for adding a Windows Deployment Services server.

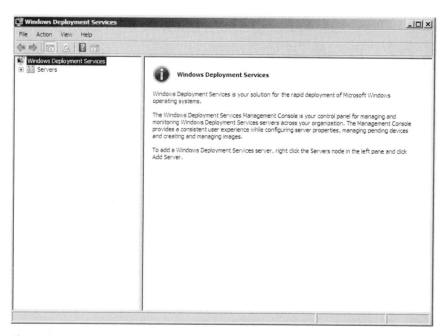

Figure 2-8 Windows Deployment Services – Servers
© Cengage Learning 2012

2. Right-click **Servers** in the left pane.

3. Click **Add Server** (Figure 2-9).

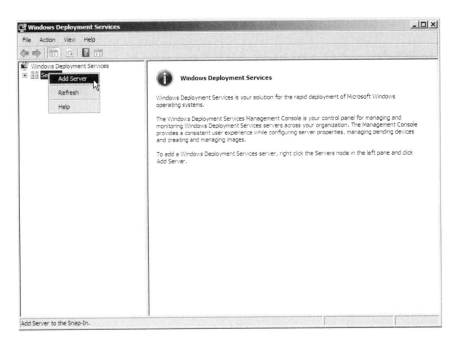

Figure 2-9 Add Server

© Cengage Learning 2012

4. The Add Server(s) Wizard walks you through adding a WDS server to the console. Select the server to add (Figure 2-10) and click **OK**. The associated figure reflects the default, Local computer option. However, you can use any of the other server options to add a specific server type.

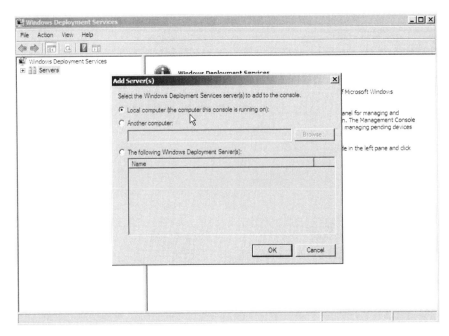

Figure 2-10 Select WDS server to add to the console

© Cengage Learning 2012

5. The WDS server displays in the console (Figure 2-11).

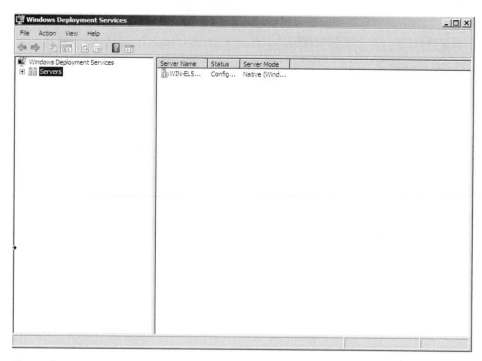

Figure 2-11 WDS Server displays in the console
© Cengage Learning 2012

6. Expand **Servers** in the left pane.
7. Right-click the server name you just added.
8. Click **Configure Server** (Figure 2-12).

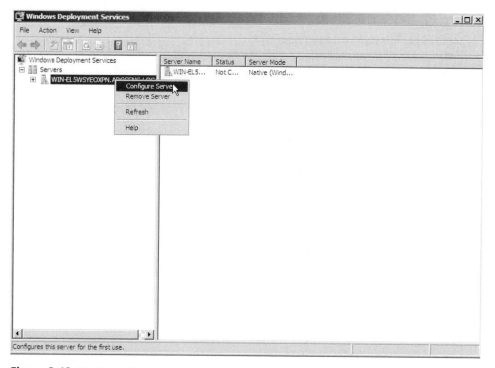

Figure 2-12 Configure Server
© Cengage Learning 2012

9. The Configuration Wizard Welcome Page displays (Figure 2-13). The wizard will walk you through the configuration steps. Click **Next**.

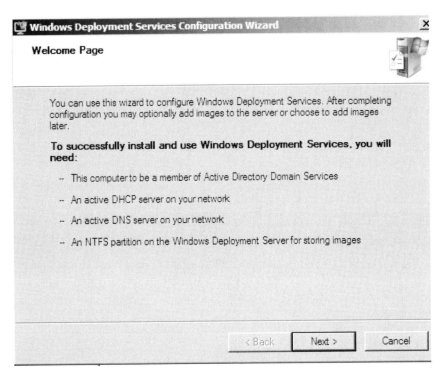

Figure 2-13 WDS Configuration Wizard Welcome Page
© Cengage Learning 2012

10. Select the remote installation folder location. Click **Next** (Figure 2-14).

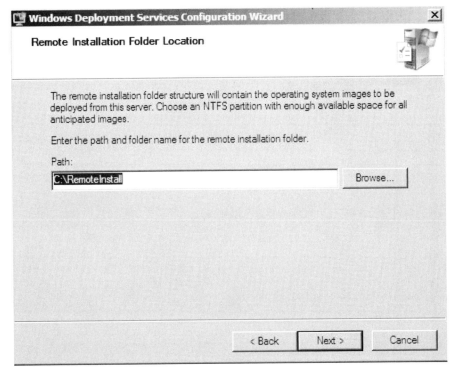

Figure 2-14 Remote Installation Folder Location
© Cengage Learning 2012

11. On the PXE Server Initial Settings screen, select the desired answer policy (Figure 2-15). Click **Finish**.

If you choose the setting, *Do Not Respond to Any Client Computer*, PXE will be essentially disabled; however, you might desire this setting before you are ready for WDS to respond to client requests. If you choose the setting, *Respond only to known client computers*, the client computer will have to be added to AD before PXE can boot to the WDS server. If you choose the setting, *Respond to all (known and unknown) client computers*, all clients can boot to the WDS server; however, the associated check box can be selected to require administrator approval for unknown clients.

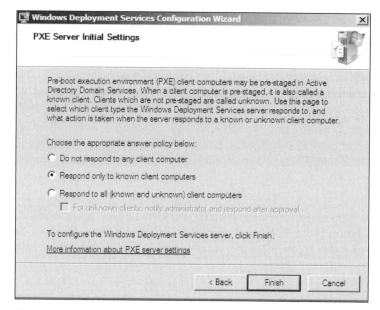

Figure 2-15 PXE Server Initial Settings

© Cengage Learning 2012

12. The Configuration Wizard displays that the configuration is complete (Figure 2-16). Click **Finish**.

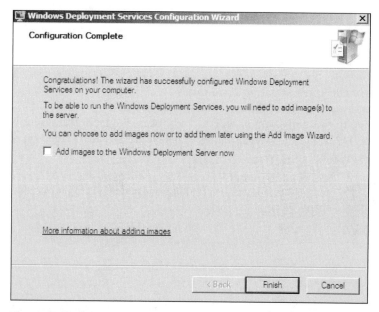

Figure 2-16 Configuration Complete

© Cengage Learning 2012

Capturing and Deploying WDS Images

After the WDS server is configured, you can add images to the server. Many administrators are familiar with images and often use other third-party applications for managing the distribution of system images. An image is basically a copy of an existing operating system and the associated configurations. Thus, with images, administrators do not have to spend time configuring each system individually. When an image is captured, the capture wizard begins and enables the image to be captured, or saved, as a .wim file.

There are four types of image types that are generally considered:

- **Boot image.** Client computers will boot into a boot image in order to install the operating system.
- **Install image.** Install images are deployed to the client computer; they are the operating system images.
- **Discover image.** A discover image enables operating system installation on a system that cannot boot from the network using the Pre-Boot Execution Environment (PXE). When you right-click a boot image, you can select to *Create Discover Boot Image*.
- **Capture image.** A capture image enables you to create custom install images. You can capture the image of an operating system using the Image Capture Wizard and use that image as your install image. When you right-click a boot image, you can select to *Create Capture Boot Image*.

You need to install at least one boot image and one install image, though organizations often install multiple install images. The Boot.wim file is located in the \sources folder on the Windows Server 2008 installation DVD. The Install.wim file is located on the Windows Server 2008 installation DVD. You can also create a custom install image. This chapter shows how to install boot and install images.

Installing a Boot Image

Boot image guidelines include:

- The boot menu can have up to 13 boot images
- The .wim file name cannot have spaces
- You can use the Windows Server 2008 Boot.wim file
- Double-byte character sets do not always display properly

Activity 2-3: Add a Boot Image

Time Required: Approximately 20 minutes
Objective: Learn how to add a boot image to WDS
Description: In this activity, you will add a boot image from the Windows Server 2008 installation DVD. This activity assumes that you are already logged on to your server; if not, you must log on first.

You need to add at least one boot image to the WDS server. You will need the Windows Server 2008 installation DVD to provide the Boot.wim image file.

1. From the Windows Deployment Services screen, right-click the **Boot Images** node in the left pane.

2. Click **Add Boot Image** (Figure 2-17).

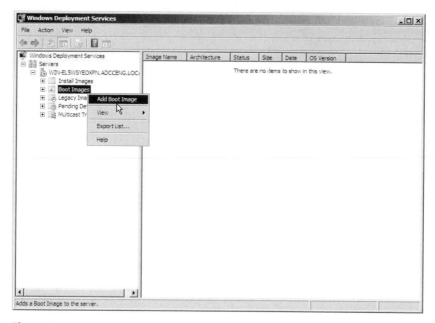

Figure 2-17 Add Boot Image
© Cengage Learning 2012

3. Click **Browse** on the Image File screen (Figure 2-18). Locate the boot.wim image in the **\sources** folder on the Windows Server 2008 DVD.

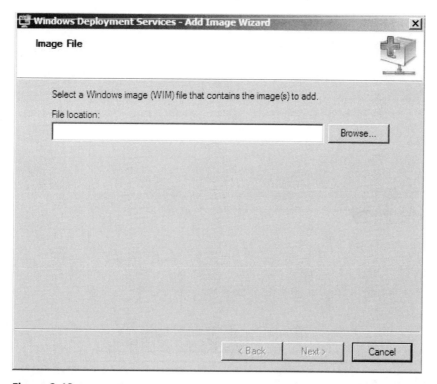

Figure 2-18 Image File
© Cengage Learning 2012

4. Click **Open,** then click **Next.**

5. Follow the Wizard instructions. Accept the default name and description on the Image Metadata screen. Click **Next** (Figure 2-19).

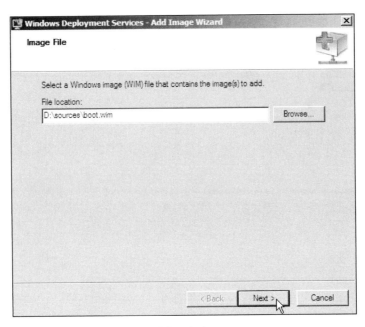

Figure 2-19 Image name and description
© Cengage Learning 2012

6. View the summary of the image settings (Figure 2-20). Click **Next.**

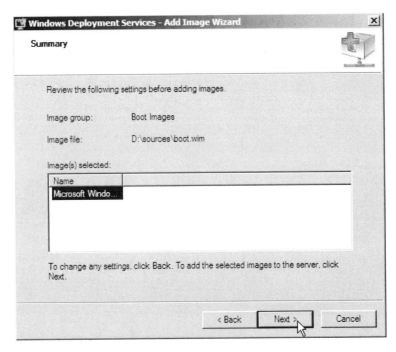

Figure 2-20 Summary of image settings
© Cengage Learning 2012

7. Repeat Steps 1–6 for any additional boot images you want to install.

8. Any boot images you have installed display under the Boot Images section of the WDS server (Figure 2-21).

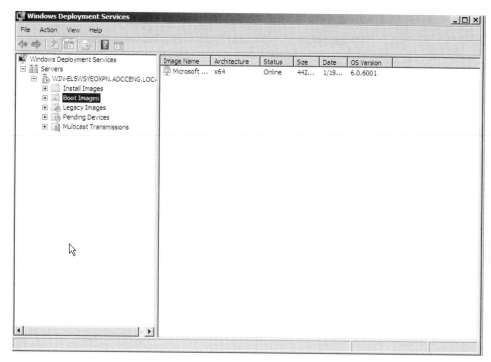

Figure 2-21 Boot Images
© Cengage Learning 2012

Installing an Install Image

The install images are the images containing the operating system and configurations that you want to deploy to the client systems. The following are prerequisites for adding an install image:

- The client must be able to do a PXE boot.
- The client must be a member of a Domain Users group.
- The client computer must have at least 512 MB RAM.
- The client computer must meet or exceed the client system requirements required for the install image for that operating system.

Activity 2-4: Add an Install Image

Time Required: Approximately 20 minutes
Objective: Learn how to add an install image to WDS
Description: In this activity, you will add an install image to WDS. You must have at least one install image. This activity assumes that you are already logged on to your server; if not, you must log on first.

You will need the Windows Server 2008 or client operating system installation DVD to provide the Install.wim image file. Organizations typically install multiple install images.

1. From the Windows Deployment Services screen, right-click the **Install Images** node in the left pane.
2. Click **Add Install Image** (Figure 2-22).

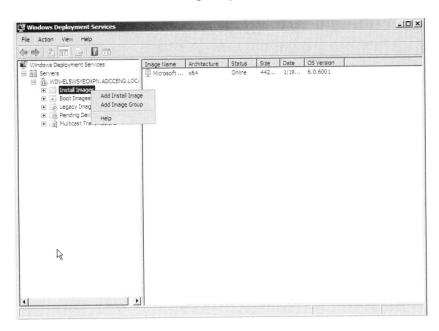

Figure 2-22 Add Install Image
© Cengage Learning 2012

3. Replace the default image group name, ImageGroup1 (Figure 2-23), with ABCentageGroup. Click **Next**.

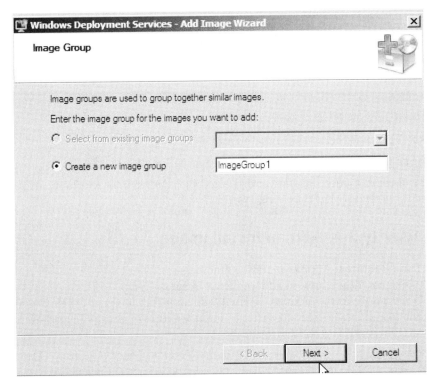

Figure 2-23 Image Group
© Cengage Learning 2012

4. Click **Browse**. Locate the install.wim image in the **\sources** folder on the Windows Server 2008 DVD or client operating system DVD, such as Windows Vista (Figure 2-24).

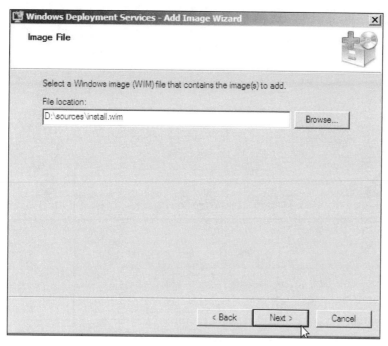

Figure 2-24 Image File
© Cengage Learning 2012

5. Click **Open**. Follow the Wizard instructions.

6. Select the images that you want to install from the list of available images (Figure 2-25). Click **Next**.

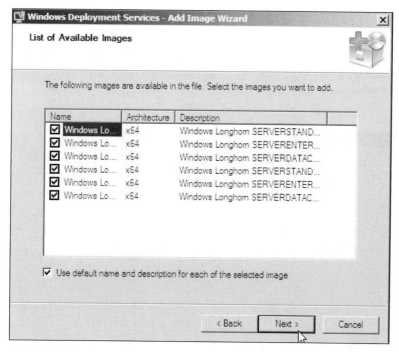

Figure 2-25 List of Available Images
© Cengage Learning 2012

7. View the summary of install image settings (Figure 2-26). Click **Next**.

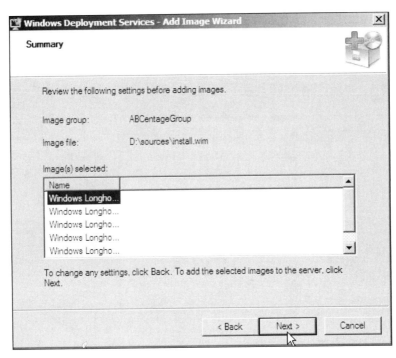

Figure 2-26 Summary of install image settings
© Cengage Learning 2012

8. Windows Server 2008 adds the images and displays the Task Progress window (Figure 2-27). Click **Finish**.

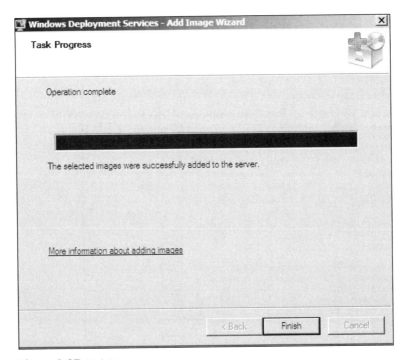

Figure 2-27 Task Progress
© Cengage Learning 2012

9. The install images display in the Install Images section of the WDS server (Figure 2-28).

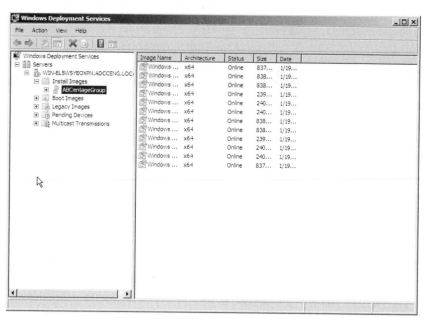

Figure 2-28 Install images

© Cengage Learning 2012

Uninstalling Windows Deployment Services

You can uninstall Windows Deployment Services using the Server Manager or through the command prompt. Make sure that you intend to uninstall the WDS role, due to the amount of time and effort required to install the WDS role on your system.

Activity 2-5: Uninstall WDS from Server Manager

Time Required: Approximately 5 minutes
Objective: Learn how to uninstall WDS from Server Manager
Description: In this activity, you will uninstall WDS from Server Manager. This activity assumes that you are already logged on to your server; if not, you must log on first.

Do not perform this activity unless you want to actually uninstall WDS.

1. From the Server Manager, click **Roles**.

2. In the Roles Summary section, click **Remove Roles**.

3. Follow the wizard. The Remove Roles Wizard will display the server roles that are installed and enable you to deselect the checkbox for that role to remove the role from your server.

To remove the WDS role from your server using the command line, enter **ServerManagerCmd -remove WDS.** If the command prompt is not displaying, click **Start,** click **Run,** enter **cmd,** and click **OK.**

Other Common Deployment Tasks

Windows Deployment Services is used for several other common deployment tasks:

- *Multicast deployments.* Multicast deployments provide the capability to deploy an image through a multicast deployment to multiple computers.
- *Custom install images.* You can create custom install images. To create a custom install image, you create a capture image, use Sysprep, and use the Image Capture Wizard.
- *Unattended installation.* You can automate the deployment using an unattend file for the user interface of Windows Deployment Services and another unattend file for the remainder of the setup.
- *Discover images.* A discover image enables an operating system installation on a system that cannot boot from the network using the Pre-Boot Execution Environment (PXE).
- *WDS Server Properties.* From Windows Deployment Services, you can right-click the WDS server and select Properties. The WDS server Properties dialog box will display with several tabs: General, PXE Response Settings, Directory Settings, Boot, Client, DHCP, Network Settings, and Advanced. The most common tabs include Boot, DHCP, and Network Settings.
    - The Boot tab includes optional settings for default boot program and default boot image.
    - The DHCP tab provides options to deconflict WDS and DCP running on the same system.
    - The Network Settings tab includes Multicast IP Address, UDP Port Range, and Network Profile sections.

Volume Activation

Volume Activation (VA) provides the capability for volume licensing, which is used for Microsoft Windows Server 2008, Windows 7, and Windows Vista. Volume activation automates the activation process and makes the management of the activation process much more efficient. With VA, you use a Multiple Activation Key (MAK) or Key Management Service (KMS) to activate the operating system.

 More detailed information is available about Volume Activation from Microsoft's Web site: http://technet.microsoft.com/en-us/library/dd772269.aspx

Key Management Service (KMS) enables volume activation within an organization's own network. When KMS is activated on a system, that system becomes the centralized system that other systems use for activation. **Multiple Activation Key (MAK)** activates the product on a system on a one-time basis. MAK uses Microsoft's hosted activation services.

With Volume Activation, end users are able to activate their products in a transparent manner. Volume Activation does not apply to or interact with invoicing or billing processes. Volume Activation needs to be properly planned during the deployment process, since upgrades and changes will affect the volume licensing.

Organizations are issued **Volume License Keys (VLKs)**, which are used with volume licensing products.

KMS Activation

KMS typically requires little configuration when the network has Dynamic DNS (DDNS) and enables automatic publishing of services. DNS publishing is enabled by default. If there are multiple KMS hosts in the network or if DDNS is not supported in the network, KMS will require more configuration. Only one KMS host is able to update DNS entries; thus, other KMS hosts will not be able to change SRV records without changing the DNS server.

KMS configuration involves the following tasks:

- Configuring KMS hosts
- Installing KMS hosts
- Configuring DNS permissions
- Configuring KMS clients

Configuring KMS Hosts

The **Software License Manager** (**Slmgr.vbs**) is a Visual Basic (VB) script that is used to configure Volume Activation. It can be run locally or remotely. The script should be run from an elevated command prompt to ensure the key operations are not prohibited when the script runs. To open an elevated command prompt, click Start, right-click Command Prompt, and select Run as Administrator.

The general syntax of Slmgr.vbs is as follows:

```
slmgr.vbs /parameter
```

The following syntax shows the additional parameters needed to run Slmgr.vbs remotely, which includes the target computer name, username, and password:

```
slmgr.vbs TargetComputerName [username] [password]
/parameter [options]
```

Slmgr.vbs has various options that you can use. Enter slmgr.vbs at a command prompt to view slmgr.vbs options (Figure 2-29). The Windows Script Host screen will display the usage of the Windows Software Licensing Manager tool, the global options available, and the advanced options available.

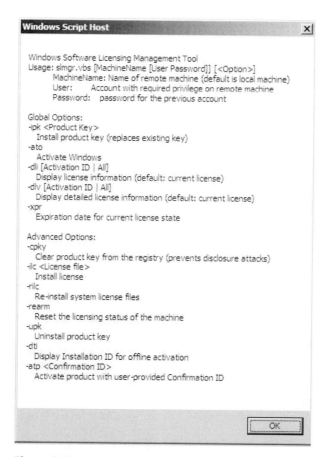

Figure 2-29 Slmgr.vbs options
© Cengage Learning 2012

Allowing WMI Traffic through the Windows Firewall Another consideration any time that you are sending traffic across a network is the security settings that might affect the transmission of the traffic. In order for VA to work and not be blocked by the Windows Firewall, the Windows Firewall must be configured to allow Windows Management Instrumentation (WMI) traffic; likewise, the same concept would apply for other security devices that you have enabled on the network. Allow the Windows Management Instrumentation (WMI) exception in Windows Firewall, in a single subnet.

For multiple subnets, allow the following connections:

- Windows Management Instrumentation (ASync-In)
- Windows Management Instrumentation (DCOM-In)
- Windows Management Instrumentation (WMI-In)
- Allow remote access in the scope

These settings can be configured using Windows Firewall with Advanced Security (Figure 2-30). Likewise, if other firewalls or security devices block traffic, they will need to be configured to allow this traffic. The purpose of this section is to address the security considerations that need to be taken into account, not to cover all potential security settings that would be necessary to allow the traffic through the network, since they will vary greatly from one network to another. Figure 2-30 depicts the Windows Firewall with Advanced Security settings.

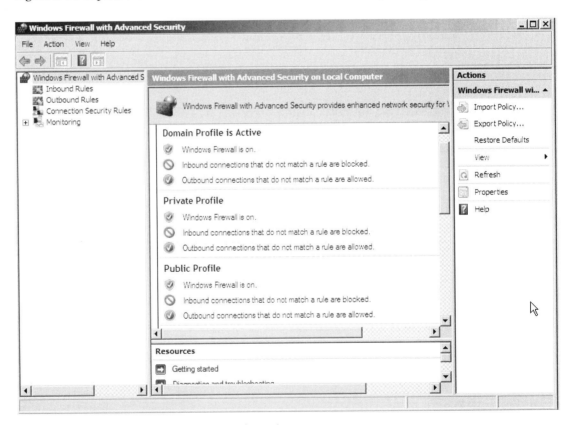

Figure 2-30 Windows Firewall with Advanced Security
© Cengage Learning 2012

Installing KMS Hosts Windows 7, Windows Server 2008 R2, Windows Server 2008, Windows Vista, and Windows Server 2003 can serve as KMS hosts. You can enable KMS functionality using Slmgr.vbs.

A KMS host on a Windows Vista system can only activate other Vista systems.

In order to install a KMS key on the host, you will first need to have the KMS key. Enter the following command to enable KMS functionality and then restart the Software Licensing Service, or restart the system:

```
slmgr.vbs /ipk <KmsKey>
```

A KMS key can activate up to six hosts on a network (the initial KMS host and five others).

To activate the host online, use **slmgr.vbs /ato.** To activate over the phone, use **slui.exe 4.**

Enter **slmgr.vbs /dli** at the command prompt to check the KMS count. Additionally, event 12290 in the Key Management Service log displays computers requesting activation and the timestamp of each request. The Key Management Service logs will appear in the applications and services logs.

Table 2-1 shows some additional KMS commands and settings.

Table 2-1   Additional Key Management Service (KMS) commands

Description	Command/Setting
Manually assign KMS host	slmgr.vbs /skms <KMS_FQDN>:<port>
Enable auto-discovery for KMS client	slmgr.vbs /ckms
Change activation interval	slmgr.vbs /sai
Change activation renewal interval	slmgr.vbs /sri
Disable DNS publishing	slmgr.vbs /cdns
Enable DNS publishing	slmgr.vbs /sdns

Changing DNS Permissions for SRV Records   If there are multiple KMS hosts, the SRV default permissions must be configured to allow updates by each SRV group member. An SRV record, which is also referred to as a Service record, is a record of data that DNS uses to identify services available. The general basic steps to enable each KMS host to update the SRV record include:

1. Create an Active Directory global security group for KMS hosts.
   a. Click **Start,** click **All Programs,** click **Administrative Tools,** and click **Active Directory Users and Computers.**
   b. Right-click **Users** in the expanded organization, click **New,** and click **Group.**
   c. Enter a name for the KMS group in the **New Object – Group** dialog box.
   d. Click **OK.**

2. Add KMS hosts to the Active Directory global security group just created.

   a. Right-click on the group and select **Properties**.

   b. On the **Members** tab, click **Add**.

   c. From the **Select Users, Contacts, Computers, or Groups** dialog box, click **Object Types**.

   d. Check **Computers** and click **OK**.

   e. Input KMS host machines names in the **Enter Object Names** dialog box.

   f. Click **Apply** and click **OK**. An SRV record will be created when the first KMS host is created.

3. Set SRV group permissions to allow updates by group members.

   a. Open DNS Manager: click **Start**, click **All Programs**, click **Administrative Tools**, and click **DNS**.

   b. Right-click the DNS server, select **Properties**, and click **Add** from the Security tab.

   c. Select permissions for the group and click **OK**.

Manually Creating SRV Records in DNS Network environments not supporting DDNS should disable auto-publishing using the **/cdns** option of the slmgr.vbs script, as described previously, to prevent failed DNS publishing events from collecting in the event log. You can manually create an SRV record in DNS.

Activity 2-6: Create an SRV Record in DNS

Time Required: Approximately 15 minutes
Objective: Learn how to manually create an SRV record in DNS
Description: In this activity, you will manually create a new SRV resource record for the location for the forwarding lookup zone (using DNS Manager).

1. Open DNS Manager: click **Start**, click **Administrative Tools**, and click **DNS**.

2. Expand the **Forward Lookup Zones** section in the left panel (Figure 2-31).

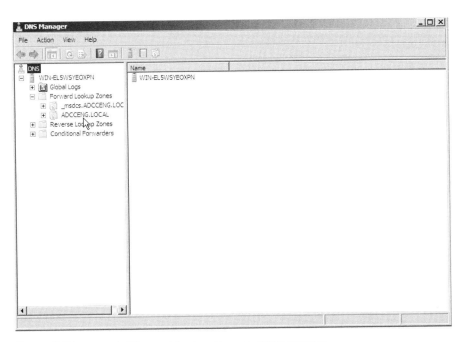

Figure 2-31 Expanded Forward Lookup Zones in DNS Manager

© Cengage Learning 2012

3. Select the computer name and then right-click the computer name and select **Other New Records**.

4. In the **Resource Record Type** dialog box, scroll down to select **Service Location (SRV)** and click **Create Record**. The **New Resource Record** dialog will display (Figure 2-32).

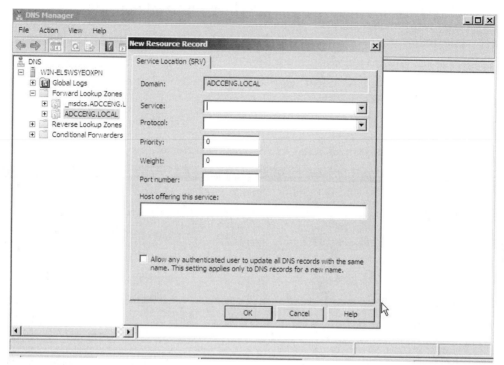

Figure 2-32 New Resource Record
© Cengage Learning 2012

5. Enter the values depicted in Table 2-2 and click **OK** to create the SRV record.

Table 2-2 contains default settings for an SRV resource record.

Table 2-2 SRV resource record settings

Name	Setting
Service	_VLMCS
Protocol	_TCP
Port number	1688
Host offering the service	FQDN of KMS Host
Priority	0
Weight	0

Deploying KMS Clients
Use the system preparation (Sysprep) tool or the Slmgr.vbs script when using the Windows Automated Installation Kit (Windows AIK) for deployment and activation. The Windows AIK enables you to create and deploy customized images for supported Windows operating systems. Windows AIK enables you to do unattended installations, capture images, and create PE images (additional information is available from Microsoft's Web site for downloading and using the Windows AIK: *http://www.microsoft.com/downloads/en/details. aspx?FamilyID=c7d4bc6d-15f3-4284-9123-679830d629f2&displaylang=en*).

Manually Activating a KMS Client KMS clients, by default, will activate themselves at defined intervals. However, you can manullay activate KMS clients using the slmgr.vbs command. Enter the following command from a command prompt to manually activate KMS:

```
slmgr.vbs /ato
```

Windows 7 and Windows Server 2008 R2 use KMS activation, by default. Install a MAK key, if you want to change KMS clients to MAK clients. To change MAK clients to KMS clients, enter the following command and run **slmgr.vbs /ato** to activate the KMS client:

```
slmgr.vbs /ipk <KmsSetupKey>
```

Table 2-3 depicts the client setup keys for Windows 7 and Windows Server 2008 R2, available from Microsoft's Web site.

Table 2-3 KMS client setup keys for Windows 7 and Windows Server 2008 R2

Operating System Edition	Product Key
Windows 7	
Windows 7 Professional	FJ82H-XT6CR-J8D7P-XQJJ2-GPDD4
Windows 7 Professional N	MRPKT-YTG23-K7D7T-X2JMM-QY7MG
Windows 7 Enterprise	33PXH-7Y6KF-2VJC9-XBBR8-HVTHH
Windows 7 Enterprise N	YDRBP-3D83W-TY26F-D46B2-XCKRJ
Windows 7 Enterprise E	C29WB-22CC8-VJ326-GHFJW-H9DH4
Windows Server 2008 R2	
Windows Server 2008 R2 HPC Edition	FKJQ8-TMCVP-FRMR7-4WR42-3JCD7
Windows Server 2008 R2 Datacenter	74YFP-3QFB3-KQT8W-PMXWJ-7M648
Windows Server 2008 R2 Enterprise	489J6-VHDMP-X63PK-3K798-CPX3Y
Windows Server 2008 R2 for Itanium-Based Systems	GT63C-RJFQ3-4GMB6-BRFB9-CB83V
Windows Server 2008 R2 Standard	YC6KT-GKW9T-YTKYR-T4X34-R7VHC
Windows Web Server 2008 R2	6TPJF-RBVHG-WBW2R-86QPH-6RTM4

MAK Activation

MAK uses Microsoft's hosted activation services for a one-time activation. MAK can be installed during the installation of the operating system or after an operating system installation. To install during initial installation, include a MAK in an unattended setup file (Unattend.xml), which can be used with Setup.exe or Windows Deployment Services.

Activity 2-7: Change the Product Key for MAK Activation

Time Required: Approximately 15 minutes
Objective: Learn how to change the product key for MAK activation
Description: In this activity, you will change the product key for MAK activation. Implied within this activity is that you already have a product key for MAK activation. To install a MAK after operating system installation, use the Control Panel System item or run the slmgr.vbs script. This activity includes the steps using the Control Panel.

1. Click **Start,** click **Control Panel,** double-click **System.**

2. Click **Change Product Key**.

3. Enter the MAK in the **Change your product key for activation** dialog box (Figure 2-33).

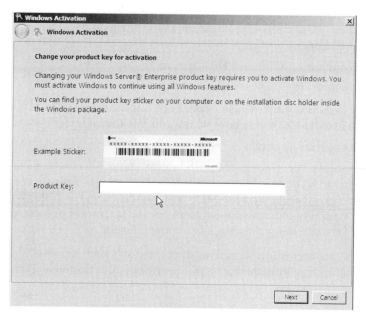

Figure 2-33 MAK activation key
© Cengage Learning 2012

4. Click **Next** and complete changing your product key for Windows Activation.

The slmgr.vbs command to change your product key is **slmgr.vbs /ipk <MAK>**

Best Practices

1. When planning WDS, ensure that your server meets the prerequisites for installing WDS.

2. When planning WDS, ensure that the client operating systems are supported by WDS.

3. Use the Boot images provided with the Windows Server 2008 DVD.

4. Organizations typically use one boot image, but multiple install images.

5. Use a discover image when the network or the system does not support PXE boot.

6. WDS image types to consider during the planning phase are boot images, install images, discover images, and capture images.

7. The PXE boot setting, *Do Not Respond to Any Client Computer*, essentially disables PXE.

8. The WDS server needs to have at least one boot image and one install image.

9. Use the Windows Automated Installation Kit to create bootable media with discover images.

Chapter Summary

- Windows Deployment Services (WDS) provides the capability to install supported Windows operating systems remotely using a network-based installation. This provides additional efficiency and consistency in the manner in which operating systems are installed within the organization.

- Installing and configuring Windows Deployment Services includes:
  - Installing Windows Deployment Services
  - Configuring Windows Deployment Services by adding the boot and install images. You need to install at least one boot image and one install image
  - Installing the operating system

- Volume Activation (VA) provides the capability for volume licensing, using a Multiple Activation Key (MAK) or Key Management Service (KMS) to activate the operating system. Volume activation is used for Microsoft Windows Server 2008, Windows 7, and Windows Vista. Volume activation automates the activation process and makes the management of the activation process much more efficient.

KMS enables volume activation within an organization's own network. MAK activates the product on a system on a one-time basis. MAK uses Microsoft's hosted activation services.

Key Terms

boot image   Client computers will boot into a boot image in order to install the operating system.

capture image   A capture image enables you to create custom install images. You can capture the image of an operating system using the Image Capture Wizard and use that image as your install image.

Deployment Server   A Deployment Server provides complete Windows Deployment Services functionality and when you select the Deployment Server option, both the Deployment Server and Transport Server are installed, which includes the WDS image store.

discover image   A discover image enables operating system installation on a system that cannot boot from the network using the Pre-Boot Execution Environment (PXE).

install image   Install images are deployed to the client computer; they are the operating system images.

Key Management Service (KMS)   KMS enables volume activation within an organization's own network.

Multiple Activation Key (MAK)   MAK enables product activation on a system on a one-time basis. MAK uses Microsoft's hosted activation services.

Pre-Boot Execution Environment (PXE)   PXE is an environment to boot computers over a network connection.

Remote Installation Services (RIS)   RIS provides a remote deployment capability available in Windows Server 2003; replaced by WDS in Windows Server 2008.

Software License Manager (Slmgr.vbs)   Slmgr is a Visual Basic (VB) script that is used to configure Volume Activation.

Transport Server   A Transport Server provides the core networking components to transmit data, such as operating system images, from a standalone server, but it does not include the WDS image store. It is used for booting from the network using PXE and TFTP and is often used in environments without AD DS, DNS, or DHCP.

Trivial File Transfer Protocol (TFTP)　TFTP is a file transfer protocol that is similar to a basic form of FTP and is used to transfer files; uses User Datagram Protocol (UDP).

Volume Activation (VA)　VA provides the capability for volume licensing; automates the activation process and makes the management of the activation process much more efficient.

Volume License Key (VLK)　VLK is a term that refers to the product key used for volume licensing, allowing one product key to be used for multiple installations.

Windows Deployment Services (WDS)　WDS is a Windows Server 2008 role that provides the capability to install supported Windows operating systems remotely using a network-based installation.

Review Questions

1. Which of the following is not a category of components in Windows Deployment Services?

    a. Server components

    b. Domain components

    c. Client components

    d. Management components

2. Which of the following is not a WDS Server component?

    a. PRE

    b. PXE

    c. TFTP

    d. Shared folder

3. Which of the following is a WDS Client component?

    a. GUI

    b. PXE

    c. TFTP

    d. Shared folder

4. Which of the following is *not* an enhancement of WDS in Windows Server 2008?

    a. Multicast functionality

    b. Enhancements to the PXE server component

    c. Enhanced client GUI

    d. Supports all client operating systems

5. Which of the following is not a benefit of Windows Deployment Services?

    a. Enables network-based Windows operating system installations

    b. Increased installation costs

    c. Reduced installation costs

    d. Consistent installation process

6. Which of the following is an option when installing Windows Deployment Services?
   a. Installation Server
   b. Boot Server
   c. Deployment Server
   d. Access Server

7. Which of the following provides complete Windows Deployment Services functionality?
   a. Deployment Server
   b. Transport Server
   c. Core Server
   d. Access Server

8. Which of the following is not a prerequisite for the default WDS installation?
   a. AD DS
   b. DHCP
   c. DNS
   d. FAT

9. How many boot images and install images do you need to add to the WDS server?
   a. One boot and one install
   b. One boot and two install
   c. Two boot and one install
   d. Two boot and two install

10. How many boot images can be in the boot menu?
    a. 1
    b. 2
    c. 12
    d. 13

11. How much RAM do you need on the client computer to install the install image?
    a. 512 MB
    b. 1 GB
    c. 5 GB
    d. 1024 MB

12. Which of the following enables an operating system installation on a system that cannot boot from the network using the Pre-Boot Execution Environment (PXE)?
    a. Multicast install
    b. No PXE install
    c. Unattended install
    d. Discover images

13. Which of the following is not a method for installing Windows Deployment Services?
    a. Initial Configuration Wizard
    b. Server Manager
    c. Volume Activation
    d. Command Line

2

14. Which of the following provides the capability for volume licensing?
    a. VL
    b. VA
    c. VBA
    d. VBS

15. Which of the following is not a KMS configuration task?
    a. Configuring KMS Hosts
    b. Configuring DNS
    c. Installing KMS Hosts
    d. Configuring WDS

16. Which of the following is a method of providing Volume Activation?
    a. KMS
    b. KVA
    c. VAK
    d. MPLS

17. Which of the following is a VB script that is used to configure Volume Activation?
    a. VBA
    b. Visual Basic
    c. Slmgr
    d. Slvba

18. If there are multiple KMS hosts, what default permissions must be configured to allow updates?
    a. SRA
    b. SRV
    c. KMS
    d. VA

19. Which of the following views the computer's activation status?
    a. slmgr.vbs /dli
    b. slmgr.vbs /dle
    c. slmgr.vbs /dmi
    d. slmgr.vbs /dlc

20. Which event in the Key Management Service log displays computers requesting activation and the timestamp of each request?
    a. 12290
    b. 19920
    c. 12090
    d. 21290

Case Projects

Case Project 2-1: Windows Deployment Services (WDS)

The IT department in New Enterprises deploys machine images by building machines by hand and on a limited basis they use the Remote Installation Service in Server 2003. They realize they cannot continue to use this process because of the growth New Enterprises is experiencing and the amount of time it takes to build machine images by hand. They would like to use WDS to build machine images when they replace server 2003 with Sever 2008 Enterprise Edition with Active Directory.

The IT department is asking you, as the Network Engineer with Peppin Associates, to explain the following:

1. Explain in a technical report how WDS should be used.

2. Provide a business justification for using WDS.

Case Project 2-2: Key Management Services (KMS) and Multiple Activation Key (MAK)

The IT department in New Enterprises also realizes the potential need for Volume Activation within the organization. Therefore, they are asking for the following information to support their decision to implement Volume Activation:

1. A technical report on how KMS will work within Server 2008 Enterprise Edition to activate machine images.

2. As part of the report they are asking you, as the Network Engineer with Peppin Associates, to provide a comparison between the use of KMS and MAK for machine activation.

Case Project 2-3: Value-Added of WDS and VA

The CIO needs to justify the benefits of WDS and Volume Activation to senior management in the organization. Therefore, they are asking for the following information in regards to WDS and Volume Activation:

1. In business terms, list the benefits of both WDS and Volume Activation.

2. In a company of 500 employees, identify the resource savings of implementing WDS and using Volume Activation.

Configuring Windows Server 2008 Storage Services

After reading this chapter and completing the exercises, you will be able to:

- Describe basic storage terminology

- Utilize the Disk Management console to perform disk management tasks

- Create new volumes and partitions

- Add a mirror to a volume

- Manage a Virtual Hard Disk (VHD) and create and attach a VHD

- Describe the use of mount points and multipath I/O (MPIO)

- Create mount points and install MPIO

- Describe the use of and configure the Microsoft Internet Small Computer System Interface (iSCSI) Software Initiator

- Manage storage devices with Storage Manager for SANs

- Define a server cluster in Storage Manager for SANs

This chapter shows you how to use the various storage management tools and utilities in Windows Server 2008 to effectively manage storage requirements in an enterprise network. Meeting today's storage requirements in organizations is a challenging task; organizations must be able to provide massive storage capabilities, they need to provide fault-tolerance and data recovery solutions, and they need to provide quality of service solutions giving priority based on application or criticality of the data. Enhanced storage capabilities and solutions in Windows Server 2008 meet the increasing storage demands from organizations.

Through the Disk Management console in Windows Server 2008, you will perform most of your storage management functions. First, you will become familiar with the Disk Management console, create new volumes and partitions, and add mirrors to a volume. Then, you will learn how to create mount points, install multipath I/O (MPIO), and describe and configure the Microsoft Internet Small Computer System Interface (iSCSI) Software Initiator. Then, you will learn about storage area network (SAN) capabilities in Windows Server 2008 and utilize the Storage Manager for SANs.

Basic Storage Terminology

Throughout this chapter, we will discuss many basic storage concepts and use basic storage terminology. Following are brief descriptions of many of the basic storage concepts and terminology:

- **Physical drive.** The hard drive is the physical drive. One physical drive can be partitioned into multiple logical drives.
- **Cluster.** A cluster is the smallest amount of disk space that can be used as an allocation unit for holding a file.
- **Partition.** One physical drive can be partitioned into multiple logical partitions.
- **Primary partition.** A primary partition contains one file system and is marked as a bootable partition.
- **Extended partition.** Extended partitions are not bootable. An extended partition can be sub-divided into logical drives. One extended partition can exist on a hard drive.
- **Volume.** A volume is a logical interface referring to data from a single logical storage area and file system.
- **Spanned volume.** A spanned volume has a single address with hard disk sections from different disks logically combined and referred to as a single element.
- **Striped volume.** A striped volume writes data across multiple disks to increase performance.
- **Mirror volume.** A mirror volume copies the data written to one disk to another disk to increase fault tolerance.
- **Redundant Array of Independent Disks (RAID).** RAID is a data storage technology that is used to increase storage performance and fault tolerance. RAID can be implemented through software or hardware to increase data reliability and input/output performance. Windows Server 2008 supports RAID 0, RAID 1, and RAID 5 through software implementation.

Overview of Disk Management Capabilities

Windows Server 2008 supports basic disks and dynamic disks. A **basic disk** can be divided into partitions and is supported by previous versions of Windows. **Dynamic disks** are divided into volumes and are supported by Windows 2000 and later versions. When Windows Server 2008 initializes a disk, it initializes the disk as a basic disk. When Windows Server 2008 creates a new fault-tolerant volume set, it converts the disks to dynamic disks. When a disk is converted to a dynamic disk, there is no data loss and the partitions are automatically converted to volumes. However, when the disk is converted back to a basic disk, data loss will occur; data needs to be backed up before converting and moved to the disk after the conversion.

You use the **Disk Management console**, Diskmgmt.msc, in Windows Server 2008 to manage the disks, create volumes, create partitions, and perform other disk management tasks. Disk Management is part of the Server Manager console.

Activity 3-1: Explore the Disk Management Console

Time Required: Approximately 3 minutes
Objective: Learn how to open and explore the Disk Management console

Description: In this activity, you will open and explore the Disk Management console in Windows Server 2008. You will use the Disk Management console to perform many of the storage management tasks.

1. Open a command prompt.

2. Enter **Diskmgmt.msc.** The Disk Management console displays, as depicted in Figure 3-1.

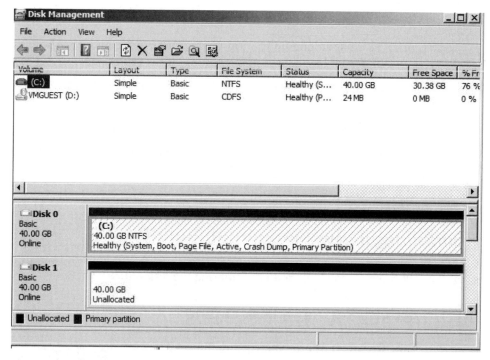

Figure 3-1 Disk Management console
© Cengage Learning 2012

3. You can also view Disk Management through the Server Manager. Open the **Server Manager**, click **Storage**, and click **Disk Management**. Disk Management displays in the Server Manager, as depicted in Figure 3-2.

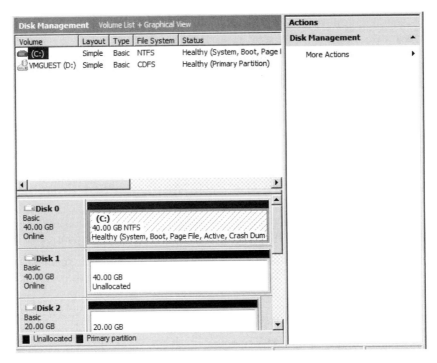

Figure 3-2 Disk Management in Server Manager
© Cengage Learning 2012

4. Click each volume in the top of the center pane and note how the corresponding volumes are highlighted in the bottom of the center pane.

5. Right-click a volume to display a context menu that displays the various actions that can be performed on disk volumes. Note that, depending on the type and status of each volume, certain actions may not be available. For example the "Mark Partition as Active" option is only available for inactive partitions.

The Disk Management Console is available on versions of Windows since Windows 2000 for managing disks.

Initializing a New Disk

When you install a new disk, you must initialize the disk if it has not been formatted. However, if the disk is offline, you will first need to bring the disk online.

Activity 3-2: Set a Disk Online

Time Required: Approximately 3 minutes
Objective: Learn how to set a disk online

Description: In this activity, you will use the Disk Management console to set a disk online. This activity requires a disk in an offline state. Perform the following steps to change a disk from offline to online:

1. Open **Server Manager**, if it is not already open.

2. Expand **Storage** and select **Disk Management**.

3. Right-click the offline disk that you want to bring online.

4. Select **Online** (Figure 3-3).

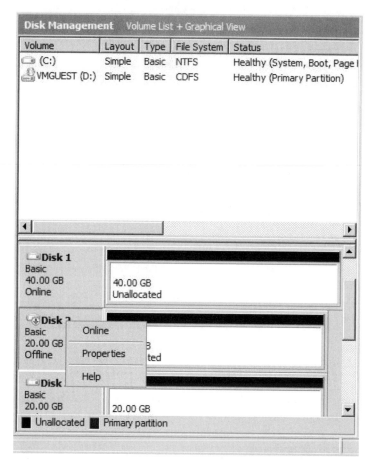

Figure 3-3 Bringing a disk online using Disk Management
© Cengage Learning 2012

After the disk is online, you can initialize the disk. The following activity initializes a disk.

Activity 3-3: Initialize a Disk

Time Required: Approximately 10 minutes
Objective: Learn how to initialize a disk

Description: In this activity, you will use the Disk Management console to initialize a disk. This activity requires an unallocated, unknown disk.

1. Open **Server Manager**, if it is not already open.

2. Expand **Storage** and select **Disk Management**.

3. Right-click **Disk Management** and select **Rescan Disks** (Figure 3-4).

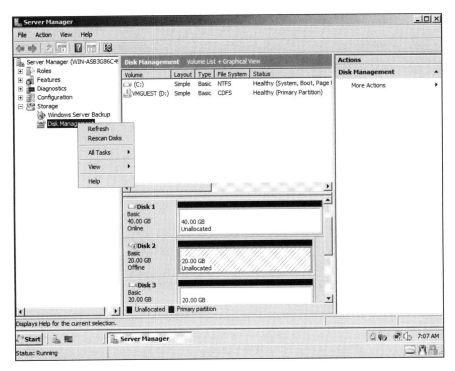

Figure 3-4 Rescan Disks
© Cengage Learning 2012

4. Right-click the unallocated disk labeled Unknown, shown as Disk 5 in the figure, and select **Initialize Disk** (Figure 3-5).

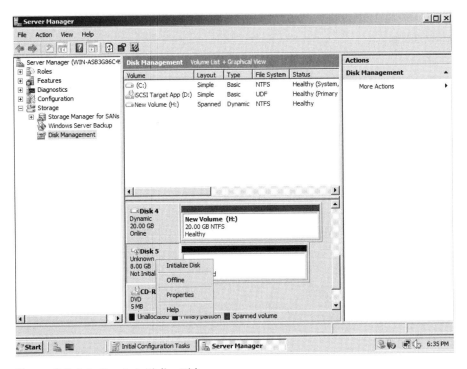

Figure 3-5 Selecting to Initialize Disk
© Cengage Learning 2012

5. The Initialize Disk dialog box lets you choose the partition style as MBR (Master Boot Record) or GPT (GUID Partition Table) (Figure 3-6).

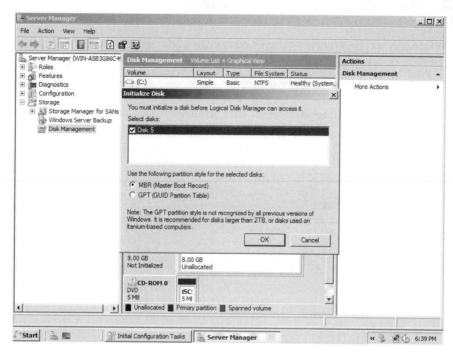

Figure 3-6 Initialize Disk dialog box
© Cengage Learning 2012

 For any disk larger than 2 TB, GPT is recommended.

6. Select **MBR (Master Boot Record)** and click **OK**.

Basic and Dynamic Disks

When working with basic disks, you will commonly perform the following tasks:

- Create partitions and logical drives
- Delete partitions and logical drives
- Format partitions and mark them as active
- Convert a basic disk to a dynamic disk

When working with dynamic disks, you will commonly perform the following tasks:

- Create volumes
- Delete or remove volumes
- Extend volumes
- Manage RAID volumes
- Convert from a dynamic disk to a basic disk

 Before converting from a dynamic disk to a basic disk, you need to back up all data. After the conversion is complete, you will need to restore that data.

Activity 3-4: Convert a Disk to a Dynamic Disk

Time Required: Approximately 10 minutes
Objective: Learn how to convert a disk to a dynamic disk

Description: In this activity, you will use the Disk Management console to convert a disk to a dynamic disk. This activity requires a basic disk to be converted.

1. Open **Server Manager**, if it is not already open.

2. Expand **Storage** and select **Disk Management**.

3. Right-click the disk you want to convert (Disk 2 as shown in the figure) to a dynamic disk and select **Convert to Dynamic Disk** (Figure 3-7).

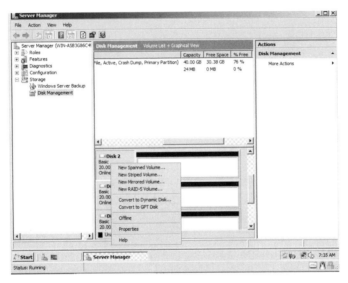

Figure 3-7 Selecting Convert to Dynamic Disk
© Cengage Learning 2012

4. The **Convert to Dynamic Disk** dialog box displays and you can select the disks you want to convert to dynamic disks. Select the desired disk(s) and click **OK** (Figure 3-8). Click **Convert** if necessary, in the Disks to Convert dialog box.

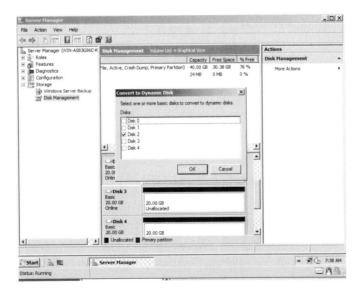

Figure 3-8 Convert to Dynamic Disk dialog box
© Cengage Learning 2012

5. Microsoft Server 2008 will display a warning about converting to a dynamic disk. Click **Yes**. The disk will display in Disk Management as a dynamic disk (Figure 3-9).

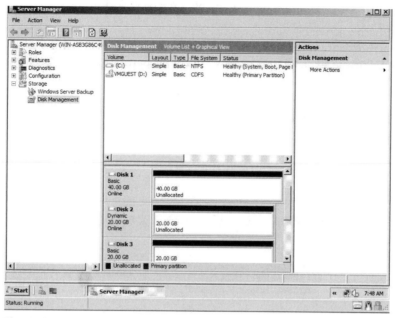

Figure 3-9 Disk displays as a dynamic disk
© Cengage Learning 2012

Creating a Volume or Partition

You can create a new volume or partition on a disk that has empty space. If the disk is a basic disk, Windows Server 2008 creates a primary partition. If the disk is a dynamic disk, Windows Server 2008 creates a volume. If the space is part of an extended partition, Windows Server 2008 creates a logical drive. Extended disks, primarily used for only data storage, provide additional storage space to a volume without having to make it bootable. They are also transferrable to another server with the same server specifications.

Potential volume types include:

- **Simple volume**. A simple volume includes space from only one disk.

- **Spanned volume**. A spanned volume extends across multiple disks; you can use up to 32 disks in a spanned volume.

- **Mirrored volume**. A mirrored volume duplicates data across two disks to increase fault-tolerance.

- **Striped volume**. A striped volume writes data to two or more disks to increase performance.

- **RAID-5 volume**. A RAID-5 volume stripes data across three or more disks and uses **parity** to be able to recover data if a disk fails.

Windows Server 2008 supports RAID-0 (striped volume), RAID-1 (mirrored volume), and RAID-5 (RAID-5 volume). RAID can be used to enhance performance or provide fault tolerance in the event of a disk failure.

Disk Management does not provide the option to create an extended partition. You need to use Diskpart.exe to create an extended partition.

Activity 3-5: Create a New Volume or Partition

Time Required: Approximately 20 minutes
Objective: Learn how to create a new volume or partition

Description: In this activity, you will see the steps to use the Disk Management console to create a new volume or partition. This activity requires two dynamic disks with unallocated space. Perform the following steps to create a new volume or partition:

1. Open **Server Manager,** if it is not already open.

2. Expand **Storage** and select **Disk Management.**

3. Right-click the unallocated disk.

4. Select the type of volume or partition to create (Figure 3-10 reflects New Striped Volume).

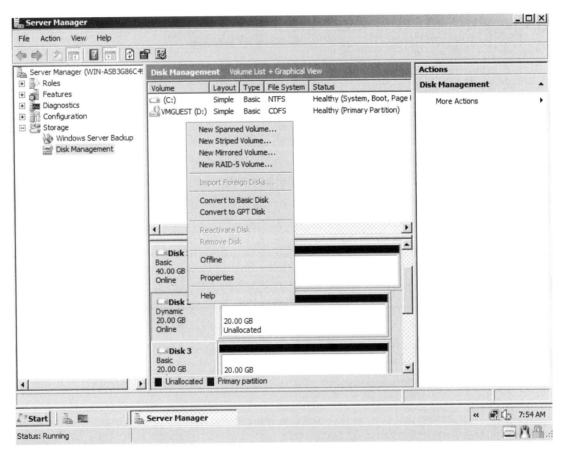

Figure 3-10 Type of volume to create

© Cengage Learning 2012

The options available and steps in this activity will depend on the type of disks and the number of unallocated volumes. Options available include: New Simple Volume, New Spanned Volume, New Striped Volume, New Mirrored Volume, and New RAID-5 Volume.

5. The New Striped Volume Wizard displays. Click **Next** to start the Wizard (Figure 3-11).

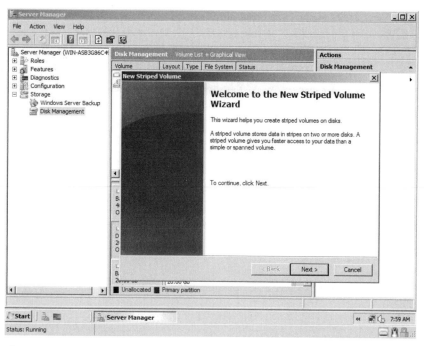

Figure 3-11 The Wizard begins
© Cengage Learning 2012

6. From the **Select Disks** dialog box (Figure 3-12), select the disk that you want to add to the volume set and click **Add**. Repeat for additional disks to add to the volume set. When finished adding disks and selecting other attributes, click **Next**.

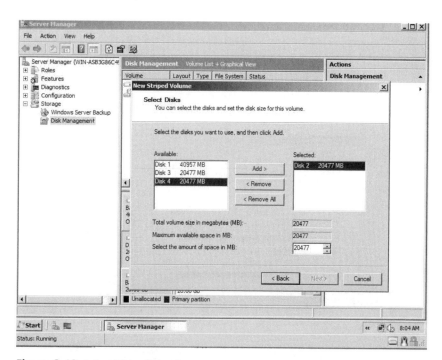

Figure 3-12 Select Disks dialog box
© Cengage Learning 2012

7. From the **Assign Drive Letter or Path** page, you can select the desired drive letter or mount point (Figure 3-13). Click **Next**.

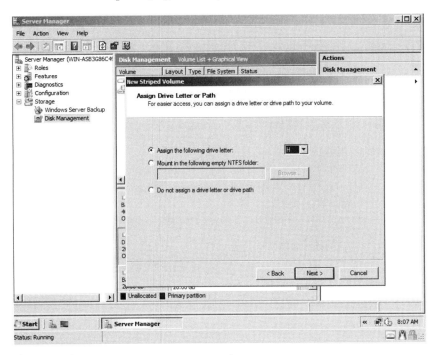

Figure 3-13 Select drive letter or mount point
© Cengage Learning 2012

8. From the **Format Volume** page, select the desired formatting options. Click **Next** and then click **Finish**.

9. Click **Yes**, when the message displays (Figure 3-14), if you are converting to a dynamic disk.

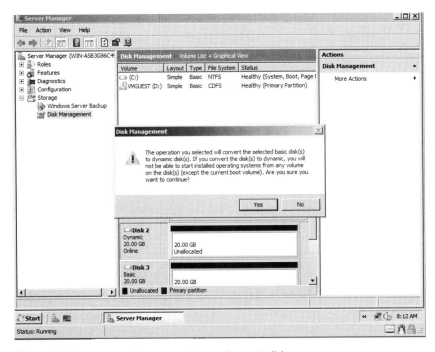

Figure 3-14 Message when converting to dynamic disk
© Cengage Learning 2012

10. The new volume is displayed in Disk Management (Figure 3-15).

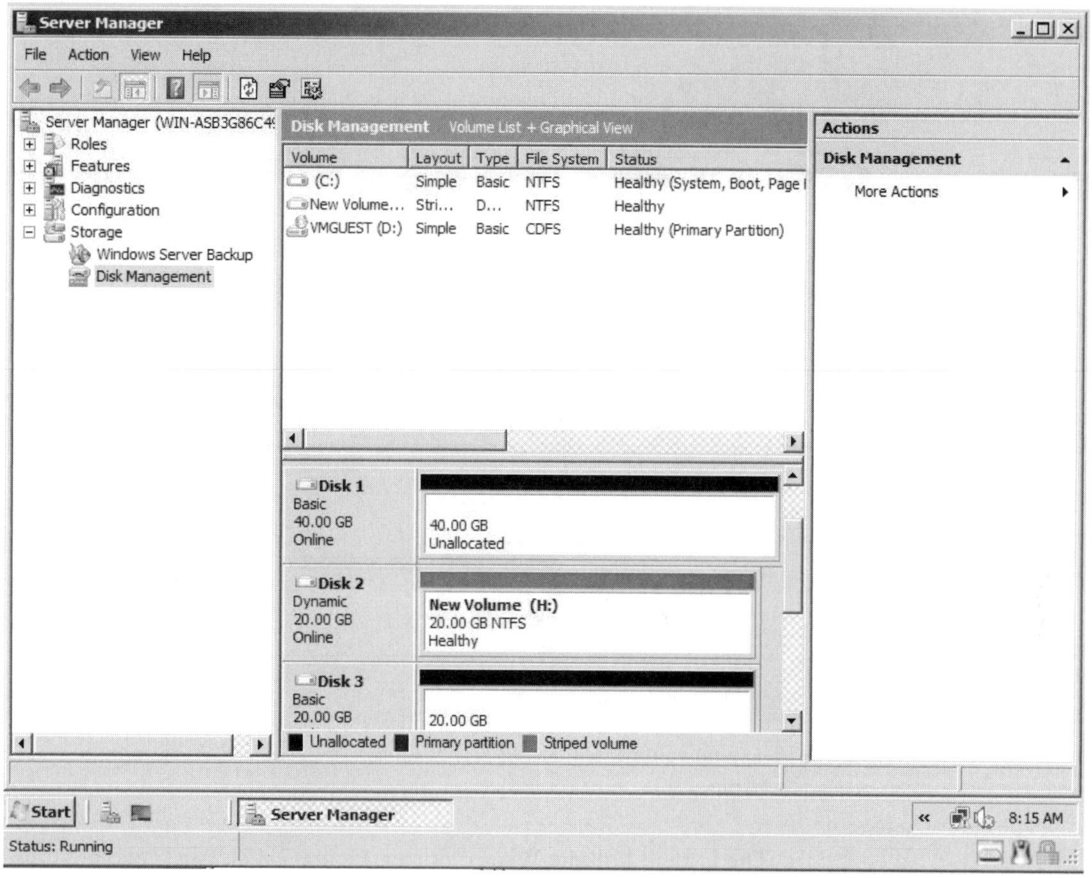

Figure 3-15 New volume displays in Disk Management
© Cengage Learning 2012

Extending a Volume

Frequently, growing businesses require additional space on drives and servers for data storage. A common task, as organizational requirements change, is to add space to a volume using an extended volume. If the volume is a simple volume or a spanned volume, you can easily extend the volume and you do not have to back up or restore your files and you do not need to reboot the system. However, many organizations back up their data before performing any major operation for additional security.

Activity 3-6: Extend a Volume

Time Required: Approximately 20 minutes
Objective: Learn how to extend a volume in Windows Server 2008

Description: In this activity, you will use the Disk Management console to extend a volume. This activity requires two formatted, basic disks. Perform the following steps to extend a volume:

1. Open **Server Manager**, if it is not already open.

2. Expand **Storage** and select **Disk Management**.

3. Right-click the volume.

4. Select **Extend Volume** (Figure 3-16).

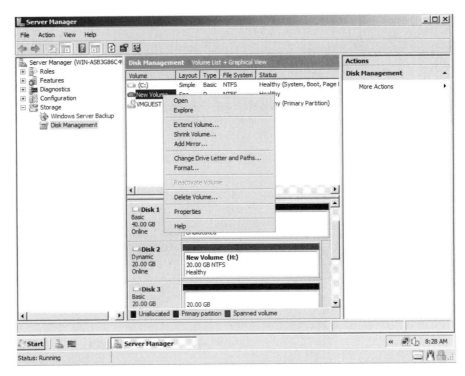

Figure 3-16 Extend Volume
© Cengage Learning 2012

5. The **Extend Volume Wizard** opens (Figure 3-17). Click **Next**.

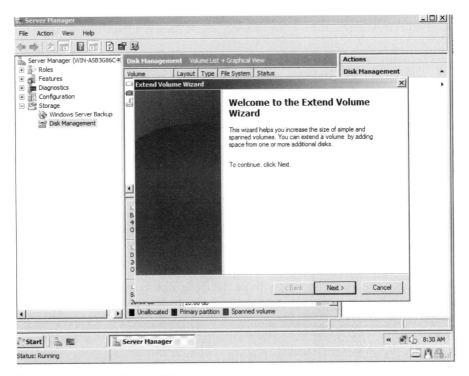

Figure 3-17 Extend Volume Wizard
© Cengage Learning 2012

6. If necessary, highlight the desired disks that have unallocated space and click **Add**.

7. Additionally, you can specify the amount of space to add (Figure 3-18). Click **Next**.

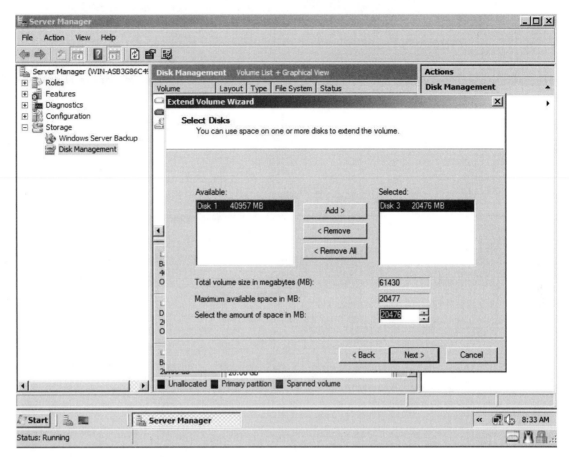

Figure 3-18 Select disks and space to add
© Cengage Learning 2012

8. From the final **Extend Volume Wizard** confirmation page, click **Finish**.

 If disk needs to be converted to a dynamic disk before extending, you will receive a confirmation message.

Adding a Mirror to a Volume

Adding a mirror to a volume increases fault-tolerance; if one disk fails, that data will be available on the mirrored disk. A mirror volume stores an exact copy of the data, and is used primarily to back up critical data. Companies use a mirror volume to decrease the odds of losing data. Although mirror volumes cost more, as they require double the disk storage, the value of having an exact copy of critical data typically far outweighs the cost. You can add a mirror to a volume when you create the volume or you can add a mirror to an existing volume.

Activity 3-7: Add a Mirror to a Volume

Time Required: Approximately 15 minutes
Objective: Learn how to add a mirror to a volume in Windows Server 2008

Description: In this activity, you will see the steps to use the Disk Management console to add a mirror to a volume. This activity assumes that you have an existing volume, which are the steps completed in the previous two activities of creating a volume and expanding a volume.

1. Open **Server Manager,** if it is not already open.

2. Expand **Storage** and select **Disk Management.**

3. Right-click the desired volume and select **Add Mirror** (Figure 3-19).

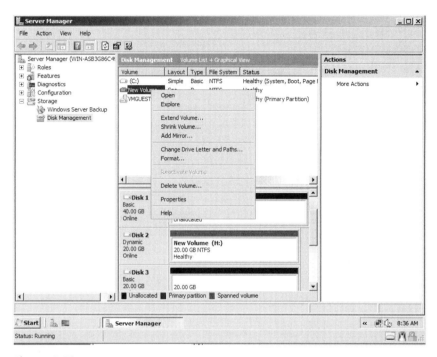

Figure 3-19 Add Mirror
© Cengage Learning 2012

4. The **Add Mirror** dialog box displays (Figure 3-20).

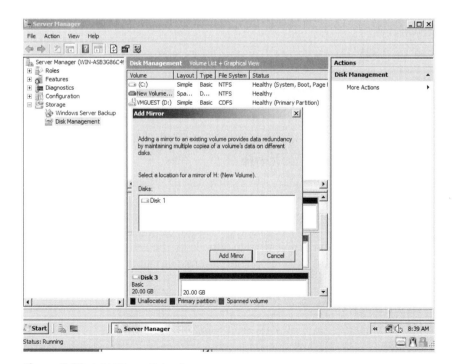

Figure 3-20 Add Mirror dialog box
© Cengage Learning 2012

5. Select the disk you would like to use as the mirror disk (Figure 3-20 reflects Disk 1). Click **Add Mirror**. If prompted to convert to a dynamic disk, click **Yes** (Figure 3-21).

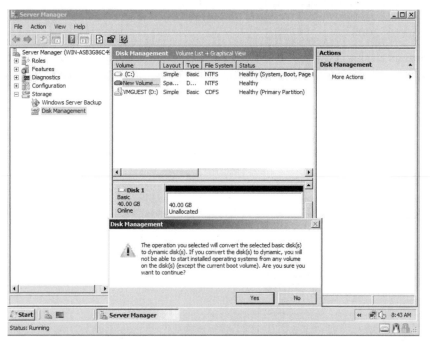

Figure 3-21 Creating the mirrored disk

© Cengage Learning 2012

Once the mirror is created, Windows Server 2008 will begin copying the data from one disk to the mirror disk.

Manage Virtual Hard Disks

The **Virtual Hard Disk (VHD) format** is a format specification commonly used with the Hyper-V functionality for supporting a virtual machine hard disk and file systems. A virtual machine hard disk is seen as a hard disk but is implemented as a single file on the native host file system. Virtual Hard Disk allows multiple operating systems to reside on the host. The VHD is encapsulated in a single file and it can then support the native file system without conflict from the server's file system. In Disk Management, the VHD will display as a physical disk and will be color coded based on its availability. It will appear blue when it has been attached and is available. It will appear gray when it is detached.

A VHD has the following advantages:

- *Restoration and backup:* Contents of a VHD are easily restored and backed up from the host server.

- *Deployment:* Virtual machines are pre-built with configurations. Multiple machines can be configured and deployed as necessary with different sets of installed tools to avoid unnecessary additional installations.

- *Isolation:* A user can be given a unique version of VHD instead of a logon with varying permissions. Each user can have a tailored version of VHD.

Use Disk Management to manage your VHD. In order to perform these actions, you will need membership in the Backup Operators or Administrators groups.

Activity 3-8: Create and Attach a VHD in Disk Management

Time Required: Approximately 20 minutes
Objective: Learn how to create and attach a VHD in Disk Management in Windows Server 2008

Description: In this activity, you will use the Disk Management console to create and attach a VHD. This activity includes two portions; you will first perform the steps to create the VHD, and then perform the steps to attach the VHD.

Steps to create a VHD:

1. Select **Create VHD** on the Disk Management console's **Action** menu. The **Create and Attach Virtual Hard Disk** dialog box displays (Figure 3-22).

Figure 3-22 Create and Attach Virtual Hard Disk dialog box
© Cengage Learning 2012

2. Specify the location to store the VHD (clicking Browse will open the default location of Libraries\Documents) and the size of the VHD (Figure 3-23 reflects 10 MB).

3. In the **Virtual hard disk format section,** select desired option (**Dynamically expanding** or **Fixed size**) (Figure 3-23 reflects Dynamically expanding).

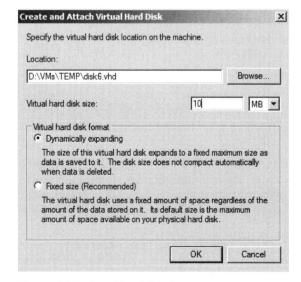

Figure 3-23 Virtual hard disk format
© Cengage Learning 2012

4. Click **OK**.

Steps to attach a VHD:

1. Select **Attach VHD** on the Disk Management console's **Action** menu. The Create and Attach Virtual Hard Disk dialog box displays (Figure 3-24).

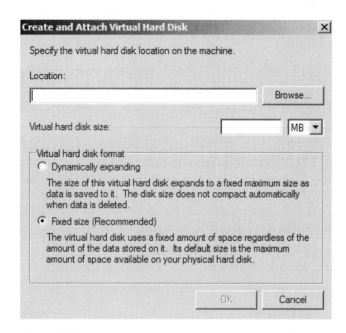

Figure 3-24 Create and Attach Virtual Hard Disk dialog box
© Cengage Learning 2012

2. Click the **Browse** button, navigate to and click the VHD file, and click **Open** to specify the VHD's file location (fully qualified path) as shown in Figure 3-25.

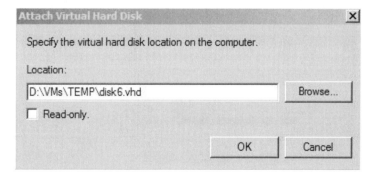

Figure 3-25 Specify the VHD location
© Cengage Learning 2012

3. Click **OK**.

A VHD can only be a basic disk.

Mount Points

Mount points enable you to access a volume from a folder on another disk; a mount point folder can be assigned to a drive. Mount points are often used to extend beyond the 26-drive letter limitation. Following are a few additional points to remember about mount points:

- Mount points can be used on basic or dynamic volumes
- Mount point volumes must have an NTFS format
- Mount point folders must be created on empty folders
- After created, mount point folder paths cannot be modified

Activity 3-9: Create a Mount Point

Time Required: Approximately 10 minutes
Objective: Learn how to create a mount point in Windows Server 2008

Description: In this activity, you will create a mount point. Complete the following steps to create a mount point.

1. Open **Server Manager**, if it is not already open.

2. Expand **Storage** and select **Disk Management**.

3. Right-click the volume and select **Change Drive Letter and Paths**.

4. Click **Add...** (Figure 3-26).

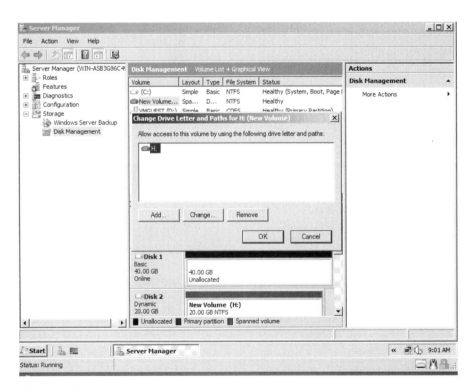

Figure 3-26 Change Drive Letter and Paths dialog box
© Cengage Learning 2012

5. In the Add Drive Letter or Path dialog box (Figure 3-27), enter the path to an empty folder.

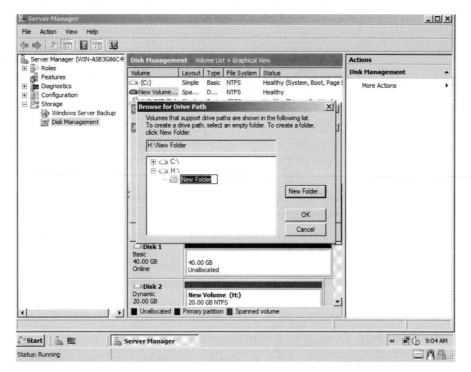

Figure 3-27 Add Drive Letter or Path dialog box
© Cengage Learning 2012

6. Click **OK** to add the path and close the dialog box.

Multipath I/O (MPIO)

In order to provide reliable access to organizational data, organizations must eliminate single points of failure. **Multipath I/O (MPIO)** provides the capability to read and write data using multiple paths to a storage device, providing redundant physical paths to the storage device. This capability increases fault tolerance against single points of failure within the communication path and the devices on the communication path to the storage device by having redundant paths accessible to a storage device. MPIO supports iSCSI, Fibre Channel and serial attached storage (SAS) connectivity options.

MPIO Major Enhancements

Windows Server 2008 R2 MPIO major enhancements include:

- *Health reporting.* Health reporting enables better diagnosis and information gathering techniques in regards to the health of the communication path to the storage device.

- *Load-balancing policy settings through the command line.* Load-balancing policy settings can be displayed and configured more easily from a command line; the MPCLAIM utility provides this capability.

- *Configuration.* The MPIO configuration report includes various elements of information including **Device Specific Module (DSM)** file information and path information. The configuration report can be saved as a text file. Additionally, you can configure MPIO settings before connecting a storage device using MPIO datacenter automation.

MPIO Load Balancing Policies

The Device Specific Module (DSM) is a new feature in Microsoft Server 2008. The Microsoft DSM driver communicates with the storage devices. DSM works with storage arrays following the **asymmetric logical unit access (ALUA)** controller model and the Active/Active controller model. Load balancing policies supported through Windows Server 2008 DSM include failover, failback, round-robin, round-robin with a subset of paths, dynamic least queue depth, and weighted path.

- **Failover.** The failover load balancing policy is not an actual load balancing method; instead, it specifies the primary path and standby paths. It is not load balancing, since the primary path is always used unless there is a failure of the primary path. If the primary path fails, a standby path is used.

- **Failback.** Failback is a similar method to failover. The primary difference being that it will switch back to the primary path when the primary path is restored.

- **Round-Robin.** The round-robin load balancing policy is an actual load balancing method. It uses each available path for input/output operations. It performs the input/output in a balanced, round-robin method.

- **Round-Robin with a Subset of Paths.** The round-robin with a subset of paths load balancing policy is similar to round-robin, but with standby paths ready for use if the primary paths fail. For normal operations, it uses a subset of paths for input/output. The standby paths are then used in the event that a primary path fails or is otherwise unavailable.

- **Dynamic Least Queue Depth.** The dynamic least queue depth performs load balancing based on the least queued path. It will forward input/output to the path with the least number of requests.

- **Weighted Path.** The weighted path load balancing policy uses weights to determine the path chosen. A path with a higher number, or weight, has less priority. When performing input/output, the path with the least weight is selected.

Activity 3-10: Install MPIO and Display MPIO Properties

Time Required: Approximately 20 minutes
Objective: Learn how to install MPIO and display MPIO properties in Windows Server 2008

Description: In this activity, you will install MPIO and display MPIO properties. This activity includes two portions; you will first install MPIO, then you will display MPIO properties.

1. Open Server Manager. If it is not open, click **Start**, click **Administrative Tools**, and click **Server Manager** (Figure 3-28).

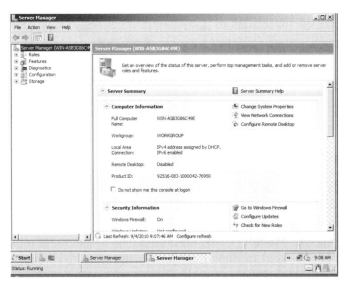

Figure 3-28 Server Manager
© Cengage Learning 2012

2. Right-click **Features** and select **Add Features** to open the Add Features Wizard (Figure 3-29).

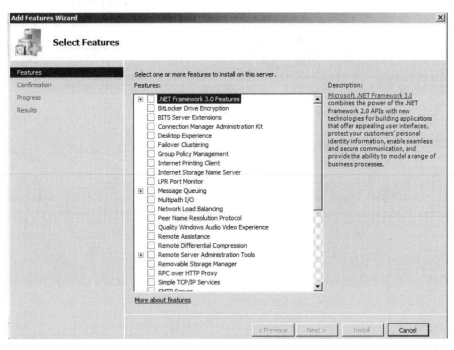

Figure 3-29 Add Features Wizard
© Cengage Learning 2012

3. The Add Features Wizard opens to the Select Features page. You can select one or more features to install on the server. Select **Multipath I/O** and click **Next** (Figure 3-30).

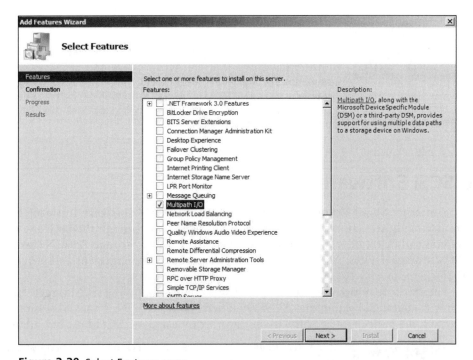

Figure 3-30 Select Features page
© Cengage Learning 2012

4. The Confirm Installation Selections page displays. Verify the features selected to install—Multipath I/O in this case—and click **Install**.

5. Click **Close** and click **Yes** to restart, if prompted to restart.

6. To display the **MPIO Properties**, click **Start**, click **Administrative Tools**, and click **MPIO** to show the MPIO Properties dialog box (Figure 3-31). Close the dialog box after exploring the options available.

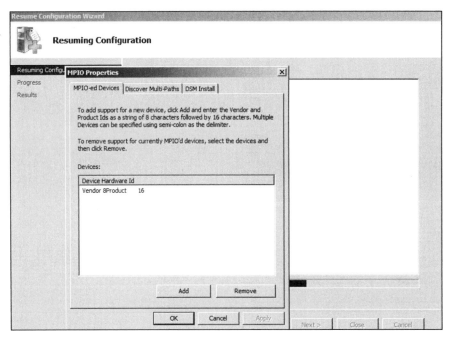

Figure 3-31 MPIO Properties dialog box
© Cengage Learning 2012

 The MPIO Properties dialog box has four tabs: MPIO Devices, Discover Multi-Paths, DSM Install, and Configuration Snapshot. Windows Server 2008 uses a Device Specific Module (DSM) that will work with storage arrays that are Active/Active and SPC-3 (SCSI Primary Commands 3) compliant. You can install third-party DSMs using the DSM Install tab. You can check for devices with multiple paths to the storage array from the Discover Multi-Paths tab. You can use the MPIO Devices tab to manually add a device.

Microsoft iSCSI Software Initiator

The **Internet Small Computer System Interface (iSCSI) Software Initiator** is a protocol for connecting host computers to an external storage array through the network adapter. You can dynamically expand your storage capacity using iSCSI **Storage Area Networks (SANs)** and iSCSI storage devices. Additionally, it can provide better management and provide more scalable performance.

The software initiator is used to establish a connection to the iSCSI target. Each software initiator is identified by a unique **iSCSI Qualified Name**, or IQN. An iSCSI session can be initiated through the built-in iSCSI software initiator or by using an iSCSI **host bus adapter (HBA)**.

 iSCSI software initiator requires more CPU utilization than using an iSCSI HBA.

The iSCSI software initiator is a feature built into Windows Sever 2008 and requires no additional installation steps. A major benefit of iSCSI is that it supports block-level access to storage devices; many applications, such as Microsoft Exchange, need the performance advantage of block-level access to storage devices. Thus, from an application performance perspective, this would be a major consideration in an organization. Another major benefit of iSCSI is the support for security protocols using **Challenge Handshake Authentication Protocol (CHAP)** and **Internet Protocol Security (IPSec)**. CHAP is used for authentication and IPSec is used for encryption.

iSCSI uses TCP port 3260.

New Features of Microsoft iSCSI Initiator

Following are the new features for the Microsoft iSCSI Initiator in Windows Server 2008 R2 and Windows 7, as defined by Microsoft:

- *GUI Redesign.* The Microsoft iSCSI Initiator GUI has been redesigned for better access to common settings.

- *Quick Connect.* Quick Connect enables one-click connections to storage devices. This does not apply to storage devices requiring additional advanced settings, such as Internet Protocol Security (IPSec) and Challenge Handshake Authentication Protocol (CHAP).

- *Configuration tab.* From the Configuration tab, you can generate configuration reports of connected devices.

- *iSCSI Digest Offload Support.* Microsoft iSCSI Initiator digest offload support features provide interoperability for network adapters.

- *iSCSI can boot up to 32 paths with MPIO.* This increases fault tolerance as redundant paths are needed to provide the required level of redundancy within an organization.

- *iSCSI/Remote Boot.* Supports remote booting from online storage on computers that are running Windows Server 2008 R2.

- *Support for IPV6 addressing.* Uses IPv6 and IPv4 addresses.

Components and Protocols of Microsoft iSCSI Initiator

The Microsoft iSCSI Initiator system includes the needed components and protocols to initiate requests and receives responses from iSCSI targets.

- *iSCSI driver.* The Microsoft iSCSI Initiator includes an **iSCSI driver,** which is used to send iSCSI commands over the network.

A gigabit Ethernet adapter that transmits 1000 megabits per second (Mbps) is recommended for the connection to an iSCSI target.

- *iSCSI target.* An **iSCSI target** is any device that receives iSCSI commands.

Each iSCSI host is identified by a unique **iSCSI Qualified Name (IQN)**.

- *iSNS.* The **iSCSI Naming Service (iSNS)** enables better management by automatically discovering targets on the network, thus providing central registration. iSNS will find available targets and it will maintain a list of registered clients (registration through DHCP discovery or manual registration).

Use the *iscsicl* command to manually register a client.

- *CHAP and IPSec.* CHAP and IPSec provide better security through authentication and encryption. CHAP provides authentication and Microsoft iSCSI Initiator supports one-way and mutual CHAP. IPSec provides authentication and encryption at the Network layer.

Activity 3-11: Configure Microsoft iSCSI Initiator

Time Required: Approximately 15 minutes
Objective: Learn how to configure Microsoft iSCSI initiator in Windows Server 2008

Description: In this activity, you will configure Microsoft iSCSI initiator. The Quick Connect feature can be used to quickly establish an iSCSI connection. This activity requires a device formatted with a drive letter and IP address to connect to.

Do not use the Quick Connect feature if you require advanced settings, such as MPIO, CHAP, and IPSec.

1. Click **Start,** click **Administrative Tools,** and click **iSCSI Initiator.**

2. Click **Continue** on the **User Account Control** page, if it appears.

If this is the first time that you have launched Microsoft iSCSI Initiator, you will see a prompt that says the Microsoft iSCSI service is not running. You must start the service for Microsoft iSCSI Initiator to run correctly. Click **Yes** to start the service.

3. The iSCSI Initiator Properties dialog box displays (Figure 3-32). Select the **Targets** tab, if necessary.

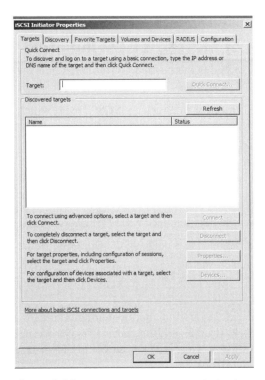

Figure 3-32 iSCSI Initiator Properties dialog box
© Cengage Learning 2012

4. In the **Target** text box, enter the IP address of the target device (your IP address will vary) and click **Quick Connect**.

5. Select the desired target and click **Connect**.

If only one target is available, it is automatically connected.

6. Click **Done** and close the iSCSI Initiator Properties dialog box.

If the device was not formatted, before you can use the device, you must format it and assign a drive letter.

Storage Area Networks (SANs)

Organizations will often require an extensive storage environment to support the storage needs within their organization. Windows Server 2008 provides tools to administer and manage a storage environment. The **Storage Manager for SANs** is used to manage the physical storage arrays and the Storage Explorer enables you to manage available connections, such as Fibre Channel connections and iSCSI connections.

Network Attached Storage (NAS) is very different from a Storage Area Network. A NAS device accesses data at the file level, not the block level.

Storage Manager for SANs

Storage Manager for SANs is a tool in Microsoft Server 2008 that enables you to create and manage **logical unit numbers (LUNs)** on Fibre Channel and iSCSI storage devices supporting the Virtual Disk Service (VDS) in the SAN. The Virtual Disk Service includes application programming interfaces (APIs) for managing storage devices from different vendors. This provides the capability for centralized management in an environment with storage devices from different vendors.

Windows Server 2008 storage management tools that use VDS include:

- Disk Management
- DiskPart
- DiskRAID
- Storage Manager for SANs

Fibre Channel and iSCSI Connections

Both Fibre Channel and iSCSI storage devices allow block-level data access. Additionally, MPIO policies can be implemented to provide for better data storage management. Configuring and managing LUNs are different in Fibre Channel and iSCSI environments. In a Fibre Channel environment, LUNs are assigned directly to a server or cluster. Access to the LUN is provided through Fibre Channel host bus adapter (HBA) ports. In an iSCSI environment, LUNs are first assigned to targets, which are logical entities. The target is created for managing connections (IP addresses and applicable security settings) between the iSCSI device and the server. In the SAN, the server connecting to the target will use the iSCSI initiator.

Storage Manager for SANs will automatically discover Fibre Channel ports. Additionally, you can manually add ports using the World Wide Name (WWN). Configuring iSCSI connections involves identifying the server accessing the LUN and the associated iSCSI initiator adapter. In order to perform this configuration, you need to be, at a minimum, a member of the local **Administrators** group. Additionally, in order to add and configure fibre channel connections or a server with iSCSI connections you will need to have associated hardware devices and connections.

Server Cluster Access in Storage Manager for SANs

With Storage Manager for SANs, you can enable LUN access for a **server cluster.** Failover clustering needs to be installed on each server in the cluster (see Chapter 10). To do this, you will need membership in the local Administrators group at a minimum. Also, in order to define a server cluster in Storage Manager for SANs, you will need to have associated hardware devices and connections. In the Server Manager for SANs, from LUN Management, you can manage the server clusters and add a new server cluster.

Best Practices

1. Due to the processing requirements of duplicating a disk, create mirrors during low utilization time periods, such as on weekends or after normal business hours.

2. When possible, consider using separate disk controllers for the mirrored disks, to increase reliability.

3. When configuring Microsoft iSCSI Initiator, deploy on a fast network.

4. Use CHAP authentication to ensure that each host has its own password.

5. Use iSNS to discover and manage access to iSCSI targets.

6. Ensure that your storage array is optimized for the best performance for your workload.

7. Choose iSCSI arrays that include RAID functionality.

8. Be careful when configuring high demand applications such as Microsoft Exchange and other applications sensitive to latency; consider placing them in a separate pool on the array.

9. Utilize security features when using Microsoft iSCSI Initiator: one-way and mutual CHAP, IPsec, and access control.

10. Access control to a specific LUN is configured on the iSCSI target from the Windows host prior to logon. This is also referred to as LUN masking.

Chapter Summary

- Windows Server 2008 provides support for the latest storage technologies and concepts including volumes, partitions, and RAID technologies.

- Windows Server 2008 supports basic disks and dynamic disks. A basic disk can be divided into partitions and is supported by previous versions of Windows. Dynamic disks are divided into volumes and are supported by Windows 2000 and later versions. Use the Disk Management console in Windows Server 2008 to manage the disks, create volumes, create partitions, and perform other disk management tasks.

- You can create a new volume or partition on a disk that has empty space. If the disk is a basic disk, Windows Server 2008 creates a primary partition. If the disk is a dynamic disk, Windows Server 2008 creates a volume. If the space is part of an extended partition, Windows Server 2008 creates a logical drive.

- Adding a mirror to a volume increases fault tolerance; if one disk fails, that data will be available on the mirrored disk.

- The Virtual Hard Disk (VHD) format is a format specification commonly used with the Hyper-V functionality for supporting a virtual machine hard disk and file systems. A virtual machine hard disk is seen as a hard disk but is implemented as a single file on the native host file system.

- Mount points enable you to access a volume from a folder on another disk; a mount point folder can be assigned to a drive.

- Multipath I/O provides the capability to read and write data using multiple paths to a storage device. This capability increases fault tolerance against single points of failure within the communication path and the devices on the communication path to the storage device by having redundant paths accessible to a storage device.

- The Internet Small Computer System Interface (iSCSI) Software Initiator is a protocol for connecting host computers to an external storage array through the network adapter. You can dynamically expand storage capacity using iSCSI Storage Area Networks (SANs) and iSCSI storage devices.

- The Storage Manager for SANs is used to manage physical storage arrays and the Storage Explorer enables you to manage available connections, such as Fibre Channel connections and iSCSI connections. Storage Manager for SANs enables you to create and manage logical unit numbers (LUNs) on Fibre Channel and iSCSI storage devices supporting the Virtual Disk Service (VDS) in the SAN.

- With Storage Manager for SANs, you can enable LUN access for a server cluster.

Key Terms

Asymmetric Logical Unit Access (ALUA)   ALUA occurs when the characteristics to access a device differ from one port to another port. For example, SCSI target devices might need to define different access characteristics when the target ports are in separate physical units.

basic disk   A physical disk which contains partitions (primary and extended) and/or logical drives. A basic disk can contain up to four primary partitions or three primary partitions and an extended partition.

Challenge Handshake Authentication Protocol (CHAP)   Provides authentication; Microsoft iSCSI Initiator supports one-way and mutual CHAP.

cluster   The smallest amount of disk space that can be used as an allocation unit for holding a file.

Device Specific Module (DSM)   Contains hardware specific information about the device that is used to optimize connectivity. It is recommended to use the DSM provided by the vendor for optimal connectivity results.

Disk Management console   Used to manage disks, create volumes, create partitions, and perform other disk management tasks. Disk Management is part of the Server Manager console.

dynamic disk   A physical disk, which manages its volumes using a database, supports many features a basic disk does not, such as volumes spanning multiple disks. Dynamic disks do not use partitions or logical drives, and because they use a database to store information, they offer greater flexibility for volume management.

dynamic least queue depth   Performs load balancing based on the least queued path. It forwards input/output to the path with the least number of requests.

extended partition   Extended partitions are not bootable. An extended partition can be subdivided into logical drives. One extended partition can exist on a hard drive.

failback A load-balancing method similar to failover. The primary difference is that failback will switch back to the primary path when the primary path is restored.

failover The failover load balancing policy is not an actual load balancing method; instead, it specifies the primary path and standby paths. It is not load balancing, since the primary path is always used unless there is a failure of the primary path. If the primary path fails, a standby path is used.

Fibre Channel A high-speed network technology that is commonly used in storage area networks for high-speed connections to storage devices.

GUID Partition Table (GPT) Defines the physical hard disk's partition table layout. The GPT is often used to overcome the 2.2 TB limitation of MBR partition tables.

Host Bus Adapter (HBA) Used to connect a system to other network and storage devices.

Internet Protocol Security (IPSec) A protocol that provides authentication and encryption at the Network layer.

iSCSI driver The Microsoft iSCSI Initiator includes an iSCSI driver, which is used to send iSCSI commands over the network.

iSCSI Naming Service (iSNS) Enables better management by automatically discovering targets on the network.

iSCSI Qualified Name Each software initiator is identified by a unique iSCSI Qualified Name, or IQN.

iSCSI Software Initiator A protocol for connecting host computers to an external storage array through the network adapter.

iSCSI target Any device that receives iSCSI commands.

logical unit number (LUN) Number that identifies a device being addressed, such as those being addressed by Fibre Channel or iSCSI.

Master Boot Record (MBR) The first sector of a partitioned storage device; it contains partition entry information.

mirror volume Copies the data written to one disk to another disk to increase fault tolerance.

mount points Enable you to access a volume from a folder on another disk; a mount point folder can be assigned to a drive.

multipath I/O Provides the capability to read and write data using multiple paths to a storage device. This capability increases fault tolerance against single points of failure within the communication path and the devices on the communication path to the storage device by having redundant paths accessible to a storage device.

parity A fault-tolerance technique that performs a logical operation on the data and stores the result of the operation on either a dedicated or a main data disk.

partition One physical drive can be partitioned into multiple logical partitions.

physical drive The physical hard drive. One physical drive can be partitioned into multiple logical drives.

primary partition A primary partition contains one file system and is marked as a bootable partition.

Redundant Array of Independent Disks (RAID) A data storage technology that is used to increase performance and fault tolerance. RAID can be implemented through software or hardware. Windows Server 2008 supports RAID 0, RAID 1, and RAID 5 through software implementation.

round-robin A load balancing method that uses each available path for input/output operations. It performs the input/output in a balanced, round-robin method.

round-robin with a subset of paths A load balancing policy similar to round-robin, but with standby paths ready for use if the primary paths fail. For normal operations, it uses a subset of paths for input/output. The standby paths are then used in the event that a primary path fails or is otherwise unavailable.

Serial Attached Storage (SAS)   A bus technology for transferring data between storage devices and disk drives.

server cluster   The virtual combination of multiple servers that appear as one server.

simple volume   A simple volume includes space from only one disk.

spanned volume   A spanned volume has a single address with hard disk sections logically combined and referred to as a single element. You can use up to 32 disks in a spanned volume.

Storage Area Network (SAN)   A group of remote storage devices that are accessible to servers and appear to be locally attached to the server.

Storage Manager for SANs   Windows Server 2008 console used to manage the physical storage arrays and the Storage Explorer enables you to manage available connections, such as Fibre Channel connections and iSCSI connections.

striped volume   A striped volume writes data across multiple disks to increase performance.

Virtual Hard Disk (VHD) format   A format specification commonly used with the Hyper-V functionality for supporting a virtual machine hard disk and file systems. A virtual machine hard disk is seen as a hard disk but is implemented as a single file on the native host file system.

volume   A logical interface referring to data from sections of multiple disks.

weighted path   A load-balancing policy that assigns weights to determine the path chosen. A path with a higher number, or weight, has less priority. When performing input/output, the path with the least weight is selected.

Review Questions

1. Through which console in Windows Server 2008 will you perform most of your disk management tasks?

    a. Disk Management console

    b. iSCSI console

    c. MPIO console

    d. Terminal Services

2. Which of the following refers to the smallest amount of disk space that can be used as an allocation unit for holding a file?

    a. Byte

    b. Bit

    c. File

    d. Cluster

3. Which of the following is not supported in Windows Server 2008?

    a. RAID 0

    b. RAID 1

    c. RAID 3

    d. RAID 5

4. Which of the following writes data across multiple disks to increase performance?

    a. Striped volume

    b. Mirrored volume

    c. Partition

    d. Mirrored partition

5. A simple volume includes space from _____ disk(s).

    a. One

    b. Two

    c. Three

    d. Unlimited

6. A spanned volume extends across multiple disks; you can use up to _____ disk(s) in a spanned volume.

    a. 1

    b. 8

    c. 16

    d. 32

7. Which RAID level stripes data across three or more disks and uses parity to be able to recover if a disk fails?

    a. RAID 0

    b. RAID 1

    c. RAID 5

    d. All RAID levels

8. Adding a mirror to a volume increases _____.

    a. fault tolerance

    b. performance

    c. peace of mind

    d. complexity

9. The _____ format is a format specification commonly used with the Hyper-V functionality for supporting a virtual machine hard disk and file systems.

    a. Virtual Hard Disk (VHD)

    b. Virtual Hard Data (VHD)

    c. Machine Hard Disk (MHD)

    d. Machine Hard Data (MHD)

10. Which of the following is not true about mount points?

    a. Mount points can be used on basic or dynamic volumes

    b. Mount point volumes must have an NTFS format

    c. Mount point folders must be created on empty folders

    d. After created, mount point folder paths can be modified

11. Which of the following is supported by MPIO?

    a. iSCSI

    b. Fibre Channel

    c. Serial Attached Storage (SAS)

    d. All of the above

12. Which load balancing policy uses each available path for input/output operations and performs the input/output in a balanced, round-robin method?

    a. Round-Robin

    b. Round-Robin with a Subset of Paths

    c. Dynamic Least Queue Depth

    d. Weighted Path

13. Which load balancing policy performs load balancing based on the least queued path and forwards input/output to the path with the least number of requests?

    a. Round-Robin

    b. Round-Robin with a Subset of Paths

    c. Dynamic Least Queue Depth

    d. Weighted Path

14. Which load balancing policy uses weights to determine the path chosen, where a path with a higher number, or weight, has less priority and the path with the least weight is selected?

    b. Round-Robin

    c. Round-Robin with a Subset of Paths

    d. Dynamic Least Queue Depth

    e. Weighted Path

15. iSCSI can boot up to _____ paths with MPIO.

    a. 8

    b. 16

    c. 32

    d. 64

16. LUN stands for which of the following?

    a. Logical Unit Number

    b. Logical Unit Network

    c. Logical Unique Number

    d. Logical Unique Network

17. IQN stands for which of the following?

    a. Internet Qualified Name

    b. Internet Qualified Network

    c. iSCSI Qualified Name

    d. iSCSI Qualified Network

18. Which of the following is a protocol for connecting host computers to an external storage array through the network adapter?

    a. NIC adapter

    b. iSCSI software initiator

    c. Layer 2 adapter

    d. Interoperable adapter

19. The Microsoft iSCSI Initiator system includes which of the following?

    a. CHAP and PAP

    b. WEP and IPSec

    c. CHAP and IPSec

    d. WEP and CHAP

20. Which of the following includes application programming interfaces (APIs) for managing storage devices from different vendors?

    a. Virtual Disk Service

    b. Virtual Disk System

    c. Storage Area Network

    d. Disk Management

Case Projects

Case Project 3-1: Storage Performance and Reliability

The IT manager in New Enterprises is considering expanding the storage capabilities in the organization. In particular, the IT manager is concerned about the performance and reliability of the storage solution implemented.

The IT department is asking you to explain the following:

1. Explain the different levels of RAID that are supported in Windows Server 2008.

2. Describe the pros and cons of a mirrored volume.

3. Explain the benefits of implementing an extended volume.

Case Project 3-2: MPIO, DSM, and iSCSI

The IT manager has more questions about the storage capabilities in Windows Server 2008. The IT manager is primarily concerned about the ability to dynamically expand the storage capacity and to ensure that a storage device is not getting overwhelmed.

To address the IT manager's concerns, you provide the following explanation about MPIO, DSM, and iSCSI capabilities in Windows Server 2008.

1. Describe MPIO and DSM capabilities.

2. Describe the load balancing policies supported by DSM.

3. Explain the Internet Small Computer System Interface (iSCSI) Software Initiator and how it can be used to dynamically expand your storage capacity.

Case Project 3-3: Storage Area Networks

The IT manager discussed the potential for expanding the storage capabilities with the CIO. However, the CIO needs to justify the additional expense to senior management in the organization. Therefore, they are asking for the following information in regards to storage expansion.

1. In business terms, list the costs and benefits of implementing RAID and implementing a storage area network within the organization.

2. Develop a technical report that describes the costs and benefits of a storage area network, including your recommendation for implementing a SAN within the organization.

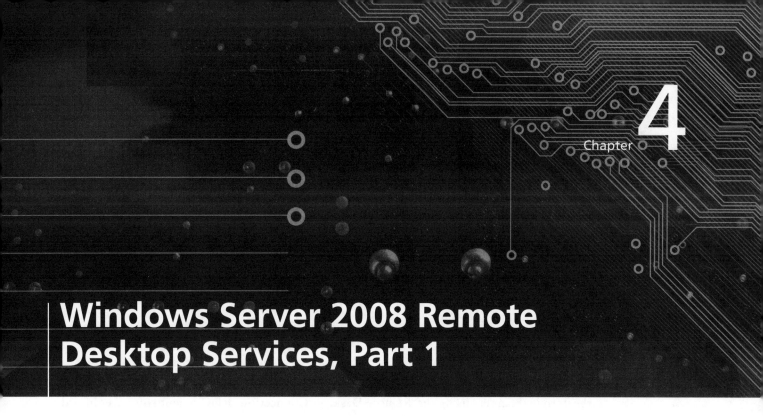

Chapter 4

Windows Server 2008 Remote Desktop Services, Part 1

After reading this chapter and completing the exercises, you will be able to:

- Describe the Remote Desktop Services capabilities in Windows Server 2008
- Explain the enhanced Remote Desktop Services capabilities in Windows Server 2008
- Describe the Remote Desktop Connection settings and Desktop Experience enhancements
- Publish remote applications
- Package Remote Desktop Services RemoteApp programs
- Explain the Remote Desktop Services Web Access capabilities and install RD Web Access
- Describe Remote Desktop Gateway functionality and install the RD Gateway role service

This chapter shows you how to use the Remote Desktop Services capabilities in Windows Server 2008. **Remote Desktop Services** is essential for organizations needing remote access to other computer systems and the applications they host. Remote Desktop Services capabilities are used for many different purposes; most users have used or have heard of Remote Desktop Services or Terminal Services as it was previously named. Remote Desktop Services is commonly used for remote access, remote administration, remote assistance, and virtual desktop hosting. Users or administrators use Remote Desktop Services to remotely log into another system. Additionally, users commonly use Remote Desktop Services to remotely access business applications available through the server. Remote Desktop Services might also be used to adhere to regulatory requirements by limiting access that a remote user has to specific applications, or it can be used to support complex or legacy applications. Depending on the organization, Remote Desktop Services could be used to help provide data security by reducing the need to store data on laptops or other devices that could be removed or stolen. Remote Desktop Services is a key component of a business application infrastructure.

Remote Desktop Connection

A client computer will connect to the **Remote Desktop Session Host** (previously referred to as the Terminal Server) using the Remote Desktop Connection (RDC) client software. In order to take advantage of the most recent updates to Remote Desktop Services, you should ensure that you have the most recent update of the RDC client software (RDC 7.0); however, most of the functionality from older versions of the client software will work with Server 2008 and Server 2008 R2.

The **Remote Desktop Connection (RDC)** client communicates with the Remote Desktop Session Host through virtual channels that operate in user mode (with restricted access) or kernel mode (without restricted access); the virtual channel is a communication path in the Remote Desktop Protocol (RDP). There are many enhancements in RDC 6.0 and carried over into RDC 7.0. From a security perspective, Network Level Authentication (NLA) is a capability supported in RDC 6.0 and later and it enables users to have to authenticate before connecting to the Remote Desktop Session Host.

Activity 4-1: Display Remote Desktop Connection Properties

Time Required: Approximately 10 minutes
Objective: Learn how to display the Remote Desktop Connection properties

Description: In this activity, you learn how to display the Remote Desktop Connection properties and check which version of RDC is installed.

1. Click **Start**, point to **All Programs**, point to **Accessories**, and click **Remote Desktop Connection** to display the Remote Desktop Connection dialog box (Figure 4-1).

After pointing to Accessories, you might have other folders to click on, such as Communications to display Remote Desktop Connection, depending on your computer's configuration.

Figure 4-1 Remote Desktop Connection

© Cengage Learning 2012

 If the tabs are not displaying, click Options to expand the dialog box and display the full dialog box with the tabs.

 To display the current version of the installed RDC, right-click the computer icon in the left corner of the Remote Desktop Connection dialog box and select About; the current version installed displays.

2. View the tabs available from the Remote Desktop Connection dialog box and see which settings are available from each tab:

- General
- Display
- Local Resources
- Programs
- Experience
- Advanced

3. Close all open windows.

The Desktop Experience

The Microsoft **Desktop Experience** improves end user experiences when using Remote Desktop Services; it is intended to look and feel like a Windows 7 desktop, which many users are familiar with using.

There are many display enhancements when using a Remote Desktop Connection. Remote Desktop Connection display enhancements include:

- *Enhanced display resolution.* Widescreen monitor resolutions (1680 × 1050 and 1920 × 1200) and a maximum resolution of 4096 × 2048 are supported.

- *Custom display resolutions.* Custom display resolutions can be set using the RDP file or the command prompt.

- *Monitor spanning.* **Monitor spanning** is the capability to span multiple monitors with a total maximum resolution of 4096 × 2048.

- *Font smoothing.* **Font smoothing** supports ClearType fonts if ClearType is enabled on the server and font smoothing is enabled.

- *Display data prioritization.* **Display data prioritization** controls the bandwidth ratio of input versus output prioritization; the default is a 70:30 ratio of input to output. You can modify these settings in the Registry.

Table 4-1 shows RDC commands to modify the display resolution and set monitor spanning.

Table 4-1   Display and monitor commands configured in RDC

Action	Command syntax	Example
Desktop width	desktopwidth:i:<width>	desktopwidth:i:1280
Desktop height	desktopheight:i:<height>	desktopheight:i:800
Monitor spanning	span:i:<0-disable; 1-enable>	span:i:1

Table 4-2 shows the Microsoft Remote Desktop Connection (mstsc.exe) commands to modify the display resolution and the monitor spanning.

Table 4-2   Display and monitor commands configured in mstsc.exe

Action	Command syntax	Example
Desktop width	mstsc.exe /w:<width>	mstsc.exe /w:1280
Desktop height	mstsc.exe /h:<height>	mstsc.exe /h:800
Monitor spanning	mstsc.exe /span	mstsc.exe /span

At a command prompt, enter *mstsc.exe /?* to display other commands available using mstsc.exe.

Desktop Experience Enhancements

The Desktop Experience was greatly enhanced for Remote Desktop Services in Windows Server 2008, for users with Remote Desktop Connection 6.0 or above. Among other enhancements, users can customize their desktop themes and use the new Desktop Composition feature in Windows Server 2008.

Microsoft Windows 7 features that are included in the Desktop Experience are the Windows Media Player, desktop themes, video for Windows (AVI support), Windows SideShow, Windows Defender, Disk Cleanup, Sync Center, Sound Recorder, Character Map, and the Snipping Tool. Microsoft wants to make the user's desktop experience on a remote desktop the same or very similar to the experience they get from their Windows 7.

 By default, these features are not automatically turned on and configured when you install Desktop Experience; you will need to configure them after Desktop Experience is installed.

4

You can configure Remote Desktop Session Host to provide the Windows Aero desktop functionality; the Remote Desktop Connection requires a Vista or higher client computer to take advantage of this functionality.

In order to configure Desktop Composition, you must perform the following general steps:

1. Enable Desktop Experience on the Remote Desktop Services server.
2. Use the Windows Vista theme on the Remote Desktop Services server.
3. Enable Desktop Composition on the host client.

Activity 4-2: Install Desktop Experience

Time Required: Approximately 15 minutes
Objective: Learn how to view and configure Desktop Experience settings

Description: In this activity, you learn how to display and configure Desktop Experience settings.

1. Click **Start**, point to **Administrative Tools**, and click **Server Manager** to open Server Manager.
2. Right-click **Features** and select **Add Features**.
3. From the **Add Features Wizard**, if necessary, add any features required for Desktop Experience (Figure 4-2) then check the box for **Desktop Experience**.

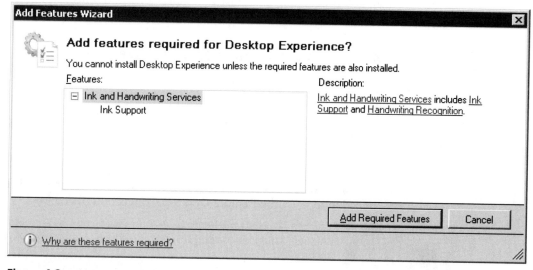

Figure 4-2 Add Features Wizard
© Cengage Learning 2012

4. Click **Next**.

5. Click **Install** and then click **Close**.

6. Click the **Yes** button when prompted to restart.

7. After the computer reboots, click **Close** in the Installation Results dialog box.

The Windows Vista theme can be set on the Remote Desktop Services server by opening the Control Panel, clicking Personalization, and then clicking Theme.

Desktop Composition is enabled by opening the Remote Desktop Connection dialog box on the client computer, then selecting the Experience tab, and checking both Desktop Composition and Themes.

Device Redirection

Device redirection is an essential capability that enables a device to be connected to the local device but be accessible through the Remote Desktop Services session. Plug and Play devices, Microsoft Point of Sale for .NET devices, and print devices are common devices that need to be redirected from the local device to the Remote Desktop Services session. Plug and Play device redirection and Remote Desktop Easy Print were designed to help reduce the problems associated with differing device and print drivers on the client and the Remote Desktop Services session.

- **Plug and Play (PNP) device redirection.** Users may want to redirect Plug and Play devices such as media players or digital cameras from the local device to the Remote Desktop Services session, so they can remotely control these devices. This capability is based on the Media Transfer Protocol (MTP) and Picture Transfer Protocol (PTP). Additionally, devices can be redirected when they are attached after the session has been established.

- **Microsoft Point of Sale for .NET device redirection.** This enhancement enables supported point of sale devices, such as bar code readers, to be used with Remote Desktop Services. You need to ensure that you have the most recent version of the Microsoft POS for .NET software downloaded from the Microsoft Web site.

- **Remote Desktop Easy Print.** This enhancement enables redirection of the default printer without having to match print drivers on the client computer and the server. Printers have been a common problem for administrators; previously administrators would need to map the print devices from the client to the server.

Activity 4-3: Redirect Plug and Play Devices

Time Required: Approximately 10 minutes
Objective: Learn how to redirect plug and play devices

Description: In this activity, you learn how to redirect Plug and Play devices. You can redirect devices even if the device is plugged in after the session has been established.

1. Click **Start**, point to **All Programs**, point to **Accessories**, and click **Remote Desktop Connection** to open the Remote Desktop Connection dialog box.

You can also start the Remote Desktop Connection by entering **mstsc** in the Run dialog box or in the Search programs and files box on the Start menu.

2. Click **Options**.

3. Click the **Local Resources** tab (Figure 4-3).

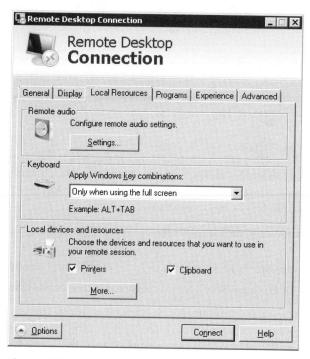

Figure 4-3 Local Resources tab
© Cengage Learning 2012

4. Click **More**.
5. Expand **Supported Plug and Play Devices** in **Local devices and resources**.
6. Choose the device to redirect.
7. Enter a check in the **Devices that I plug in later** box (Figure 4-4).

Figure 4-4 Local devices and resources
© Cengage Learning 2012

This enables a device to be redirected even if it is plugged in after the session has been established.

8. Click **OK** and close the Remote Desktop Connection dialog box.

Authentication and Single Sign-On

Single sign-on (SSO) capabilities have become expected in many organizations. SSO enables a user to enter credentials once and be able to access other systems and services, based on the user's rights and permissions, without having to reenter their credentials each time. The credentials of the user are passed to the application or system being accessed, such as Remote Desktop Session Host server.

For single sign-on to work, the following must exist:

- The client system must be Windows Vista or higher (or Windows XP with SP3) or be a Server 2008 system.
- The user rights and permissions must be adequate to access the application or system.
- The client and the Remote Desktop Session Host server must be in the same domain.

To configure SSO, you will need to configure authentication settings for the Remote Desktop Session Host server and you will need to configure the SSO capability for the client computer. The following two activities walk you through the process of accomplishing those two tasks.

Activity 4-4: Set Remote Desktop Session Host Server Authentication

Time Required: Approximately 10 minutes
Objective: Learn how to set Remote Desktop Session Host Server authentication settings

Description: In this activity, you learn how to display the Remote Desktop Services configuration options and select the appropriate authentication option.

1. Click **Start,** point to **Administrative Tools,** point to **Remote Desktop Services,** and click **Remote Desktop Session Host Configuration** to display the screen shown in Figure 4-5.

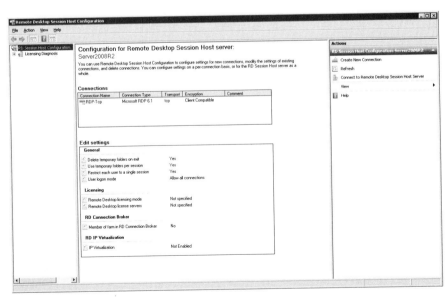

Figure 4-5 Remote Desktop Session Host Configuration

© Cengage Learning 2012

2. In the Connections section, right-click the name of the connection, such as **RDP-Tcp** and click **Properties** to display the RDP-Tcp Properties window.

3. Click the **General** tab, if it is not already selected. Ensure that the **Security Layer** value is set to either **Negotiate** or **SSL (TLS 1.0)**.

4. Click the **Log on Settings** tab (Figure 4-6). Ensure that the **Always prompt for password** check box is not selected.

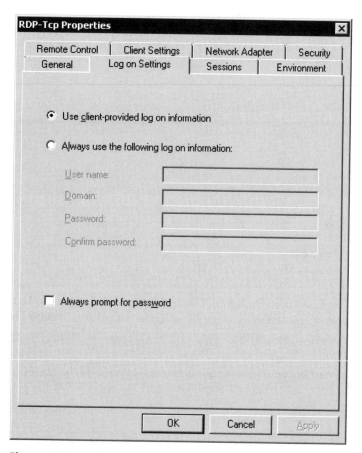

Figure 4-6 RDP-Tcp Properties
© Cengage Learning 2012

5. Click **OK**.

6. Close all windows.

After you have configured the Remote Desktop Session Host authentication options, you can enable single sign-on capabilities.

Activity 4-5: Enable Single Sign-On Capabilities

Time Required: Approximately 10 minutes

Objective: Learn how to enable single sign-on capabilities: After authentication is configured on the Remote Desktop Session Host server, you need to use Group Policy to allow default credential usage on the Remote Desktop Session Host server.

Description: In this activity, you learn how to enable single sign-on capabilities through credentials delegation.

1. Click **Start**, click **Run**, type **gpedit.msc** and press **Enter** to open the Local Group Policy Editor (Figure 4-7).

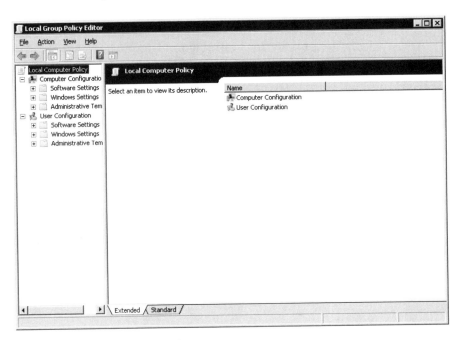

Figure 4-7 Local Group Policy Editor
© Cengage Learning 2012

2. In the left pane, expand **Computer Configuration, Administrative Templates, Windows Components, Remote Desktop Services, Remote Desktop Session Host,** and **Security.** Note the Group Policy settings that can be configured. Figure 4-8 shows the Security settings.

The Group Policy settings can be configured using the Local Group Policy Editor or the Group Policy Management Console (GPMC).

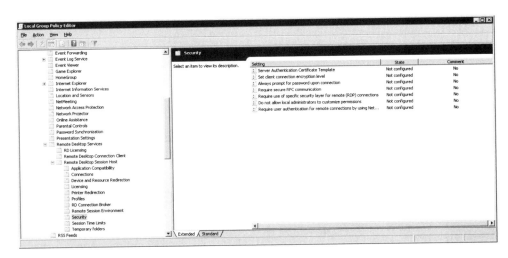

Figure 4-8 Security settings
© Cengage Learning 2012

3. Close all open dialog boxes, and the Local Group Policy Editor window.

Remote Desktop Services Role

Remote Desktop Services is one of the server roles available in Windows Server 2008 R2. You will need to install the Remote Desktop Services role in order to perform many of the activities in the chapter, and in general when installing and configuring the Remote Desktop Services capabilities on your system.

The Remote Desktop Services role is installed in a similar manner as other roles that you have previously installed. The Add Role Wizard walks you through the process. Activity 4-6 covers the steps of installing the Remote Desktop Services role.

Windows 2000 Server was the first version that incorporated Terminal Services as a server role, instead of as a separate product. Windows 2000 Server also introduced Remote Administration.

The Remote Desktop Services consists of many role services for providing remote desktop features and functionality. The role services include:

- RD Session Host
- RD Web Access
- RD Licensing
- RD Gateway
- RD Connection Broker
- RD Virtualization Host

The different role services will be discussed in this chapter and in Chapter 5.

Activity 4-6: Install Remote Desktop Services

Time Required: Approximately 10 minutes
Objective: Learn how to install the Remote Desktop Services and the Remote Desktop Session Host role

Description: In this activity, you learn how to use the Server Manager to install the Remote Desktop Session Host role.

1. Click **Start,** point to **Administrative Tools,** and click **Server Manager** to open the Server Manager (Figure 4-9).

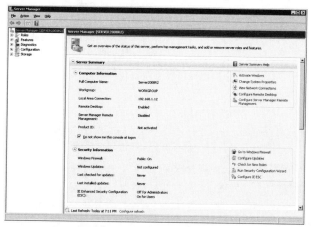

Figure 4-9 Server Manager
© Cengage Learning 2012

2. Click **Roles** in the left pane, then click **Add Roles** in Roles Summary.

3. The Add Roles Wizard's Before You Begin page displays. Click **Next**.

4. Check the **Remote Desktop Services** box on the wizard's Select Server Roles page (Figure 4-10).

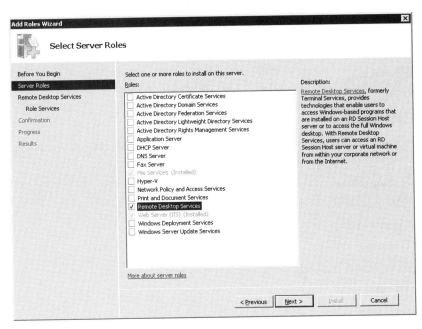

Figure 4-10 Select Server Roles

© Cengage Learning 2012

5. Click **Next**.

6. Click **Next** on the Remote Desktop Services page.

7. Check **Remote Desktop Session Host** on the Select Role Services page (Figure 4-11).

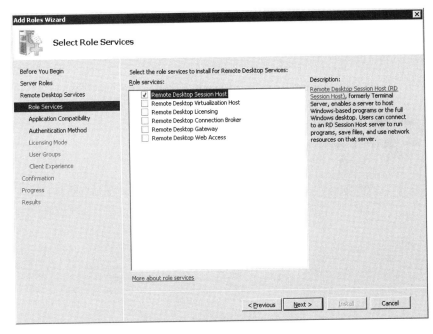

Figure 4-11 Select Role Services

© Cengage Learning 2012

8. Click **Next**.

9. The Uninstall and Reinstall Applications for Compatibility page displays. Click **Next**.

10. The Specify Authentication Method for Remote Desktop Session Host page displays (Figure 4-12). Select the desired authentication method and click **Next**.

Available options are Require Network Level Authentication and Do not require Network Level Authentication. Read the description for each before selecting desired option.

NOTE

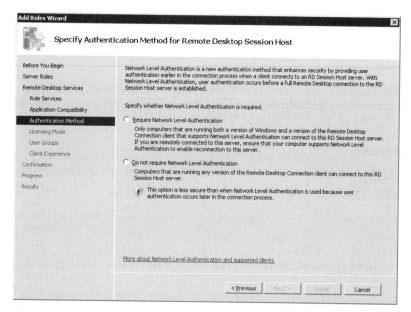

Figure 4-12 Specify Authentication Method for Remote Desktop Session Host

© Cengage Learning 2012

11. The Specify Licensing Mode page displays (Figure 4-13). Select the desired licensing mode and click **Next**.

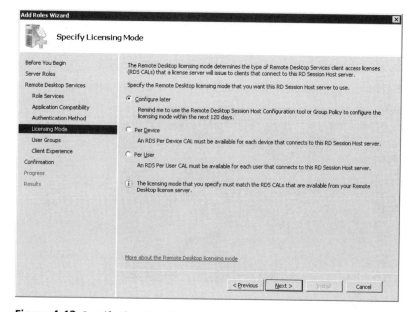

Figure 4-13 Specify Licensing Mode

© Cengage Learning 2012

Licensing mode options are Configure later, Per Device, and Per User. Read the description for each before selecting desired option.

Windows Server 2008 provides a license management system for Remote Desktop Services known as **Remote Desktop Licensing (RD Licensing).** This system allows Remote Desktop Session Host servers to obtain and manage client access licenses (RD CALs) for devices and users that are connecting to a server.

12. The Select User Groups Allowed Access to This Remote Desktop Session Host Server page displays. Add the desired users or groups and click **Next.**

13. The Configure Client Experience page displays. Select the desired functionality and options. Click **Next.**

14. The Confirm Installation Selections page displays. After you confirm that the settings are correct, click **Install,** click **Close,** and click **Yes** to restart. Once the server reboots, close the Installation Results window.

Execute mode is when clients are connected and applications are being executed by users. Install mode is when applications are being installed for use by clients.

After the Remote Desktop Services role has been installed, you can change the user mode, such as changing the user mode from Execute to Install, then back to Execute. You will need to change the server mode to Install mode to install a program on the server; after the application is installed, you need to change the server back to Execute mode.

Activity 4-7: Change between Install Mode and Execute Mode

Time Required: Approximately 5 minutes
Objective: Learn how to change between Install and Execute mode

Description: In this activity, you will learn the Command Prompt commands to change between Install mode and Execute mode.

1. Click **Start,** click **Run,** type **cmd,** and click **OK** to open the command prompt.

2. To see help information about user modes, enter **change user /?** (Figure 4-14).

3. To change to Install mode, enter **change user /install.**

4. To change to Execute mode, enter **change user /execute.**

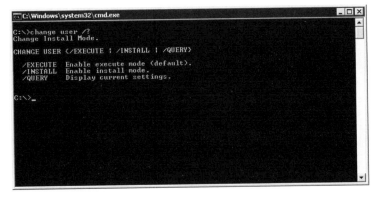

Figure 4-14 /install and /execute commands
© Cengage Learning 2012

5. Close the command prompt.

Publishing Remote Applications

Remote Desktop Services **RemoteApp** is a newer capability introduced in Windows Server 2008, but is supported only by clients running RDC 6.1 or higher. RemoteApp enables you to publish individual applications instead of having to publish the entire desktop, which was the only option available in previous versions. In previous versions, you could have an RDP file connect to a single application; however, the session would end when that application was closed.

The method in which profiles are managed will affect the applications and the data associated with the applications, which needs to be taken into account when configuring Remote Desktop Services. There are three types of profiles: local, roaming, and mandatory.

- *Local.* Stored on a single computer
- *Roaming.* Stored on a network drive and available to any computer that can access that network drive
- *Mandatory.* Stored on a network drive, but are read-only profiles

If the Remote Desktop Session Host server role is not yet installed on Windows Server 2008, you will need to install the role before proceeding with RemoteApp and the following activities.

When an application is installed on the Remote Desktop Session Host server, the application can be added to a published list of programs. Other users will have access to the published list of programs through Remote Desktop Services.

Since some applications, especially older applications, might not operate on a Remote Desktop Session Host server, it is essential to thoroughly test the applications before deployment. Many applications were designed for single users and might not work on a Remote Desktop Session Host server. Since multiple applications run concurrently, there are potential resource, file, memory, and performance issues in a Remote Desktop Session Host server environment that should be tested before deployment.

The RemoteApp Manager is a tool available for managing the applications being published for remote user to access. The next two activities work with RemoteApp program lists and packaging applications for RemoteApp.

Activity 4-8: Add to the RemoteApp Programs List

Time Required: Approximately 10 minutes

Objective: Learn how to choose programs to add to the RemoteApp Programs list

Description: In this activity, you will use the RemoteApp Manager to choose programs to add to the RemoteApp Programs list.

1. Click **Start,** point to **Administrative Tools,** and click **Server Manager** to open the Server Manager.

2. Expand **Roles,** expand **Remote Desktop Services,** and click **RemoteApp Manager** (*servername*) (Figure 4-15).

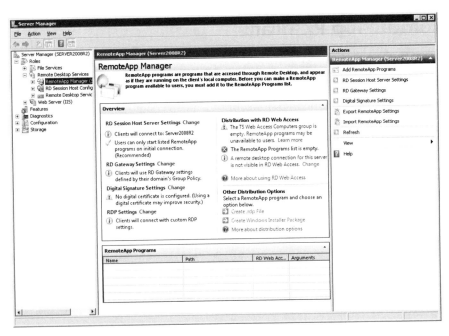

Figure 4-15 RemoteApp Manager
© Cengage Learning 2012

3. Click **Add RemoteApp Programs** in the Actions pane.

4. The RemoteApp Wizard opens. Click **Next**.

5. Select the desired applications to add to the RemoteApp program list (Figure 4-16).

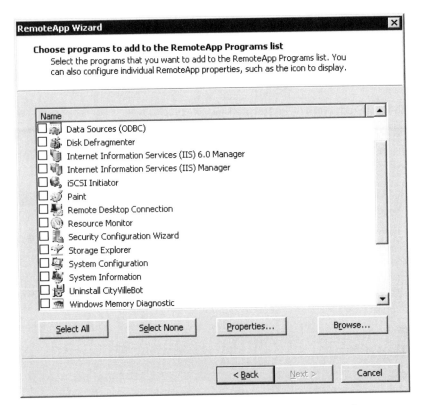

Figure 4-16 Choose programs to add to the RemoteApp Programs list
© Cengage Learning 2012

6. Click **Next** and click **Finish**.

Packaging RemoteApp Programs

When you package RemoteApp programs, you will define the location where the package will be saved, the Remote Desktop Session Host settings, the Remote Desktop Gateway settings, and the certificate settings. In the following activity, you package RemoteApp programs and create a Windows Installer file (MSI); group policies can then be used to deploy this file to clients. RDP files can also be used, which are self-contained distribution files.

 Client computers must have RDC 6.0 or higher to run these package files.

Activity 4-9: Package RemoteApp Programs

Time Required: Approximately 10 minutes
Objective: Learn how to package RemoteApp programs

Description: In this activity, you learn how to use the RemoteApp Manager to package RemoteApp programs.

1. Open the **RemoteApp Manager,** if it is not already open (Figure 4-17).

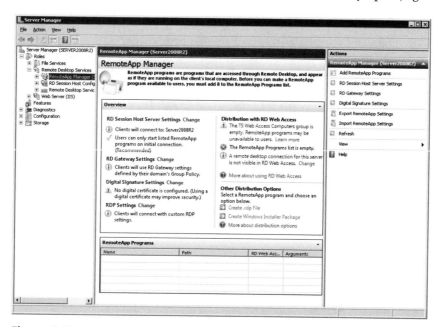

Figure 4-17 RemoteApp Manager
© Cengage Learning 2012

2. In the RemoteApp Programs list, select the application that you want to create a package for and click **Create Windows Installer Package** from the Actions pane.

 When you package RemoteApp programs, you can use the Windows Installer file (MSI) or use the Remote Desktop file (RDP).

3. The RemoteApp Wizard displays. Click **Next.**

4. The Specify Package Settings page displays (Figure 4-18). From this page, you will select the location to save the package, modify Remote Desktop Session Host settings, modify RD Gateway settings, and change Certificate settings.

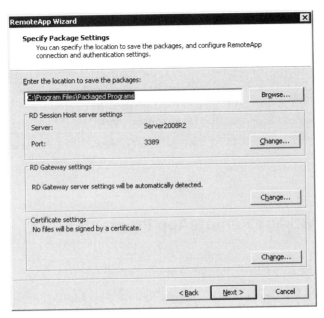

Figure 4-18 Specify Package Settings

© Cengage Learning 2012

5. Click **Next**.

6. The Configure Distribution Package page displays. Select where the shortcut icons will appear on the client computer. In this case, select **Start menu folder** and enter a folder name, such as Remote Programs (Figure 4-19).

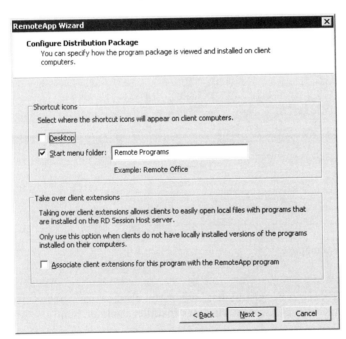

Figure 4-19 Configure Distribution Package

© Cengage Learning 2012

7. Click **Next** and click **Finish**.

You can use Group Policies to deploy this .msi file to client computers.

Remote Desktop Web Access

In addition to the methods of packaging and deploying RemoteApp programs mentioned previously, you can use **Remote Desktop Web Access (RD Web Access)** to distribute RemoteApp programs. Remote Desktop Web Access will be installed as a server role on the server that users will connect to when they access the RemoteApp programs. When using Remote Desktop Web Access, client computers must have RDC 6.1 or higher installed.

RD Web Access integrates with Internet Information Services (IIS) to provide access to applications as icons available in the Web browser (Internet Explorer). The RD Web Access server displays the application icon for the client. When the client clicks the icon, the RD Web Access server creates the RDP file so the client can launch the application from the server. When the application is launched from Remote Desktop Web Access, the current settings in the RemoteApp Manager of the Remote Desktop Session Host Server are used; thus, they are always up to date. In other scenarios, the RDP files would need to be redistributed when changes occur. The launched applications will be independent of the browser window.

 When the Remote Desktop Web Access role is installed, Internet Information Services (IIS) is also installed on the server and the server will act as a Web server.

 Remote Desktop Web Access can also be used to provide remote access to computers with Remote Desktop enabled.

Microsoft enhanced Remote Desktop Web Access in Windows Server 2008 by embedding ActiveX controls on Web pages hosted on IIS.

Activity 4-10: Install Remote Desktop Web Access

Time Required: Approximately 10 minutes
Objective: Learn how to install Remote Desktop Web Access

Description: In this activity, you use the Server Manager to install Remote Desktop Web Access.

1. Click **Start,** point to **Administrative Tools,** and click **Server Manager** to open Server Manager.

2. Click **Remote Desktop Services** in Roles Summary (if the Remote Desktop Services role is not installed, it will need to be installed first; see Activity 4-6).

3. Click **Add Role Services** in the Role Services area.

4. The **Select Role Services** page displays. Select the **Remote Desktop Web Access** check box (Figure 4-20).

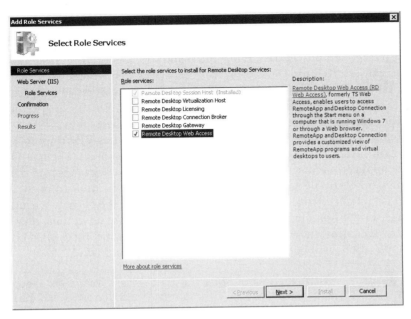

Figure 4-20 Select Role Services
© Cengage Learning 2012

5. If required roles for Remote Desktop Web Access are not currently installed, you will get a prompt to install them (Figure 4-21). If so, click **Add Required Role Services** to install the required roles.

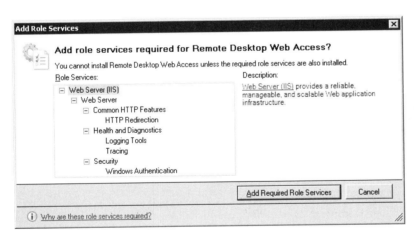

Figure 4-21 Add Role Services
© Cengage Learning 2012

6. Click **Next**.

7. If IIS needs to be installed, click **Next** on the introduction page, click **Next** on the Role Services Selections for IIS page, and click **Install** on the Confirm Installation Selections page.

8. Click **Close** on the Installation Results page (Figure 4-22).

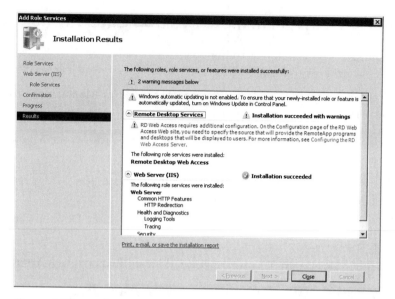

Figure 4-22 Installation Results

© Cengage Learning 2012

Remote Desktop Gateway

Remote Desktop Gateway (RD Gateway) establishes an HTTPS connection; it encapsulates Remote Desktop Protocol (RDP) traffic with SSL encryption. This creates a secure connection for remote users to use to access the server without having to create a Virtual Private Network (VPN) connection. By default, the client and the server will negotiate the highest level of mutually supported encryption.

- *Low security.* 56-bit key encryption and server authentication is not supported

- *High security.* 128-bit encryption, encrypts traffic in both directions, and it supports server authentication

- *FIPS-compliant security.* FIPS-compliant encryption between the server and the client

 RD Gateway uses port 443, which is typically open for HTTPS traffic. With older versions, RDP listened on port 3389, which is often blocked for security purposes.

The Remote Desktop Gateway server will receive the RDP packets, authenticate the user by checking the **Network Policy Server (NPS)** and Active Directory, and will allow the remote user access to the RemoteApp programs that have been Remote Desktop Web Access-enabled. Remote users can connect to internal resources behind the firewall and network address translators (NATs). You should use the Remote Desktop Gateway for secure access to RemoteApps available through Remote Desktop Web Access. Remote Desktop Gateway can be implemented with an ISA Server or other VPN solution for additional security. Additionally, you can install an SSL certificate on the Remote Desktop Web Access server for secure HTTPS connections.

When you install the Remote Desktop Web Access role, the following role services are also required:

- Remote Procedure Call over HTTP Proxy service

- Internet Information Services 7.5

- Active Directory Domain Services (if the clients must be a member of a domain-based group)

- Network Policy and Access Services

- Remote Desktop Gateway servers and clients must be configured with Network Access Protection (NAP)

Activity 4-11: Install Remote Desktop Gateway Role Service

Time Required: Approximately 10 minutes
Objective: Learn how to install the Remote Desktop Gateway role service

Description: In this activity, you will learn how to use the Server Manager to install the Remote Desktop Gateway role service.

1. Click **Start,** point to **Administrative Tools,** and click **Server Manager** to open the Server Manager.

2. Click **Remote Desktop Services** in Roles Summary.

3. Click **Add Role Services** in the Role Services area.

4. The Select Role Services page displays. Select the **Remote Desktop Gateway** check box.

5. Click **Next.**

6. The Add Role Services Wizard displays. Click **Add Required Role Services** (Figure 4-23).

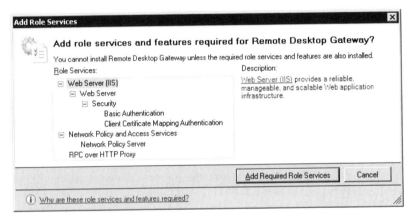

Figure 4-23 Add Role Services
© Cengage Learning 2012

7. Click **Next.**

8. The Choose a Server Authentication Certificate for SSL Encryption page displays. Select the desired SSL encryption (Figure 4-24).

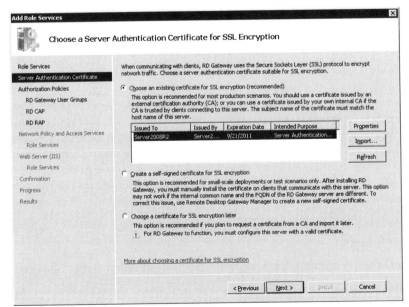

Figure 4-24 Choose a Server Authentication Certificate for SSL Encryption
© Cengage Learning 2012

9. Click **Next**.

10. The Create Authorization Policies for RD Gateway page displays (Figure 4-25). Click **Next**.

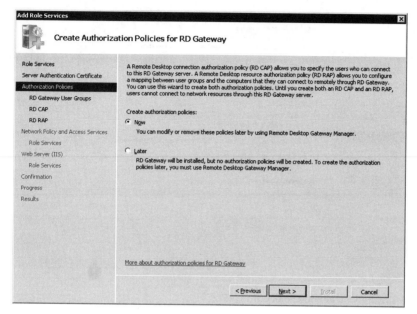

Figure 4-25 Create Authorization Policies for RD Gateway
© Cengage Learning 2012

11. Click **Add** and select the groups that can connect through the Remote Desktop Gateway. Click **Next**.

For most of the remaining steps, you can select desired options, change settings, or use the default values entered before clicking Next to proceed to the next wizard step.

12. The Create an RD CAP for RD Gateway page displays. Select desired options. Click **Next**.

13. The Create an RD RAP for RD Gateway page displays. Select desired options. Click **Next**.

14. The Network Policy and Access Services page displays. Click **Next**.

15. Confirm that the **Network Policy Server** role is selected. Click **Next**.

16. The **Web Server (IIS)** page displays. Click **Next**.

17. Change or accept the default roles. Click **Next**.

18. Review your installation selections, then click **Install** (Figure 4-26), and click **Close** when the installation is complete.

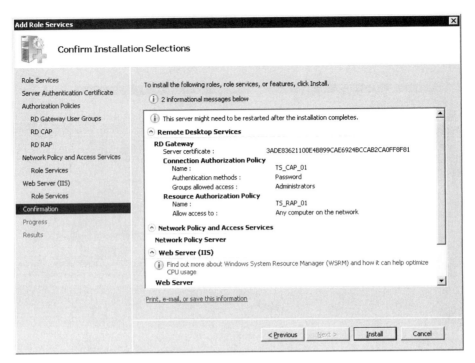

Figure 4-26 Confirm Installation Selections
© Cengage Learning 2012

After you have installed the Remote Desktop Gateway role service, the Remote Desktop Gateway will need a valid digital certificate. Follow your organizational procedures for obtaining a valid digital certificate. You can purchase the digital certificate from a third-party certificate authority or create a self-signed certificate.

The following Web site has a list of Windows root certificate program members: *http://support.microsoft.com/kb/931125.*

Because trust between a client and the server is a critical component, the digital certificate will ensure that the client and the server are who they are saying that they are.

RD CAPs and RD RAPs

Remote Desktop Connection Authorization Policies (RD CAPs) and **Remote Desktop Resource Authorization Policies (RD RAPs)** must be created after you have installed the Remote Desktop Gateway role service. You will use the Remote Desktop Gateway Manager, available through Administrative Tools and Remote Desktop Services.

- RD CAPs enables you to specify which users can connect to the Remote Desktop Gateway server, specify the requirements that users must meet to connect, and specify whether to enable or disable client device redirection. These options are available from the New RD CAP dialog (from the Remote Desktop Gateway Manager, expand the Remote Desktop Gateway server, expand Policies and click Connection Authorization Policies, click Create New Policy in the Action pane and select Custom).

- RD RAPs enables you to specify the network resources that users can connect to, specify the user groups and computer groups, and specify whether to use the default TCP port 3389 or allow a connection through another port. These options are available from the New RD RAP dialog (from the Remote Desktop Gateway Manager, expand the Remote

Desktop Gateway server, expand Policies and click Resource Authorization Policies, click Create New Policy in the Action pane and select Custom).

- Together, RD CAPs and RD RAPs define who can access what resources. You can define multiple RD CAPs and RD RAPs for more customized network access.

RD CAPs and RD RAPs are covered in more detail in Chapter 5.

4

Best Practices

1. Ensure that client computers have the most up-to-date Remote Desktop Connection (RDC) version.

2. Use Remote Desktop Services Desktop Experience if you want users to connect to the Remote Desktop Session Host server and have the Windows Vista desktop look.

3. Use the single sign-on capability to allow domain users to only have to log on once and have access to the resources available on the server.

4. It is not recommended to install the Remote Desktop Session Host server role on a domain controller; if you try to, you will get a warning message.

5. You can use a Remote Desktop Gateway server with Microsoft Internet Security and Acceleration (ISA) Server to provide enhanced security options.

6. RemoteApp programs can be made available through Remote Desktop Web Access; however, the client must be running at least RDC 6.1, which is included on Windows Server 2008, Windows Vista SP 1 and higher, and Windows XP SP 3.

7. When you are determining which programs to include in your RemoteApp programs, ensure that you properly test the programs to ensure they operate properly in this environment.

8. When you make RemoteApp programs available over the Internet, use the Remote Desktop Gateway to ensure that you properly secure the remote connections to the server.

9. Remote Desktop Gateway provides a secure encrypted connection for remote users; remote users do not need to configure virtual private network (VPN) connections.

10. Network Access Protection (NAP) can be used to further enhance security when using the Remote Desktop Gateway and Remote Desktop Services clients.

Chapter Summary

- Remote Desktop Services is an essential capability for organizations needing to remotely access another system and access programs on the remote system. Remote Desktop Services is a key component of a business application infrastructure.

- A client computer connects to the Remote Desktop Server using the Remote Desktop Connection (RDC) client software.

- The Windows Desktop Experience gives users a better feel and experience using a Remote Desktop Connection. Remote Desktop Connection display enhancements include enhanced display resolution, custom display resolutions, monitor spanning, font smoothing, and display data prioritization.

- Device redirection is an essential capability that enables a device to be connected to the local device but be accessible through the Remote Desktop Services session. Plug and Play devices, Microsoft Point of Sale for .NET devices, and print devices are common devices that need to be redirected from the local device to the Remote Desktop Services session.

- Single sign-on (SSO) enables users to enter their credentials once and be able to access other systems and services, based on their rights and permissions, without having to reenter their credentials each time. For single sign-on to work, the client system must be Windows Vista or higher or be a Server 2008 system, the client must have adequate rights and permissions, and the client and the Remote Desktop Session Host server must be in the same domain.

- Remote App is a new capability introduced in Windows Server 2008. RemoteApp enables you to publish individual applications instead of having to publish the entire desktop, which was the only option available in previous versions of Remote Desktop Services (Terminal Services).

- When you package RemoteApp programs, you will define the location where the package will be saved, the server settings, the Remote Desktop Gateway settings, and the certificate settings.

- You can use Remote Desktop Web Access to distribute RemoteApp programs. Remote Desktop Web Access will be installed as a server role on the server that users will connect to when they access the RemoteApp programs.

- Remote Desktop Gateway can be used to provide security and encryption when remote users access the server; it will establish an HTTPS connection, which will encapsulate Remote Desktop Protocol (RDP) traffic with SSL encryption.

Key Terms

Desktop Experience   The Desktop Experience feature includes features common on client operating systems, such as Windows 7. Common features include Windows Media Player, desktop themes, Video for Windows (AVI support), Windows Defender, Disk Cleanup, Sync Center, Sound Recorder, Snipping Tool, and others.

device redirection   A capability that enables a device to be connected to the local device but be accessible through the Remote Desktop Services session.

display data prioritization   A feature that controls the bandwidth ratio of input versus output prioritization; the default is a 70:30 ratio of input to output.

font smoothing   A setting that creates anti-aliasing on screen text to make fonts smoother and easier to read. ClearType fonts are supported if ClearType is enabled on the server and Font Smoothing is enabled.

Microsoft Point of Sale for .NET device redirection   This enhancement enables supported point of sale devices, such as bar code readers, to be used with Remote Desktop Services. You need to ensure that you have the most recent version of the Microsoft POS for .NET software downloaded from the Microsoft Web site.

monitor spanning   The capability of spanning multiple monitors with a total maximum resolution of 4096×2048.

Network Policy Server (NPS)   The Microsoft implementation of a Remote Authentication Dial-in User Service (RADIUS) server and proxy in Windows Server 2008.

Plug and Play (PNP) device redirection   PNP devices can be redirected from the local device to the Remote Desktop Services session. This capability is based on the Media Transfer Protocol (MTP) and Picture Transfer Protocol (PTP).

RemoteApp   Enables you to publish applications for client access; with RemoteApp you can publish individual applications instead of having to publish the entire desktop, which was the only option available in previous versions of Remote Desktop Services.

Remote Desktop Connection Authorization Policies (RD CAPs)   Enables you to specify which users can connect to the Remote Desktop Gateway server, specify the requirements that users must meet to connect, and specify whether to enable or disable client device redirection.

Remote Desktop Easy Print   This enhancement enables redirection of the default printer without having to match print drivers on the client computer and the Remote Desktop Session Host Server.

Remote Desktop Gateway (RD Gateway)   A role service in the Remote Desktop Session Host server role that allows authorized remote users to connect to resources on an internal corporate or private network from any Internet-connected device.

Remote Desktop Licensing (RD Licensing)   A license management system for Windows Server 2008 Remote Desktop Services that allows Remote Desktop Session Host servers to obtain and manage client access licenses (RD CALs) for devices and users that are connecting to a server.

Remote Desktop Resource Authorization Policies (RD RAPs)   Enables you to specify the network resources that users can connect to, specify the user groups and computer groups, and specify whether to use the default TCP port 3389 or allow a connection through another port.

Remote Desktop Services   One of the server roles available in Windows Server 2008 R2. In Server 2008 and earlier, this feature was called Terminal Services.

Remote Desktop Session Host   One of the server roles available in Windows Server 2008 R2.

Remote Desktop Web Access (RD Web Access)   A role service in the Remote Desktop Services role that lets you make RemoteApp programs, and a connection to the Remote Desktop Session Host server desktop, available to users from a Web browser.

single sign-on (SSO)   A feature that enables users to enter their credentials once and be able to access other systems and services, based on their rights and permissions, without having to reenter their credentials each time.

Review Questions

1. Network Level Authentication (NLA) makes users have to authenticate before connecting to the Remote Desktop Session Host. NLA is a capability supported in which RDC versions?

   a. RDC 5.0 or higher

   b. RDC 5.1 or higher

   c. RDC 6.0 or higher

   d. RDC 7.0 or higher

2. Which of the following is not a tab available from the Remote Desktop Connection dialog box?

   a. General

   b. Display

   c. Options

   d. Experience

3. What is the maximum resolution of the enhanced desktop resolution when using RDC?

   a. 1680 × 1050

   b. 1920 × 1200

   c. 4096 × 2048

   d. 8192 × 4096

4. What is the default display data prioritization?

   a. 40:60

   b. 50:50

   c. 70:30

   d. 80:20

5. Which of the following commands will modify the display resolution to a 1280 width?

   a. desktopwidth:i:1280

   b. width:i:1280

   c. desktopw:i:1280

   d. desktop1280:i:width

6. Which of the following mstsc.exe commands will modify the display resolution to a 1280 width?

   a. mstsc.exe /h:1280

   b. mstsc.exe 1280 /w

   c. mstsc.exe 1280

   d. mstsc.exe /w:1280

7. Which of the following is not required to configure Desktop Composition?

   a. Disable Desktop Experience

   b. Enable Desktop Experience

   c. Use the Windows Vista theme

   d. Enable Desktop Composition on the host client

8. Which of the following capabilities enables a device to be connected to the local device but be accessible through the Remote Desktop Services session?

   a. Device remote connect

   b. Device anywhere

   c. Device redirection

   d. Device session

9. Which of the following enhancements enable supported point of sale devices, such as bar code readers, to be used with Remote Desktop Services?

   a. Microsoft Bar Code for .NET Device Redirection

   b. Microsoft Point of Sale for .NET Device Redirection

   c. Microsoft Point of Sale for Bar Code Device Redirection

   d. Microsoft Point of Sale for .DOC Device Redirection

10. With device redirection, the Plug and Play capability is based on which of the following protocols?

    a. FTP

    b. FTP and MTP

    c. FTP and PTP

    d. MTP and PTP

11. Which of the following capabilities enables a user to enter their credentials once and be able to access other systems and services, based on their rights and permissions, without having to reenter their credentials each time?

    a. Single sign-on

    b. Tokens

    c. Digital signatures

    d. Device sign-on

12. What mode do you need to be in to install an application?

    a. Administrator

    b. Install

    c. Execute

    d. Transfer

13. Which new capability enables you to publish individual applications instead of having to publish the entire desktop?

    a. RemoteApp

    b. RD App

    c. RD Desktop

    d. RD Remote

14. Which of the following is not a Remote Desktop Session Host server role service?

    a. RD Session Broker

    b. RD Gateway

    c. RD Routing

    d. RD Web Access

15. Which RDC version is needed to run a RemoteApp package?

    a. RDC 5.0 or higher

    b. RDC 6.0 or higher

    c. RDC 4.0 or higher

    d. Any version

16. When the RD Web Access role is installed, which other service must also be installed?

    a. Internet Information Services (IIS)

    b. File Transfer Protocol (FTP)

    c. Domain Name Service (DNS)

    d. Dynamic Host Configuration Protocol (DHCP)

17. Which port does RD Gateway use?

    a. 20

    b. 21

    c. 443

    d. 433

18. Which of the following enables you to specify which users can connect to the RD Gateway server, specify the requirements that users must meet to connect, and specify whether to enable or disable client device redirection?

    a. RD CAPs

    b. RD RAPs

    c. RD MAPs

    d. RD GAPs

19. Which of the following enables you to specify the network resources that users can connect to, specify the user groups and computer groups, and specify whether to use the default TCP port 3389 or allow a connection through another port?

    a. RD CAPs

    b. RD RAPs

    c. RD MAPs

    d. RD GAPs

20. Which of the following can be used to further enhance security when using the RD Gateway and Remote Desktop Services clients?

    a. Network Access Protection (NAP)

    b. Network Prioritization (NP)

    c. Internet Information Services (IIS)

    d. File Transfer Protocol (FTP)

Case Projects

Case Project 4-1: Business Need for Implementing Remote Desktop Services

The IT manager in New Enterprises is considering implementing Remote Desktop Services capabilities within the organization. In order for the IT manager to prepare a proposal for management, the IT Department is asking you to explain the following:

1. In business terms, explain the benefits of implementing Remote Desktop Services.

2. In business terms, explain the risks with implementing Remote Desktop Services.

3. In business terms, state your recommendation for implementing Remote Desktop Services.

Case Project 4-2: Authentication and Single Sign-On

The IT manager has more questions about Remote Desktop Services in Windows Server 2008. The IT manager is primarily concerned about the authentication and single sign-on capabilities. To address the IT manager's concerns, provide the following information about authentication and single sign-on capabilities in Windows Server 2008:

1. Describe the authentication and single sign-on capabilities in Windows Server 2008.

2. Describe the concerns with implementing authentication and single sign-on capabilities in Windows Server 2008.

3. Describe a recommended approach for mitigating the concerns with implementing authentication and single sign-on capabilities in Windows Server 2008.

Case Project 4-3: RD Web Access and RD Gateway

The IT manager remains concerned about the security issues associated with implementing Remote Desktop Services, especially as it relates to RD Web Access. He has stated that he is convinced that the organization needs to provide that capability; however, he needs to ensure that management is fully aware of the potential risks.

1. In business terms, describe the security risks and vulnerabilities of implementing RD Web Access.

2. In technical terms, describe the security risks and vulnerabilities of implementing RD Web Access.

3. Describe the security capabilities in Windows Server 2008, as it relates to RD Web Access and RD Gateway.

Windows Server 2008 Remote Desktop Services, Part 2

After reading this chapter and completing the exercises, you will be able to:

- Describe the tools available for managing Remote Desktop Services in Windows Server 2008

- Explain how to manage, monitor, and terminate services in Remote Desktop Services

- Describe the options available in the RD Gateway Manager to securely manage and operate the RD Gateway

- Describe how the RD Connection Broker can be used to handle increased loads and provide fault tolerance for your servers

- Explain how RD Licensing is used to manage Client Access Licenses (CALs)

In Chapter 4, you learned about many of the basic concepts of using Remote Desktop Services within Windows Server 2008. In this chapter, you will learn about additional Remote Desktop Services concepts and capabilities, including additional tools for managing the Remote Desktop Connection Host, monitoring and terminating processes and user sessions, additional Remote Desktop Gateway configurations, the Remote Desktop Connection Broker, and Remote Desktop Licensing.

Managing the Remote Desktop Session Host

To properly manage the Remote Desktop Session Host, the administrator will need to perform many tasks. The administrator needs to ensure that authorized users are able to connect to the Remote Desktop Session Host, track the user sessions, and ensure that the applications and processes are available for users. Additionally, administrators often need to remotely control a user session.

Windows Server 2008 provides command-line and graphical user interface (GUI) tools for managing the Remote Desktop Session Host. This chapter focuses on the GUI tools that are available for managing the Remote Desktop Session Host.

The Remote Desktop Services Manager is the primary GUI tool for managing the Remote Desktop Session Host. After the Remote Desktop Services role has been installed (see Chapter 4), the Remote Desktop Services Manager is available. The following activity shows how to access and view the tabs and settings in the Remote Desktop Services Manager.

Activity 5-1: Display the Remote Desktop Services Manager

Time Required: Approximately 10 minutes
Objective: Learn how to display the Remote Desktop Services Manager

Description: In this activity, you will see the steps to display the Remote Desktop Services Manager. You will use the Remote Desktop Services Manager to manage and set various options affecting the operation of the Remote Desktop Session Host.

1. Click **Start**, click **All Programs**, click **Administrative Tools**, click **Remote Desktop Services**, and click **Remote Desktop Services Manager** to open the Remote Desktop Services Manager (Figure 5-1).

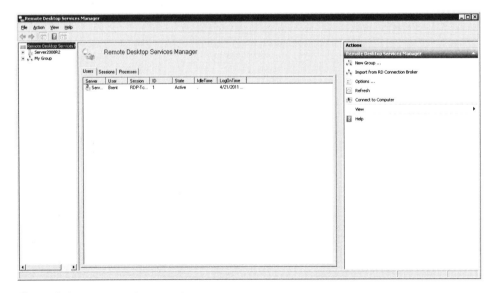

Figure 5-1 Remote Desktop Services Manager
© Cengage Learning 2012

2. Click each of the following tabs to view the data displayed in the Remote Desktop Services Manager: **Users**, **Sessions**, and **Processes**. (See descriptions below.)

3. Close all open windows.

The Remote Desktop Services Manager is organized into three panes. The left pane displays the servers and groups that you can manage. The center pane has the three tabs you just explored for managing the Users, Sessions, and Processes of the selected server. The right pane is the Actions pane, and provides different actions based on which items you have selected in the other two panes.

The Users tab in the center pane displays user data and server and session data associated with the user:

- *Server.* Displays the server that the user is connected to
- *User.* Displays the user name
- *Session.* Displays the session for the user
- *ID.* Displays the session ID for that session
- *State.* Displays the state of the session: active, disconnected, reset, or idle
- *Idle Time.* Displays the time that the session has been idle
- *LogOn Time.* Displays the date and time that the user connected to the session

The Sessions tab in the center pane displays similar information as in the User tab; however, the Sessions tab displays more information relating to the session:

- *Server.* Displays the server running the session
- *Session.* Displays the type of session running
- *User.* Displays the user name
- *ID.* Displays the session ID for that session
- *State.* Displays the state of the session: active, disconnected, reset, or idle
- *Type.* Displays the session client, such as RDP client
- *Client Name.* Displays the name of the client establishing the session
- *Idle Time.* Displays the time that the session has been idle
- *LogOn Time.* Displays the date and time that the user connected to the session
- *Comment.* Displays additional session information

The Processes tab in the center pane displays information about the processes, sessions, and users connected to the sessions:

- *Server.* Displays the server running the process
- *User.* Displays the user initiating the process
- *Session.* Displays the session number associated with the process
- *ID.* Displays the session ID
- *PID.* Displays the process ID
- *Image.* Displays the executable file that runs the process

Monitoring and Terminating Processes

Administrators often need to monitor or terminate a process or a user session. A common concern about remote sessions is about the processes that are being executed from within the session. Administrators often need to view the active processes and, if necessary, terminate a process. Likewise, they might need to monitor, connect to, or terminate a user session. The following two activities show how to monitor and terminate a running process and a user session.

Activity 5-2: Monitor and Terminate a Process

Time Required: Approximately 10 minutes
Objective: Learn how to monitor and terminate a process

Description: Administrators commonly need to manage or terminate an active process. In this activity, you will see the steps to manage and terminate a process.

1. Display the Remote Desktop Services Manager, if it is not already displayed (see Step 1 in Activity 5-1).

2. Click the **Processes** tab to view the active processes (Figure 5-2).

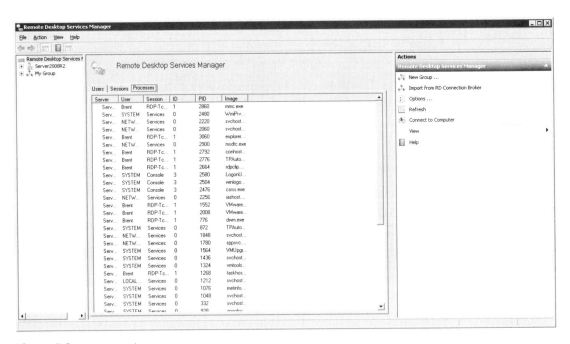

Figure 5-2 Processes tab
© Cengage Learning 2012

You can also display active processes through the command prompt using the *query process* command (for example, the following command would display all visible processes on the RDS Corp1 server: *query process * /server:RDSCorp1*).

3. Start a command prompt window.

4. Type **ping –n 200** www.cengage.com and press **Enter** to start a PING process that will attempt 200 times to reach the www.cengage.com server.

5. In the Remote Desktop Services Manager window, click the **Processes** tab.

6. Click the **PING.EXE** process and click **End Process** in the Actions pane.

7. Click **OK** to confirm ending the process (Figure 5-3).

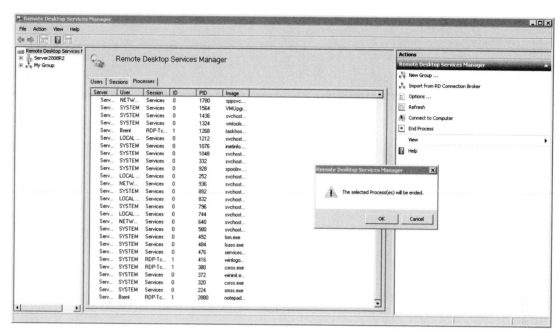

Figure 5-3 End Process

© Cengage Learning 2012

8. Navigate to the command prompt window. You will see the PING command has stopped execution.

In the same manner that administrators often need to monitor and terminate a process, they might also need to view the sessions and, if needed, terminate a session. In the Remote Desktop Services Manager, the three types of sessions include:

- *Console*, which is the session that you connect to if you log on to the physical console
- *Services*, which is the session that contains system processes on the RD Session Host
- *Listener*, which is the session that listens for and accepts new client connections

If you encounter a session that is not active, or orphaned, you can choose to disconnect the session or terminate the session. If you disconnect the session, it will use fewer resources but leave the applications and data in use open in the session. If you terminate the session, all resources being used by the session will be available.

Activity 5-3: Manage and Terminate a Session

Time Required: Approximately 10 minutes
Objective: Learn how to manage and terminate a session

Description: Just as administrators need to manage and terminate processes, they might need to do the same for sessions. In this activity, you will see the steps to manage and terminate a session.

1. Display the Remote Desktop Services Manager, if it is not already displayed (see Step 1 in Activity 5-1).

2. Click the Users or Sessions tab (in this example, click **Users**), view the information, and find the user or session you desire to manage (Figure 5-4).

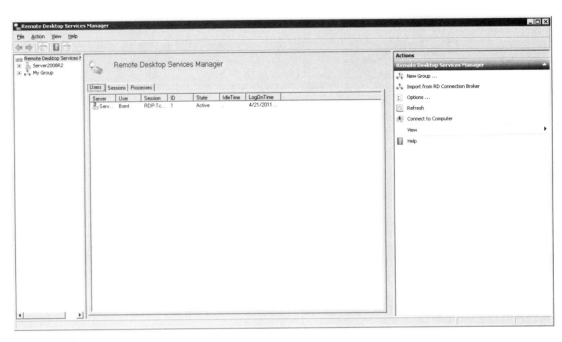

Figure 5-4 Users tab
© Cengage Learning 2012

3. Right-click the session and select **Connect** to connect to that session (Figure 5-5).

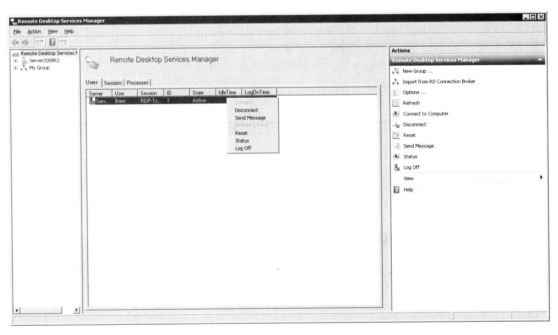

Figure 5-5 Connect to a session
© Cengage Learning 2012

When you connect to a session, you will need to enter the user session password if the session is not your own.

4. Right-click the session and select **Reset**. From the dialog box telling you that you are resetting the session (Figure 5-6), click **OK**. The session resets and all processes will be terminated for that session.

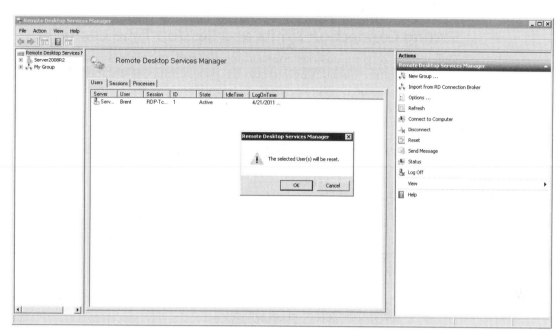

Figure 5-6 Resetting the session

© Cengage Learning 2012

 You can also select Disconnect, which will not terminate the active processes of that session.

In addition to using the Remote Desktop Services Manager, you can use the command line to perform common actions. Following are some common commands that you can use from the command line:

- *change logon* – enable or disable session logons
- *change port* – list or change COM port for applications
- *logoff* – log off a user from a session
- *msg* – send user(s) a message
- *reset session* – terminate a session
- *tscon* – connect to another session
- *tsdiscon* – disconnect a session
- *tskill* – terminate a process

Here is an example of command-line syntax:

```
tskill processid | processname | [/SERVER:servername] [ID:sessionid] [/V]
```

There are also common *query* commands from the command line to query for process, session, or user information:

- *query process*
- *query session*
- *query user*

Here is an example of *query* command syntax:

```
query process [* | processid | username | sessionname | /ID:nn |
programname] [/SERVER:servername]
```

Setting Connection Limits and Session Time Limits

The number of simultaneous connections allowed and the session time limits affect the overall availability of the server. Administrators typically limit the number of simultaneous connections and enforce session time limits for performance reasons, for security reasons, and due to licensing requirements.

Activity 5-4: Specify Connection Limits and Session Time Limits

Time Required: Approximately 10 minutes
Objective: Learn how to specify connection limits and session time limits

Description: To control the number of users connected to the server, administrators need to specify connection limits and session time limits. In this activity, you will see how to specify connection limits and session time limits.

1. To view the Remote Desktop Session Host Configuration window, click **Start,** click **Administrative Tools,** click **Remote Desktop Services,** and click **Remote Desktop Session Host Configuration** (Figure 5-7).

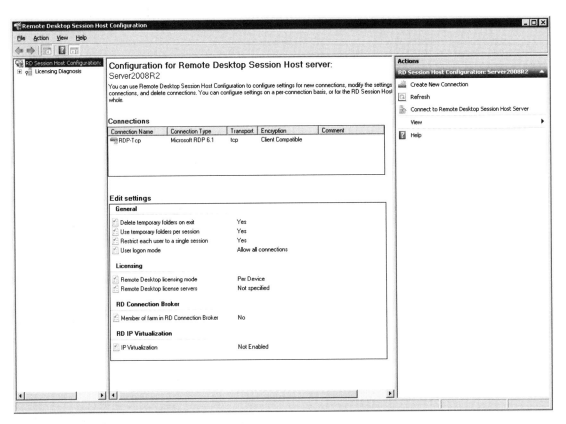

Figure 5-7 Remote Desktop Session Host Configuration
© Cengage Learning 2012

2. Double-click a setting, such as **Use temporary folders per session,** and the Properties dialog box for that setting displays (Figure 5-8).

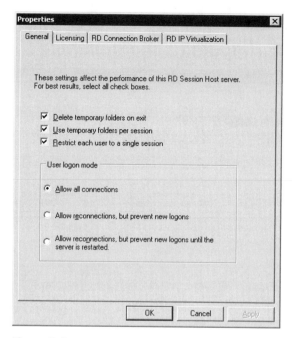

Figure 5-8 Remote Desktop Session Host Configuration Properties
© Cengage Learning 2012

3. View the settings available and click **OK** when complete.

4. Click **Start,** click **Run,** type **gpedit.msc,** and click **OK** to open the Local Group Policy Editor (Figure 5-9).

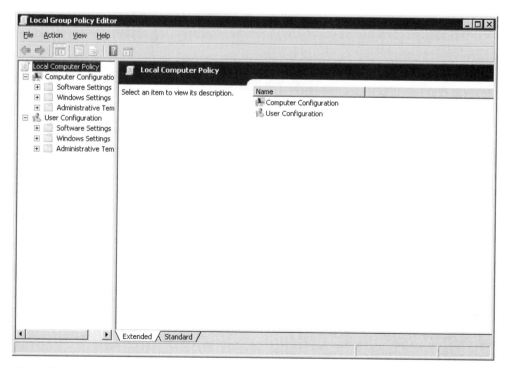

Figure 5-9 Group Policy Editor
© Cengage Learning 2012

5. To limit the number of simultaneous connections, click **Computer Configuration**, click **Administrative Templates**, click **Windows Components**, click **Remote Desktop Services**, click **Remote Desktop Session Host**, and click **Connections** (Figure 5-10).

6. Double-click **Limit number of connections**. Enable the setting and enter the desired value for the number of connections and click **OK**.

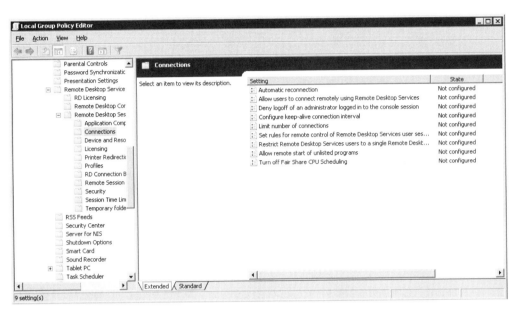

Figure 5-10   Connections

© Cengage Learning 2012

7. To limit the session time limit, click **Computer Configuration**, click **Administrative Templates**, click **Windows Components**, click **Remote Desktop Services**, click **Remote Desktop Session Host**, and click **Session Time Limits** (Figure 5-11).

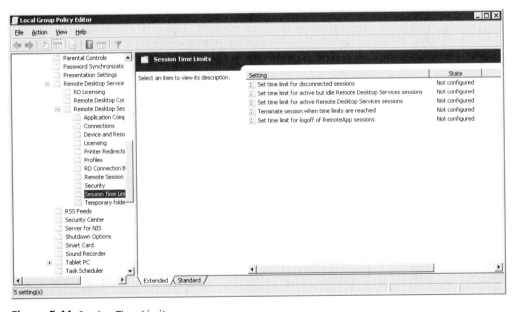

Figure 5-11   Session Time Limits

© Cengage Learning 2012

8. Double-click the desired setting, modify the configuration and the desired value for the session time limit, and click **OK**.

Remotely Controlling a User Session

Administrators, tech support personnel, and others might need to remotely control another user's session. You can monitor or take control of another user's session through Remote Control settings in **Group Policy** (Remote Desktop Session Host Configuration), and Active Directory User and Computers (user account properties).

Through Group Policy, you can control a session through user or computer configuration:

- User Configuration > Policies > Administrative Templates > Windows Components > Remote Desktop Services > Remote Desktop Session Host > Connections
- Computer Configuration > Policies > Administrative Templates > Windows Components > Remote Desktop Services > Remote Desktop Session Host > Connections

Using Active Directory User and Computers, you can enable and configure remote control through User Account Properties:

- On the Remote control tab of the Properties dialog box, you can select Enable remote control (which is selected by default), Require user's permission (which is selected by default), or specify the level of control (View the user's session or Interact with the session).

RD Gateway

For Remote Desktop Gateway (RD Gateway) and remote clients to establish a secure, encrypted connection, the RD Gateway will need to install a certificate in the RD Gateway's server computer certificate store. The RD Gateway acts as a proxy between a remote user establishing a remote connection and the resources internal to the network. When users connect, they will validate the authenticity of the certificate. The purpose of the RD Gateway is for authorized users to be able to connect to internal resources from a remote location on devices that run the Remote Desktop Connection (RDC) client. The server authentication certificate must meet the following criteria:

- Must be a computer certificate
- The extended key usage must be Server Authentication (OID 1.3.6.1.5.5.7.3.1)
- The Subject name of the certificate must match the DNS name the client will use to establish the connection

When you install and configure the RD Gateway, you will be prompted to provide the server authentication certificate for SSL connections (installing and configuring the RD Gateway was covered in Chapter 4).

A Remote Desktop Connection Authorization Policy (RD CAP) defines which user can connect through RD Gateway, optionally from which computers a connection can be made, the authentication method, and the client devices that will be redirected.

A Remote Desktop Resource Authorization Policy (RD RAP) defines the resources that a user group is allowed to access after connecting through the RD Gateway. At least one RD CAP and one RD RAP is required for a user to connect to a resource on the network; the RD CAP authorizes the user to connect through the RD Gateway and the RD RAP enables access to the resources after they have connected.

The following activity is similar to Activity 4-11 in Chapter 4, with a little more information on RD CAP and RD RAP; thus, if you have already installed the RD Gateway Role Service, you can skip this activity. If the RD Gateway has not been already installed, the following steps will install the RD Gateway and define the RD CAP and RD RAP.

Activity 5-5: Install the RD Gateway Role Service

Time Required: Approximately 20 minutes
Objective: Learn how to install the RD Gateway role service

Description: In this activity, you will use the Server Manager to install the RD Gateway role service.

1. Click **Start**, click **Administrative Tools**, and click **Server Manager** to open the Server Manager.
2. Click **Remote Desktop Services** in Roles Summary.
3. Click **Add Role Services** in the Role Services area.
4. The Select Role Services page displays (Figure 5-12). Select the **Remote Desktop Gateway** check box.
5. Click **Next**.
6. The Add Roles Wizard displays. Click **Add Required Role Services**.

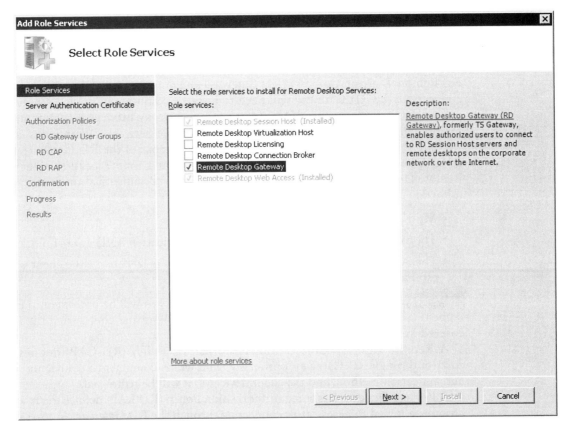

Figure 5-12 Select Role Services
© Cengage Learning 2012

7. Click **Next**.
8. The Choose a Server Authentication Certificate for SSL Encryption page displays (Figure 5-13). Select the desired SSL encryption.

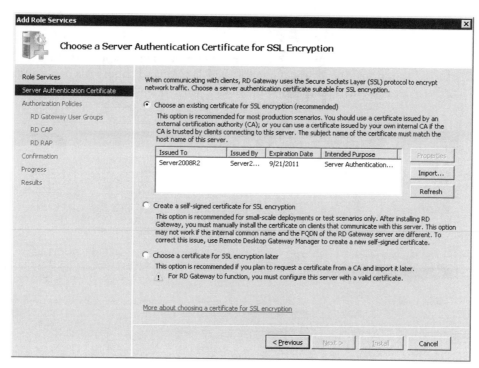

Figure 5-13 Choose a Server Authentication Certificate for SSL Encryption
© Cengage Learning 2012

9. Click **Next**.

10. The Create Authorization Policies for RD Gateway page displays (Figure 5-14). Click **Next**.

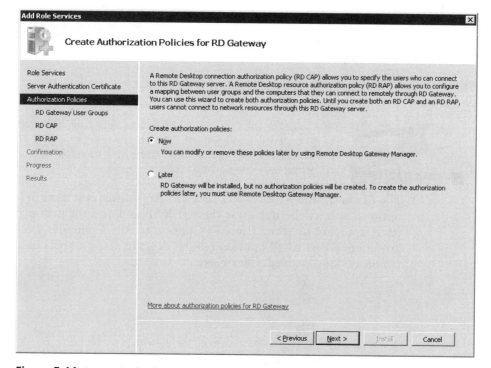

Figure 5-14 Create Authorization Policies for RD Gateway
© Cengage Learning 2012

11. Click **Add** and select the groups that can connect through the Remote Desktop Gateway. Click **Next**.

12. The Create an RD CAP for RD Gateway page displays (Figure 5-15). Select desired options. Specify the name for the RD CAP and choose the desired Windows Authentication method (Password, Smart Cards, or both). Click **Next**.

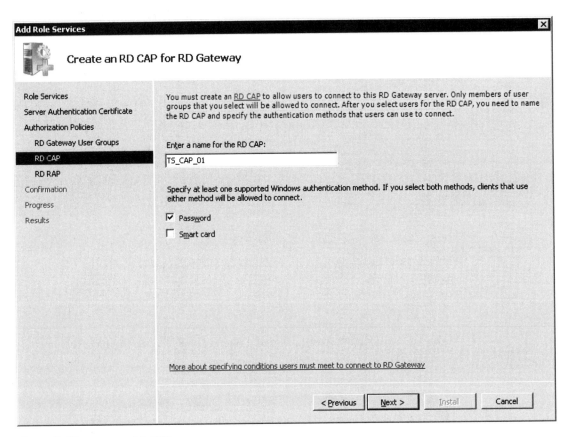

Figure 5-15 Create an RD CAP

© Cengage Learning 2012

You can define the RD CAP and RD RAP options later, if desired, through the RD Gateway Management Console. However, one RD CAP and one RD RAP must be defined for users to be able to establish a connection and get access to resources.

13. The Create an RD RAP for RD Gateway page displays (Figure 5-16). Select desired options. Specify the name for the RD RAP and add the group that contains the resources (choose Allow Users To Connect to Any Computer On The Network, to give users access to all internal remote desktop session hosts and computers with remote desktop enabled. Click **Next**.

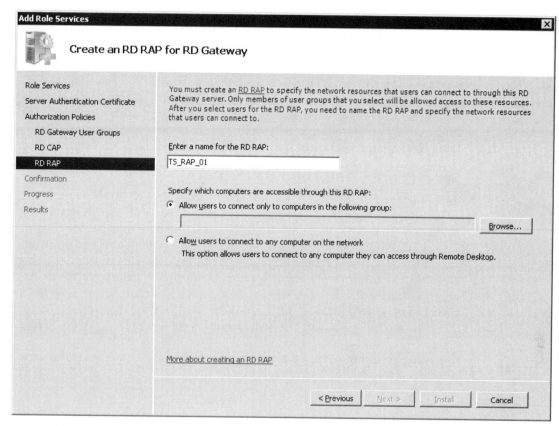

Figure 5-16 Create an RD RAP
© Cengage Learning 2012

14. The Network Policy and Access Services page displays. Click **Next**.

15. Confirm that the **Network Policy Server** role is selected. Click **Next**.

16. The Web Server (IIS) page displays. Click **Next**.

17. Change or accept the default roles. Click **Next**.

18. Click **Install**.

RD Gateway Options

You will commonly manage the RD Gateway using the RD Gateway Manager. To open the RD Gateway Manager, click Start, click Administrative Tools, click Remote Desktop Services, and click Remote Desktop Gateway Manager.

The RD Gateway Manager displays the RD Gateway server, policies (RD CAPs and RD RAPs), and Monitoring in the left pane, the RD Gateway Server Status in the center pane, and the Actions available in the right pane. Additionally, you can right-click the RD Gateway server and select Properties to display the Properties dialog box for the RD Gateway server.

Remote Desktop Connection Broker

An organization might decide to have more than one Remote Desktop Session Host to handle the increased load on the server and to provide additional fault-tolerance. In a small organization, one server might suffice; however, in a medium to large organization, a server farm might be necessary to support the demands of the users. A server farm consists of two or more servers with the same configuration. They will appear to the client as a single entity.

In an environment with a single server, the client creates an RDP file for connecting to the specific server. In a multi-server environment, the connection request will go through a connection broker and the load balancer.

Server farms are integrated with the load balancing feature in order to ensure that the workload is distributed among each of the servers in the server farm, thus providing additional fault tolerance, increased performance, and scalability within the organization.

In order to feasibly install the **Remote Desktop Connection Broker (RD Connection Broker)** role service, you will need to be working in an environment with an Active Directory domain setup. With that environment, you can add the Remote Desktop Connection Broker role service.

Server Farms and Load Balancing

As you learned in Chapter 1, *network load balancing (NLB)* provides increased performance, availability, and scalability for the clients supported. NLB distributes, or load balances, client traffic across several servers; the available server will take turns responding to the client requests. There can be up to 32 servers in a cluster. The client will not necessarily know they are working with a server farm; clients will have one IP address they communicate with and each of the servers in the server farm will have an internal IP address, which the clients do not necessarily know about. Additionally, RD Connection Broker tracks disconnected sessions and can reconnect clients to those sessions.

Large organizations with heavy demands on the servers will need to configure servers to join a server farm and configure load balancing accordingly in order to improve performance and other characteristics discussed above. However, in order to configure this capability, you need to be working in a multiple-server environment.

RD Licensing

Remote Desktop Licensing (RD Licensing) is used to manage the **Client Access Licenses (CALs)** that are required for devices or users to connect to a Remote Desktop Session Host server. When connecting to a Remote Desktop Session Host server, the server will request a CAL, if needed, from an RD Licensing server so the client can connect to the Remote Desktop Session Host server. You must have at least one license server deployed to enable clients to get the client access license and connect to the Remote Desktop Session Host server environment.

Two concurrent connections are supported through Remote Desktop for remote administration.

In order to provide time to configure your RD Licensing server, Remote Desktop Services includes a grace period for licensing. During the grace period, the Remote Desktop Session Host server can connect unlicensed clients. The grace period begins when the first client connection is accepted by the Remote Desktop Session Host server and it ends when a permanent CAL is issued or after the grace period has expired.

The grace period for Server 2003 and Server 2008 is 120 days.

General steps to configure RD Licensing are as follows:

1. Install the RD Licensing service
2. Activate the licensing server
3. Install licenses on it
4. Ensure that the license server can be discovered

Managing Client Access Licenses

Installing client access licenses will be discussed, but not provided as an activity, since most readers would not be going through the process at this point to actually get the client access licenses.

Here are some tips for other common licensing actions:

- After you have installed RD Licensing, use the RD Licensing Manager to manage the RD Licensing servers.

- To change RD Licensing properties, right-click the desired server from the RD Licensing Manager and select Properties.

- You might need to change the discovery scope of the RD Licensing server. You change the scope through the RD Licensing Manager; then select the desired server and select Review Configuration on the Action menu. The discovery scope options include: *This domain* or *The forest*.

- RDS Per User CAL tracking. The RDS Per User CAL information is stored in the user account information in Active Directory Domain Services (AD DS).

- Review Configuration can help to identify RD Licensing configuration problems. Review Configuration will check many configuration items, including the discovery scope, whether the server is installed on a domain controller (if discovery scope is Domain), if the server is published in Active Directory Domain Services (if discovery scope is Forest), if the server is a member of the RD License Servers group in AD DS, and check the security group Group Policy setting.

- For increased security, through the security group Group Policy setting, you can control which servers can receive an RD CAL through group policy settings.

- Use the RD Licensing Manager to revoke an RDS Per Device CAL, so it will become available to other users. You can revoke up to 20 percent of the available RDS Per Device CALs at any given time.

- To revoke an RDS Per Device CAL, open the RD Licensing Manager, select the node for the desired CALs (such as Windows Server 2008—Installed RDS Per Device CALs), select the RDS Per Device CAL that you want to manage (such as revoke), and select to revoke the CAL.

You can revoke an RDS Per Device CAL; you cannot revoke an RDS Per User CAL.

Best Practices

1. For performance purposes, install the RD Licensing role service on a server separate from the Remote Desktop Session Host, especially in larger environments.

2. Become familiar with the three panes in the Remote Desktop Services Manager and the tabs and settings available. There are many settings in each of these panes and tabs for managing your server.

3. Frequently monitor processes and user sessions to determine if corrective actions need to be taken or if a process or session needs to be terminated.

4. Many of the actions that you frequently perform can be performed faster through the command-line interface; thus, learn and use command-line commands for actions that you perform frequently.

(continues)

(continued)

5. Understand your operational environment and limit the number of simultaneous connections allowed and the session time limits accordingly.

6. Establish a corporate policy for remotely controlling a user's session so all employees are aware of the potential and the activities performed when remotely controlling a session.

7. Establish a corporate policy for controlling and maintaining the CALs.

8. Ensure that the settings for the RD Gateway adhere to the corporate security standards and policies to ensure that remote clients establish a secure and encrypted connection, if applicable.

9. Explore the RD Gateway server properties to see which settings are needed to adhere to security standards and policies, such as SSL Certificate, Auditing, and SSL Bridging.

10. Configure network load balancing (NLB) to increase performance, availability, and scalability for the clients supported. Ensure that this is monitored to verify the desired results.

Chapter Summary

- In order to properly manage the Remote Desktop Session Host, the administrator needs to perform many tasks, such as tracking the user sessions, ensuring that the applications and processes are available for the users, and terminating processes and sessions. Windows Server 2008 provides command-line tools and graphical user interface (GUI) tools for managing RD Session Host server.

- Additionally, administrators need to limit the number of simultaneous connections allowed and specify the session time limits, as these affect the overall availability of the server.

- Administrators, tech support personnel, and others might need to remotely control another user's session. Thus, you can monitor or take control of another user's session. Remote Control settings are configured in Group Policy, Remote Desktop Session Host Configuration, and Active Directory Users and Computers (user account properties).

- For RD Gateway and remote clients to establish a secure, encrypted connection, the RD Gateway must install a certificate in the RD Gateway's server computer certificate store. The RD Gateway acts as a proxy between a remote user establishing an RDP connection and the resources internal to the network.

- You will commonly manage RD Gateway using the RD Gateway Manager. The RD Gateway Manager displays the RD Gateway server, policies (RD CAPs and RD RAPs), and Monitoring in the left pane, the RD Gateway Server Status in the center pane, and the Actions available in the right pane.

- An organization might decide to have more than one Remote Desktop Session Host to handle the increased load on the server and to provide additional fault-tolerance. A server farm consists of two or more servers with the same configuration. They appear to the client as a single entity.

- Network load balancing (NLB) provides increased performance, availability, and scalability for the clients supported. NLB distributes, or load balances, client traffic across several servers; the available server will take turns responding to the client requests. There can be up to 32 servers in a cluster.

- Remote Desktop Licensing (RD Licensing) is used to manage the Client Access Licenses (CALs) for connecting to a server. When connecting to a server, the server will request a CAL, if needed, from an RD Licensing server so the client can connect to the server. You must have at least one license server deployed to enable clients to connect to the Remote Desktop Session Host environment.

Key Terms

Client Access License (CAL) Gives a client or device the rights to use or access the services of a server; required for devices or users to connect to a Remote Desktop Session Host server.

Group Policy Microsoft Group Policy provides centralized management and control of users and groups.

RD Connection Broker Remote Desktop Connection Broker (RD Connection Broker) is a role service that enables a user to reconnect to an existing session in a load-balanced server farm.

RD Licensing A Windows Server 2008 license management system for Remote Desktop Services. This system allows servers to obtain and manage Client Access Licenses (CALs).

Review Questions

1. Which of the following is the primary GUI tool for managing Remote Desktop Services?
   a. Remote Desktop Services Manager
   b. TS GUI
   c. TS Gateway Manager
   d. TS Licensing Manager

2. Which pane of the Remote Desktop Services Manager displays the servers and groups that you can manage?
   a. Right pane
   b. Center pane
   c. Left pane
   d. All panes

3. From the center pane of the Remote Desktop Services Manager, which tab displays the amount of time a session has been idle?
   a. User tab
   b. Session tab
   c. Process tab
   d. Both a and b

4. Which of the following commands will terminate a process?
   a. tskill
   b. killprocess
   c. prkill
   d. processkill

5. Which of the following will connect to another session?
   a. logon
   b. tskill
   c. tscon
   d. tsdiscon

6. Which of the following commands will query for session information?
   a. query all
   b. qsession
   c. query session
   d. session query

7. For RD Gateway and remote clients to establish a secure, encrypted connection, the RD Gateway will need to install a _____ in the RD Gateway's server computer certificate store.

   a. Connection

   b. Certificate

   c. Application

   d. Driver

8. The Subject name of the server authentication certificate must match the _____ name the client will use to establish the connection.

   a. RDP

   b. TCP

   c. DNS

   d. DHCP

9. The RD Gateway acts as a proxy between a remote user establishing an RDP connection and the resources _____ to the network.

   a. external

   b. internal

   c. foreign

   d. untrusted

10. Which of the following defines which user can connect through TS Gateway?

    a. RD CAP

    b. RD RAP

    c. RD HAP

    d. RD SAP

11. Which of the following defines the resources that a user group is allowed to access after connecting through the RD Gateway?

    a. RD CAP

    b. RD RAP

    c. RD HAP

    d. RD SAP

12. In the RD Gateway Manager, which pane displays the available Actions?

    a. All panes

    b. Left pane

    c. Right pane

    d. Center pane

13. A server farm consists of _____ or more servers with the same configuration.

    a. 1

    b. 2

    c. 3

    d. 32

14. Which of the following is used to provide increased performance, availability, and scalability for the clients supported.

    a. UDP

    b. TCP

    c. NLB

    d. DNS

15. Up to how many servers can be in a cluster?

    a. 2

    b. 6

    c. 32

    d. 64

16. What is the licensing grace period in Windows Server 2008?

    a. 30 days

    b. 60 days

    c. 120 days

    d. 180 days

17. Which of the following is used to manage the Client Access Licenses (CALs)?

    a. RD Licensing

    b. RD Access

    c. RD Client Access

    d. RD Gateway

18. How many concurrent connections are supported through Remote Desktop for remote administration?

    a. 1

    b. 2

    c. 4

    d. 8

19. You can revoke up to _____ of the available RDS Per Device CALs at any given time.

    a. 10 percent

    b. 20 percent

    c. 50 percent

    d. 75 percent

20. You can revoke up to _____ of the available RDS Per User CALs at any given time.

    a. 10 percent

    b. 20 percent

    c. 50 percent

    d. You cannot revoke an RDS Per User CAL

Case Projects

Case Project 5-1: Business Need for Expanding Remote Desktop Services

The IT manager in New Enterprises is considering expanding the Remote Desktop Services capabilities within the organization. In order for the IT manager to prepare a proposal for management, the IT department is asking you to explain the following:

1. In business terms, explain the costs of expanding the organization's ability to manage their Remote Desktop Services implementation.

2. In business terms, explain the benefits of expanding the organization's ability to manage their Remote Desktop Services implementation.

3. In business terms, explain the different methods, described in this chapter, for managing Remote Desktop Services; also, explain the additional resources needed to provide these capabilities.

Case Project 5-2: Security and RD Gateway

The Security manager has many questions about security in Windows Server 2008. The Security manager is primarily concerned with the RD Gateway and the security methods that can be provided through the RD Gateway.

To address the Security manager's concerns, you provide the following descriptions of security and RD Gateway in Windows Server 2008.

1. Describe the ability to provide encrypted connections in RD Gateway in Windows Server 2008.

2. Describe how the RD CAP and RD RAP settings affect security.

3. Describe SSL Certificate, Auditing, and SSL Bridging RD Gateway Properties and how they affect security.

Case Project 5-3: Network Load Balancing

There have been some connection problems in the organization that the IT manager feels would be solved with network load balancing. The IT manager desires to provide additional resources to increase performance, availability, and scalability for the clients supported. However, he needs to support this decision from a technical perspective and a business perspective.

1. In business terms, describe the performance, availability, and scalability enhancements provided to the organization through the implementation of NLB.

2. In technical terms, describe the performance, availability, and scalability enhancements provided to the organization through the implementation of NLB.

Chapter 6

Configuring Windows Server 2008 Web Services, Part 1

After reading this chapter and completing the exercises, you will be able to:

- Create and configure Web applications utilizing application pools on IIS 7

- Manage IIS Web sites including publishing, configuring virtual directories, and migrating sites and Web applications

- Create and configure FTP 6 sites

- Create and configure FTP 7 sites

- Create and configure SMTP virtual servers

In today's world, it is highly unlikely for an organization to not have a Web site, or even multiple sites. From providing marketing information about an organization on the Internet, providing employees information internally, to selling product and providing on-demand support, a Web site is a must have rather than a nice-to-have. The question is not "Should we have a Web site?" but, "What capabilities should our Web site have?" In the Windows Server environment, the Internet Information Server (IIS) server role is a powerful and flexible tool to answer that question and to provide the needed capabilities for an organization's Web site.

Configuring Web Applications

IIS is a server role available in all versions of Server 2008. The architecture of IIS is modular, which allows you to install only the components you require to conserve server resources, maintain peak performance, and reduce security risks. It is important to communicate with your Web developers to understand their needs when choosing which components to deploy when setting up Web application configurations.

A Web application is not the same thing as a Web site. The application runs within the context of a site, but the site can have different areas that do not require the user to interact with any particular Web application. In addition, within a single Web site, there can be multiple Web applications. To determine how a user accesses a Web application, it can be configured as either directory-dependent or URL-specified.

Directory-Dependent Applications

A directory-dependent application is accessed by directly referring to the directory where it resides within the URL. An example that directs a user to a login page might look something like this:

```
http://www.yourcompany.com/login
```

In this simple case, the application residing in the login directory presents the user with a form to enter their username and password. The login directory might be the only area within the Web site that runs the login application.

URL-Specified Applications

A URL-specified configuration determines the appropriate application to execute by looking at parameters passed in the URL. Using this configuration, directing a user to a login page might look something like this:

```
http://www.yourcompany.com?uid=0
```

In this case, the application looks at the uid (User ID), and seeing that it is 0, automatically directs the user to the login page. If the uid had been greater than 0, indicating the user was already logged on, the user may have been redirected to a home page or a welcome page.

.ASP (Classic ASP) vs. .ASPX (ASP.NET)

Active Server Pages are one of the most common types of Web application in the Windows Server environment. There are two types of Active Server Pages: Classic ASP and ASP.NET. While they may look similar, Classic ASP files have an extension of .ASP, while ASP.NET files have an extension of .ASPX. Most Classic ASP files will run as ASP.NET pages, although they may need some minor changes. The big difference is the additional functionality available to ASP.NET.
While IIS7 can support basic ASP.NET applications directly, additional functionality is available by installing the Application Server role.

Installing this role should only be done if your application developers require the features for their applications. These additional features use server resources and increase the **attack surface** (code that can be run by an unauthenticated user) of the server.

Role services that are available with this role include the following:

- *.NET Framework 3.5.1* which includes the Windows Communication Foundation (WCF), Windows Workflow Foundation (WF), and Windows Presentation Foundation (WPF). These create an infrastructure developers can use to create powerful Web applications.

- *Web Server (IIS) support* integrates IIS with the Application Server and makes the application server features available to Web applications. If this option is chosen, you will be prompted to install IIS if it isn't already installed.

- *Com+ network access* which enables the Application Server to host or allow remote invocation of applications built with COM+ or Enterprise Services components. Component Access Model (COM) allows developers to access code from a distributed infrastructure.

- *TCP port sharing* allows multiple .NET applications to share the same TCP port. Applications can co-exist on the same server in separate, isolated processes.

- *Windows Process Activation Service Support (WAS)* enables the Application Server or IIS itself to access applications remotely on the network using different types of protocols and services such as TCP Activation, HTTP Activation, Named Pipes Activation and Message Queuing Activation. This allows applications to start and stop dynamically in response to incoming requests.

- *Distributed transactions* provides services for transactions over multiple databases on multiple computers on the network.

Activity 6-1: Create a Web Application

Time Required: 5 minutes

Objective: Create a Web application within a Web site

Description: You will create a Web application that identifies a physical path on the server to find the application and how to connect to it.

1. Create the following directory on the server's C drive: **C:\websites\example**. This is the directory where the Web application code would be placed.

2. Click **Start**, point to **Administrative Tools**, and click **Internet Information Services (IIS) Manager** to start IIS Manager. Then, if it is not already expanded, expand the server node in the Connections pane, and expand **Sites**. Select **Default Web Site** in the Connections pane; this is where the Web application will be created.

3. Right-click the **Default Web Site** and click **Add Application** to open the Add Application dialog box shown in Figure 6-1.

4. Type **example** in the Alias text box. The application would be accessed by users via the URL http://yourdomain.com/example.

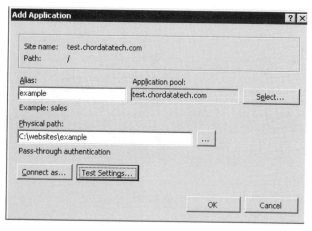

Figure 6-1 Add Application dialog box

© Cengage Learning 2012

5. Type **c:\websites\example** in the Physical path text box.

It is recommended that the physical path be separate from where the actual Web site or other Web sites reside. This gives you more control over the access to the application vs. just placing it in a sub-folder underneath the main site.

6. Click **Connect as** to open the Connect As dialog box (Figure 6-2).

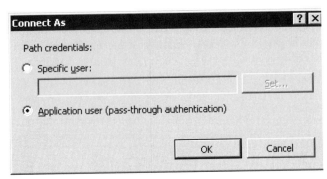

Figure 6-2 Connect As dialog box

© Cengage Learning 2012

7. Click on the option button next to **Application user (pass-through authentication)** if it is not selected by default. Click **OK**. The built in IIS user uses pass-through authentication. If the application required a specific user to run, you can select **Specific user** and enter the appropriate user in that text box.

8. Click the **Test Settings** button in the Add Application dialog box (refer to Figure 6-1) to open the Test Connection dialog box, as shown in Figure 6-3. The authentication test should have a green check box next to it. Authorization will probably have a yellow triangle with an exclamation mark in it, with a message that the access to the path cannot be verified. This is normal since the default IIS user context is not defined until a user actually tries to access the page.

9. Click **Close**, and then click **OK** to close the Add Application dialog box.

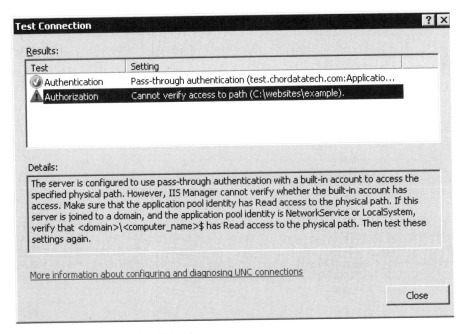

Figure 6-3 Test Connection dialog box

© Cengage Learning 2012

Application Pools

One of the most powerful features of Web applications in the Windows Server 2008 environment that not only aids development but maximizes overall uptime for all sites and applications running on a server is Application Pools. **Application Pools** isolate your Web sites from your Web applications. Each Application Pool contains its own worker processes independent of the other pools, preventing problems with one site or application from creating trouble or performance problems for other sites. You can troubleshoot or restart an Application Pool independently. Maintenance on one site need not affect other sites on the same server.

When IIS is installed on the server it automatically includes the DefaultAppPool (which is associated with the Default Web site). If the Application Development Role Services are already installed, the Classic .NET AppPool will also be included. The Classic .Net AppPool is used to support older applications that use .NET Framework 2.0 using Classic Managed Pipeline mode. The DefaultAppPool also supports .NET Framework 2.0 but uses the newer integrated pipeline mode. Some older applications may require the Classic .NET AppPool in order to function properly, depending on how they were written.

When you create a new site in IIS7, an Application Pool is automatically created for that site. When you create a Web application you can configure it to use any of the available Application Pools. A Web application can have its own pool.

Occasionally bugs or defects may be introduced into an application that cause it to use an inordinate amount of resources, or have a memory leak. **Recycling** allows you to restart an Application Pool gracefully while allowing it to complete requests that are already in the pipeline before restarting. This provides a seamless experience for users who may be accessing the affected site or applications and prevents them from receiving an error message. The recycling settings can be set for either Fixed Intervals and/or Memory Based Maximums.

The best practice would be to have a misbehaving application rewritten to address the issue but when this is not possible, or it will take some time to address the problem, the recycle settings can be adjusted to minimize the impact. Recycling events can be logged. You can review event logs to see which applications are recycling frequently in order to determine where the problems are.

Settings related to system resources and CPU and memory usage can also be adjusted. These settings are not to be changed without due consideration. It is possible to assign more server resources to the pool than is warranted and negatively affect other sites and applications. For most situations, the default settings are fine.

Activity 6-2: Create an Application Pool

Time Required: 5 minutes

Objective: Create an Application Pool that is not assigned to a particular application

Description: You will create an Application Pool and configure the recycling parameters as well as the logging of recycling events.

1. Open IIS Manager.
2. Right-click the **Application Pools** node in the Connections Pane and choose **Add Application Pool.**
3. Type **Example2** in the Name text box.
4. Select **.NET Framework v2.0.50727** in the .NET Framework version drop-down list (this may differ on your server. If so, simply choose the highest version).
5. Select **Integrated** in the Managed pipeline mode: drop-down list.
6. Click the check box next to **Start application pool immediately** if it is not already checked. Click **OK.**
7. The Application Pools screen appears. Select the **Example2** application pool, as shown in Figure 6-4.

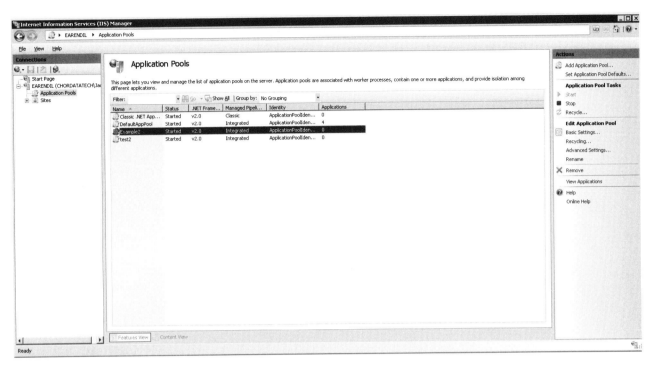

Figure 6-4 Application Pools

© Cengage Learning 2012

8. Click **Recycling** under Edit Application Pool in the Actions pane.

9. As shown in Figure 6-5, click the check box next to **Regular time intervals** and **Fixed number of requests** and type **1740** and **15000** in the respective corresponding text boxes. Ensure that the **Regular time intervals** check box is also selected and that its corresponding text box contains the value **1740**.

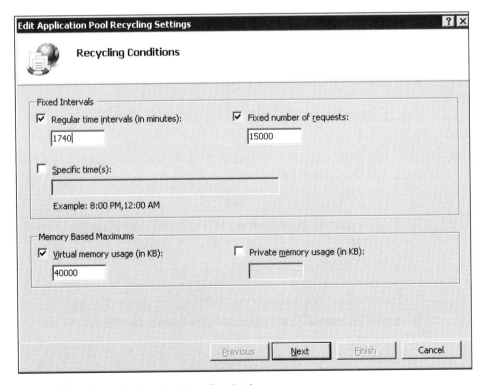

Figure 6-5 Edit Application Pool Recycling Settings

© Cengage Learning 2012

10. Click the check box next to **Virtual memory usage** and enter **40000** in the corresponding text box. Click **Next**.

11. As shown in Figure 6-6, ensure that the **Regular time intervals** and **Virtual memory usage** check boxes are selected. Click **Finish**.

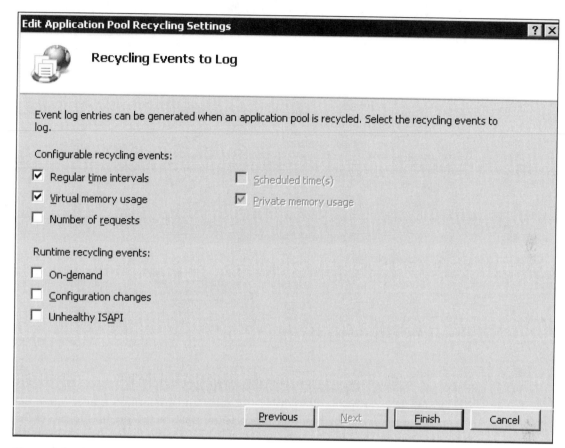

Figure 6-6 Edit Application Pool Recycling event logging
© Cengage Learning 2012

Managing Web Sites

Having the HTML and Web application code written is a necessary first step, but without having a properly configured and managed Web site infrastructure, the huge amount of effort involved in creating a powerful Web site can be wasted.

Publishing IIS Web Sites

Publishing a Web site starts with creating the appropriate folders on the server and moving the content into them. Once the content is there, the actual publishing is done through IIS Manager. The general steps to publish a Web site are as follows:

1. Open IIS Manager, right-click the **Sites** node in the Connections pane, and choose **Add Web Site**. The Add Web Site dialog box appears, similar to Figure 6-7.

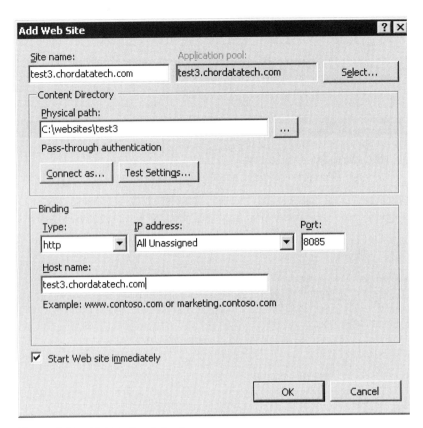

Figure 6-7 Add Web Site dialog box
© Cengage Learning 2012

2. Enter the site name, the physical path, and the binding information, and click **OK**.

Bindings refer to the IP address and port, and sometimes a host name that a Web site will communicate over. The binding information must be unique on the server in order for the site to function. In the Binding section of the Add Web Site dialog box, the site must be bound to a unique IP address, a unique port, or a unique host name. If any of these settings conflict with an existing site you will be warned when you click **OK** and you will have the option to change whatever is causing the conflict.

You can test the site by choosing the Browse link in the Browse Web Site section of the Actions Pane of IIS Manager.

If you choose the host name as the unique element you will not be able to access the site until you create a DNS (Domain Name System) record telling the network the specific IP address of this site. DNS is the TCP/IP protocol that resolves host and domain names to IP addresses.

Configuring Virtual Directories

In some instances it might be desirable to share content between multiple Web sites or Web applications (e.g., common images or documents). **Virtual directories** allow a Web site or Web application to access content outside of the default file structure, allowing you to create common areas.

To create a virtual directory:

1. Open IIS Manager.

2. Right-click the site or application to add the virtual directory to in the Connections Pane and choose **Add Virtual Directory**. The Add Virtual Directory dialog box appears similar to Figure 6-8.

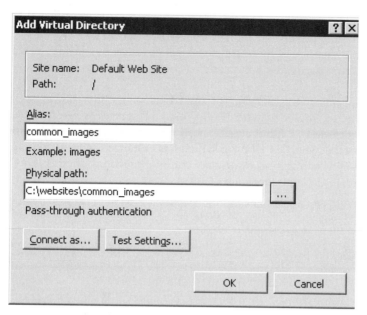

Figure 6-8 Add Virtual Directory dialog box
© Cengage Learning 2012

3. Type the name by which you wish to refer to this Virtual Directory in the text box beneath **Alias** and type or select the file path in the text box beneath **Physical path**. You can place images such as a company logo here and make them available to other sites on the server by creating similar virtual directories pointing to the same folder.

 The virtual directory can be a powerful tool but best practice is to keep your site structures as simple and intuitive as possible. Nesting virtual directories is possible but could make managing the site more difficult in the long term.

Migrating Sites and Web Applications

In most cases migrating a Web site requires copying the folders from the old server to the new one and then recreating any additional sites, Web applications, and virtual directories required for the site to function. If changes from the default server settings were made in the Web.config file in the root of the site or Web application, that will need to be moved as well. If there are differences in the server-level configurations between the original server and the new one, then those settings may need to be adjusted.

 Web.config changes are covered in the next chapter.

Configuring an FTP Server

Within an internal network, copying files to a Web site is a simple matter of opening the source and destination folders, selecting the appropriate files, and copying them through keyboard or menu commands or drag and drop. When the file source is outside of the network, it becomes a little more problematic. An external Web developer could be given remote access to the server, but that can create security issues.

One answer to this problem is the **File Transfer Protocol (FTP)**. FTP is a simple protocol designed specifically to transfer files. An FTP user does not have access to the command line of the system they are connecting to, and permissions can be limited to a small set of directories where files can be copied to or from.

This is not to say having FTP running on your server is without risks. Use of the FTP server requires careful planning because of security concerns. Since an FTP site allows authorized users to upload content to your server there are performance issues to consider as well. It is important to determine who truly needs this access and to configure the service in a way that makes it as secure as possible.

Server 2008 contains a Role Service for the FTP server under IIS7 that provides the same functionality as the one included with IIS 6. This FTP service is referred to as FTP 6. Server 2008 R2 does not include FTP 6 but an enhanced version (which is available for download from Microsoft for Server 2008) called FTP 7.5 which has enhanced security and administration features. Since the 70-643 certification exam may contain questions about both versions, you need to be familiar with how to configure each of them.

The two versions cannot coexist on a single server, so if you install one version and then decide to install the other you must first uninstall the first version.

In FTP 6 there are certain limitations you need to be aware of. FTP does not keep its own list of users (except for Anonymous), so you must create a local Windows user or a Domain user if you wish to have people log in to specific FTP accounts. If there will be multiple FTP sites on a single server, each site must have a unique combination of IP address and port number. Generally, it is recommended that you assign a unique IP address rather than a unique port, since most FTP clients will be expecting port 21 to be the FTP port. Configuring which directories a user can access from FTP is controlled through FTP User Isolation. A site can be configured to not isolate users; all users are able to access the FTP home directory of all other users. Users can be isolated; users are assigned an FTP home directory within the FTP root directory. Users can be isolated using Active Directory; users are assigned an FTP home directory configured using their Active Directory user account (this option requires the FTP users to be Domain users). This configuration option cannot be changed after a site is created, so the decision as to what option to use must be made before creating the site.

Activity 6-3: Add FTP 6 Role Service (Server 2008 only)

Time Required: 5 minutes
Objective: Add the FTP 6 role service in Windows Server 2008

Description: You will add the FTP 6 role service on Windows Server 2008 to make the FTP service available on this server. The FTP 6 role service is only for Windows Server 2008. Refer to Activity 6-5 for instructions on adding the FTP 7 role service on Server 2008 or Server 2008 R2.

1. Open Server Manager.
2. Right-click **Web Server (IIS) Role** and choose **Add Role Services**. The Add Role Services screen appears.
3. Check the boxes for **FTP Server**, **FTP Service** and **FTP Management Console**.
4. Click **Next** to add the Role Service.

With FTP 6 the service is managed using the IIS 6 Management Console. If you open IIS Manager and select the FTP Sites node in the Connections Pane you will see a message, "FTP Management is provided by the Internet Information Services (IIS) 6.0 Manager," and the link "Click here to launch" that launches the other console. You can also choose the IIS 6.0 Manager directly from the Administrative Tools program group.

When you first open the IIS 6.0 Manager you will see the server listed in the left side navigation pane and a node called FTP Sites with Default FTP Site below that. When initially added, the default FTP site is not running, there will be a small red x over the FTP icon to the left of

Default FTP Site and (Stopped) will be to the right of it. To start the site, right-click Default FTP Site and choose Start. You will be prompted that the service is set for Manual Startup and asked if you wish to start the service. Choose Yes. The service will start and the red x will disappear from the icon.

Activity 6-4: Create a New FTP 6 Site

Time Required: 15 minutes
Objective: Create and configure an FTP site

Description: You will create a public FTP site where all users will have access to the same directories. The users connecting to this site will only be able to download content.

1. Open IIS 6.0 Manager.

2. Click **Default FTP Site,** and click the small square icon on the bar underneath the menu options to stop the default FTP site. The screen should appear similar to Figure 6-9.

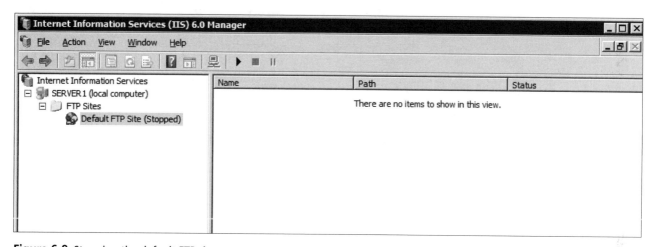

Figure 6-9 Stopping the default FTP site
© Cengage Learning 2012

3. Right-click the **FTP Sites** node, choose **New,** then **FTP Site.** The FTP Site Creation Wizard starts.

4. Click **Next** to proceed past the FTP Site Creation Wizard welcome screen. The FTP SiteDescription dialog box appears.

5. In the text box underneath Description: type **test.** Click **Next.** The IP and Port Settings dialog box appears.

6. Select **(All Unassigned)** from the Enter the IP address to use for this FTP site: dropdown if it is not already selected. This allows the FTP server to respond to requests on the assigned port on all unassigned IP addresses.

7. Type **21** in the text box under Type the TCP port this FTP site (Default = 21): if it is not already entered. Click **Next.** The FTP User Isolation dialog box appears.

8. Click the option button next to **Do not isolate users** if it is not already selected. Click **Next.** The FTP Site Home Directory dialog box appears.

9. Type **C:\inetpub\ftproot\test.** Click **Next.** The FTP Site Access Permissions dialog box appears.

10. Click the check box next to **Read.** Click **Next.**

11. Click **Finish** to close the wizard.

Configuring Your FTP Site Using IIS Manager

Once an FTP site is created it can be managed from IIS 6.0 Manager. You can start or stop the site and adjust the site configuration. To adjust the site configuration, right-click the site in the left panel and choose Properties. This will open the Properties dialog for the site, similar to Figure 6-10. There are five tabs available in the FTP site Properties dialog, each of which is discussed in the following sections.

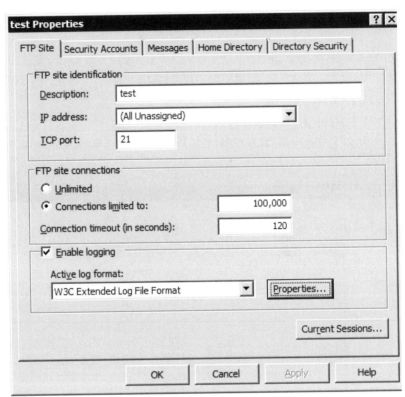

Figure 6-10 FTP site Properties dialog box

© Cengage Learning 2012

FTP Site The FTP Site tab is divided into three sections. The FTP site authentication section allows you to see and modify the site description and IP address and port. The FTP site connections section allows you to set a maximum number of connections to the site, or allow unlimited connections. You can also specify the connection timeout in seconds. The default choices are to limit connections to 100,000 and a timeout value of 120 seconds. If you are planning on a small number of users, limiting the number of connections can help reduce the opportunity for the site to be attacked. The third section deals with logging. To enable logging you click the check box next to Enable logging. The default choice for the Active log format dropdown is W3C Extended Log File Format. This format allows for some additional information to be logged. Adding to the default set can reduce performance, however. If you click the Properties button the Logging Properties dialog box will appear. There are two tabs available on the dialog box, General and Advanced. The General tab allows you to set how often the log file will roll over, either by time (hourly, daily, weekly, or monthly) or by file size. You can specify the log file directory, and there is a check box to specify using local time as part of the log filename.

Security Accounts The Security Accounts tab is where you choose to allow anonymous connections or not. Anonymous access is useful for access to FTP sites where the content is meant to be openly available to users. By allowing anonymous access you do not need to create a new user for each person who wants to access the content on the FTP site. If anonymous access is allowed, by default the server will use the IUSR_MachineName (where MachineName is the name of the local computer) account permissions but you can choose another user. If you check the box next to Allow only anonymous connections, then those permissions will always be used regardless of the actual credentials provided by the user.

Messages   The Messages tab allows you to specify the messages that will be sent to the client at different parts of their session. The banner message is displayed when the user initially connects to the site. The Welcome message is displayed when the user has successfully logged in. The Exit message displays as the connection is terminated. And the Maximum Connections message displays if the server exceeds its limits.

Home Directory   The Home Directory tab allows you to adjust the home directory location. By default this is a folder on the local system but you can also choose a network location using the Universal Naming Convention (UNC) network path. If you choose this option you will see a connect as button that allows you to specify credentials for the client connection. The default choice is to use the user's credentials. The network choice is useful if you want multiple sites to be able to access the same content. The directory listing style determines how the FTP client will see the directory listing; either UNIX or MS-DOS format.

Directory Security   The Directory Security tab allows you to grant or deny access to the site by different computers based on IP address. By default, all computers will be granted access to the site.

FTP 7

The latest FTP Server for Windows Server 2008 is called FTP 7 (as of this writing, the version of FTP is 7.5.5). It is included in Server 2008 R2 but is also available as a download for Windows Server 2008 from *www.iis.net/downloads*. If FTP 6 is already installed, you must uninstall it. To uninstall FTP 6:

1. Open the Server Manager.
2. Right-click **Web Server,** and choose **Remove Role Services.**
3. Uncheck the FTP Publishing Service option and complete the wizard to remove FTP 6.

Uninstalling FTP 6 removes all aspects of the application from the server. Any sites, and/or configuration information will be destroyed. If you have been using FTP 6, take note of all site information and configuration before uninstalling it.

The FTP 7 Role Service is installed in much the same way as FTP 6.

Activity 6-5: Add FTP 7 Role Service

Time Required: 5 minutes
Objective: Add the FTP 7 role service

Description: You will add the FTP role service to make the FTP service available on this server.

1. Open Server Manager.
2. Right-click **Web Server (IIS) Role** and choose **Add Role Services.** The Add Role Services screen appears as in Figure 6-11.

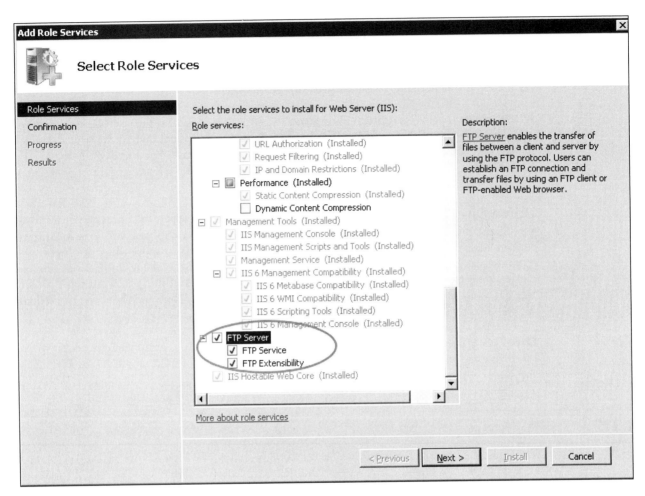

Figure 6-11 Add Role Services
© Cengage Learning 2012

3. Check the boxes for **FTP Server, FTP Service,** and **FTP Extensibility.**

4. Click **Next** to add the role service.

The FTP Extensibility option is needed if you want to use IIS Manager Users with the FTP server. (You also must verify that the Management Service Role service is installed for this.)

There are several improvements in FTP 7 over FTP 6. Multiple sites on a single server can now share an IP address and port similar to the way Web sites can. Enabling virtual host names allows you to enter a unique name for an FTP site.

 If you use virtual host names for your FTP sites, a DNS record is required for users to access the sites.

Unlike in FTP 6, User Isolation can now be configured after the site is created. A new feature is the ability to use **SSL (Secure Sockets Layer)** with FTP 7, allowing for more secure encrypted file transfers. SSL is a protocol that allows identification of a site, and encryption of data passed between the client and the site. To make administration easier, there is no longer a separate management console. All management functions of FTP 7 are done in IIS Manager. Table 6-1 compares the features of FTP 6 and FTP 7.

Table 6-1 Major feature differences between FTP 6 and FTP 7

Feature	FTP 6	FTP 7
Shared IP addresses and port	N	Y
FTPS	N	Y
Management in IIS Manager	N	Y
Requires Windows or Domain users	Y	N
User Isolation set up post-install	N	Y

Activity 6-6: Create a New FTP 7 Site

Time Required: 15 minutes

Objective: Create and configure an FTP 7 site

Description: You will create a public FTP site where all users will have access to the same directories. The users connecting to this site will only be able to download content.

1. First, create a folder named **test2** in the C:\inetpub\ftproot folder. This will serve as the physical path for the FTP site.

2. Open IIS Manager, right-click the server node, and then click **Add FTP Site**.

3. Right-click the **FTP Sites** node, choose **New**, then **FTP Site**. The FTP Site Creation Wizard starts. The FTP Site Description dialog box appears.

4. Click **Next** to proceed past the FTP Site Creation Wizard welcome screen. 5. In the text box underneath Description: type **test**.

5. Type **test2** in the **FTP site name** text box. In the Physical path text box, type **C:\inetpub\ftproot\test2** and then click **Next** to display the Binding and SSL Settings dialog box.

6. Ensure that (**All Unassigned**) is displayed in the IP Address: drop-down field if it is not already selected. This allows the FTP server to respond to requests on the assigned port on all unassigned IP addresses.

7. Type **21** in the Port text box if it is not already displayed.

8. Click the **Enable Virtual Host Names** check box to select it. Type **ftp.mydomain.com** in the Virtual Host text box (substituting your domain for mydomain as appropriate).

9. Ensure that the check box next to **Start FTP site automatically** is checked.

10. Click the **Allow SSL** option button.

This option cannot be changed after site setup. It is suggested you choose Allow SSL even if you aren't sure if you will be using SSL, to avoid having to delete and re-add the site later.

11. Since we currently don't have a SSL certificate, select **Not Selected** in the drop-SSL Certificate drop-down list. Click **Next** to display the Authentication and Authorization Information dialog box.

12. Click the **Anonymous** check box, if it isn't checked already. Ensure that the **Basic** check box is *not* checked.

13. Select **Anonymous users** in the **Allow access to** drop-down list if it isn't already selected.

14. Under Permissions, click the **Read** if it isn't already checked. Ensure that the **Write** checkbox is *not* checked.

15. Click **Finish** to close the wizard.

Once a site is created, you can choose it in the Connections pane of IIS Manager and see the various configuration and edit options in the Features View pane and Actions pane.

Managing FTP 7 Virtual Directories

Folders can be created underneath the physical root, or you can create virtual directories physically outside the main folder structure that appear to the users as subfolders in the site. To create a virtual directory, right-click the site node in the Connections pane and choose Add Virtual Directory. Enter an alias for the folder and the physical path to the folder in the file system. By default, pass-through authentication is used but a particular user can be entered by clicking the Connect as button. You can also test the settings by clicking the **Test Settings button**. Click **OK** and the virtual directory is created.

FTP 7 Advanced Settings

Clicking on **Advanced Settings** from the Actions pane displays the Advanced Settings dialog box similar to Figure 6-12.

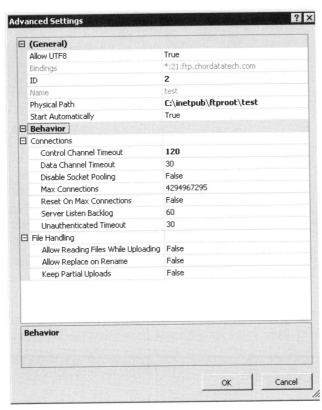

Figure 6-12 FTP Advanced Settings

© Cengage Learning 2012

The Behavior section contains fine tuning options including the timeout values and connections settings as well as file handling options affecting partial uploads and whether a session can read files while an upload is going on.

Adding FTP Publishing to a Web Site

Another new feature in FTP 7.5.5 is the ability to add FTP publishing to an existing Web site. The FTP service can be managed and restarted independently of the Web site. Using this feature, a Web developer or remote administrator can upload content to the Web site without having to create an independent FTP site or configure virtual directories to access the Web site folders. To add this capability:

1. Choose an existing Web site in IIS Manager's Connections pane, right-click it and choose **Add FTP Publishing**.

2. In the Binding and SSL Settings dialog box assign an IP address and port, if required, and if appropriate, enable Virtual Host Names and enter a name. You also make

basic SSL choices here. Click **Next** to move to the Authentication and Authorization Information dialog box.

3. Choose the Authentication types and Authorization settings, and click **Finish** to complete the wizard.

 It is advisable to check Basic Authentication and make sure Anonymous is not checked when adding FTP publishing to a Web site. You don't want just anyone uploading content to your site!

Authentication Options

Authentication settings can be adjusted beyond the options given in the wizard. Choose the site in the Connections pane of IIS Manager and then double-click **FTP Authentication** from the Features View. This will list the available authentication methods as well as their status. By default, Anonymous and Basic will be listed in the Features View pane but if you choose Custom Providers from the Actions pane you can add IIS Manager and ASP.NET.

Anonymous Authentication allows all users to access the FTP site. It uses the built-in IUSR user account for the permissions unless you specify a different user account. If you want to provide access to anyone this is the method to choose.

Basic Authentication sends the username and password in clear text so you want to consider using SSL if you are allowing connections over the Internet. This option lets you restrict access to either local users or domain users.

IIS Manager Authorization allows you to create users in the IIS Manager section of the Features View of the server node. This creates users that are not part of Active Directory or the local computer and are specific to the Web service. This is detailed in more depth in Chapter 7. This method also uses plain text to send credentials so it is best to use SSL if you choose this method for an Internet facing site.

The final custom provider is ASP.NET Authorization. This method uses the .NET user management framework and is appropriate for an ASP.NET Web site that validates credentials internally.

Authorization Rules

You can configure who should have access to a particular site's content and whether they have Read and/or Write permission. Choose the site in the Connections pane, and double-click **FTP Authorization Rules** in the Features View. Either edit an existing rule or add a new Allow or Deny rule by clicking the appropriate link from the Actions pane. In the Edit Allow Authorization dialog that appears, the choices include:

- All users
- All Anonymous users
- Specified roles or user groups
- Specified users
- You then choose Read and/or Write permissions for the rule.

FTP User Isolation

This feature allows you to provide individual directories to the users and prevent other users from accessing the content. Choose the site in the Connections pane and then double-click **FTP User Isolation** in the Features view to configure this option. If you choose to not isolate users, you have two options:

- *FTP root directory*. This sets the starting folder to the FTP root folder, and allows all users to access content there. Other permissions on specific folders can be configured if required.
- *User name directory*. This sets the starting folder to a folder with the username provided at login if it exists. If it does not then the user starts in the root folder.

If you choose to isolate users, you have three options:

- *User name directory (disable global virtual directories).* The user starts in their user folder and cannot navigate above it or to any global virtual directories.

- *User name physical directory (enable global virtual directories).* The user starts in their home folder but will have access to global virtual directories that you create.

- *FTP home directory configured in Active Directory.* If the user is a member of the Active Directory domain they will start in the folder specified in AD.

FTP SSL Settings

While useful, FTP can be a security risk. With user names and passwords as well as data being passed in the clear, it is desirable to add some level of security. One way is to use SSL encryption for the connections. The ability to use **FTPS**, encrypting the login to the FTP server and the file transfer using the SSL protocol and a certificate, is new to FTP 7.5 and was not available in previous versions of IIS. While this can create performance issues because of increased processing overhead, it is better to have the security, particularly for an Internet-facing server.

To configure SSL, choose a site that is enabled for SSL from the Connections pane in IIS Manager and then double-click the **FTP SSL Settings** icon in the Features View. On the FTP SSL Settings screen choose the SSL certificate to use. Choose an SSL Policy setting: Allow SSL Connections, Require SSL Connections, or a custom option.

Allow SSL Connections makes the use of SSL an option but doesn't force the client to use it. Require SSL Connections will not allow connections without SSL. Custom lets you adjust the setting separately for the control channel and the data channel. You could for example require encryption only for the credentials, protecting the usernames and passwords. This would make the server less vulnerable to hacking since login information would be encrypted, but would not affect performance as much since the remainder of the transaction would be unencrypted. While this is an improvement over no encryption it still leaves you vulnerable to brute force hacking attempts since other control channel data can easily be read and the encrypted parts identified by the hacker. The entire control channel could be encrypted which would make a hack attempt more difficult and still not require that the data being uploaded or downloaded be encrypted. This would still leave some vulnerability, but would have less of an impact on performance. Encryption of the data channel can be allowed, required, or denied. Requiring it is the most secure but the trade-off is the performance. The final setting is the checkbox to use 128-bit encryption for SSL connections. If this is not checked, 40-bit is used which decreases security but improves performance.

FTP Firewall Support

Firewalls are a necessity whenever there is exposure to the Internet. For FTP to function through a firewall various ports need to be opened. This applies to every firewall between your FTP server and its destination, including a Windows firewall on the server itself and a firewall you are using for your whole network.

While active FTP connections can work through the firewall for non SSL connections they may not work for FTPS when you are using a device to translate network addresses between networks (Network Address Translation or NAT). Passive Mode connections will work with FTPS through a NAT device but you must specify the port range for the Passive data connections as well as the control channel (default is 21) including an FTP Firewall Support section that allows you to configure the FTP service for this. To configure it select the Server node in the Connections pane of IIS Manager. Double-click the FTP Firewall Support icon in the Features view to access the settings. Specify a port range to use for passive connections. This should be above 1023 so as not to interfere with standard services. You can also specify the External IP Address of your firewall. This is needed for passive mode connections when SSL is enabled and your firewall doesn't support modifying packets. The Port setting is global but the External IP Address setting can be set here and also at the site level.

Once you set these ports be sure to restart the Microsoft FTP Service from the Services Console on the server in order for the changes to take effect. You will then need to set up matching settings in the Windows Firewall and your network firewall.

FTP IPv4 Address and Domain Restrictions

In some cases, it may be desirable or necessary to limit FTP access to a known number of IP addresses or domains. FTP 7 provides that flexibility. To set address or domain restrictions:

1. Choose the site in the Connections pane of IIS Manager and double-click **FTP IPv4 Address and Domain Restrictions**.

2. To set rules for a specific IP address or a range of IP addresses, choose **Add Allow Entry** or **Add Deny Entry** in the Actions pane, and type in the IP addresses you want to restrict or allow.

To enable domain name restrictions:

1. Choose **Edit Feature Settings** from the Actions pane and select the check box next to **Enable domain name restrictions** in the dialog box that appears. Click **OK**. A dialog box warns you that this feature requires the use of DNS reverse lookups, which can be resource intensive. To proceed, click **Yes**.

2. Click either **Add Allow Entry** or **Add Deny Entry**. On the Add Allow Restriction Rule or Add Deny Restriction Rule dialog, entering a domain entry will now be an option. The permissions you set are inherited and can be overwritten by creating new rules at folder and virtual directory levels.

FTP Current Sessions

To see the status of FTP sessions currently running on the server, click the site node in the Connections pane, and double-click **FTP Current Sessions** from the Features View.

FTP Messages   There are four times during an FTP session where you can control the content of the messages displayed to the user: when they connect to the server (the Banner message), when they actually log in to the server (the Welcome message), when they exit (the Exit message), and when the maximum number of connections has been reached (the Maximum Connections message). To customize these messages, click the site node in the Connections pane of IIS Manager, and double-click **FTP Messages** from the Features View. The FTP Messages screen will appear in the Features View, similar to what is shown in Figure 6-13.

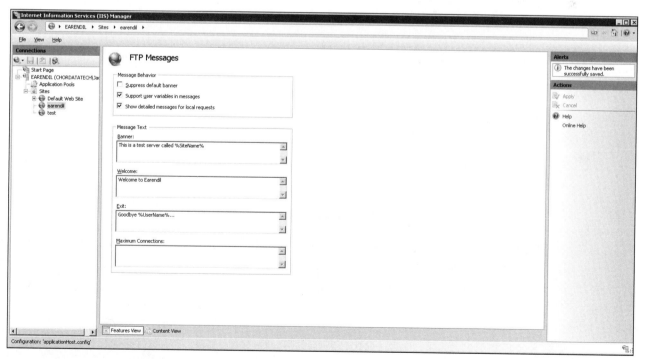

Figure 6-13 FTP Messages screen
© Cengage Learning 2012

In the Message Behavior section, you can click check boxes to suppress the default banner, support user variables in messages, and show detailed messages for local requests. The Support user variables choice allows you to personalize the message by inserting certain variables. Available variables are:

%BytesReceived%
%BytesSent%
%SessionID%
%SiteName%
%UserName%

FTP Logging

An important part of managing an FTP server is logging its usage. FTP 7 creates a W3C format log file that can be read with any text editor, or by any number of third-party log analysis tools.

To configure logging options, click the server node in the Connections pane of IIS Manager then double-click FTP Logging. The FTP Logging screen appears in the Features view. The drop-down under One log file per: gives you the choice of one log file per site, or one log file per server. If you choose one log file per site you will be able to modify some of the settings on a site-by-site basis. The Log File section allows you to customize which fields that will be logged as well as the location of the log file and the encoding. Clicking the **Select W3C Fields** button displays the Information To Log dialog similar to Figure 6-14.

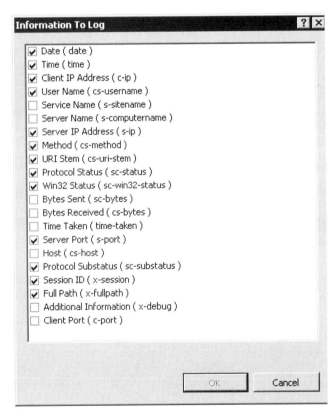

Figure 6-14 Information To Log dialog

© Cengage Learning 2012

The Log File Rollover section allows you to specify the conditions when a new log file is created. The options are by time (e.g., daily, weekly) or when the file reaches a certain size in bytes. Clicking the check box next to Use local time for file naming and rollover will incorporate the local time in the filename of the log files when they roll over.

FTP Directory Browsing

Depending on your user base, they may be comfortable with one kind of directory listing from within an FTP connection. The FTP Directory Browsing feature is available at both the server level and the site level and as with other settings is hierarchical. The site setting overrides the inherited setting from the server. The Directory Listing Style can either be the default MS-DOS or the UNIX style. There are also several Directory Listing options:

- *Virtual directories.* You can choose to hide virtual directories or show them here
- *Available bytes.* This displays available space, when quotas are enabled it shows the current user's available space
- *Four-digit years.* Displays years in four digits rather than two

Configuring an SMTP Server

E-mail is truly a universal communication tool. It is particularly useful in the Web environment where user response to contact forms may require an opt-in, or where it is preferable to receive an acknowledgment to a request that can be reviewed at the user's leisure. E-mail is sent using the **Simple Mail Transport Protocol (SMTP)**. SMTP defines the format of, and what information is included along with the text of the message. Windows Server 2008 contains an SMTP feature that allows you to send e-mail messages from Web applications. The SMTP server on Windows Server 2008 can be configured to provide this functionality and also secured using various combinations of authentication, as well as relay and address restrictions to prevent unauthorized use by spammers.

Activity 6-7: Install SMTP Server

Time Required: 15 minutes
Objective: Install SMTP Server

Description: You will install SMTP Server, along with any other required services.

1. Open Server Manager from the Administrative Tools program group. Right-click the **Features** node in the left navigation pane and choose **Add Features** to launch the Add Features Wizard.

2. Check the box next to **SMTP Server.** You will be prompted to add the role services and features required for SMTP Server. Click the button that says **Add Required Role Services** to continue. This returns you to the Select Features screen. Click **Next** to continue.

3. The Introduction to Web Server (IIS) screen that provides information about the feature appears. Click **Next**. The Select Role Services dialog appears, similar to Figure 6-15.

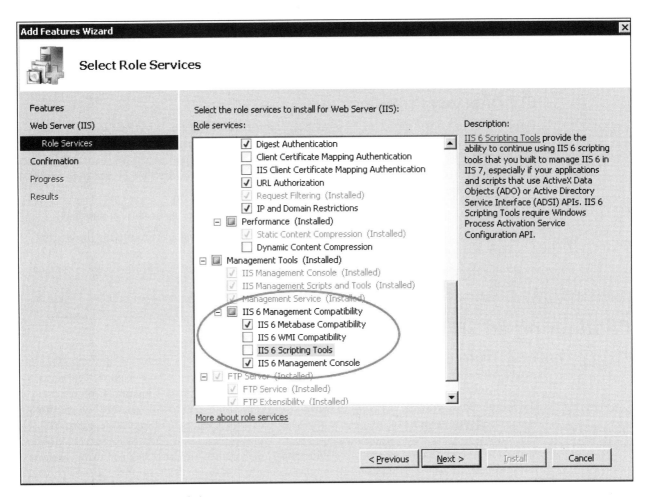

Figure 6-15 Select Role Services dialog
© Cengage Learning 2012

IIS 6 Management Compatibility is selected since this is required to manage the SMTP server.

4. Click **Next** to continue to the confirmation dialog which lists the roles, role services, and/or features that are about to be installed. What is displayed will depend on what roles, role services, and features are already installed, but it will appear similar to Figure 6-16.

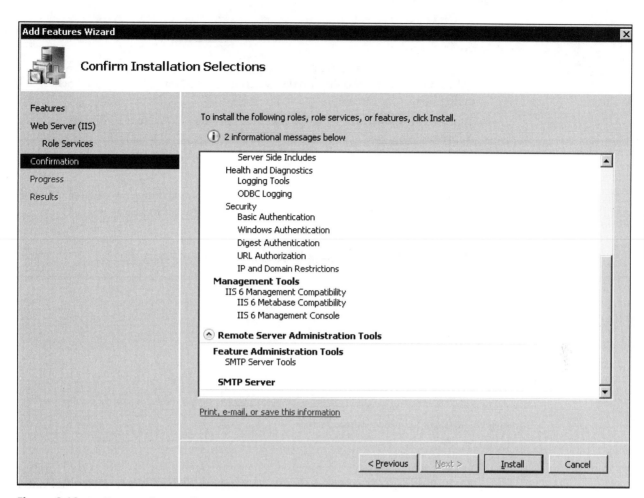

Figure 6-16 Confirm Installation Selections
© Cengage Learning 2012

5. Click **Install** to begin the installation. The next screen shows the progress of the installation. When complete it automatically advances to the Installation Results screen. Click **Close** to complete the wizard.

Configure SMTP Server

When SMTP Server is installed a default virtual server is created. You can configure this for your purposes or create specialized SMTP virtual servers that may have particular restrictions or configuration options set to meet the particular needs of a Web application, or different sites being hosted on the server.

Activity 6-8: Create an SMTP Virtual Server

Time Required: 15 minutes
Objective: Create and configure an SMTP Virtual Server

Description: You will create an SMTP Virtual Server available for use by Web applications on a Windows 2008 server.

1. Open Internet Information Services (IIS) 6.0 Manager from the Administrative Tools program group.

2. In the left navigation pane, right-click the server node, point to **New**, and then click **SMTP Virtual Server** to display the Welcome to the New SMTP Virtual Server Wizard dialog box.

3. Type **WebResponse** in the Name text box and then click **Next** to display the Select IP Address dialog box.

4. Select [**All Unassigned**] in the Select the IP address for this SMTP virtual server dropdown list, and then click **Next**.

5. Click **Yes** to proceed past the SMTP Configuration warning message regarding the IP address and port number already being used, as shown in Figure 6-17.

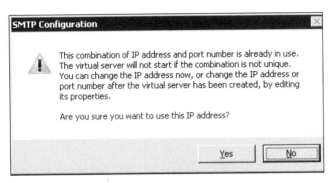

Figure 6-17 SMTP Configuration warning screen
© Cengage Learning 2012

6. The Select Home Directory dialog box is displayed. Type **C:\INETPUB\Mailroot** in the Home directory text box and click **Next** to display the Default Domain dialog box.

7. Type **test.yourdomain.com** (where yourdomain.com is the domain you are using for these test exercises) in the Domain text box.

8. Click **Finish**.

Once an SMTP Virtual Server is created, it can be managed through IIS 6.0 Manager. To access the configuration options, open IIS 6.0 Manager, right-click the **SMTP Virtual Server** you wish to modify, and click **Properties** to bring up the Properties dialog box for this SMTP Virtual Server.

There are six tabs that contain the various configuration options: General, Access, Messages, Delivery, LDAP Routing, and Security.

General The General tab, as shown in Figure 6-18, allows you to configure the IP address of the server, limit the number of connections to the server, set the time-out for those connections, and enable or disable logging. In Activity 6-8 we received a warning message that there was a conflict with another server for the IP address and port. In the General tab you can correct this, by assigning a particular IP address to the server. By clicking the **Advanced** button, you can create multiple paths to access the server by specifying multiple IP addresses and/or ports. For performance considerations you can set a limited number of connections to the server, as well as a shorter timeout (the default is 10 minutes).

It is suggested that you enable logging only if you are trying to troubleshoot a particular issue with the server, otherwise you will negatively impact server performance, and the logs will use a large amount of disk space.

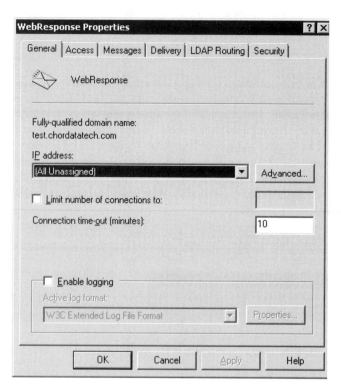

Figure 6-18 General tab
© Cengage Learning 2012

Access The Access tab, shown in Figure 6-19, allows you to configure the ways in which the server can be accessed.

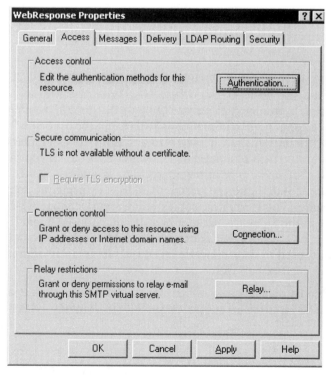

Figure 6-19 Access tab
© Cengage Learning 2012

Proper configuration of Access control, Connection control, and Relay restrictions are the primary defense against spammers using your server.

Clicking the **Authentication** button brings up the Authentication dialog box. Anonymous access is enabled by default. Typically this setting should only be used if the server is going to be accessed within a trusted network. It is not recommended for a server that can be accessed from the Internet. Basic authentication requires that the client send a username and password in clear text. This can be secured by clicking the text box next to **Requires TLS encryption**. However using **Transport Layer Security (TLS)**, the successor to SSL, requires a certificate. Integrated Windows Authentication uses standard Windows accounts to access the server. This is most useful when your applications will run under a particular Windows account or when all of your users are members of an Active Directory domain.

Clicking the **Connection** button brings up the Connection dialog box which appears similarly to Figure 6-20.

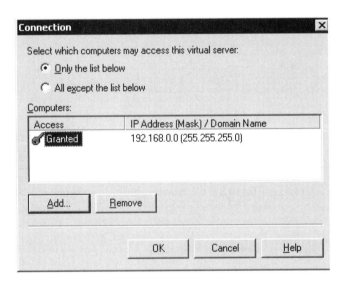

Figure 6-20 Connection dialog box
© Cengage Learning 2012

You can click the option button next to either "Only the list below" to limit access to a particular computer, group of computers or domains, or "All except the list below" to deny access to a specific computer, network or domain. Clicking **Add** brings up the Computer dialog box. Here you can click the option button next to either Single computer, Group of computers, or Domain. If you choose a single computer, you type in the appropriate IP address in the text box below IP Address or click the **DNS Lookup** button to get the IP address by using the domain name. If you choose a group of computers, you type in the subnet address in the Subnet address text box and type in the subnet mask in the Subnet mask text box. If you choose Domain, type the domain name in the Domain text box. The **subnet address** is the address that specifies a logical IP network. The **subnet mask** is used to determine which of the bits in an IP address are part of the subnet address and which bits are part of the host address.

Using a domain name rather than an IP address will decrease server performance since a DNS lookup will be required for each e-mail transaction.

Click the **Relay** button to access the settings, as shown in Figure 6-21. As with the Connection control section you can create exclusive or inclusive rules. There is a check box at the bottom that is checked by default that allows authenticated computers to relay regardless of the settings. Relaying is when the "from" address of a message is from a domain other than the one the SMTP Virtual Server is responsible for. An unsecured relay is the way that most spammers are able to co-opt your server for their purposes, which can result in your server being blocked from sending e-mail into certain domains, so it is extremely important to configure this properly.

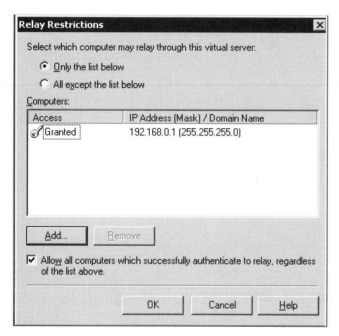

Figure 6-21 Relay restrictions screen
© Cengage Learning 2012

Messages The Messages tab allows you to configure the options for messages sent through the server. The options here include the maximum size of the message (including attachments), the maximum amount of data that can be sent through one connection to the server, the number of messages per connection, and the number of recipients per message. You can also specify an address that will receive non-delivery reports and you can specify the Badmail directory where non-deliverable messages will be stored so that you can troubleshoot problems.

Delivery The Delivery tab, shown in Figure 6-22 allows you to configure the delivery options for the server. By default, if the server cannot reach the recipient server when it tries to send a message it will retry at set intervals for 2 days. The first retry is at 15 minutes, the second at 30, the third at 60 and subsequent attempts will be made every 4 hours thereafter. The sender will receive a delay notification if the message has not gone through after 12 hours. All of these parameters can be adjusted in the Outbound section of the screen. There is a separate Local section to adjust the delay notification and expiration timeout for local mail.

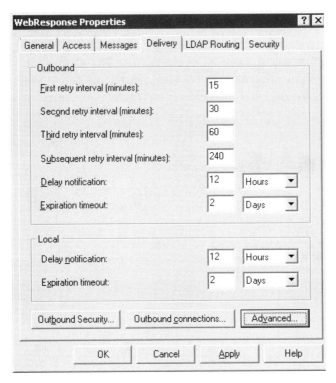

Figure 6-22 Delivery tab
© Cengage Learning 2012

At the bottom of the Delivery tab screen are three buttons dealing with outbound connections: Outbound Security, Outbound connections, and Advanced. Clicking the **Outbound Security** button allows you to enter authentication settings for connecting to smart hosts that require authentication as shown in Figure 6-23.

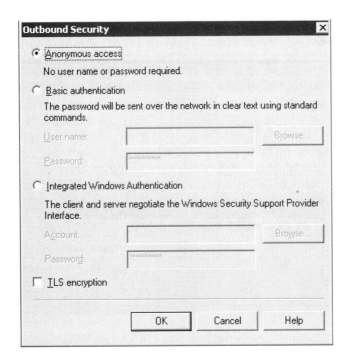

Figure 6-23 Outbound Security screen
© Cengage Learning 2012

The Outbound Connections button allows you to limit the number of connections to other SMTP servers and how long those connections will be active, as shown in Figure 6-24.

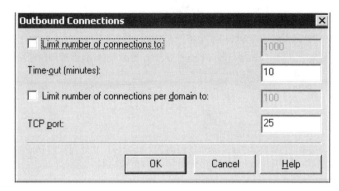

Figure 6-24 Outbound Connections screen
© Cengage Learning 2012

The Advanced button allows you to set the following:

- *Maximum hop count.* Each time a message is relayed through an SMTP server it includes a hop count. If this maximum is exceeded then the message is made non-deliverable.

- *Masquerade domain.* This setting automatically changes the From address to the domain entered here. If you want all messages from this server to have a consistent domain, you would use this setting.

- *Fully Qualified Domain Name (FQDN).* This is the server name that you create in your DNS Address (A) and Mail Exchanger (MX) records. The **Fully Qualified Domain Name (FQDN)** is a domain name reference that includes the host (e.g., www), the domain (e.g., mydomain), and the top level domain (e.g., .com). This must match those records to avoid problems with Spam filtering at your recipient's servers.

- *Smart host.* With this setting you can route all of the mail through another specific SMTP server. This allows you to secure multiple SMTP servers by only exposing one for external addresses. You can check the box that allows you to attempt direct delivery first. The Smart host option is also useful if your network is not using a static IP address. You can route the mail to an SMTP server where you are allowed to connect and relay that it has a static address, either one you own or from your hosting or access provider. Mail that comes from a server with a dynamic IP address will generally be flagged as spam on most systems today.

- *Perform reverse DNS lookup on incoming messages.* This option causes the SMTP server to perform a **reverse DNS lookup** to match the users' domain name against the IP address in the header. A reverse DNS lookup resolves a host's IP address to its name. This creates more overhead for the server but it decreases the risk of sending spam when message headers have been spoofed. **Spoofing** is a method used by hackers to gain access to a system by masquerading as someone or something trusted by the system.

LDAP Routing The LDAP Routing tab allows you to configure settings when using the LDAP protocol for routing messages. **Lightweight Directory Access Protocol (LDAP)** is the standard by which directory services software communicates with each other. Active Directory and Microsoft Exchange are both compliant with this standard.

Security The Security tab allows you to specify the users and accounts that can configure the SMTP Virtual Server. By default this will include the Administrators Group, Local Service, and Network Service built-in accounts. You can add other users and groups and designate control to them.

Monitoring Performance

There are three main ways you can monitor the performance of an SMTP Virtual Server:

1. Open IIS 6.0 Manager and choose the Current Sessions object.
2. Open the Windows Performance Monitor and select the SMTP Server.
3. Periodically review the messages that are in the various folders in the server root directory. These folders include:

   - Badmail
   - Drop
   - Pickup
   - Queue

The Badmail directory in particular should be reviewed to identify and troubleshoot delivery problems.

Configuring SMTP for ASP.NET

If you have installed Application Development role services for ASP.NET on your server, there is a section in the Features View on both the server level and the site levels for ASP.NET. In that section there is an icon for SMTP E-mail. Choosing the server node in the Connections panel and double-clicking the **SMTP E-Mail** icon in the Features View allows you to access the settings that your ASP.NET applications will use for sending e-mail as shown in Figure 6-25.

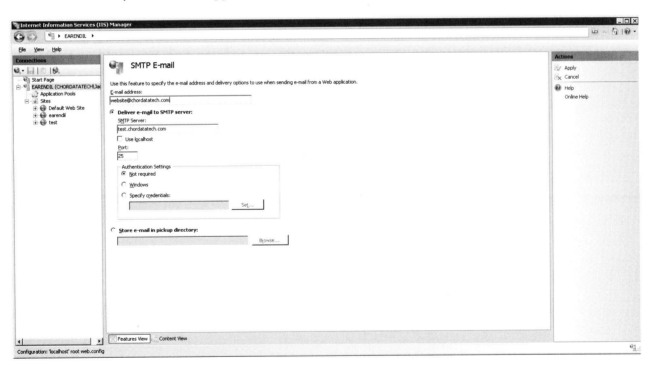

Figure 6-25 SMTP for ASP.NET

© Cengage Learning 2012

These settings do not change the configuration of the SMTP server, they simply specify the connection settings the Web applications will use. The first setting is the e-mail address that the site or application will use in the from field. Below this is an option button to Deliver e-mail to SMTP Server or to Store e-mail in pickup directory. If you make the first choice you specify the name of the SMTP server and the port and Authentication settings to use. If you choose the pickup directory option you specify that location.

Best Practices

1. Avoid installing the Application Server Role unless your application developers require the features for their applications. These additional features use server resources and increase the attack surface of the server.

2. Keep your site directory structures as simple and intuitive as possible. Nesting virtual directories is possible but can make managing the site more difficult in the long term.

3. If you are still running Server 2008, and you need to install FTP, FTP 7 is preferred since it has more robust security and functionality.

4. Create Virtual Directories with FTP 7 so that user directories can be isolated away from the physical root of the site.

5. If FTP Publishing is enabled for a site, ensure that Anonymous access is not allowed to the site, so that only properly credentialed users can actually upload or download content to and from the site.

6. When using SMTP virtual servers, only enable logging when trying to troubleshoot a particular issue with the server. Logging can negatively impact server performance, and consume large amounts of disk space.

7. When possible use Integrated Windows Authentication for access to the SMTP server.

8. Always try to restrict connections to the SMTP server to select groups of IP addresses (such as a subnet of Web servers hosting applications that require the ability to send e-mail).

9. Always try to restrict relaying to select groups of IP addresses. Allowing spammers to utilize an unsecured relay can result in the server being blocked from sending e-mail to some domains.

10. Use the Smart host setting to relay to a single SMTP server that faces the Internet when there are multiple SMTP servers in the network, to minimize the number that are actually exposed to the Internet. If some SMTP servers do not have static IP addresses, use the Smart host setting to relay to one that does to avoid messages being labeled as spam.

Chapter Summary

- Web applications can be accessed based on the directories they are placed in, and/or through the URL the user enters to access the site.

- Application Pools separate the worker processes of Web applications so they do not affect each other. If there is a problem with one, it won't affect the whole server, and maintenance can be done to an application without affecting other applications or sites.

- Publishing a Web site involves creating the directories where the content will reside and setting the bindings (what IP address and ports will be used to reference the site) in IIS Manager.

- Virtual directories allow a Web site or Web application to access content outside of the default file structure, allowing you to create common areas.

- Migrating a Web site involves duplicating the directory structure where the content resides, and recreating the sites, Web applications, and any virtual directories required for the site to function.

- FTP provides a simple method for copying content to Web sites when you do not have direct access to the directories on the server (remote access).

- FTP 6 requires all authenticated users (except Anonymous) to be either Windows users on the server, or domain users.

- Each FTP 6 site requires a unique IP address/port number combination.
- FTP 7 allows you to create virtual directories.
- FTP 7 can use the IIS Manager list (users that are not Windows or domain users) to authenticate a user.
- FTP 7 can be added to a Web site to allow remote access to the Web directories.
- FTP 7 can be configured to use SSL, encrypting the contents of the control channel, the data channel, or both.
- SMTP virtual servers allow Web applications to be able to easily send e-mail.
- Proper configuration of Access control, Connection control, and Relay restrictions, specified in the Access tab of the SMTP properties are important aspects in protecting an SMTP server against spammers.
- Limits on message size, the maximum amount of data that can be sent through one connection to the server, the number of messages per connection, and the number of recipients per message can be specified in the Messages tab.
- The Delivery tab allows you to configure how a message will be sent out, including setting a consistent domain, and the ability to use smart hosts, where multiple SMTP servers are configured to relay mail via a single server.
- ASP.NET applications can access the settings used to send e-mail.

Key Terms

Application Pool   A list of one or more URLs served by a worker process or group of worker processes that is isolated from other groups of worker processes.

attack surface   Code in a Web application that can be run by unauthenticated users.

bindings   The IP address, port, and sometimes a host name over which a Web object (Web, FTP, SMTP site) will communicate with the client.

File Transfer Protocol (FTP)   A simple protocol designed specifically to transfer files.

FTPS (FTP over SSL)   Encrypting the login to the FTP server and the file transfer using the SSL protocol and a certificate.

Fully Qualified Domain Name (FQDN)   A domain name reference that includes the host (e.g., www), the domain (e.g, mydomain), and the top level domain (e.g., .com).

LDAP (Lightweight Directory Access Protocol)   The standard by which directory services software communicates with each other.

recycling   An operation in IIS7 that allows you to restart an Application Pool while allowing it to complete requests that are already in progress.

Reverse DNS lookup   Resolves a host's IP address to its name.

SMTP (Simple Mail Transfer Protocol)   A protocol that defines how email is sent across a network.

spoofing   A way hackers can try to gain access to a system by masquerading as someone or something trusted by the system. (e.g., using an email address of someone within the domain).

SSL (Secure Sockets Layer)   A protocol that allows identification of a site, and encryption of data passed between the client and the site.

subnet address   The address that specifies a logical IP network.

subnet mask   Used to determine which of the bits in an IP address are part of the subnet address and which bits are part of the host address.

TLS (Transport Layer Security)   The successor to SSL.

virtual directories   Allow a Web site or Web application to access content outside of the default file structure, allowing you to create common areas.

Review Questions

1. Access to a Web application is controlled through what two methods?
   a. Directory-dependent and ASP.NET configuration
   b. Directory-dependent and URL-specified
   c. Host Names and SSL
   d. DNS and URLs

2. Which two extensions are used by Active Server pages (depending on whether they are ASP.NET)?
   a. .ASP and .ANT
   b. .ASP and ASPN
   c. .ASPX and .ASP
   d. None of the above

3. Which user is used by default in Web applications?
   a. The default IIS user
   b. The Windows user connecting to the site
   c. The domain user connecting to the site
   d. The user specified in the login box the application presents

4. One of the main advantages of using Application Pools is:
   a. You don't need to remember the names of all of the worker processes
   b. The worker processes know which site to work with
   c. The worker processes for a site/application are isolated from other sites/applications
   d. There are no advantages, it just needs to be done

5. Virtual directories allow you to _____.
   a. Store content to be accessed by a single Web application
   b. Fool hackers into looking in the wrong area on a server
   c. Make a Web application work
   d. Create common areas for multiple Web sites or Web applications

6. Virtual directories are referenced in the URL by _____.
   a. Preceding them with the pound sign (#)
   b. Preceding them with an exclamation point (!)
   c. Preceding them with a percent sign (%)
   d. An alias created when you configured the Virtual Directory

7. Best practice for Virtual Directories is _____.
   a. Limiting them to 10 deep
   b. Avoid nesting directories too deeply
   c. Use a numbering scheme to determine the directory level
   d. None of the above.

8. FTP 6 sites must have two unique settings:
   a. The name of the site and the IP address
   b. The IP address and the port
   c. The port and the name of the site
   d. None of the above

9. The default port for an FTP site is _____.

    a. 21

    b. 22

    c. 98

    d. 25

10. FTP is a security risk because _____.

    a. Data is bounced between multiple servers along a transfer route

    b. User name and password information is transferred in the clear

    c. Data is transferred in the clear

    d. b and c

11. Using SSL with FTP 7, what parts of a transaction can be encrypted?

    a. The user name and password

    b. The entire connection channel

    c. The data channel

    d. All of the above

12. FTP 6 is a good choice for an Internet-facing file transfer program because _____.

    a. The user name and password are hidden

    b. Users must have a Domain account

    c. Users don't need a Domain account, but must have a Windows account

    d. It isn't. There are too many limitations to make it an easy and effective tool

13. The method used by FTP 7 to allow for duplicate bindings is _____.

    a. Virtual server names

    b. Virtual host names

    c. Unique host names

    d. FTP 7 has the same limitations as FTP 6.

14. The FTP server available for Windows Server 2008 is _____.

    a. FTP 6

    b. FTP 6 is included but there is an optional download from Microsoft for FTP 7

    c. FTP 5

    d. FTP 6.5

15. Which two bindings must be unique for each SMTP server?

    a. The host name and the port

    b. The port and the authentication option

    c. The IP address and the host name

    d. The IP address and the port

16. The default port for SMTP is _____.

    a. 21

    b. 22

    c. 25

    d. 38

17. An SMTP server can be assigned multiple _____.

    a. Combinations of IP addresses and ports

    b. Virtual host names

    c. a and b

    d. None of the above

18. Spammers can use your SMTP server by taking advantage of _____.

    a. An open port in your firewall

    b. An unsecured relay

    c. A reverse DNS lookup

    d. All of the above

19. To enhance security against spammers you should _____.

    a. Use Integrated Windows Authentication for access to the SMTP server

    b. Restrict connections to select groups of IP addresses

    c. Restrict relaying to select groups of IP addresses

    d. All of the above

20. To take advantage of special features for ASP.NET you need to have installed _____.

    a. Application Development Role services for ASP.NET

    b. SMTP for ASP.NET Role services

    c. ASP.NET extensions for SMTP

    d. There are no special features for ASP.NET

Case Projects

CASE PROJECTS

Case Project 6-1: Create a Web Site for ASP.NET Applications

You are the administrator for the Web server at Your Company Inc. You have been asked to create a Web site that will be running an ASP.NET Web application. The site must be configured to handle ASP.NET, and the following role services are needed: .NET Framework 3.5. and Web Server (IIS). The development team has told you that the application will be directory-dependent, and that four subdirectories are needed: login, application, reports, and logout. There will be several other sites in the near future, and they should all share a common image area.

Document what roles and role services are needed, and what the directory structure will look like (including any virtual directories), assuming that the base directory structure is: C:\webs\site1.

Case Project 6-2: Create FTP 7 Sites

You have been asked to give two groups FTP access. The first group is visitors who wish to download free content (such as a white paper, driver software for a device). The other group is development personnel uploading new content and application code to a Web site.

Document what features the sites will require, what type of authentication makes sense for each, and where they can be accessed from.

Case Project 6-3: Create an SMTP Virtual Server

You have been asked to create an SMTP virtual server for a specialized Web application. Only the application may use the server to send e-mail, but it needs the capability to send e-mails using From names that are not part of the domain. Document what features the server will require, as well as authentication and relay settings.

Chapter 7

Configuring Windows Server 2008 Web Services, Part 2

After reading this chapter and completing the exercises, you will be able to:

- Back up and restore IIS Web site configurations
- Monitor the performance of an IIS Web site
- Configure SSL security utilizing certificates
- Configure site permissions and authentication
- Configure application permissions

Once an IIS Web site is initially configured to serve Web pages, there are several administrative tasks that should be performed. The site must be regularly backed up, and a way to restore it put into place. The performance of the site should be monitored to ensure that pages are served efficiently.

Depending on the sensitivity of the data being transferred to and from the site, not only should the data be encrypted as it passes over the Internet, but users connecting to the site should be confident that they are indeed connecting to your site and not being redirected somewhere else. What the site itself can access and how applications within the site behave need to be determined and configured. Similarly, the site needs to verify that users connecting to the site are authorized for access.

Configuring these administrative tasks properly is critical to ensuring site integrity and availability.

Managing Internet Information Services (IIS)

Just as you would want to back up configuration data for an application, you need to back up IIS configuration data. Having a complete configuration backup will speed recovery in case of loss or damage from a security breach, and minimize the amount of work required if a site needs to be moved to a different server or directory.

IIS 7 configuration data is stored in **XML** text files. XML is a format for representing, describing, and classifying Web-delivered information. There are two files that you need to be concerned with. Application Host.config contains the full server configuration and is located in

```
%SystemDrive%\%SystemRoot%\System32\inetsrv\config
```

Each site hosted by the server will have a file called Web.config located in the site's root directory. Web application folders can contain this file as well. The server-level settings are used by an individual site but can be overridden by changing them in the Web.config file. This is also true for applications. Having these files available allows for a smooth transfer of the site to another server or directory.

IIS itself monitors the files for changes and backs up the files to the %SystemDrive%\InetPub\ History folder whenever a change is detected. By default, IIS checks for changes every 2 minutes and keeps 10 prior versions of the file. The %SystemDrive%\InetPub\History folder should be included in your system and configuration backup to ensure proper site and server configuration in the case of a system restore. If a change to the configuration needs to be rolled back, the server can be restored to a prior configuration by copying the appropriate backup version over the file in the

```
%SystemDrive%\%SystemRoot%\System32\inetsrv\config
```

directory and restarting the Web server.

A backup can be performed on demand in the case of migrating a site (or multiples sites) to another server or to ensure the last stable configuration can be restored to undo problematical changes to the server configuration.

IIS Configuration Backup

The command line tool AppCmd.exe is used to manually back up and restore the full server configuration. By default AppCmd.exe is located in the

```
%SystemDrive%\%SystemRoot%\System32\inetsrv
```

directory. To initiate a backup as shown in Figure 7-1, open a command-line window and type the command:

```
AppCmd add backup "BackupName"
```

 AppCmd.exe only backs up site configuration files. The files that make up the site (code and images) must be backed up separately.

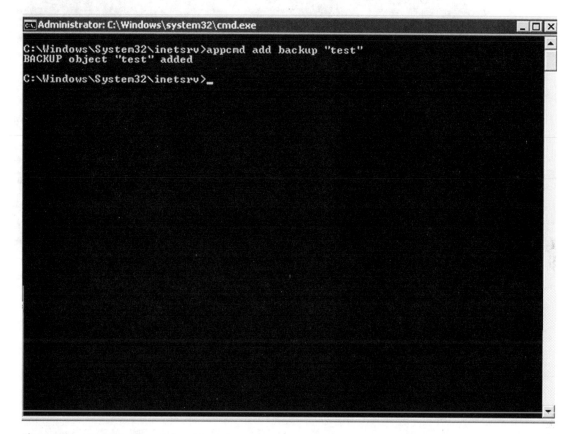

Figure 7-1 Creating a new manual backup
© Cengage Learning 2012

The "BackupName" parameter is optional. If no name is given, one will be generated automatically, uniquely identified by a timestamp. You should consider coming up with a standard naming convention to make it easier to identify particular backups. The backup created consists of a set of .xml files and .config files. The files are stored in a folder created in the

```
%SystemDrive%\%SystemRoot%\System32\inetsrv\backup\
```

folder. To restore a backup as shown in Figure 7-2, open a command prompt window and type the command:

```
AppCmd restore backup "BackupName"
```

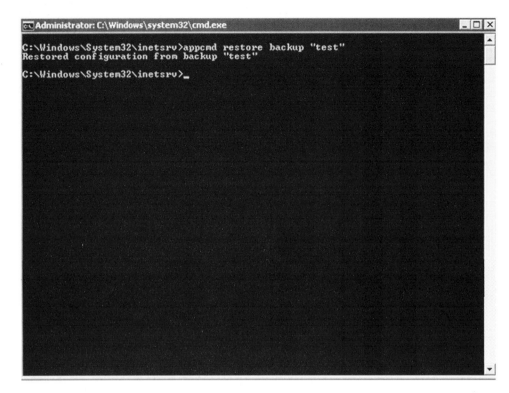

Figure 7-2 Restoring a configuration from backup
© Cengage Learning 2012

You can review available backups. To review a backup as shown in Figure 7-3, open a command prompt window and type:

```
AppCmd list backups
```

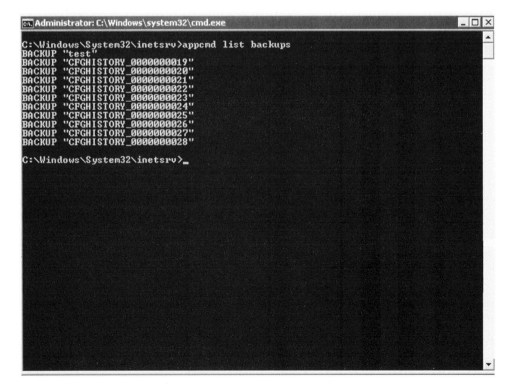

Figure 7-3 Listing available backups
© Cengage Learning 2012

Activity 7-1: Restore from an Automatic Backup

Time Required: 15 minutes

Objective: Restore a Web site from the backup performed automatically by IIS

Description: You will create a test Web site, delete it, and restore it from the automatic backup performed by IIS.

1. Create a new folder in C:\inetpub\wwwroot (or the name of the root folder for your server if different) called **test**.

2. Copy the files iisstart.htm and welcome.png from c:\inetpub\wwwroot to that folder.

3. Open IIS manager.

4. Right-click **sites** and choose **Add Website**. (If necessary, click to expand the server node in the left pane.)

5. Name your new site **test.yourdomain.com**.

6. Set the physical path to **C:\inetpub\wwwroot\test** (replace C:\inetpub\wwwroot with the name of your root folder if different).

7. A **port** is a number assigned to a resource (in this case a server application) to identify it within the network. To avoid conflicts with other applications on the server, change the port to **8081** and click **OK**.

Write down the time, you will use this to help choose the correct backup in Step 10.

8. On the right side under **Manage Web Site** click **Browse *;8081 (http)**. You should see the IIS7 welcome page.

9. Go back to the IIS Manager window and right-click the **test** Web site and click **remove** to delete the site. Click **OK** to confirm deletion.

10. Refresh the Web browser. The site should no longer exist. Keep the Web browser open. Again, note the time to help choose the correct backup in Step 11.

11. Navigate to **C:\Inetpub\history**. Locate the last folder created prior to removing the site. Select and copy the file **applicationHost.config**.

12. Navigate to **C:\Windows\system32\inetsrv\config**.

13. Paste the file, overwriting the one that is there.

14. Go to IIS Manager, right-click the server and choose **refresh**.

15. Expand the list of sites. The **test** site should be in the list again.

16. Return to your Web browser and refresh the page. The IIS7 welcome page should appear.

Activity 7-2: Create a Manual Backup and Restore a Site from It

Time Required: 15 minutes

Objective: Create a manual backup of a site, and restore the site from it

Description: Using the test Web site from Activity 7-1, create a manual backup of the site configuration using AppCmd.exe, delete the site, and restore it from the backup you just performed.

1. Click the **Start** button, then click **run** and type **cmd** to open a command prompt window.

2. Change the directory to **C:\Windows\system32\inetsrv**.

3. Enter the command **AppCmd add backup "Test01"**. Minimize the command prompt window but don't close it.

4. Open IIS Manager.

5. Choose the site **test**.

6. On the right side under **Manage Web Site** click **Browse *;8081 (http)**. You should see the IIS7 welcome page.

7. Right-click the **test** Web site and click **remove** to delete the site.

8. Refresh the Web browser. The site should be gone. Leave the Web browser open.

9. Restore the command prompt window and type **AppCmd restore backup "Test01"**.

10. Go to IIS manager, right-click the server, and choose **refresh**.

11. Expand the list of sites. The **test** site should be in the list again.

12. Return to your Web browser and refresh it. The IIS7 welcome page should appear.

13. Leave this Web site on the server for use in other activities.

Monitoring IIS

The ability to observe how sites and applications are running and consuming resources is an important tool in maintaining server performance. Two monitoring features have been added to IIS7 that help dramatically with diagnosing and troubleshooting both site and application issues. The first is the ability to look at the real-time status of application pools, sites, worker processes, application domains, and running requests. The second is the ability to create detailed trace event logs in XML format for failed requests.

Monitoring Real-Time Status

This feature allows you to drill down into the individual worker processes running on the server to check metrics like the percentage of the CPU or the amount of memory they are consuming. Troubleshooting in real time saves you an enormous amount of time and energy versus hoping to recreate the error under controlled circumstances.

To check real-time status, start by viewing a list of the currently running Worker Processes. Open IIS Manager and click on the server in the tree view of the Connections pane on the left. A set of choices will appear in the Features View window. Double-click Worker Processes. The current Worker processes, their Process ID, State, CPU percentage and memory usage will appear in the Features View pane of the window as shown in Figure 7-4. Reviewing this display you can check to see if any processes are using an inordinate amount of processing time or memory, causing slow server times or crashes.

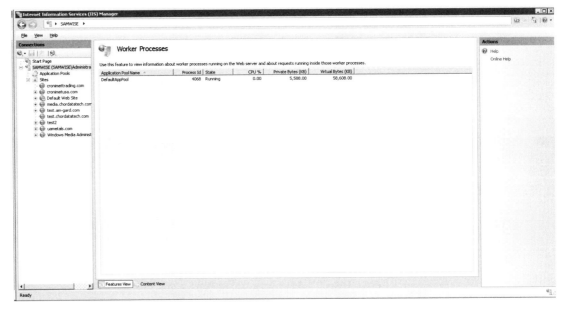

Figure 7-4 Checking the real-time status of worker processes

© Cengage Learning 2012

Failed Request Tracing

Trying to locate specific error transactions in a log file that could be recording thousands of transactions from multiple sites can be frustrating and time consuming. Failed Request Tracing allows you to create a log file of failed requests for a specific site, enabling you to quickly identify problem areas.

Activity 7-3: Enable Failed Request Tracing

Time Required: 10 minutes
Objective: Enable Failed Request Tracing

Description: You will enable Failed Request Tracing for a single site on the Web server. You will specify a particular directory to store the log file for this site, and set a specific number of trace files to keep.

1. Open IIS Manager.
2. In the Connections Pane click **Sites**.
3. In the **Features View,** double-click the site you wish to troubleshoot.
4. In the Actions pane under configure, click **Failed Request Tracing**.
5. In the dialog box that opens (see Figure 7-5) click the check box to **Enable** logging for this site.

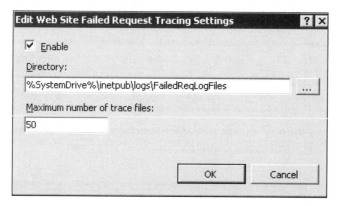

Figure 7-5 Web Site Failed Request Tracing Settings
© Cengage Learning 2012

6. The default location of the log file is %SystemDrive%\inetpub\logs\FailedReqLogFiles. Change this to a new location with a directory named to identify the site.
7. Specify the Maximum number of trace files to keep.

The number of versions of the trace file to keep is largely a matter of taste and space requirements, but it is recommended for ease of management to keep no more than 10.

8. Click **OK**. The server will begin logging failed requests to the site.

Configuring Logging

The transaction log file created by the Web server is one of the most useful tools to track server performance over time, helping identify sites that may have higher resource needs and should be moved to a less crowded or more powerful server. It can also show you usage trends to help in capacity planning and resource allocation.

Each time a request is made to the server a log entry is made. By default, logging is configured for the entire server, but it can be modified on a site-by-site basis. The standard location for the log files is %SystemDrive%\inetpub\logs\LogFiles. Configuration changes are made from IIS Manager.

The industry standard **W3C log file format** is the default. The W3C format is a customizable text-based format. Other choices include IIS, **NCSA** (a fixed text-based log file format), and a custom choice. (The custom choice requires registering a new COM component that implements the ILogPlugin or ILogPluginEx interface.) In the W3C format certain logging fields are included by default but additional fields can be chosen.

 When selecting optional fields to be included, be aware that some involve additional processor time or require DNS resolution, which can affect server performance. You can actually cause more of a problem than you are trying to solve!

Time stamps in the logs are in Coordinated Universal Time (UTC) by default, but you can choose local server time.

The log file can be set to rollover (close out and start a new version and file) on a schedule, when a maximum file size is reached, or not at all. The default is to rollover daily, but you can select weekly or monthly as well. If you choose not to rollover the log file, it will continue to grow in size with each log transaction. Choosing to not rollover the log file may cause problems with disk space management and usage reporting, so take those issues into consideration before deciding to select that option.

Log files can be viewed in any text editor, making it easy to check individual transactions. For more meaningful analysis of usage over time or aggregate usage, there are several third-party log analysis software packages available that can provide the desired data.

 There is a wide range of third-party log analysis packages, both open-source (free), and commercial. Two examples are AWStats (open source) and Sawmill (commercial). Open-source packages may require specific scripting languages like Perl or PHP to be installed on your server. A Web search on "log file analysis tools" will provide a good selection.

Click on a server or an individual site in the Connections pane, shown on the left side of Figure 7-6. You can then choose logging from the Features View pane.

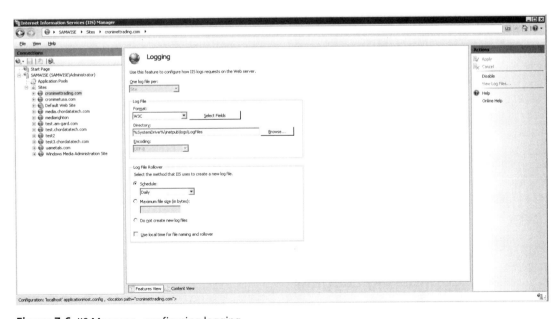

Figure 7-6 IIS Manager—configuring logging

© Cengage Learning 2012

Here you can make changes to the log file format, the location and the Log File Rollover settings. The available fields are shown in Figure 7-7 with the default ones selected.

In general, the W3C log file format is recommended. It is almost universally compatible with third-party log analysis software, and is the default for IIS.

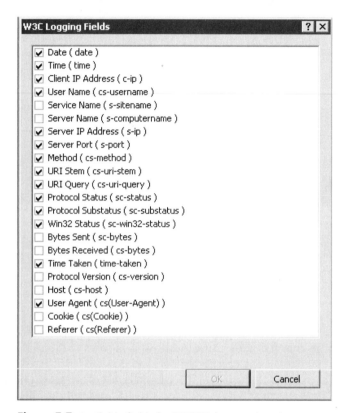

Figure 7-7 Available fields for W3C Web server logging
© Cengage Learning 2012

Delegation of Administrative Rights

IIS 7 is administered locally by default on Microsoft Server 2008. If you have multiple administrators or multiple sites that might have several administrators, or servers or sites that need be administered by outside users, you can delegate administrative rights.

To delegate administrative rights you must install the Management Service if it is not already installed. The Management Service is one of the role services available to the Web Server Role under Management Tools. It can be installed using the Add role services Wizard in Server Manager. In Figure 7-8, under Management Tools, you can see where you will need to select the Management Service to install it. The IIS Management Scripts and Tools role service is required to install the Management Service.

If you only install the IIS Management Console, you will not be able to manage the server remotely. Likewise, no outside users can be created to manage the server.

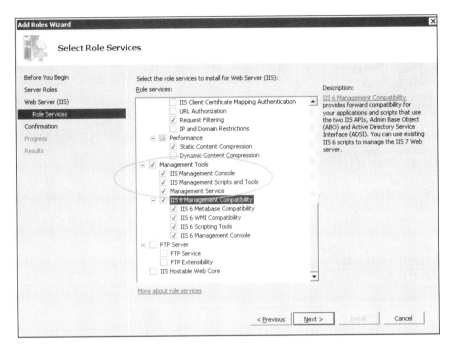

Figure 7-8 Adding the Management Service
© Cengage Learning 2012

The server needs to be able to identify any administrator with access. There are two types of identity credentials available. The type of access required and the location of the user will determine which credential type is appropriate. You can limit access to users within your domain structure by allowing Windows credentials only. If you need to allow outside users such as consultants, Web developers, or clients to manage portions of their Web sites and Web applications, remote connections can be enabled, and you can allow Windows credentials or IIS Manager credentials.

You create IIS Manager users in IIS Manager. IIS Manager users are stored in IIS itself. Unless you create them in your domain, they only have access to IIS, and only to the features you delegate permission for.

The Management Service is available in IIS Manager from the Features View pane which appears when you click on the server you want to work with. Click the **Management Service** check box to start the service. The service starts as shown in Figure 7-9.

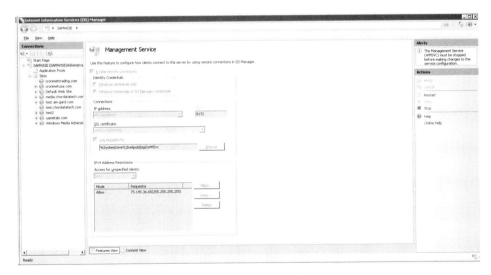

Figure 7-9 Management Service used to delegate administrative rights
© Cengage Learning 2012

Each feature of a server element can have permissions delegated with different levels of access. The features are displayed in the Features View pane as shown in Figure 7-10. Generally there will be three choices: Read/Write, Read Only, or Not Delegated. Certain features will have a slightly different set of three: Configuration Read/Write, Configuration Read Only, or Not Delegated. Using a combination of access levels to various features allows a Web developer to adjust different site settings for their applications and databases without giving them full control over the server or site.

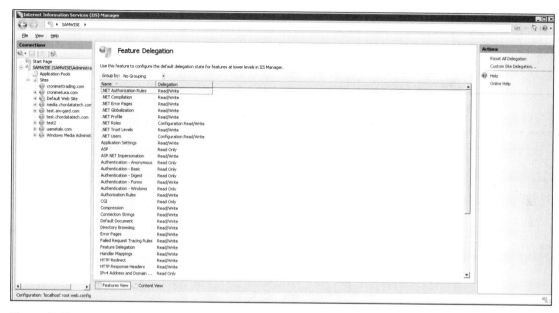

Figure 7-10 Feature Delegation in IIS Manager
© Cengage Learning 2012

Features do not need to be delegated on a server-wide basis. Custom site delegation is available to adjust the settings on a site-by-site basis. Click **Custom Site Delegation** in the Actions pane to bring Custom Site Delegation into the Features View pane as shown in Figure 7-11.

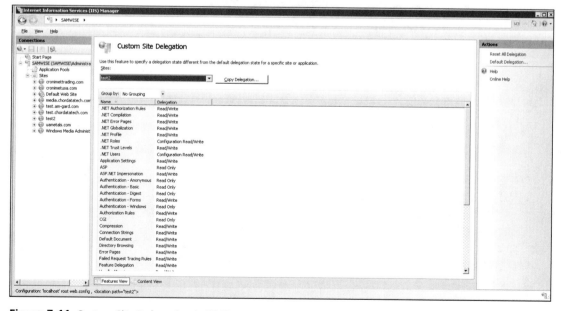

Figure 7-11 Custom Site Delegation in IIS Manager
© Cengage Learning 2012

If needed, you can reset the settings back to the ones inherited by the site from the server by clicking **Default Delegation** in the Actions pane, or reset all delegation for the server by clicking **Reset All Delegation** in the Actions pane.

Click on the site in the Connections pane, then click **IIS Manager Permissions** in the Management section of the Features View pane as shown in Figure 7-12. Click **Allow User** in the Actions pane, and the Allow User dialog box appears as shown in Figure 7-13. Select the type of user you are giving permissions to (Windows or IIS Manager), and select the appropriate user from the Select User dialog box that appears as shown in Figure 7-14.

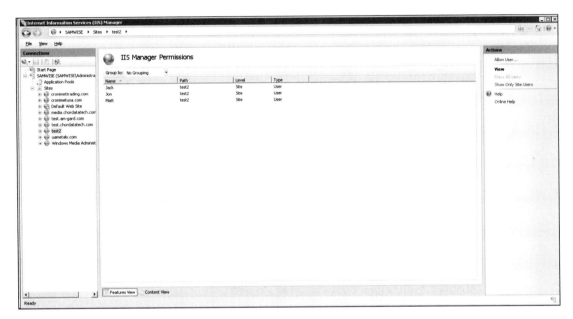

Figure 7-12 IIS Manager Permissions in IIS Manager

© Cengage Learning 2012

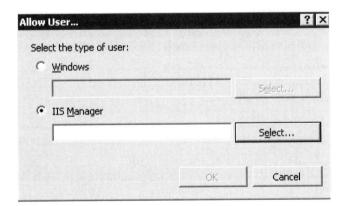

Figure 7-13 Allow User dialog box

© Cengage Learning 2012

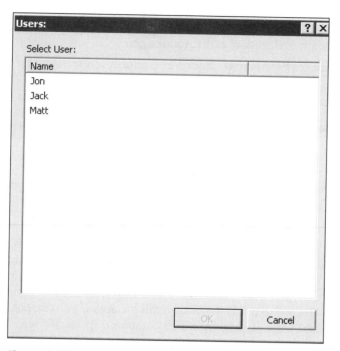

Figure 7-14 Select User dialog box
© Cengage Learning 2012

Users who want to manage sites remotely can download Internet Information Services (IIS) 7 Manager from the Microsoft Download Center (http://www/microsoft.com/downloads). The download page lists the system requirements and prerequisites for the software. This is available for Windows XP SP2, Windows Vista SP1, Windows Server 2003 SP1 and Windows 7. Windows 7 and Vista users must first install the Internet Information Services Management Console from the Windows Features (select **Programs and Features** from Control Panel to access Windows Features), and then install the download. Using the IIS Manager they will be able to connect remotely to a server, site, or application to which they have access rights.

You can choose to enable remote connections as well as specify what identity credentials to use. The default remote management port is 8172 but this can be customized for your network. It is also possible to restrict access to specific IP addresses in order to reduce the attack surfaces on the server. If the users needing access have static IP addresses, this can be a useful tool.

Activity 7-4: Delegate Site Administrative Rights to a Web Developer Outside of the Domain

Time Required: 15 minutes
Objective: Create a user and delegate the default site level administrative rights to the user for a single Web site

Description: You have been asked to allow a Web developer rights to the Web server named test. The Web developer does not have a user name in the domain. You will use IIS Manager to create an administrative user and delegate the default rights that appear.

1. Open IIS Manager.
2. Choose the server in the Connections pane.
3. Choose **IIS Manager Users** in the Features View pane.
4. Open the Feature and choose **Add User** from the Actions pane.
5. Enter the user name **Tom** and password **tomtesting** and confirm the password. This username is locally stored in IIS so you don't need to specify a domain.

6. Select a site in the Connections pane.

7. Click **Custom Site Delegation** in the Actions pane.

8. Select **IIS Manager Permissions** under Management in the Features View pane.

9. Click **Open Feature**.

10. Click **Allow User** in the actions pane.

11. Select the user from IIS Manager.

12. Click **OK**.

Configuring SSL Security

A standard **HTTP** connection transmits data in plain text. Anyone who can intercept the transmission (for example by using a network sniffer in the network where the Web server or client is located) can read what is transmitted. For most sites this is not a problem since the information is probably meant to be in the public domain. However, when personal information such as usernames and passwords or financial information like credit card numbers are being transmitted, it is important to encrypt the data so that it is not easily read by anyone who manages to intercept it.

Secure Sockets Layer (SSL) is a method by which communications between a Web server and Web client can be secured. SSL provides two levels of protection. First, it encrypts the data being transmitted between the client's browser and the Web server. Encryption makes it much harder for someone to steal sensitive information since the data will need to be decrypted after it is stolen. Second, SSL reliably identifies the server to the client so clients can be reasonably sure they are indeed connected to the server they were requesting the connection to. This minimizes the threat of "spoofing," where Web traffic is redirected to another server masquerading as the intended destination.

There are multiple levels of certificate encryption available, ranging from 384 bit to 16384 bit. The higher the encryption bit level, the more secure and harder to break it is. However, the higher the bit level, the more computing resources will be required for encryption and decryption, of the certificate itself, which can have an impact on system performance and response time. The default is 1024-bit encryption. It is often recommended to use 2048-bit encryption as it is less vulnerable to brute force attacks and the additional amount of processing will not make a noticeable difference in the response time or load on the server.

In order to use SSL the server must have a Server Certificate. For Web sites serving pages to users on the Internet, this certificate is usually generated by a third-party **Certificate Authority (CA)**. A CA is a trusted entity that issues digital certificates that can be used by Web sites to establish their identity to users connecting to them. Thawte and Verisign are two well-known CAs. Since these CAs are trusted by the client browsers, the certificates that they issue are also trusted, and the client can be sure they are connecting to the correct server. Information regarding your site and company is needed for a CA to generate a certificate. This information is formatted into a **Certificate Signing Request (CSR)** which is sent to the CA. The CSR is a block of encrypted text that contains information that will be included in the certificate plus the public key that will be used. The information is validated, a certificate is generated, and sent to you to install on the server. When you request a certificate from a CA, one of the parameters is the level of encryption for the certificate (mentioned above). Many CAs are suggesting that you use 2048-bit encryption for the best combination of security and performance.

Certificates are issued with expiration dates. Once the expiration date is reached a user connecting to a site using that certificate will get a warning that the certificate is no longer valid. Certificates can be renewed by the server or site owner by creating a renewal request and sending it to the CA that issued the certificate.

For a test or development environment, Microsoft Server 2008 allows you to create a self-signed certificate. Data transmitted will still be encrypted but the client browser will display a warning that the site's security certificate is not trusted, that is, it does not come from a trusted CA. The user can choose to proceed but their browser will indicate that the SSL certificate has an error.

In an enterprise environment where you have control of both the servers and the client computers, Microsoft Server 2008 can make use of the Active Directory Certificate Services Server role. This allows you to maintain your own certificate-based security infrastructure.

Certificates are handled by IIS at the server level. You assign a certificate to a Web site by specifying the https protocol in the **site bindings** (site configuration information that defines what protocols are connected to a particular port number, IP address and optional host header) for the site. If you have more than one site that requires SSL on the server and you want to use unique certificates for them, you will need to either assign a different port or a unique IP address for each site. Using a port other than the default SSL port (443) will require the client to specify the port in the URL (e.g., https://www.yourwebsite.com:460). This can severely limit the availability of the site to the general population since they will need to know the port number to connect. Unless there is a specific reason to use a unique port (for example, you only want specific users to know how to connect to the secure site), assigning a different IP address for each site is preferred.

Activity 7-5 Request a Certificate from a Third-Party Certificate Authority (CA)

Time Required: 15 minutes
Objective: Create a Certificate Signed Request (CSR) for the main Web site of the domain

Description: You have been asked to request a certificate from a Certificate Authority for one of the sites on the server. Use IIS Manager to create a Certificate Signed Request (CSR).

1. Click on the server in the Connections pane of IIS Manager.

2. Choose the **Server Certificates** icon under IIS in the Features View pane.

3. Click **Open Feature** in the Actions pane.

4. Choose the **Create Certificate Request** choice in the Actions pane. In the Request Certificate Wizard it is vital that you make no errors in the information you provide.

5. Creating a CSR starts with entering information about your organization. The information requested is shown in Figure 7-15. Type **www.yourdomain.com** in the Common name field. This is also known as the **Fully Qualified Domain Name (FQDN)**. This should be the URL that users will be entering to reach your site.

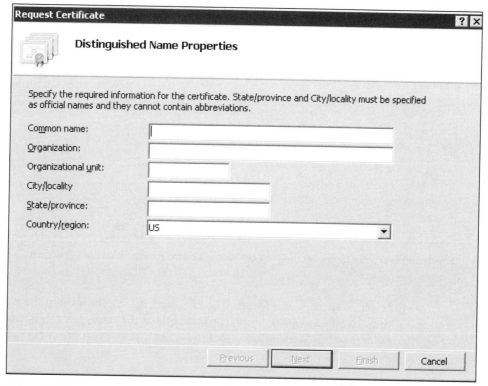

Figure 7-15 Distinguished Name Properties dialog box from request certificate wizard
© Cengage Learning 2012

6. Type **My Company Inc.** in the Organization field. This is the full legal company or personal name of the organization you are requesting the certificate for as it is legally registered in your locality.

7. Type **Information Technology** in the Organizational unit field. This is whatever branch or department of your company you are ordering the certificate for. (Other examples would be marketing, accounting, etc.)

8. Type **Bigcity** in the City/locality field. The contents of this field must not be abbreviated (for example, do not use NY for New York).

9. Type **New York** in the State/province field. The contents of this field also must not be abbreviated.

10. Keep the default **US** in the Country/region field.

11. Click **Next.**

12. Choose the **Cryptographic service provider** that is supported by your CA, as shown in Figure 7-16. (The default choice, **Microsoft RSA SChannel Cryptographic Provider**, is supported by most CAs.)

 A **cryptographic service provider (CSP)** is a means of providing hardware- or software-based encryption and decryption.

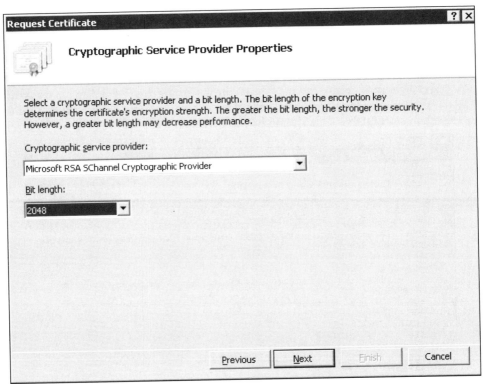

Figure 7-16 Cryptographic Service Provider dialog box from request certificate wizard
© Cengage Learning 2012

13. Select **2048** as the **Bit length.** The bit length affects the level of the certificate's encryption. Larger values increase the strength of the encryption but also require greater amounts of processing resources to implement and can affect performance.

14. Click **Next.**

15. Type **test.txt** into the Specify a file name for the certificate request: field. (You can choose the location where the file will be saved using the Browse button labeled . . .). The dialog box appears as shown in Figure 7-17.

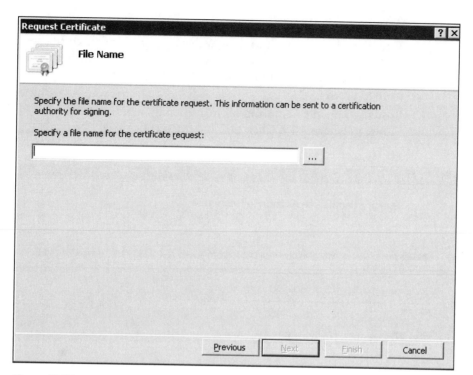

Figure 7-17 CSR File Name dialog box from request certificate wizard
© Cengage Learning 2012

16. Click **Finish** to generate the file and complete the wizard.

At this point, if you were actually requesting a certificate from a third-party CA, you could e-mail the request or cut and paste it into the Web site of the CA depending on the CA's particular procedures. The Certificate Signing Request (CSR) itself will look similar to Figure 7-18.

Figure 7-18 Sample Certificate Signing Request (CSR)
© Cengage Learning 2012

17. Once your CA processes your request they will either e-mail you the certificate or send you a link to log in to their Web site to retrieve the certificate. Save this text file to the server hard drive using a **.cer** extension. From the Server Certificates view in IIS Manager you would then click the **Complete Certificate Request** from the Actions pane.

18. Browse to the file name and fill in a Friendly name to keep track of the certificate as shown in Figure 7-19. Click **OK** and the certificate will be ready to use.

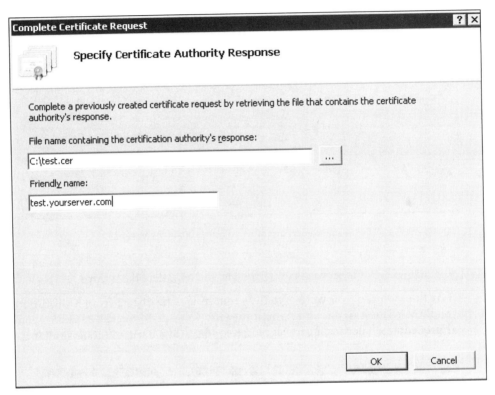

Figure 7-19 Completing the certificate request
© Cengage Learning 2012

Activity 7-6: Configure a Self-Signed Certificate

Time Required: 5 minutes
Objective: Create a self-signed certificate for use in a test environment

Description: You have been asked to create a certificate for an internal testing site so the developers can verify how everything works with SSL. Use IIS Manager to create a self-signed certificate for the internal Web site.

1. Click the server in the connections pane of IIS manager.

2. Choose the **Server Certificates** icon under IIS in the Features View pane.

3. Click **Open Feature** in the Actions Pane. A list of the available certificates will appear in the Features View pane and the commands needed to generate certificates in the Actions pane.

4. Choose **Create Self-Signed Certificate** from the Actions pane.

5. The wizard will launch, requesting a friendly name for the certificate, as shown in Figure 7-20.

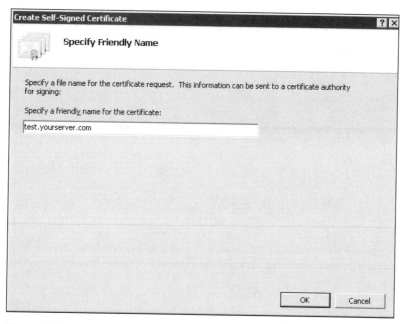

Figure 7-20 Creating a self-signed certificate
© Cengage Learning 2012

6. Enter the Web site name **test** that you created in the previous activities.

7. Click **OK** and the certificate is created and available for use.

Renewing a Certificate

To renew a certificate, you need to generate a request, similar to a CSR. Go to the server node in the Connections pane of IIS Manager and choose **Server Certificates** from the Features View pane. Click **Open Feature** in the Actions pane to display the list of Server Certificates. Choose the certificate you wish to renew and click on the **Renew** choice in the Actions Pane. The Renew an existing certificate Wizard will start as shown in Figure 7-21. Choose **Create a renewal certificate request** and click **Next**. Figure 7-22 shows the Specify save as file name dialog box.

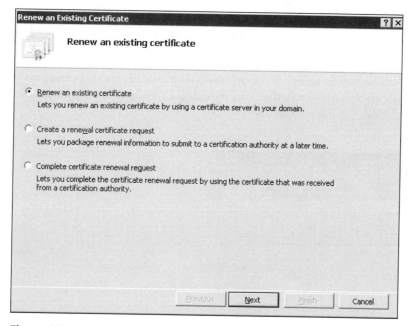

Figure 7-21 Renew an existing certificate dialog box
© Cengage Learning 2012

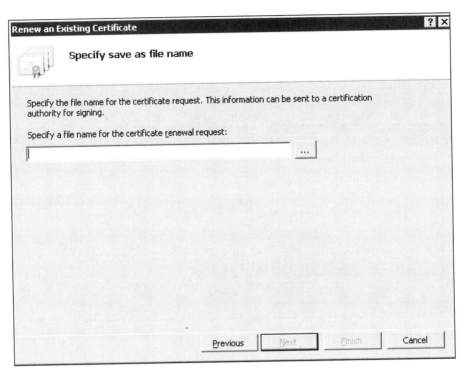

Figure 7-22 Saving a certificate renewal request
© Cengage Learning 2012

Enter a file name for the request and click **Finish**. You then submit that file to your CA the same way you did for the original certificate. When the CA sends you the new file, you initiate the same wizard but this time choose **Complete certificate renewal request** and browse to the .cer file that you received and click **Finish** to import the renewed certificate.

Importing and Exporting Certificates

Certificates are not bound to a server by the hardware configuration. This allows you to export and import certificates in the event that a Web site or sites need to be moved to another physical server.

To export a certificate, simply select it from the list of certificates and choose **Export** from the Actions pane. Enter a file name (it will automatically append the .pfx extension) and type a password to secure the certificate. Click **OK**. You can then transport this file to another server.

To import a certificate, choose **Import** from the Actions pane. The Import Certificate dialog box appears as shown in Figure 7-23. Browse to the .pfx file and type the password. You can use the check box to determine whether you would like to allow the certificate to be exported later or not. Click **OK** to complete the import.

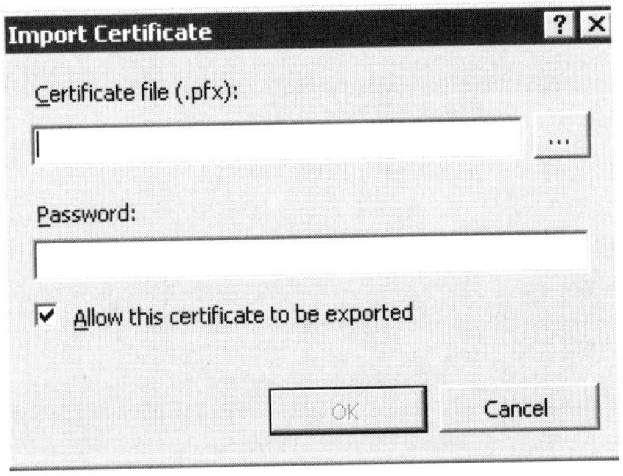

Figure 7-23 Import Certificate dialog box
© Cengage Learning 2012

Configuring Web Site Permissions and Authentication

By default, IIS will allow anyone who can reach the server through the port assigned to HTTP (typically port 80) access to the site. There are situations where access to the site or parts of the site needs to be restricted to certain users. For example, you might want to restrict access to a membership site, or a part of the site that is reserved for employees or selected customers. Access can be restricted by using one of the available authentication methods.

There are currently seven authentication methods that are supported by IIS and each requires different modules to be installed using the server roles. Listed below are the available authentication methods:

1. Anonymous

   In IIS7, anonymous authentication allows any user to access content on a Web site. Requests from users are presented to the server as the IUSR built-in account. As long as content is available to this user using NTFS permissions, it is available to all users who access through the Web server.

2. ASP.NET Impersonation

   This method allows you to specify a user account or authenticated user when executing code through a Web request. When it is not enabled the code is executed using the same user account as the ASP.NET process. (**ASP.NET** is a Microsoft Web application framework for building dynamic Web sites, Web applications, and Web services.)

3. Basic

   Basic authentication uses a standard method of challenging the user for credentials that all browsers support. There is no encryption of the username and password. To securely use this method you should either be in a secure network or use SSL encryption for the site.

4. Client certificates

   Just as the server's identity can be verified via a server certificate, IIS7 can validate the identity of a Web user by using client certificates. IIS automatically queries the certificate if the method is enabled. There are three usage modes:

   - One-to-one mappings
   - Many-to-one mappings
   - Active Directory mappings

   We will discuss these later in this chapter in the Client Certificate Mappings section.

5. Digest

   Digest authentication requires a Windows domain controller to authenticate users and relies on HTTP 1.1 to securely transmit credentials. Most modern Web browsers support this so it can be used for both requests coming from the internet or an intranet.

6. Forms

   Forms-based authentication uses standard http forms to transmit login information. This can be secured using SSL encryption. When a user attempts to access content they are redirected to a login page that is specified in the form's authentication settings. Once the information is submitted with this form and validated, the user is given access to the requested information. The default settings are designed for ASP. NET Web applications. The user provides the login information and cookies are sent to the Web server with each request. This proves that the client has authenticated with the Web server. Cookie options include:

   - Do not use cookies
   - Use cookies
   - Auto Detect
   - Use device profile

7. Windows

Windows authentication uses NTLM or Kerberos authentication protocols to validate credentials. It can work with either a Windows domain or a local security database. This is primarily used for intranet or extranet settings where all of the users are part of the same Active Directory domain or part of a trusted domain.

NTLM (NT LAN Manager) is an older Windows challenge/response style authentication protocol. **Kerberos** is a newer authentication protocol that uses tickets for client authentication.

Each object within the Web server hierarchy can be configured to require authentication before it can be accessed by the Web server. This includes the server, a site within the server, an application, a virtual directory, a physical folder, or even a particular file. Enabling any authentication method besides anonymous requires that anonymous authentication be disabled for that object.

Settings are inherited downward in the server hierarchy but can be overridden by setting a different method at a lower level. A common example would be to set anonymous authentication for the site itself, but to require one of the more restrictive authentication types on a folder of content that only specific users (such as paid or registered members or certain employees) are allowed to access.

Configuring Application Permissions

The .NET Framework provides a robust set of features that can be implemented in Web applications. Given this flexibility it is essential to restrict the permissions of these Web applications to protect the server itself from defective code, attacks, and accidental erasure of files. To this end IIS7 supports **Code Access Security (CAS)** policy. CAS policies define what operations are accessible to Web applications written with .NET code.

There are five trust levels that can be set at the server, site, application, or virtual directory and folder level. Like other security settings, trust levels are hierarchical so explicit settings at the lower levels override inherited permissions. Settings for the various levels are defined within XML-based .config files and can be viewed or edited with an XML editor. The five trust levels are Full, High, Medium, Low, and Minimal. Each subsequent level is more restrictive and thus more secure.

Table 7-1   NET trust level definitions

Trust Level	Description
Full	Specifies unrestricted permissions. Grants the ASP.NET application permissions to access any resource that is subject to operating system security. All privileged operations are supported
High	Specifies a high level of code access security; the application cannot do any of the following things by default:
	• Call unmanaged code
	• Call serviced components
	• Write to the event log
	• Access Message Queuing service queues
	• Access ODBC, OleDb, or Oracle data sources
Medium	Specifies a medium level of code access security; in addition to High Trust Level restrictions, the ASP.NET application cannot do any of the following things by default:
	• Access files outside the application directory
	• Access the registry
	• Make network or Web service calls

(continues)

Table 7-1 NET trust level definitions (*continued*)

Trust Level	Description
Low	Specifies a low level of code access security, which means that, in addition to Medium Trust Level restrictions, the application cannot do any of the following things by default:
	• Write to the file system
	• Call the Assert method
Minimal	Specifies a minimal level of code access security; the application has only execute permissions

Activity 7-7 Assigning .NET Trust Levels to a Specific Site

Time Required: 5 minutes

Objective: Assign .NET trust levels to a specific directory in a site

Description: You have been asked to set a specific .NET trust level to a directory to ensure that the .NET application running there cannot accidentally do damage elsewhere on the server.

1. Click on the server in the Connections pane of IIS Manager.

2. Select a site from the list in the Connections pane.

3. Double-click the **.NET Trust Levels** icon in the Features View pane.

4. Select **Medium (web_mediumtrust.config)** from the drop-down menu as shown in Figure 7-24.

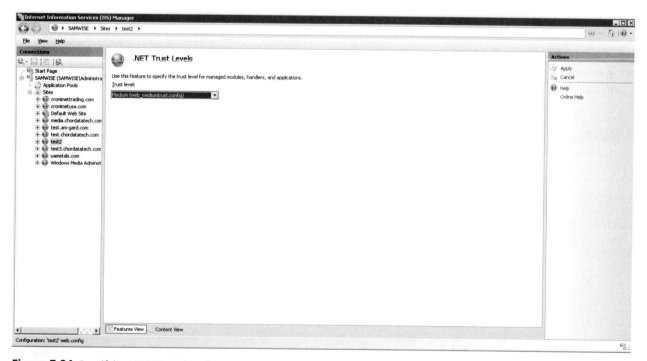

Figure 7-24 Specifying .NET Trust Levels

© Cengage Learning 2012

5. Click **Apply** in the Actions pane.

Client Certificate Mappings

As stated earlier there are three types of client certificate mappings.

- *One-to-one.* For one-to-one mappings, the server has a matching certificate for every user that will access the restricted content. When a request is made the server validates the client certificate against its own copy and if they match it allows access. This is most useful when there are a small number of users that require access to the material.

- *Many-to-one.* Many-to-one mappings involve the server authenticating users based on particular information found in the client certificate. Validating based on the organization is one way in which the user can be shown to be from a trusted organization.

- *Active Directory.* In a domain environment the Active Directory mappings can greatly simplify the use of client certificates. In order to use this method, the domain administrator must set up their own certificate-based infrastructure. This is accomplished by installing the Active Directory Certificate Services role on the domain controller which includes the Certification Authority and the Certification Web Enrollment services. This allows for the creation, distribution, and validation of the certificates.

Configuring Site Permissions and Authentication

To configure authentication, you choose the appropriate object in the Connections pane (such as the server, site, application, virtual directory, or physical folder or file). Double-click **Authentication** in the Features pane, then choose the appropriate available authentication method from the list and choose **Enable** from the Actions pane.

To use the higher forms of authentication you must also disable Anonymous authentication at that level.

Best Practices

1. If transferring a site or sites to another server, or making significant changes to server configuration, perform a manual backup of the site(s) configuration to ensure the latest version is available for restore or roll back if there is a problem with a new configuration.

2. For ease of management, set the maximum number of failed trace log files the system should keep to 10 or less.

3. When configuring logging options for Web transactions, use the W3C log file format, and keep the use of optional fields to a minimum, unless there is a special need to track something, or you are debugging an issue.

4. The optimum rollover period for Web transaction log files is daily. This allows for flexible disk space management, especially when there are large numbers of transactions being logged.

5. If the Web server is only going to be administered locally, then do not install the Management service. This will reduce the ways server administration can be attacked remotely.

6. Use SSL whenever possible when sending usernames, passwords, or sensitive information (e.g., credit card numbers) via the Web. This makes it much more difficult to intercept the information.

(Continues)

(Continued)

7. Whenever possible, use a well-known Certificate Authority (CA) like Verisign or Thawte for certificates rather than self-signed certificates. This will give users a much stronger feeling of confidence when connecting to your site.

8. When requesting certificates from a Certificate Authority (CA) set the certificate encryption level to 2048 bits. This gives better protection of the certificate without adversely affecting system performance.

9. If there will be ASP.NET applications running in a site, set .NET trust levels to ensure that the applications have the minimum amount of privilege they need to run.

Chapter Summary

- Once IIS is installed and running on a server, there are a variety of administrative tasks that must be considered. These include backing up and restoring sites, monitoring server performance, restricting access to different parts of the server, and encrypting data coming to and from the server.

- IIS configuration is maintained in XML text files that can easily be backed up or copied to other servers.

- Site configuration backups can be set to run automatically or be performed manually.

- Server performance metrics such as percentage of CPU and memory usage can be observed in real time.

- Failed requests can be logged to a specific error log file to assist in troubleshooting Web application errors.

- Extensive logging of Web transactions can be configured giving detailed views of Server performance, trends, and traffic volume.

- Server management by default is the role of the server administrator, but different levels of management can be delegated to users both inside a Windows Server 2008 domain, and outside of a domain.

- Remote server management is available and configurable.

- SSL security can be configured using certificates. Using certificates provides two levels of protection: 1. Data is encrypted over the Internet. 2. The client connecting to the server can be sure that they are connecting to the correct server.

- A self-signed certificate can be generated internally to encrypt data, however, it will not be considered to be trusted by users connecting to the site.

- Trusted certificates are issued by several different Certificate Authorities (CAs). These CAs are known to the various client browsers (Internet Explorer, Firefox, Google Chrome, etc.) and users connecting to a site using a certificate issued by one of these CAs can be reasonably sure they are connecting to the site they think they are connecting to.

- Access to Web sites, folders within a Web site, or applications can be restricted to certain users or groups by the use of authentication. There are seven different kinds of authentication.

Key Terms

ASP.NET   A Microsoft Web application framework for building dynamic Web sites, Web applications, and Web services.

Certificate Authority (CA)   A trusted entity that issues digital certificates that can be used by Web sites to establish their identity to users connecting to them.

Certificate Signing Request (CSR)   A block of encrypted text that is generated on the server that the certificate will be used on. The CSR contains information that will be included in the certificate plus the public key that will be used. The corresponding private key is created at the same time.

Code Access Security (CAS)   A security mechanism within the .NET Framework that helps protect computers from malicious code.

cryptographic service provider (CSP)   A means of providing hardware or software based encryption and decryption.

Fully Qualified Domain Name (FQDN)   The complete domain name of a specific host on the internet (i.e. www.mydomain.com).

Hypertext Transport Protocol (HTTP)   Protocol used to transfer Web pages from the server to the client.

Kerberos   A protocol for clients to present network credentials for authentication. Tickets are obtained from a Kerberos Key Distribution Center and presented to the server to authenticate the client.

NCSA   Fixed text-based log file format developed by the National Center for Supercomputing Applications at University of Illinois at Urbana-Champaign.

NTLM   NT LAN Manager; an older Windows challenge/response authentication protocol used on networks that include Windows operating systems as well as stand-alone systems.

port   Number assigned to user sessions and server applications in an IP network.

Secure Sockets Layer (SSL)   A cryptographic protocol that provides secure communication over the Internet.

site bindings   Site configuration information that defines what protocols are connected to a particular port number, IP address and optional host header.

W3C log file format A   customizable text-based format that is the default log file format for IIS. W3C is an organization that develops Web standards based on feedback from member organizations and the public.

XML (Extensible Markup Language)   A format for representing, describing, and classifying Web-delivered information.

Review Questions

1. IIS 7 configuration data is stored in files that are in what format?

    a.   HTML

    b.   Binary

    c.   XML

    d.   MDB

2. IIS checks for changes to server configuration files how often?

    a.   30 seconds

    b.   2 minutes

    c.   5 minutes

    d.   1 hour

3. How many versions of the configuration files are kept?

   a. 3

   b. 5

   c. 7

   d. 10

4. The command line tool to manually back up and restore configuration files is called:

   a. AppCmd.exe

   b. AppCmd.com

   c. AppCommand.exe

   d. ApplCmd.exe

5. Which log file format does IIS generate by default?

   a. IIS

   b. W3C

   c. NCSA

   d. Custom

6. What is the default period for log file rollover?

   a. Daily

   b. Weekly

   c. Monthly

   d. Bi-weekly

7. What are the potential issues with some of the optional logging parameters?

   a. Intermittent incorrect values reported

   b. Processing load and network latency

   c. Interruption of the HTTP session

   d. There are no issues

8. What service must be installed to delegate IIS feature management?

   a. The Delegation service

   b. The Feature Service

   c. FTP

   d. The Management Service

9. Why would you want to create an IIS Manager user vs. adding them to the domain?

   a. Domain users aren't recognized by IIS administration

   b. So that they only have access to the administrative functions of their web site

   c. So they have sufficient privilege to administer their Web site

   d. None of the above

10.   What tool is required on the client side to manage an IIS server remotely?

    a.   IIS 7 Manager

    b.   Control Panel

    c.   IIS 7 Server Monitor

    d.   None of the above

11.   What two ways does a server certificate and SSL enhance Web site security?

    a.   Detect unauthorized access and verification of site identity to user

    b.   Encrypts/decrypts incoming/outgoing data and detects unauthorized access

    c.   Verifies site identity to the user and encrypts/decrypts incoming/outgoing data

    d.   None of the above

12.   How can you assign different certificates to different Web sites within a server?

    a.   Bind SSL to different ports for each OR assign a unique IP address to each site

    b.   Bind SSL to different ports for each AND assign a unique IP address to each site

    c.   Assign the certificate to the site—no other action is required

    d.   You can't assign different certificates to different Web sites within a server

13.   What is the biggest issue with a self-signed certificate?

    a.   It does not encrypt data

    b.   The Certificate is not signed by a trusted CA

    c.   Both a and b

    d.   self-signed certificates only work inside a domain

14.   What is the information generated to request a certificate called?

    a.   Certificate Signing Request (CSR)

    b.   Signed Certificate Request (SCR)

    c.   Authenticated Certificate Request (ACR)

    d.   Request For Certificate (RFC)

15.   By default who can access a site open to the Internet?

    a.   Only people you tell about it

    b.   Anyone

    c.   Authenticated users

    d.   Certain IP addresses

16.   How many authentication methods does IIS support?

    a.   1

    b.   5

    c.   25

    d.   7

17.   With anonymous authentication which user's privileges are used to access content?

    a.   The administrator account

    b.   The domain privileges of the user connecting

    c.   The built in IUSR account

    d.   A guest account

18. Which authentication method would work best for a private intranet restricted to users within a domain?

   a. Windows authentication

   b. Client certificates

   c. Anonymous

   d. Forms

19. Which of these objects (or groups of objects) within the web server hierarchy can access be restricted to?

   a. Server or a site within the server

   b. An application

   c. A virtual directory, a physical folder, or a particular file

   d. All of the above

20. What are the five trust levels a .NET application can have related to accessing Web server objects?

   a. Full, High, Medium, Low, Minimal

   b. Complete, General, Restricted, Limited, None

   c. Maximum, High, Medium, Low, Minimum

   d. There are no trust levels; .NET applications can access any Web server object

Case Projects

Case Project 7-1: Delegating Permissions for a Web Server

You are the administrator for the Web server at Your Company Inc. You have been asked to create four sites: the company Web site, a site for another company (othercompany.com), the company intranet, and a testing site for the Web developers.

Two employees from the other company need remote access to their Web site only. Another administrator needs to administer the overall server, and the entire Web development team (three developers), who are domain users, need access to administer the testing Web site. Decide the type of IIS Manager user each person should be, create the appropriate IIS Manager users and domain users, and grant the appropriate rights to each, making sure they only have access to appropriate Web site(s).

Case Project 7-2: Configuring Access to Site Content

Using the four sites created in Case Project 7-1, you will now configure how users may access the content.

The outside company site requires only Anonymous authentication. The company Web site requires a folder that requires encrypted transactions. You are free to choose any name for the folder. You can choose to create a self-signed certificate, or both Thawte (*http:// www.thawte.com*) and VeriSign (*http://www.verisign.com*) offer test or trial certificates. These are typically limited to a number of days before they expire and may limit the level of encryption. VeriSign offers two different kinds of trials—choose the "test" certificate.

The main customer site should be set for Anonymous authentication. Set up a customer folder under the company Web site and use Basic authentication to allow registered users access to the content in that folder. Use Windows authentication for access to the company intranet site, and the testing site.

Case Project 7-3: Web Server Security Review

You have been asked to review the security for a company Web server within a domain containing two sites and to write a report covering what changes you might suggest for each site. The specifics are:

- Site 1 is an internal intranet site, using forms authentication with no SSL to restrict access. There are several .NET applications running that are accessed from a variety of directories in the site, no trust .NET levels set. The .NET applications do not require any files outside of the application directory, but do write to the file system. There is one administrator for the site, but they would like to add two more employees to the list.

- Site 2 is a site accessible from the Internet, with a members-only page using forms authentication without SSL. A specific directory within the site contains a .NET application and no trust level is set. The .NET application accesses a database and writes to the error log as part of its normal operation. There is one administrator who is an employee and an administrator who is a consultant and accesses the server remotely. Both administrators have domain accounts.

Chapter

Configuring Windows Server 2008 Network Application Services

After reading this chapter and completing the exercises, you will be able to:

- Install and configure a Windows Media Server

- Stream broadcast and on-demand content, with and without advertisements

- Use cache and proxy streaming to maximize server performance

- Install and use Active Directory Digital Rights Management Service to protect content from unauthorized access

- Configure a wide variety of Windows SharePoint options including incoming and outgoing e-mail

Important additions to standard Web content (text and images) include various types of multimedia such as audio and video, as well as the ability to use the Web as a collaboration tool. Audio and video are probably now the top ways to communicate ideas and pass information on the Web, and including them on Web sites is often no longer optional. Being able to use the Web for collaboration, whether on the Internet or on an intranet, is also becoming a must-have rather than a nice-to-have. The need for these services creates the dual challenges of managing these services and being able to provide them without taxing server resources beyond reasonable levels.

Windows Server 2008 provides two services to help you manage media and collaborative content: Windows Media Server and Windows SharePoint. Configuring these services properly can help you manage and deliver this important content effectively.

Configuring Windows Media Server

Users today often prefer having media "streamed" to their browsers rather than having to download the entire video or audio clip before they can view or listen to the content. **Streaming** allows the user to almost immediately start enjoying or using the content on-demand instead of waiting until the entire clip is downloaded (the time difference can be significant, especially with video).

The platform to accomplish this in Windows Server 2008 is the Streaming Media Services role. This role is not included in Windows Server 2008 but is an optional downloadable add-on available at *http://www.microsoft.com/downloads*. You must search for Windows Media Services 2008 and choose the download that matches your operating system. Once you have downloaded this and installed it you can open the Server Manager and add the appropriate roles as shown in Figure 8-1.

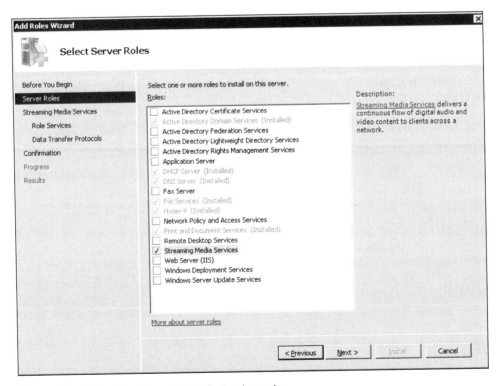

Figure 8-1 Adding the Streaming Media Services role
© Cengage Learning 2012

The Streaming Media Services role has three role services under it: Windows Media Server, Web-based Administration, and Logging Agent. Depending on the version of Windows Server 2008 you are using, there may be some limitations on the services you can offer. For example, multicast streaming is not available under Windows Server 2008 R2 Standard Edition.

Both the Web-based Administration and Logging Agent role services require the Web Server role (IIS) to be installed on the server as well. If you haven't already installed the Web Server role, and your choices require it, the wizard will add the needed components without leaving the installation of the Media Services roles. Streaming media data is delivered through one of two data transfer protocols: **Real Time Streaming Protocol (RTSP)** or **Hypertext Transfer Protocol (HTTP)**. You can choose either or both protocols. Which protocol you will use for particular content will depend on what the content is and how the content needs to play for the user. For example, since the HTTP protocol does not lose packets, it may be the preferred protocol when data loss is unacceptable, but RTSP may be preferred for events streaming in real time. Another caveat is if another program is using the HTTP protocol, you will need to do some additional configuration to stream media over that protocol. The wizard also shows what versions of Windows Media Player or Windows Media Services is required for the different protocols.

Activity 8-1: Install Windows Media Services

Time Required: 30 minutes

Objective: Install Windows Media Services on the server

Description: You will install the Streaming Media Services role and configure Windows Media Services.

1. Download the installer from **http://www.microsoft.com/downloads** and execute the installer.

The Microsoft Download Center references a large number of downloads. Depending on what you are looking for, it may or may not be listed on the home page. At the top of the page are various categories of downloads (e.g., Product Families), and a search box. You may need to use some of these tools to locate the download you are interested in. Try searching for Windows Media Services 2008.

2. From the **Start** menu, launch **Server Manager**. Click **Roles**, click **Add Role**, then click **Next** if you see the Before You Begin window.

3. On the Select Server Roles Screen, click the check box next to **Streaming Media Services** (refer to Figure 8-1).

4. Click **Next** to start the Wizard.

5. Review the Introduction to Streaming Media Services.

6. Click **Next**.

7. Click the check boxes next to **Windows Media Server, Web-based Administration**, and **Logging Agent** as shown in Figure 8-2.

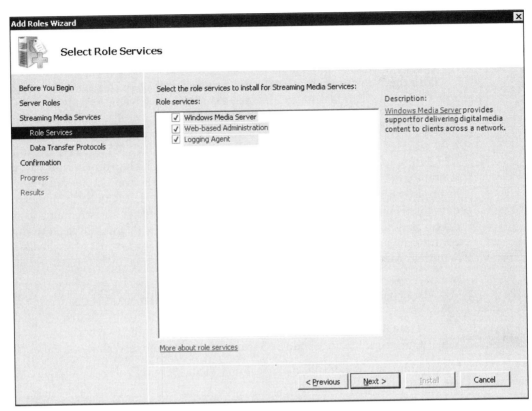

Figure 8-2 Selecting the role services under Streaming Media Services

© Cengage Learning 2012

If IIS is not installed at this point, when you select the check box for Web-based Administration, a pop-up will appear asking if you wish to add role services required for Web-based Administration, as shown in Figure 8-3. Click the Add Required Roles Services button to install the Web Server (IIS) Service.

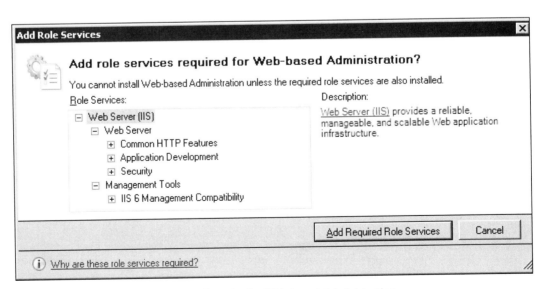

Figure 8-3 Adding the Web Server (IIS) service for Web-based Administration

© Cengage Learning 2012

8. Click **Next**.

9. Click the check boxes next to **Real Time Streaming Protocol (RTSP)** and **Hypertext Transfer Protocol (HTTP)**.

The choice for Hypertext Transfer Protocol (HTTP) will be grayed out if you have not yet installed IIS.

10. Click **Next**.

11. Click **Install**. The wizard completes the installation.

Once the Role and Role services are installed, you can begin to manage the media server. Testing access to the content can be done from the server or from a client machine. However, testing access to the content on the server via the Windows Media Services Console requires Windows Media Player. Windows Media Player can be installed by installing the Desktop Experience feature through Server Manager. In terms of verifying access to content, it is better if testing is done from a client machine rather than from the server itself, since that gives a more realistic view of how the content will generally be accessed. If you choose not to test the streaming on the server you will not need to install Windows Media Player.

The installation in Activity 8-1 installed both the Windows Media Services Console and the Web-based Administration role service. While functionality is comparable between the two interfaces, the Web interface is generally used for remote administration. The Windows Media Administration site needs to be started from IIS Manager, and it is recommended that you protect the site using SSL. For our configuration and management of the server, we will concentrate on using the Windows Media Services console. The Windows Media Services console is launched from the Administrative Tools program group.

To identify the physical path on the server and other characteristics of the content being streamed, Windows Media Services uses what are called **publishing points**. The client connects to a publishing point, and Windows Media Services manages the connection and streams the content. Two types of publishing points are supported: on-demand, and broadcast. Which type is used depends on how you want the playback of content to be controlled. **On-demand** publishing points are generally used when the client will control playback, and broadcast publishing points are generally used when playback will be controlled on the server. On-demand publishing points can be thought of like playing back music on your PC; you control when a piece of music starts, you can fast forward, rewind, or stop it at any point. **Broadcast** publishing points are used when content streaming is controlled on the server side. Broadcast content streaming can be thought of as more like television (without a DVR!) or radio. The content delivery is controlled at the source; it starts when it is scheduled to start at the source, and runs until is complete or is stopped at the source.

When a publishing point is created, the following information is needed: a name to identify it, the content type to stream, and whether logging is enabled.

The publishing point name not only identifies the publishing point for reference, it will be used in the URL a client uses to connect to the content, so do not use special characters like question marks, brackets, braces, etc. in the name because that could cause problems in the location name for a browser.

The content type can be one of four basic choices: Encoder, Playlist, One file, or Files in a directory:

• The Encoder type enables a publishing point to connect to a PC, server, or appliance that is running Windows Media Encoder and broadcast the Encoder output. **Encoding** is where digital content is converted into an appropriate format for creating a live stream or **live streaming**. The Encoder type is a broadcast publishing point; the playback is controlled at the server.

Windows Server 2008 Enterprise gives you the choice of Unicast or Multicast. Given our scope is Windows Server 2008 (rather than Enterprise) we will only be covering Unicast here. **Unicast** is a method of streaming where each client connects to the primary source and has its own dedicated stream of content. Unicast publishing points can be on-demand or broadcast. **Multicast** is a method of streaming that sends a single stream from the source to a point that clients connect to and receive content from. Multicast publishing is only broadcast.

- The Playlist type enables a publishing point to take a mix of files and live streams from a **playlist** (a list of content to be streamed) and stream them.

- The One file type enables a publishing point that streams one file (as you might guess). Valid extensions of files that can be streamed by default include .wma, .wmv, .asf, .wsx, and .mp3.

- The Files in a directory type enables a publishing point to stream digital media or playlists in a specific directory. Multiple pieces of content can be streamed, and all files in the directory are accessible to clients. A single file can be streamed by including the file name in the URL, or all of the files in the directory can be streamed.

The content type you select will depend on the type of media and how you want to present it to users. Here are some guidelines for selecting the various types:

- The Encoder type is for live-stream broadcasts, such as a live video or audio feed from an event. As mentioned above, you will need Windows Media Encoder to encode the data being streamed.

- The Playlist type is needed to stream multiple pieces of content in a sequence. You must use Playlist if you want to intersperse advertising with regular content.

- The One file type is best when there is only a single piece of media to stream, and you don't want to include advertising. A single file can be on-demand or broadcast.

- Files in a directory is best when there are multiple pieces of media to stream and you want to easily allow the client to choose particular content or have all content streamed on-demand rather than setting up individual publishing points and trying to maintain them.

To direct a client to your publishing point with a more friendly looking URL, you can create an announcement file. Announcement files have a file extension of .asx and are based on XML. The most important piece of information in the file is the URL of the content, but you can also insert tags using a text editor to provide additional features or information to client players like author or copyright information.

Activity 8-2: Create an On-Demand Publishing Point and an Announcement File

Time Required: 25 minutes
Objective: Create a publishing point and verify the media content streams to a client

Description: Utilizing the demonstration files included with Windows Server 2008 Media Services, you will create an on-demand publishing point that streams content to a client system, and an announcement file to make it easy for users to access the content.

1. Open the **Windows Media Services** console from the **Administrative Tools** program group. The left pane shows your server and a list of Publishing Points. There are two default publishing points (an on-demand and a broadcast publishing point).

2. Right-click **Publishing Points** in the left pane.

3. Choose **Add Publishing Point**.

4. Click **Next** to move past the Welcome page.

5. Type **SingleFile** into the Name text box and click **Next**. Do not use special characters in the name. The wizard will show you a list of characters to avoid.

6. Click the option button next to **One file** on the Content Type screen and click **Next**.

7. Click the option button next to **On-demand publishing point** on the Publishing Point Type screen and click **Next**.

8. Click the option button next to **Add a new publishing point** on the Existing Publishing Point screen, and click **Next**.

9. Type **C:\WMPub\WMRoot\pinball.wmv** into the File name text box on the File Location screen or click the **Browse** button and navigate to the **C:\WMPub\WMRoot** directory and select **pinball.wmv**.

10. Click **Next**.

11. Make sure the **yes** box is checked, then click **Next** on the Unicast Logging screen.

12. The Publishing Point Summary should appear similar to Figure 8-4. Click **Next**.

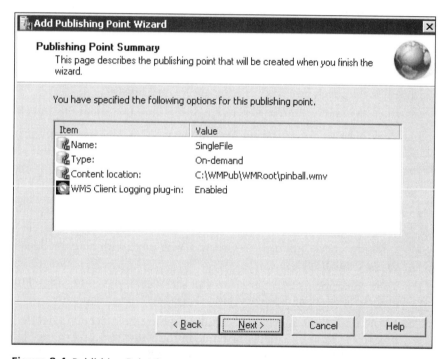

Figure 8-4 Publishing Point Summary

© Cengage Learning 2012

13. Make a note of the URL shown in the Completing the Add Publishing Point Wizard screen shown in Figure 8-5. At this point the content can be streamed to a client player via that URL. Do not exit the wizard yet.

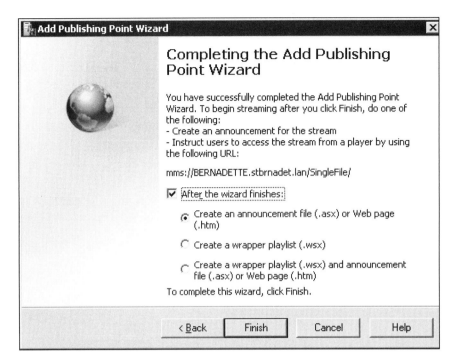

Figure 8-5 Completing the Add Publishing Point Wizard
© Cengage Learning 2012

14. Click the check box next to **After the wizard finishes.**

15. Click the option button next to **Create an announcement file** and click **Finish.**

16. Click **Next** to move past the Welcome page. The Unicast Announcement Wizard will automatically launch.

17. Type the URL from Step 13 into the **URL to content** text box if what is displayed is not correct and click **Next.**

18. Type the appropriate directory for the Web server on this server in the **Announcement file (.asx) name and location** text box if it is not pre-filled in by the wizard.

19. Click the check box next to **Create a Web page with an embedded player and a link to the content.**

20. Type the appropriate directory for the Web server and **SingleFile.htm** if it is not already filled in, and click **Next.**

21. In the Edit Announcement Metadata dialog box, type **SingleFile** in the Value text box to the right of Title, your name in the Value text box to the right of Author, and **today's date** in the Value text box to the right of Copyright and click **Next.**

22. If you have installed Windows Media Player on this server, click the check box to **Test files when this wizard finishes.** If not, leave the check box unchecked.

To make testing easier, it is recommended that you install Windows Media Player (WMP) on the server. Install WMP by installing the Desktop Experience feature through Server Manager.

23. Click **Finish.**

24. If you clicked the check box in Step 22, the Test Unicast Announcement dialog box will appear. You can select **Test announcement** to start Windows Media Player and connect to the stream. Select **Test Web page with an embedded player** to open the Web page and test the publishing point with the embedded player.

25. If you do not have Windows Media Player installed on the server, you can point a browser on a machine with network access to the server to the URL from Step 21 to test the Web page with an embedded player.

Depending on the content you are delivering and the circumstances you are delivering it under, adding advertising to the content may be desirable. There are several ways to deliver advertising with your content:

- Wrapper ads play before and/or after the regular content. Wrapper ads always play, even if used with a broadcast publishing point, so the client will always see your advertisements no matter when they join the broadcast.

- Interstitial ads are streaming content placed in a playlist. The ads can be interspersed with regular content within the playlist.

- Banner ads appear in the player rather than as part of the content. The ads can be static text, images, or multimedia and are independent of the content being streamed.

ACTIVITY

Activity 8-3: Create an On-Demand Publishing Point with a Wrapper Ad

8

Time Required: 15 minutes
Objective: Create a publishing point with multiple pieces of content and ads wrapped around the content

Description: Utilizing the demonstration files included with Windows Server 2008 Media Services, you will create an on-demand Files in a directory publishing point that streams content and advertising via wrapper ads to a client system.

1. Open the Windows Media Services console from the Administrative Tools program group. The left pane will show your server and a list of Publishing Points. There will be two default publishing points (an on-demand, and a broadcast publishing point).

2. Right-click **Publishing Points** in the left pane.

3. Choose **Add Publishing Point (Wizard)**.

4. Click **Next** to move past the Welcome page.

5. Type **On-DemandPublishingPoint1** into the Name text box and click **Next**. Do not use special characters in the name. The wizard will show you a list of characters to avoid.

6. Click the option button next to **Files (digital media or playlists) in a directory** on the Content Type screen and click **Next**.

7. Click the option button next to **On-demand publishing point** on the Publishing Point Type screen and click **Next**.

8. Type **C:\WMPub\WMRoot** in the Location of directory text box on the Directory Location screen and click **Next**.

9. Click the check box next to **Loop (content plays continuously)** and click **Next**.

10. Make sure the **yes** box is checked, then click **Next** to move past the Unicast Logging screen.

11. The Publishing Point Summary should appear similar to Figure 8-4. Click **Next** after reviewing the list.

12. Click the check box next to **After the wizard finishes**.

13. Click the option button next to **Create a wrapper playlist (.wsx) and announcement file (.asx) or Web page (.htm)** and click **Finish**.

14. Click **Next** to move past the Create Wrapper Wizard welcome screen. The Unicast Announcement Wizard will launch.

15. The Wrapper Playlist File screen appears, similar to Figure 8-6. Click **Add Advertisement**.

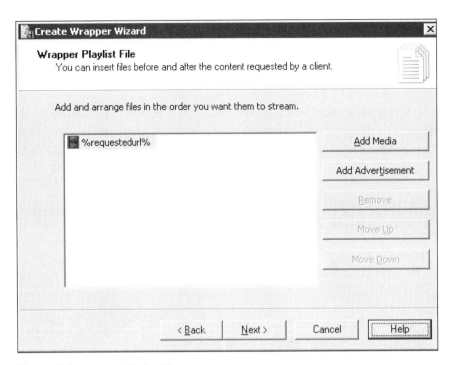

Figure 8-6 Wrapper Playlist File screen

© Cengage Learning 2012

16. The Add Advertisement screen appears, similar to Figure 8-7. Click **Browse**. Choose the file named **encoder_ad.wmv**, then click **OK** to close the Add Advertisement screen.

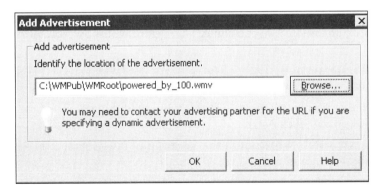

Figure 8-7 Add Advertisement

© Cengage Learning 2012

17. From the Wrapper Playlist File screen, click **Add Media**.

18. The Add Media Elements screen appears, similar to Figure 8-8. Click **Browse**. Choose the file named **fupgrade.asf**, select File under Content type examples, then click **OK** to close the Add Media Elements dialog box.

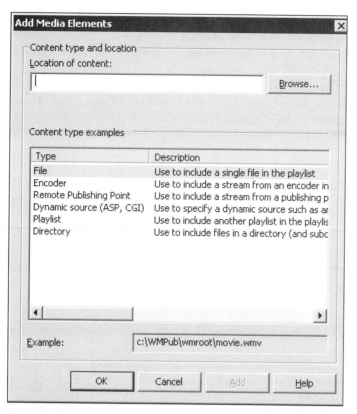

Figure 8-8 Add Media Elements
© Cengage Learning 2012

19. From the Wrapper Playlist File screen, click **Add Media**.

20. On the Add Media Elements screen, Click **Browse**. Choose the file named **powered_ by_100.wmv**, select File under Content type examples, then click **OK** to close the Add Media Elements dialog box.

21. From the Wrapper Playlist File screen, click **Add Advertisement**.

22. On the Add Advertisement screen, Click **Browse**. Choose the file named **industrial.wmv**, then select File under Content type examples, then click **OK** to close the Add Media Elements dialog box.

23. Click **Next**.

24. Type **C:\WMPub\WMRoot\On-DemandPublishingPoint1_wrapper.wsx** in the File name text box in the Save Wrapper Playlist File screen, and click **Next**.

25. Click the check box next to **Enable wrapper playlist when wizard finishes** and click **Finish**.

26. Complete the Unicast Announcement Wizard as in Steps 16 through 25 in Activity 8-2, replacing the filename SingleFile.htm with **on-DemandPublishing Point1. htm**, and the title SingleFile with **OnDemand** in Step 21.

Caching and Proxy Settings

One of the bigger challenges of serving streaming video and audio is the load it puts on both the server itself and on the network bandwidth available to that server. Large numbers of requests for streaming content can overload a server and cause delays in delivering the content. Windows Server 2008 Media Services addresses this through caching and proxies.

A **caching server** copies content from the primary server and stores it in a local cache. It then serves the media directly to client computers and devices. This reduces the load on the primary server since it only needs to send content to the caching server initially and when the content changes.

A **proxy server** works with live streams. When a client requests access to a live stream from the proxy server, the proxy server connects to the origin server and sends the stream to the client. If the proxy server is already handling a requested stream, it splits the stream to the additional client and maintains a single connection to the origin server. There is no caching since the live stream is not a file source.

Whether using cache or proxy servers, clients can access the media server closest to them to reduce network latency.

To configure cache/proxy settings you must enable the plug-in as follows:

1. Open Windows Media Services console from the Administrative Tools program group and choose the server node in the left panel.

2. Select the Properties tab in the main window and then select Cache/Proxy Management from the Category list as shown in Figure 8-9.

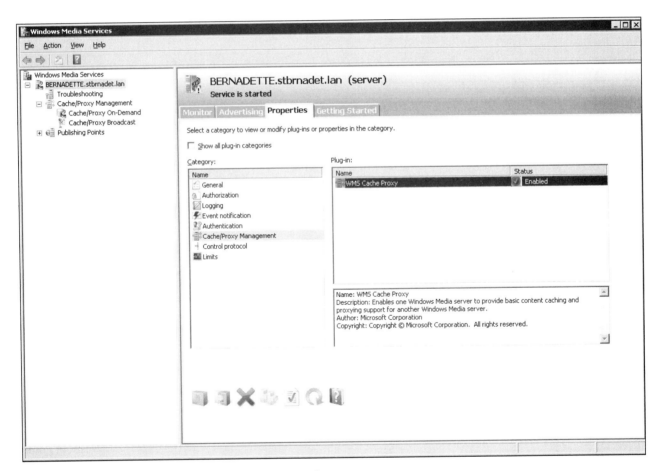

Figure 8-9 Properties tab in Windows Media Services console

© Cengage Learning 2012

3. The first icon on the bottom left of the screen is the enable icon. Click this to enable the plug-in for access to the configuration options. Once enabled, double-click the WMS Cache Proxy in the Plug-in window and the WMS Cache Proxy Properties screen displays as in Figure 8-10.

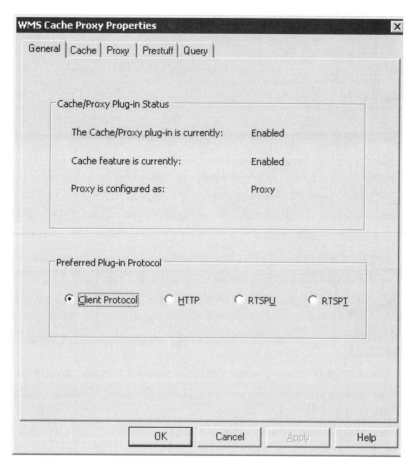

Figure 8-10 WMS Cache Proxy Properties
© Cengage Learning 2012

The General tab allows you to specify which protocol to use when streaming between servers. The default setting is Client Protocol, which means the stream between servers will use the same protocol requested by the client.

The second tab is the Cache tab. Here you can set storage limits for the cache. There are no limits by default but if you are dealing with a lot of content it makes sense to consider some limits. You can also specify the location of the Cache directory, adjust the caching speed, and clear the cache from this tab.

There are three options on the Proxy tab:

- *Proxy*. This default setting presents media to clients and identifies the proxy server as the same computer that is the origin server.

- *Proxy Redirect*. This option allows you to redirect a client request to another server in the array. This is used for load balancing.

- *Reverse Proxy*. Reverse proxy is used as a security measure. It isolates the origin server from the client and as far as the client is concerned the reverse proxy is the origin server. All client requests are made to the reverse proxy, which then requests the data from the origin server and then serves it to the client. This can also help with load balancing. This is usually used as an Internet-facing server so that the origin server can remain safe on the internal network.

The Prestuff tab allows you to specify settings for caching content prior to client requests. This allows you to bring content over before going into production. You can prestuff from a stream source or a file source.

The Query tab allows you to search for cached content on the server and gives you the option for deleting specific content from the cache.

Activity 8-4: Cache an On-Demand Publishing Point

Time Required: 10 minutes

Objective: Configure an on-demand Publishing Point for caching

Description: Install and configure caching and direct the on-demand publishing point created in Activity 8-3 to the cache.

1. Enable caching if you have not already.
2. Open Windows Media Services console from the Administrative Tools program group and in the left panel choose the server node where you created On-DemandPublishingPoint1 in Activity 8-3.
3. Click the plus (**+**) sign next to Publishing Points and click **On-DemandPublishingPoint1**.
4. Click the **Properties** tab.
5. Click **Cache/Proxy** in the list under Category.
6. Double-click **Cache expiration** in the list under Property.

 Cache expiration refers to how long the client can cache the content. Although deleting cached versions is not a very effective way of keeping users from redistributing your content, it is still a good idea to limit the amount of time your content can be cached on client systems.

7. Click the option button before **After (seconds)** if it is not already selected.
8. Type **86400** in the text box (if not already entered by default). This sets the cache expiration (24 hours).
9. Click **OK**.
10. Click the **Monitor** tab. The caching monitor should appear similar to Figure 8-11.

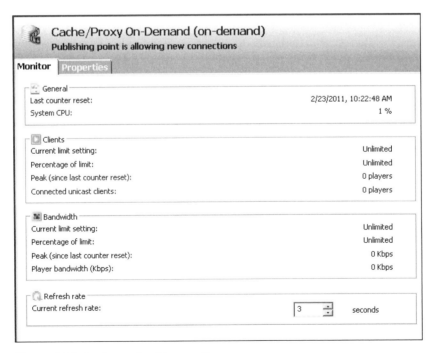

Figure 8-11 On-demand caching monitor

© Cengage Learning 2012

11. Close any open windows.

Securing Content

While you want to make useful content available to users, in some cases access to content might be by subscription or some other fee, or the content is valuable intellectual property, and you do not want it to be freely copied. Given the ease of access to digital content it is vital that there be a way to protect intellectual property from unauthorized access and distribution. Utilizing Active Directory Digital Rights Management Services (AD RMS) and Windows Media Rights Manager (WMRM) are two ways you can protect intellectual property.

Windows Media Rights Manager (WMRM)

While most of the configuration and file processing involved with WMRM is done by the content provider, it is valuable to know the overall process:

1. Packaging – The file is encrypted and a key stored in a separate encrypted license. Other information can be added, e.g., the URL of where the license can be found. Packaged media is saved in one of two formats: Windows Media Audio (.wma) or Windows Media Video (.wmv).

2. Distribution – A packaged file can be placed on a regular Web page for download, or added to a Windows Media Server as a publishing point and streamed. Other distribution methods include e-mail or CD.

3. Establishing a License Server – A license clearinghouse is chosen by the content provider. User requests for licenses are authenticated by the clearinghouse, keeping the serving of the content and the licensing separate. The specific rights (sometimes called rules) that the content provider decided on are stored at the clearinghouse as well. Rights can include how many times the content can be played, the specific computer system licensed to play it, and start times and end times.

4. License Acquisition – License acquisition can begin when the user plays the content for the first time, tries to download or stream the content, or gets a predelivered license. Depending on how the content provider configured the license, the user may be sent to a page for registration and/or payment, or the license is retrieved from the clearinghouse.

5. Playing the Media File – Similar to AD RMS, the content can only be played on a WMRM enabled player, such as Windows Media Player.

Installing and Configuring Active Directory Digital Rights Management Services (AD RMS)

To take advantage of the capabilities of AD RMS the content to be protected must be created by AD RMS-enabled applications, such as Microsoft Office 2007 or later, Microsoft Exchange 2007 or later, and Microsoft Office SharePoint Server 2007 or later. Using the AD RMS Software Development Kit (SDK), developers can make their applications AD RMS-enabled as well. On the server side, AD RMS must be installed as a Server Role and properly configured.

Activity 8-5: Install Active Directory Digital Rights Management Services

Time Required: 30 minutes
Objective: Install and do initial configuration of AD RMS

Description: To allow use of AD RMS protected content, install and do the initial configuration of the AD RMS Server Role.

1. Launch the Add Roles wizard from the Server Manager.

2. The Select Server Roles page appears. Click the check box next to **Active Directory Rights Management Services** and click **Next**.

The system on which you are installing AD RMS must be a member of a domain.

3. You may be prompted to install additional features. The wizard will guide you through any additional installs.

4. The next page appears similar to Figure 8-12. This introduction page gives a brief overview of AD RMS, some installation notes, and links to additional information if needed.

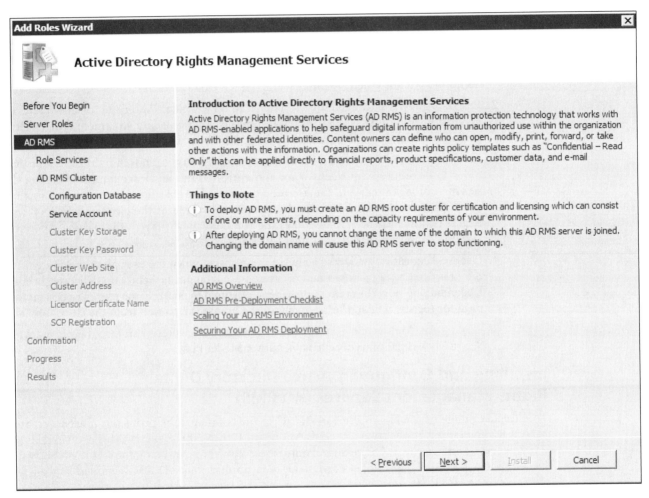

Figure 8-12 AD RMS Introduction page

© Cengage Learning 2012

5. Click **Next** to display the Select Role page. The first choice, Active Directory Rights Management Server, is preselected. The next choice is Identity Federation Support. This allows you to leverage federated trust relationships between your domain and others, provided you have configured Active Directory Federation Services (AD FS).

6. Click **Next** to display the Create or Join an AD RMS Cluster page. If there is already a root or licensing-only cluster available you will have the option to join it, or create a new licensing-only cluster. If there is not a cluster available, the only option will be to create a new one. There must be an AD RMS root cluster with one or more servers in it.

7. Click **Next** to display the Select Configuration Database page. If this will be the only AD RMS server in the root cluster, you may click the option button next to **Use Windows Internal Database on this server**. If there will be multiple servers in the cluster, you must click the option button next to **Use a different database server** and provide the server and database instance.

8. Click **Next** to display the Specify Service Account page. Type a domain user in the text box below the heading Domain User Account. The domain user should be a standard user with no additional privileges. Installing AD RMS on a domain controller is not recommended, but if that is the case, the domain account entered must be a member of the Domain Administrators group or the Enterprise Administrators group.

9. Click **Next** to display the Configure AD RMS Cluster Key Storage page. The cluster key is used to sign certificates and licenses issued by the cluster. Click the option button next to either **Use AD RMS centrally managed key storage** or **Use CSP key storage**. AD RMS centrally managed key storage will automatically share the cluster key with any new AD RMS servers joining the cluster. CSP key storage requires a cryptographic service provider (CSP) and the key will need to be distributed manually when a new server joins the cluster.

10. Click **Next**. You will be prompted for the cluster key password. Type the password in the text boxes (once to set it, the other to verify it).

11. Click **Next** to display the Select AD RMS Cluster Web Site page. Under **Select a Web site for the virtual directory,** click the Web site for the virtual directory where AD RMS will be hosted.

12. Click **Next** to display the Specify Cluster Address page. This page defines an internal address for the AD RMS cluster so that clients can communicate with the cluster over the network. Click the option button next to either **Use an SSL-encrypted connection (https://)** or **Use an unencrypted connection (http://)**. Using SSL is recommended (and required if you want to add Identity Federation Support), and will require obtaining and installing a third party certificate or using a self-signed certificate. Type the Fully Qualified Domain Name in the **Fully-Qualified Domain Name** text box and the port in the **Port** text box, and click **Validate**.

You cannot change the domain name or the port after configuration is complete. It is recommended that you create a cname record for this host name in your DNS manager. If the server is ever moved you can simply point the cname record to the new server.

13. Click **Next** to display the Name the Server Licensor Certificate page. A certificate will be created that verifies the server identity to clients based on the name entered in the Name text box. This defaults to the server name.

14. Click **Next** to display the Register AD RMS Service Connection Point page. Click the option button next to either **Register the AD RMS service connection point now** or **Register the AD RMS service connection point later**. The service connection point (SCP) provides clients with intranet URLs for the AD RMS cluster. If you are a member of the Enterprise Administrators group, and you do not plan to join other AD RMS servers to the cluster before releasing it to clients, you can register the SCP now. Otherwise select to register later.

15. Click **Next** to display the Confirm Installation Selections page, similar to Figure 8-13. Click **Install** to begin the installation.

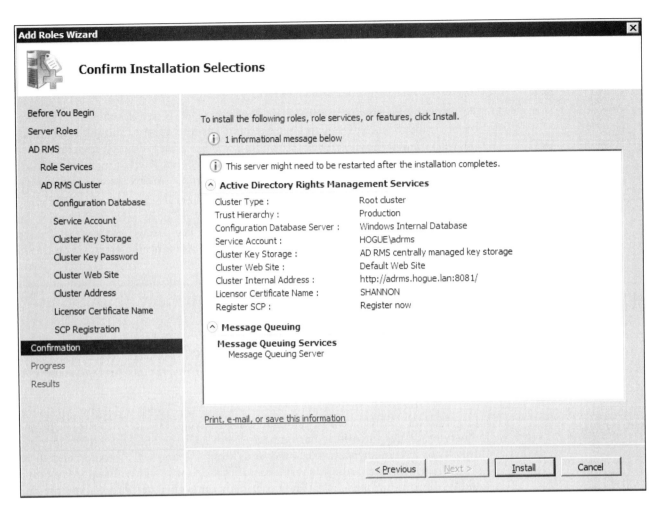

Figure 8-13 AD RMS Confirm Installation Selections

© Cengage Learning 2012

16. The Installation Progress page will appear and display status messages as the installation proceeds. When the installation is complete, it will advance automatically to the Installation Results page, similar to Figure 8-14. You will need to log off and log back on to the server to begin administering AD RMS.

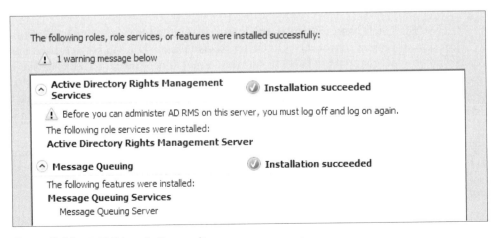

Figure 8-14 AD RMS Installation results

© Cengage Learning 2012

Managing AD RMS

Once AD RMS is installed you can begin managing the server. From the Management Console you can check general information about the **server cluster** (the group of servers administering rights policies), and see if there are recommended or optional tasks that still need to be done. The management console is also where you create policies for content. Policies control how AD RMS enabled applications access the content.

Rights policy templates are used to encrypt documents limiting access to users they have been made available to. Different levels of access can be granted to users as well, such as read, save as, or print. Content can also be made time sensitive; set to expire after a certain date or number of days.

The Active Directory Rights Management console is started from the Administrative Tools program group. The initial view in this console is information about the server cluster. Here you can see the Cluster Details including a summary, intranet URLs and Extranet URLs if present. There is also a section showing the Database configuration and logging information and finally a list of Tasks both recommended and optional. An example is shown in Figure 8-15.

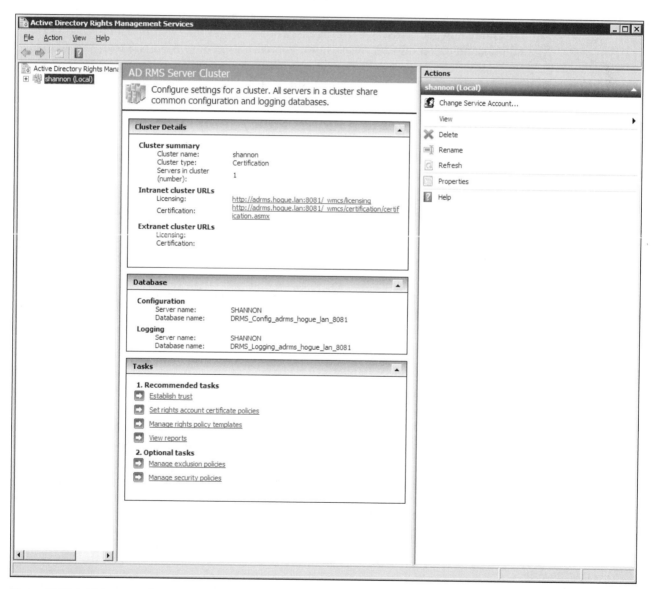

Figure 8-15 Initial screen of Active Directory Rights Management console

© Cengage Learning 2012

Clicking on the plus sign next to the server name expands the list of available options:

- *Trust Policies.* This section allows you to specify what other domains are available as Trusted User Domains as well as Trusted Publishing Domains. If Active Directory Federation Services is installed and you have installed the Identity Federation Support service you will see additional options related to it.

- *Rights Policy Templates.* This is the section where you can create rights templates with various restrictions that you will make available to your client machines. You also specify a network share for the Templates file location that your clients can access.

- *Rights Account Certificate Policies.* This section contains settings for validity periods for the **rights account certificates (RACs)** which identify trusted users and groups that can generate rights-protected content. There are both Standard and Temporary RACs available.

- *Exclusion Policies.* Here you can exclude specific users from access to protected content. You can also exclude some versions of AD RMS-enabled applications from access (for example, older versions of Office). You can also ensure that a minimum version of the AD RMS client has access using the Lockbox Version Exclusion.

- *Security Policies.* Here you can enable and configure Super Users (members of this group are granted owner licenses), perform Password Reset (in the event of data loss or disk failure), and decommission the cluster if you wish to remove AD RMS from the domain.

- *Reports.* Here you can monitor statistics for the user accounts that have received RACs from the cluster. You can also view Health and Troubleshooting reports here.

Activity 8-6: Create a Rights Policy Template

Time Required: 15 minutes
Objective: Create a rights policy template

Description: In this activity, you create a rights policy template that prevents a document from being printed, and causes the document to expire after 2 days. You should have already installed AD RMS.

1. Create a security group called **hr** with an e-mail address of **hr@yourserver.com** where yourserver.com is your server address.

2. Open the Active Directory Rights Management Console from the Administrative Tools program group.

3. Expand the list of options for this server by clicking the **plus sign** next to the server name.

4. Click **Rights Policy Templates**.

5. The Distributed Rights Policy Template page displays. Click either **Create distributed rights policy template** near the bottom of the central pane, or **Create Distributed Rights Policy Template** in the Actions pane on the right.

6. The Add Template Identification Information page displays. Click **Add**.

7. The Add New Template Identification Information page displays. Select **English (United States)** from the Language drop-down, type **Test1** in the Name text box, and type **This policy will prevent printing and will cause the document to expire after 2 days** in the Description text area, as shown in Figure 8-16.

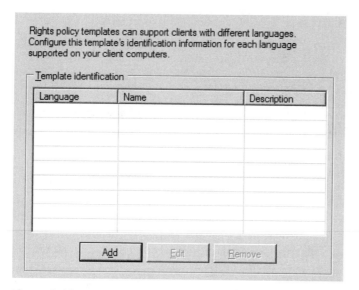

Figure 8-16 Add New Template Identification Information
© Cengage Learning 2012

8. Click **Next** to move to the Add User Rights page. Click the **Add** button. The Add User or Group screen displays. Click the option button next to **The e-mail address of a user or group**. Type **hr@yourserver.com** where yourserver.com is your server address.

9. Click **OK**. You are returned to the Add User Rights page. If necessary, click **hr@yourserver.com** to highlight it.

10. In the text area underneath the label Rights for **hr@yoursever.com** uncheck the check boxes to the right of **Full Control, Print**, and **Edit**.

11. Ensure that the check box next to the label **Grant owner (author) full control right with no expiration** is checked.

12. Click **Next** to move to the Specify Expiration Policy page. Click the option button next to **Expires after the following duration (days)**.

13. Type the number **2** in the text box after Expires after the following duration (days).

14. Click **Finish** to add the template to the configuration database, and to generate an XML file in the shared templates folder.

Configuring Microsoft Windows SharePoint Services Server Options

One of the most exciting applications of the Internet and intranets is the ability to collaborate. Prior to the Web, collaboration was a laborious project, hard to synchronize between users, often requiring either routing hardcopy versions of documents to team members or at best e-mailing versions and hoping that changes would not be accidentally overwritten or lost.

Now, with Microsoft Windows SharePoint Services (WSS) a wide variety of content types can be shared among users, and the content can be managed from a central point. This ensures that everyone is working from the same content, minimizing the chances for lost, overwritten, or duplicate changes. In addition, the feature set of WSS allows for creation of announcements, tasks, and reminders, making it ideal as a hub to coordinate work on a project. It can even be used as a platform for Web-based application development.

WSS is a server role that must be downloaded from Microsoft.

Users of Windows Server 2008 R2 must download Windows SharePoint Services 3.0 x64 with Service Pack 2. If you try to install any earlier version or the 32-bit version by mistake it will alert you of the incompatibility. Depending on your system configuration, you may need .Net Framework 3.0 SP1. This should be found at this link: *http://www.microsoft.com/downloads/en/details.aspx?FamilyID=ec2ca85d-b255-4425-9e65-1e88a0bdb72a.*

Part of the installation process is deciding whether the WSS installation will be a standalone server or part of a server farm. For a smaller organization the standalone server is the easiest to deploy; it requires only a single server and uses the Windows Internal Database for the back-end data storage. The server farm configuration provides improved performance since the back-end data storage is separate from the front-end. This allows multiple front-end Web sites connecting to a WSS database on a Microsoft SQL Server. The first front-end server hosts the SharePoint Central Administration Web site. Let's look at how to configure the standalone configuration.

Activity 8-7: Install and Complete Initial Configuration of SharePoint

Time Required: 15 minutes
Objective: Install and complete initial configuration of a SharePoint site

Description: In this activity, you install a standalone SharePoint server, and use the configuration wizard to complete initial configuration of a SharePoint site.

1. Download and start the installer for Windows SharePoint Services Server.
2. The Microsoft Software License Terms screen will display as shown in Figure 8-17. Click the check box next to the label **I accept the terms of this agreement** and click **Continue.**

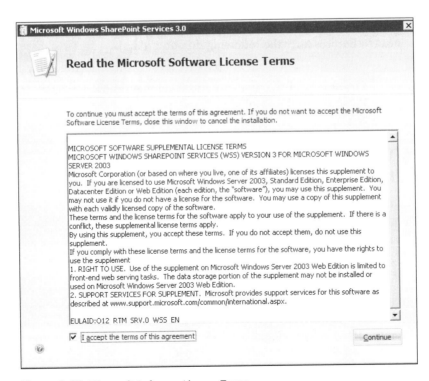

Figure 8-17 Microsoft Software License Terms
© Cengage Learning 2012

3. The Choose the Installation you want screen displays. There are two choices on this screen: Basic and Advanced. Click the **Basic** button to continue with the installation.

4. The installer displays two progress windows. The first informs you of the progress of the installation itself, the second informs you of the progress of the downloading and applying updates. There are no buttons or links displayed during the process.

5. The installer displays the completion screen as shown in Figure 8-18. Make sure the check box next to **Run the SharePoint Product and Technologies Configuration Wizard now** is checked, then click **Close**.

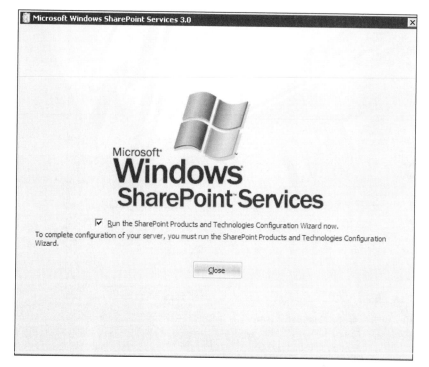

Figure 8-18 SharePoint installation complete

© Cengage Learning 2012

6. When the SharePoint Products and Technologies wizard launches, click **Next** to move past the Welcome dialog.

7. The screen displays any services that may need to be started or reset during the configuration, as shown in Figure 8-19. If any of the dependent services are not currently installed, the wizard will launch the appropriate install procedures. Click **Yes** to restart the services and continue.

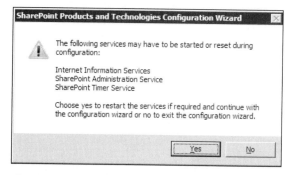

Figure 8-19 SharePoint Products and Technologies Configuration Wizard dependent services dialog box

© Cengage Learning 2012

8. The next screen shows the progress of the configuration. No action needs to be taken here unless you wish to cancel the configuration, in which case you would click Cancel.

9. After the wizard completes the configuration, the Configuration Successful screen appears, as shown in Figure 8-20. Click **Finish** to complete the configuration.

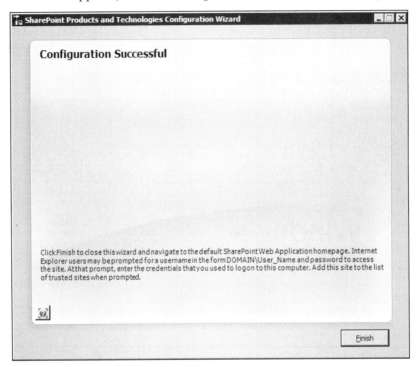

Figure 8-20 Configuration Successful screen

© Cengage Learning 2012

 The wizard can also be used to repair a SharePoint installation if the Web site becomes unavailable. The wizard is labeled SharePoint Products and Technologies Configuration Wizard under Administrative Tools in the Start menu.

At this point there are two SharePoint Web sites available:

• The default site is accessible through http://server_name (where server_name is your server), as shown in Figure 8-21. By default, this site is bound to port 80.

Figure 8-21 Default SharePoint Web site

© Cengage Learning 2012

- The SharePoint Central Administration Web site, accessible from the Administrative Tools program group of the server. The actual URL is http://server_name:port (where server_name is your server, and port is the port assigned to the Web site during the installation), as shown in Figure 8-22. This site is where WSS can be configured and different options chosen, such as for e-mail settings, user permissions, and site-by-site settings. Running the SharePoint Central Administration Web site via the Administrative Tools program group is the preferred method. Running it from this link runs your Web browser as administrator. Without the elevated permissions some of the options will not be available, for example, the ability to create new Web applications.

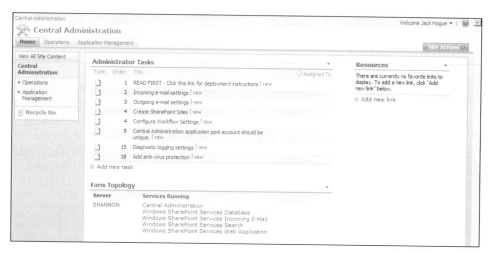

Figure 8-22 SharePoint Central Administration Web site
© Cengage Learning 2012

Upon accessing the SharePoint Central Administration site for the first time, you will be presented with a list of administrative tasks, as shown previously in Figure 8-22, that should be completed before allowing users access to the default SharePoint site. Each task listed is a link to a page with more detail about completing that task. Many of the task description pages will have links to take you to the appropriate part of the site to complete it. As each task is completed it can be deleted from the list.

The Central Administration site is divided into three sections:

- Home Page
- Operations
- Application Management

These sections are accessed via tabs near the top of the page or from the navigation pane on the left of the screen.

The Operations page is divided into the following areas related to settings that affect the entire server, each with links to associated pages:

- *Topology and Services*. Includes the server farm configuration and e-mail settings.
- *Security Configuration*. Service account management, antivirus settings, etc.
- *Logging and Reporting*. Both diagnostic and usage analysis options are available.
- *Global Configuration*. Scheduling, third-party solutions, and Web site mappings.
- *Backup and Restore*. Backup and restoration of the database as well as status monitoring of the processes.
- *Data Configuration*. Database server configuration.

The Application Management page is divided into the following areas related to specific sites, each with links to associated pages:

- *SharePoint Web Application Management*. Creating and deleting Web applications and configuring them.
- *Application Security*. Security settings for **Web parts** (predefined SharePoint components or modules), user permissions and authentication settings.
- *Workflow Management*. Settings for the workflow feature.
- *SharePoint Site Management*. Controls for creating, deleting, and managing site collections.
- *External Service Connections*. Settings for Records Center, HTML viewer, and Document Conversion.

Site Permissions

There are a number of permissions that site administrators may want to grant to certain users, as well as some that are reserved only for administrators. The User Permissions for the Web Applications page, accessed via the link in the Application Security section of the Application Management page, lists and allows you to enable or restrict which permissions site administrators can grant to users. These settings are not for particular users, but rather define what can be given or taken away from individual users by an administrator.

The permissions are divided into the following three groups:

- *List Permissions*. Permissions related to the control of adding, viewing, editing, and removing data.
- *Site Permissions*. Permissions related to which features and operations can be performed by site administrators. This includes their ability to manage permissions for other users, customizing pages, and viewing usage information.
- *Personal Permissions*. Permissions related to the default permissions. Users may have to manage Web parts and customize and rearrange views.

Authentication Settings

If your SharePoint site is delivering general content that should be openly available (either to the public or internally on an intranet), authentication may not be required, and you can stay with the default Anonymous access. If you are delivering specialized content on some pages of the site, or content to which access should be restricted to certain people or departments, you can configure Microsoft Windows SharePoint Services to require that users be authenticated before they can access content on your SharePoint site.

There are three types of authentication available:

- *Windows*. This uses the standard Windows authentication method. This is the recommended solution if the SharePoint site is only going to be accessed by users with local or domain accounts.
- *Forms*. Forms-based authentication requires users to provide a valid username and password to log on. This type of authentication is best used if Windows-based authentication is not practical; for example, if external business partners or Internet users need to access the site.
- *Web single sign on*. This allows users to authenticate against a Web service. This type of authentication simplifies things for users who must access numerous Web applications. Windows Server 2008 Active Directory Federation Services (ADFS) can provide these services.

To adjust Authentication settings click the Application Management tab and choose Authentication Providers under the Application Security category. Then click the zone name to reach the Edit Authentication Page as shown in Figure 8-23.

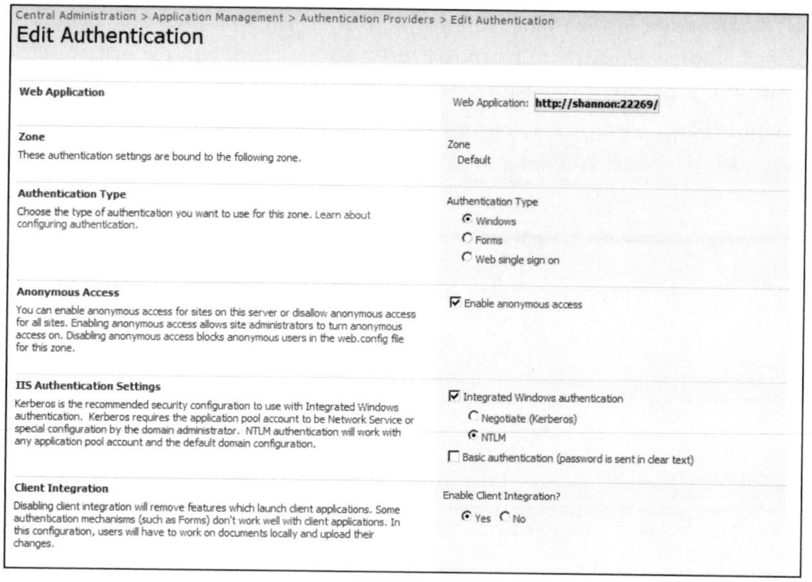

Figure 8-23 SharePoint Edit Authentication page
© Cengage Learning 2012

Backups

No computer system, disk drive, or array can be guaranteed to run forever, and sometimes outside forces come into play that shortens the time between failures. Worse, no one can predict when a catastrophe might happen. Since you can't stop systems or disks from occasionally crashing, you need to protect your SharePoint sites and data by backing them up.

Backups and restores can be configured and monitored by clicking the Operations tab and selecting the appropriate option from the Backup and Restore section.

To begin a backup:

1. Choose **Perform a backup** from the Backup and Restore section of the Operations tab. The first screen in the Perform a Backup process is displayed as shown in Figure 8-24.

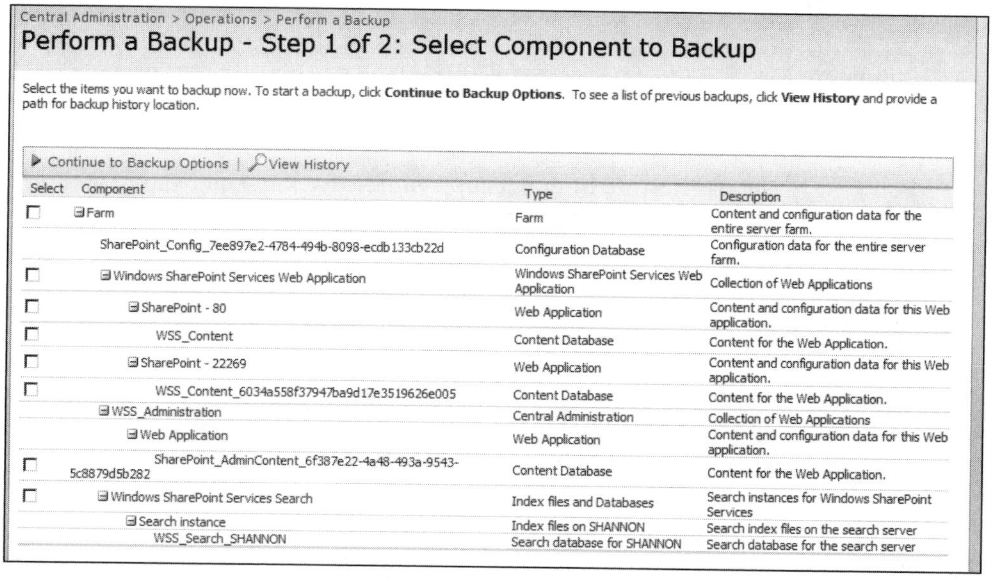

Figure 8-24 Perform a Backup Step 1 of 2
© Cengage Learning 2012

2. Choose the content you wish to include in the backup. The content is shown in hierarchical levels, starting from the most comprehensive (the entire server farm) down to individual Web applications and search instances.

3. Click **Continue to Backup Options** to continue to the Start Backup – Step 2 of 2 shown in Figure 8-25.

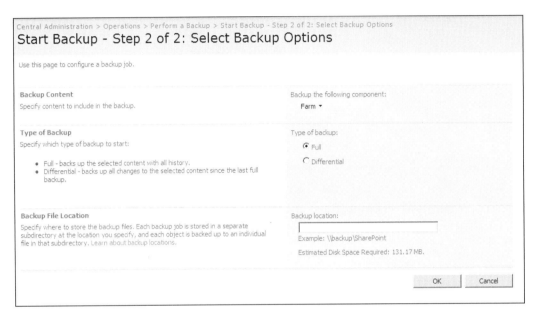

Figure 8-25 Start Backup Step 2 of 2

© Cengage Learning 2012

4. Select the type of backup, either **Full** or **Differential,** and specify the backup location. Click **OK** to start the backup.

Backups do not interrupt access to the site (by locking files for instance), but if the site is large, they can affect performance, so consider the time, the size of the site, and current system load before launching a backup.

To check the status of a backup choose **Backup and restore job status** from the Backup and Restore section of the Operations tab. The page will auto-refresh periodically to update the status.

To restore a backup:

1. Choose **Restore from Backup** from the Backup and Restore section of the Operations tab. The first screen in the Restore from a Backup process is displayed as shown in Figure 8-26.

Figure 8-26 Restore from Backup Step 1 of 4

© Cengage Learning 2012

2. Type in the location of the backup as it was entered when the original backup was performed. The restore will locate all of the subdirectories. Click **OK** to proceed to the next screen.

3. The Restore from Backup – Step 2 of 4 screen appears as in Figure 8-27. This screen lists the backups available in the location entered in step 2. Click the radio button on the line of the backup to restore.

Figure 8-27 Restore from Backup Step 2 of 4

© Cengage Learning 2012

4. Click **Continue Restore Process** to continue on to the Restore from Backup – Step 3 of 4 screen (Figure 8-28). Select the component(s) to restore. If this is not the backup set you wish to restore from, then click **Select a Different Backup Package**.

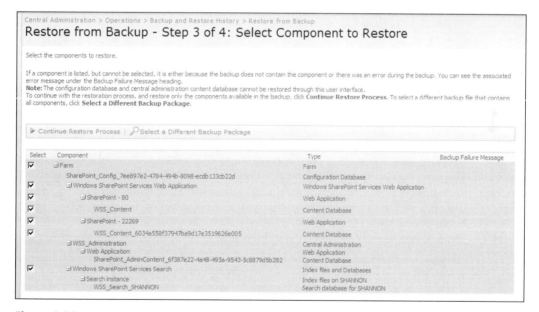

Figure 8-28 Restore from Backup Step 3 of 4

© Cengage Learning 2012

5. Click **Continue Restore Process** to continue on to the Restore from Backup – Step 4 of 4 screen (Figure 8-29). There are two restore options: **New configuration** and **Same configuration**. If you choose Same configuration, the selected content will be restored to the same set of folders it was saved from. Any changes made to the site since the backup being restored will be lost. This option is useful to restore a damaged site. The New configuration option restores the selected content to the locations specified in the New Names section. This is an easy way to clone a site, or to be able to compare files before copying them over to the original site and overwriting existing files.

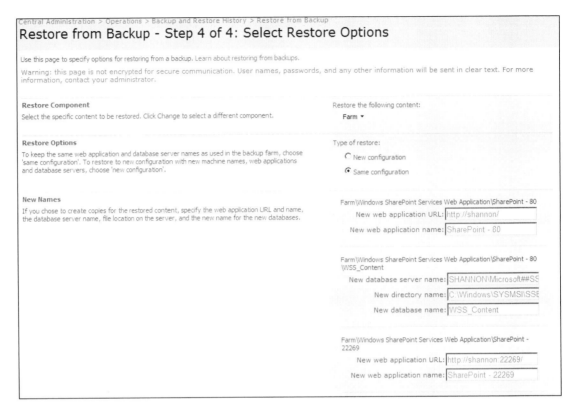

Figure 8-29 Restore from Backup Step 4 of 4
© Cengage Learning 2012

6. Click **OK** to begin the restore process.

7. Use the Backup and Restore Status page to monitor the restore process.

A history of backups and restores is available by clicking the **Backup and Restore History** choice in the Backup and Restore Status page. This page is similar to Figure 8-30. On this screen, you can click the option button on the line of a backup, and click **Continue Restore Process** to begin a restore.

Figure 8-30 Backup and Restore History
© Cengage Learning 2012

Antivirus Configuration

Viruses have become a fact of everyday life for a system administrator. The prevalence and variety of viruses makes the use of antivirus software a necessity rather than an option. Antivirus software should be installed on the (or each) Web server running Microsoft Windows SharePoint Services (WSS). WSS provides a way to centrally configure some antivirus settings.

To configure antivirus settings (antivirus software must be installed and running on the server or servers):

1. Choose **Antivirus** from the Security Configuration section of the Operations tab.

2. Select the settings you wish to enable. Your options are:
   - Scan documents on upload
   - Scan documents on download
   - Allow users to download infected documents
   - Attempt to clean infected documents

3. Type the time out value (in seconds) in the **Time out duration (in seconds)** text box. If you notice slower server response times during virus scanning, you can set this number lower.

4. Type the number of execution threads in the **Number of threads** text box. As with the time out value, if you notice slower server response times during virus scanning, you can set this number lower.

5. Click **OK**.

Service Accounts

There are five services added to the server when Microsoft Windows SharePoint Services (WSS) is installed, each using a default account to operate.

The services and the associated default accounts are shown in Table 8-1.

Table 8-1 WSS service names and accounts

Service Name	Default Account	Startup Type
Windows SharePoint Services Administration	Local System	Manual
Windows SharePoint Services Search	Local Service	Manual
Windows SharePoint Services Timer	Network Service	Automatic
Windows SharePoint Services Tracing	Local Service	Automatic
Windows SharePoint Services VSS Writer	Local System	Manual

Depending on the security policies of an organization there may be other accounts that should be used, or new specialized accounts may need to be created to properly run these services. These services can be changed from the services console of the server.

Configuring Windows SharePoint Services E-Mail Integration

E-mail often serves as one of the primary communication mediums in an organization. Microsoft Windows SharePoint Services (WSS) can use outgoing e-mail to send alerts, invitations, and administrator notifications. WSS can store incoming e-mail in lists to help organize it.

Outgoing E-mail

Outgoing e-mail requires an SMTP server to be available. This can be installed through the IIS server role, or you can use an existing SMTP server within your network that you have permission to send from. To configure outgoing e-mail:

1. Choose **Outgoing e-mail settings** from the Topology and Services section of the Operations tab.

2. Specify the following:
   - Outbound SMTP server
   - From Address
   - Reply-to address
   - Character set

3. Click **OK**.

Incoming E-mail

Incoming e-mail can be disabled or enabled for the server. Enabling incoming e-mail allows you to keep pertinent comments or information together with documents through e-mail. However, it can also allow spam messages in. To enable or disable and further configure incoming e-mail:

1. Choose **Incoming e-mail settings** from the Topology and Services section of the Operations tab.

2. Click one of the option buttons next to **Yes** or **No** under the heading Enable Sites on this server to receive e-mail? to enable or disable incoming e-mail.

3. Click one of the option buttons next to **Automatic** or **Advanced** under the heading Settings mode. All required settings are retrieved by the server when Automatic is selected, and e-mail is sent to the default mail drop folder. If you are not using the SMTP service to retrieve incoming e-mail, you must select Advanced mode, provide the e-mail drop folder, and ensure that the Windows SharePoint Services Timer has modify permissions on the e-mail drop folder.

4. WSS allows you to configure a connection to your organization's user directory through the SharePoint Directory Management Service. If this is applicable, type the appropriate information into the fields shown in Figure 8-31.

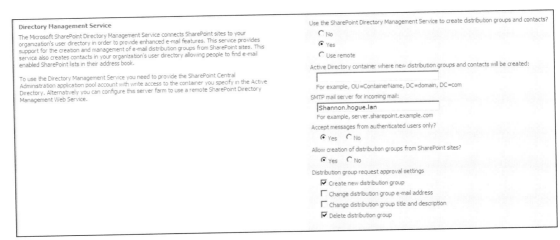

Figure 8-31 Directory Management Service connection configuration
© Cengage Learning 2012

5. Under the E-mail server display address heading, type the server address in the provided text box.

6. If you will accept e-mail from any e-mail server, click the option button next to **Accept mail from all e-mail servers**. To limit incoming e-mail to specific servers, click

the option button next to **Accept mail from these safe e-mail servers** and enter the allowable server addresses in the text area provided.

7. Click **OK**.

Configuring a Document Library to Receive E-Mail

Collaborating on documents is one part of an overall collaboration strategy. A powerful feature of Microsoft Windows SharePoint Services (WSS) is allowing a document library to receive e-mail. E-mailed suggestions, status updates, or supporting materials can be stored with the appropriate documents where they can be easily found.

To modify the settings, follow these general steps:

1. Go to the team site and open a particular document library.

2. Click Settings and under the Communications section click Incoming e-mail settings.

3. Allow incoming e-mail by clicking the option button next to Yes under the heading Allow this document library to receive e-mail?. There are several configuration options that can be adjusted as shown in Figure 8-32.

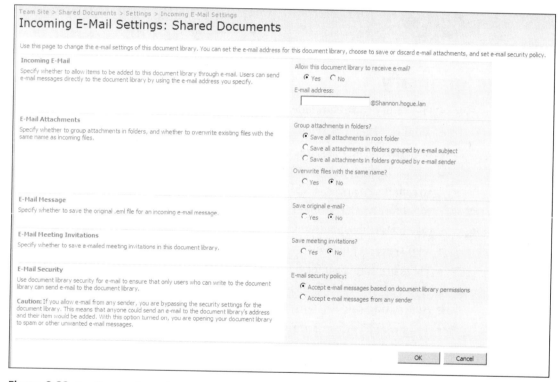

Figure 8-32 Configuring Incoming E-Mail Settings for a document library
© Cengage Learning 2012

Best Practices

1. When deciding on a protocol to use for streaming media, consider the HTTP protocol when data loss is unacceptable, but RTSP may be preferred for events streaming in real time.

2. When using the Web interface for Windows Media Services administration, protect the site with SSL to reduce the chance of unauthorized access.

3. Use an announcement file to have better control over how the content will be handled, and to make it easier to access content.

(continues)

(continued)

4. When there will be large numbers of consumers of static content, create caching servers to distribute the load.

5. When there will be large numbers of consumers of live content, create proxy servers to distribute the load.

6. Access the SharePoint Central Administration Web site via the Administrative Tools program group. This ensures access to all of the functionality of the site.

7. For SharePoint sites that will only be accessed by local Windows or Domain users, use Windows authentication.

8. Configure backups within SharePoint for all SharePoint sites.

9. Install antivirus software on all Web servers running Windows SharePoint Services.

10. Whenever possible, restrict incoming e-mail to certain senders or domains (or disable it entirely) on Windows SharePoint Services servers to minimize spam and virus-infected e-mails.

Chapter Summary

- The ability to stream video and audio to clients is an integral part of Web content today.

- Windows Media Services provides a way to effectively stream content to clients.

- Windows Media Services can be administered either locally or from the Web.

- Streaming media data is delivered through one of two data transfer protocols: Real Time Streaming Protocol (RTSP) or Hypertext Transfer Protocol (HTTP).

- Windows Media Services identifies the physical path on the server to the actual content through publishing points.

- Two types of publishing points are supported: on-demand, and broadcast.

- There are four content types that can make up a publishing point: Encoder, Playlist, One File, or Files in a directory.

- Advertising can be added via wrapper ads, which are a type of playlist.

- To improve performance and decrease server load, streaming media can be cached or delivered via a proxy.

- Content can be protected from unauthorized use or copying through the use of Active Directory Digital Rights Management Services (AD RMS).

- Rights are granted to users through rights policy templates.

- To effectively use AD RMS the content must be created and used by AD RMS-enabled applications.

- Windows SharePoint Services allows users to easily and effectively collaborate on content.

- Access can be limited to different pages in the SharePoint server by the use of Authentication.

- Some antivirus features can be configured through SharePoint.

- E-mail can be sent and received through SharePoint.

- E-mail can be sent directly to document libraries in SharePoint, making it easy to find e-mails related to documents.

Key Terms

broadcast Content streaming is controlled on the server side. Server has control of all aspects of playback.

caching server In relation to Media Services, a server that connects to the Media Services Server retrieves the content and streams it to multiple clients.

encoding The process where digital content is converted into an appropriate format for streaming.

Hypertext Transport Protocol (HTTP) Protocol used to transfer web pages or streaming media from the server to the client.

live streaming Streaming audio or video directly from an encoded source.

multicast A method of streaming that sends a single stream to a point that clients connect to and receive the content. Publishing point can only be broadcast.

on-demand Content streaming controlled on the client side. The client has control of all aspects of playback (rewind, fast forward, etc.).

playlist A list of content to be streamed.

proxy server In relation to Media Services, a server that connects to the Media Services Server, retrieves a broadcast stream, and streams it to multiple clients.

publishing point The object Windows Media Services uses to identify the physical path and other characteristics of content to be streamed.

Real Time Streaming Protocol (RTSP) Protocol used to transfer streaming media from the server to the client. Best for live streaming.

rights account certificates (RACs) are used by AD RMS to identify trusted users and groups that can generate rights-protected content.

rights policy template Where access permissions and file expirations are designated for particular media controlled by AD RMS.

server cluster In relation to AD RMS, a group of servers administering rights policies.

streaming Serving audio and video directly to a player versus requiring the content to be completely downloaded first.

unicast A method of streaming where each client connects and has its own dedicated stream of content. Publishing point can be on-demand or broadcast.

Web parts Predefined SharePoint components or modules.

Review Questions

1. What are the three roles under the Streaming Media Services role?
   a. Windows Media Server, Web-based Administration, and Logging Agent
   b. Windows Media Server, Web-based Administration, and Logging Analysis
   c. Windows Media Console, Web-based Administration, and Logging Agent
   d. Windows Media Server, Remote Administration, and Logging Agent

2. Streaming media is delivered through one of two data transfer protocols:
   a. HTTP and FTP
   b. HTTP and RTSP
   c. HTTP and SSL
   d. HTTP and SMTP

3. Publishing points _____ .

    a. determine the protocol the media will be streamed through

    b. identify the server the media is being streamed to

    c. are raw content

    d. identify the physical path to the actual content

4. On-demand publishing points _____ .

    a. allow the user to control the playback of the content

    b. are constantly streaming, when the user connects they start at the point the source is currently streaming

    c. are excellent for live presentation content

    d. none of the above

5. Broadcast publishing points _____ .

    a. allow the user to control the playback of the content

    b. are constantly streaming, when the user connects they start at the point the source is currently streaming

    c. are excellent for static pre-recorded content

    d. none of the above

6. The Files in a directory content type can pick up and stream _____ .

    a. playlists

    b. individual media files

    c. a and b

    d. only specialized playlists pointing to specific types of media

7. The Encoder content type is for _____ .

    a. live stream broadcasts

    b. playlists of media

    c. standard media files

    d. none of the above

8. What is the extension of an announcement file?

    a. .asx

    b. .ann

    c. .anf

    d. .anc

9. Announcement files contain _____ .

    a. metadata about the content (e.g., author)

    b. the URL of the content

    c. a and b

    d. a and b and pointers to .NET applications to control playback

10. To include advertising in a stream you _____ .

    a. create a standard playlist and stick advertising media in it

    b. add the advertising to your media files

    c. create a Wrapper Ad playlist

    d. add the advertising to the media content directory with a special name – it will be picked up automatically

11. Advertisements play _____.
    a. when the content is accessed
    b. when the user requests it
    c. only at the end of the content
    d. only at the beginning of the content

12. A caching server _____.
    a. picks up the content from the primary server based on a configurable timer setting and streams it to clients
    b. is sent parts of the content depending on length and streams the part it has to clients based on signals from the primary server
    c. collects requests for the content, and sends a request to the primary server when enough requests have been received
    d. copies content from the primary server, stores it locally and serves the media directly to clients

13. A proxy server _____.
    a. works with live streams
    b. connects to the origin and streams the content to the client when it receives a request
    c. can split streams between multiple clients while maintaining a single connection to the origin server
    d. all of the above

14. To avoid exposing the Media Services Server to the Internet you can _____ .
    a. put in multiple firewalls
    b. use the Proxy Redirect
    c. use the Reverse Proxy
    d. none of the above

15. AD RMS is an acronym for _____ .
    a. Active Directory Digital Rights Management Services
    b. Active Directory Rights Management System
    c. Active Directory Rights Manufacturing System
    d. Active Directory Digital Rights Markup Services

16. Using AD RMS you can exclude _____ .
    a. certain users and applications from accessing content
    b. certain domains from accessing content
    c. certain IP addresses from accessing content
    d. There are no exclusion rules

17. Super Users are granted what kind of license in AD RMS?
    a. There is no such thing as a Super User
    b. Editor
    c. Administrator
    d. Owner

18. The three types of authentication available in SharePoint Services are _____ .

    a. Basic, Windows, and Forms

    b. Web Single Sign On, Basic, and Windows

    c. Web Single Sign On, Forms, and Windows

    d. Windows, IIS users, Forms

19. Windows Authentication is best for _____ .

    a. general internet users

    b. when SharePoint will be accessed only by users with local or domain accounts

    c. it should never be used

    d. only the home page

20. To handle e-mail SharePoint requires _____ .

    a. enabling the internal SharePoint SMTP server

    b. an outside e-mail provider such as Hotmail

    c. an SMTP server accessible within your network

    d. SharePoint does not handle e-mail

Case Projects

Case Project 8-1: Streaming Media Content

You are the administrator for the Web server at Your Company Inc. You have been asked to set up a test media server that will stream both video and audio to clients. Outline creating the announcement files and how to set up the content, as well as what must be done to handle the types of content that will be streamed. Content includes a live streaming webinar, a set of static audio files that play as a group, and a replay of a past webinar. There will be ads that need to play at the beginning and the end of the list of static audio files.

Case Project 8-2: Windows Media Rights Manager (WMRM)

A business consultant has come up with a highly specialized methodology for a business to significantly increase their sales and profits. They have a very specific market they are aiming at, and the market is willing to accept some inconvenience accessing the content knowing how valuable it is. Most of the users of the content would be in the continental United States. The content is both audio and video. Reviewing the five-step process outlined in this chapter (Packaging, Distribution, Establishing a license server, License acquisition, Playing the media file), outline the considerations and choices you would make (and have the content provider do) to minimize unauthorized access and duplication of the content.

Case Project 8-3: Configuring SharePoint Services

You have been asked to configure a SharePoint server to allow only internal users who are members of the domain to access the default site. Both outgoing and incoming mail is allowed. Incoming mail is specifically for a certain document library called Corporate and it should be restricted to only users within the domain. Outline the steps required to answer the needs of this scenario.

Configuring Windows Server 2008 Hyper-V Virtualization

After reading this chapter and completing the exercises, you will be able to:

- Define common terms associated with virtualization
- Describe the role virtualization plays in the datacenter
- Install and use the Hyper-V server role
- Create and work with Hyper-V virtual machines
- Configure virtual networks
- Work with virtual hard disks
- Manage and configure virtual machines

OS virtualization has become a mainstream technology in both small and large networks. When considering whether to use virtualization in an IT datacenter, most IT managers look for a return on their investment in real money or in productivity gains. Hyper-V can deliver both.

Server virtualization can be used to achieve a variety of goals including server consolidation, application isolation, convenient testing of application installations and upgrades, and more. Because virtualization provides an ideal environment for installing, testing, and isolating network applications, the Hyper-V role is likely to be a part of most Server 2008 application scenarios.

This chapter focuses on how you can use the Windows Server 2008 Hyper-V role for your virtualization platform. We'll discuss how virtualization functions in the IT datacenter, requirements for installing Hyper-V, initial installation and configuration of the Hyper-V role, creating virtual machines, managing virtual hard disks and virtual networks, and virtual machine management and optimization.

A Virtualization Primer

Virtualization is a process that creates a software environment to emulate a computer's hardware and BIOS, allowing multiple OSs to run on the same physical computer at the same time. On Windows Server 2008, this environment is created by the Hyper-V server role. Like all technologies, virtualization has a collection of terms that define its operation and components:

- A **virtual machine (VM)** is the virtual environment that emulates a physical computer's hardware and BIOS. You create VMs with the Hyper-V management console.

- A **guest OS** is an operating system installed in a VM. Once a VM is created in Hyper-V, a guest OS can be installed in it the same way you would install any operating system on a physical computer. Hyper-V supports an expansive variety of guest OSs, discussed later under Creating Virtual Machines in Hyper-V.

- A **host computer** and **host operating system** are the physical computer and the originally installed operating system (if applicable) on which VM software is installed and VMs run.

- Virtualization software is the software for creating and managing VMs and creating the virtual environment in which a guest OS is installed.

- The **hypervisor** is the virtualization software component that creates and monitors the virtual hardware environment, which allows multiple VMs to share physical hardware resources. The hypervisor on a host computer acts in some ways like an OS kernel, but instead of scheduling processes for access to the CPU and other devices, it schedules VMs.

  o A type 1 hypervisor implements OS virtualization by running directly on the host computer's hardware and controls and monitors guest OSs. It bypasses the need to have a host operating system installed. Instead, it controls access to the host's hardware and provides device drivers for guest OSs. Also called **bare-metal virtualization**, it's used primarily for server virtualization in datacenters. Examples include VMWare Player and Workstation, Microsoft Virtual PC, and Oracle Virtualbox.

  o A type 2 hypervisor implements OS virtualization by being installed in a general-purpose host operating system, such as Windows 7 or Linux, and the host OS accesses host hardware on behalf of the guest OS. Also called **hosted virtualization**, it's used primarily for desktop virtualization solutions.

In some software, such as Xen and Microsoft Virtual Server, the hypervisor component is called the Virtual Machine Monitor (VMM).

- A **virtual disk** consists of files residing on the host computer that represent a virtual machine's hard drive.

- A **virtual network** is a network configuration created internally by virtualization software and used by virtual machines for physical and virtual network communication.

- A **snapshot** is a partial copy of a VM made at a particular moment; it contains changes made since the VM was created and can be used to restore the VM to its state when the snapshot was taken.

As a type 1 hypervisor, the Hyper-V virtualization environment sits between the hardware and the virtual machines. Each virtual machine is referred to as a child partition on the system while Windows Server 2008 with Hyper-V installed is referred to as the parent or management partition. The Hyper-V management console runs on Windows Server 2008 in the parent partition and provides an interface to manage the VMs running in the child partitions. Figure 9-1 illustrates these concepts of the Hyper-V architecture.

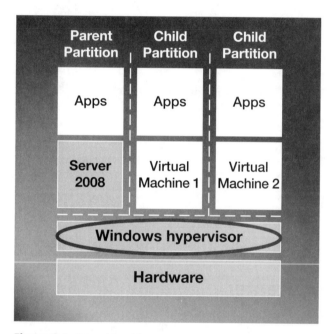

Figure 9-1 Hyper-V architecture
© Cengage Learning 2012

Hyper-V can be installed directly on a server without the Windows Server 2008 OS. Hyper-V is then managed by another server running Windows Server 2008.

Figure 9-2 shows the Hyper-V management console with four VMs; three of which are currently running. Referring to Figure 9-1, the Hyper-V management console running in Windows Server 2008 is the parent partition and each of the three running VMs are separate child partitions. Notice in the bottom of the middle pane of Figure 9-2, you see a thumbnail of the currently selected VM, named w2k8vm-01. The thumbnail shows the screen that VM is currently displaying. You can double-click the thumbnail to connect to the VM and operate the OS as if it were installed on a physical computer.

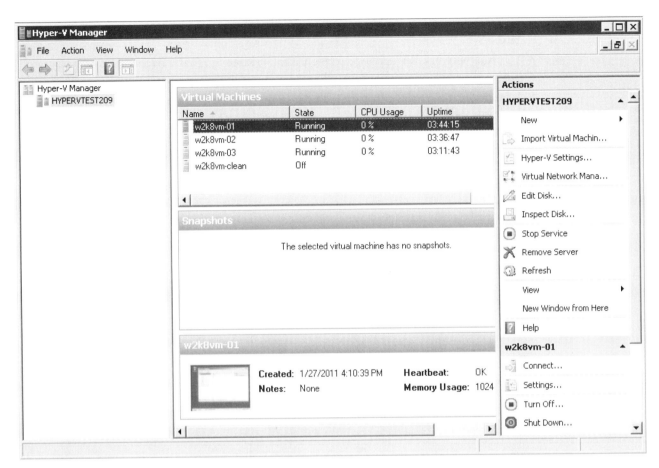

Figure 9-2 Hyper-V management console
© Cengage Learning 2012

Virtualization in the IT Datacenter

Type 1 hypervisors like Hyper-V are targeted mainly for production virtualization in datacenters. Virtualization comes with a fairly high price tag for the virtualization software, the hardware to run it on, or both. In addition, network administrators must be trained to use the virtualization software and manage the virtual machines. As mentioned earlier, IT managers are looking for a return on their investment. The following applications for type 1 hypervisors are just some of the ways that virtualization is being used in today's datacenters:

- *Consolidation of servers.* Server consolidation is probably the original reason for virtualizing servers in the datacenter and is done for the following reasons and benefits:
  - Retirement of old or unreliable hardware: Converting physical machines to VMs and running them on the latest hardware means you can get rid of old hardware, thereby gaining a reliability advantage and avoiding the tedious task of reinstalling and reconfiguring a server OS on new hardware. You might also improve performance.
  - Making optimal use of multicore, high-performance hardware: Some server roles, such as Active Directory, should be the only major network service running on a server. With multicore server CPUs, you're likely to waste a lot of the server's power if you install a single-role OS. Instead, you can run two, three, or more VMs on the same physical server, making optimal use of the available performance.
  - Maintain application separation: Some applications and services run best when they're the only major application installed on an OS. You avoid OS resource conflicts and gain stability and reliability.

     ○ Reclaim rack or floor space: By consolidating a dozen physical servers into three or four host servers, you're no longer tripping over a plethora of towers or wondering whether your rack can handle one more server.

     ○ Reduce cooling and power requirements: In most cases, by reducing the number of servers (even with higher performance machines), you save money on cooling and powering a datacenter, especially when you reduce hundreds of servers down to dozens of hosts.

- *Server Core installations.* The Windows Server 2008 Server Core installation option makes an ideal VM choice because of Server Core's relatively small footprint and fewer resource requirements. Read-only domain controllers are also good candidates for virtualization.

- *Test installations and upgrades.* Before you install a major software package or upgrade on your server, you can create a copy of the VM and go through a test run to iron out any potential problems or conflicts. If something still goes wrong on the production VM, you can revert to a snapshot.

- *Test a preconfigured application.* Not sure if the application the vendor is trying to sell you is right for your company? Some vendors offer virtual appliances that you can use to evaluate the application without the trouble of installing it.

- *Test what-if scenarios.* You can create a virtual network and run clones of your production VMs to test ideas for improving your network's performance, functionality, and reliability. This type of testing on production systems is never a good idea.

- *Live migration.* Because they are physically nothing more than data files, virtual machines can be migrated to new hardware while they're running, in a process called **live migration**. Live migration brings performance or reliability improvements with practically no downtime.

- *Dynamic provisioning.* Advanced VM management systems can deploy VMs and storage dynamically to meet application requirements. This advanced feature has uses in clustered computing (discussed in Chapter 10) and in cloud computing.

The list of possible applications for virtualization in a datacenter is too extensive to mention all of them, and new ones are cropping up all the time. Suffice to say that if you work in an IT department, virtualization is almost certain to be a part of the strategy.

Hyper-V Installation

Hyper-V is a server role that is installed like any server role in Windows Server 2008, using the Add Roles wizard in Server Manager. However, unlike some of the other roles you can install, to install and use Hyper-V your system must meet a few prerequisites:

- You must be running a 64-bit version of Windows Server 2008 Standard, Enterprise, or Datacenter Edition.

- The CPU must support virtualization extensions, such as AMD-V and Intel-VT.

- You must have free disk space at least equal to the minimum requirement for the OS you're going to install as a virtual machine. Remember, the guest OS virtual disk is a collection of files that reside on the host server's physical hard disk and the amount of space required by a guest OS is no different than the space required of an OS that is installed on physical hardware.

- The amount of RAM must be at least equal to the minimum amount required for Windows Server 2008 plus the minimum amount required for the OS you're installing. For example, the minimum amount of RAM required by Windows Server 2008 is 512 MB. If you plan to install a Windows Server 2008 guest OS, you will need another 512 MB for the guest, for a total of 1 GB. For all practical purposes though, 2 to 4 GB of RAM should be considered the minimum amount on a Hyper-V host machine.

After you have an adequately configured system running a 64-bit version of Windows Server 2008, you can install the Hyper-V role. Keep in mind that you can't install Hyper-V on Windows Server 2008 that is itself running as a virtual machine.

 The original release of Windows Server 2008 shipped with a beta version of Hyper-V. The Windows Server 2008 host OS should have at least Service Pack 1 installed, which contains the released version of Hyper-V.

Hyper-V Licensing Considerations

When you install a guest OS on a virtual machine, you must have a proper license for the guest OS. Windows Server 2008 with Hyper-V gets you started by including licenses for **virtual instances** of Windows Server 2008 with the Standard, Enterprise, and Datacenter editions:

- Standard edition includes one license for a virtual instance of Windows Server 2008, which means you can install Windows Server 2008 as a guest OS in a single VM without having to purchase an additional Windows Server 2008 license key.

- Enterprise edition includes licenses for four virtual instances of Windows Server 2008.

- Datacenter edition includes licenses for unlimited virtual instances of Windows Server 2008.

Now, it's time to install the Hyper-V role so you can begin creating and working with virtual machines.

 ## Activity 9-1: Install the Hyper-V Role on Windows Server 2008

 You must have a 64-bit version of Windows Server 2008 installed on a host computer that supports virtualization extensions to complete the activities in this chapter. In some cases the hardware virtualization extensions must be enabled in the computer's BIOS setup routine. Some activities require two VMs to run simultaneously. You must have at least 2 GB of RAM on your host computer to accommodate this. Hyper-V cannot be installed on a virtual machine.

Time Required: 15 minutes
Objective: Install the Hyper-V server role

Description: You want to install a new application on your Windows Server 2008 system. You have read about the benefits of virtualization and believe that this new application is a good candidate to install on a virtual machine, but first you need to install the Hyper-V server role.

 The instructions and screenshots used in the activities in this chapter use the released version of Hyper-V which is part of Windows Server 2008 Service Pack 1 or higher.

1. Log on to your Windows Server 2008 computer as Administrator, if necessary. If Server Manager doesn't start, click the server icon in the Quick Launch toolbar.

2. In the left pane of Server Manager, click **Roles**.

3. Click **Add Roles** in the Roles Summary pane on the right. In the Before You Begin window, review the information, and then click **Next**.

4. In the Select Server Roles window, click to select the **Hyper-V** check box, and then click **Next**. If you see a message stating that Hyper-V can't be installed, you don't have a compatible processor, or the virtualization technology isn't enabled in the BIOS, and you will have to stop the installation at this point and resolve the indicated problems (if possible).

5. The next window displays information about Hyper-V, including an overview, prerequisites, and information on configuring Hyper-V and virtual machines. Read this information, and then click **Next**.

6. In the Create Virtual Networks window, click to select the check box next to the name of your network adapter, and then click **Next**. This connects the host computer NIC to a new virtual network. You learn more about virtual networks later in the Hyper-V Virtual Networks section.

7. Now you're ready to install Hyper-V. Click the **Install** button. After a few minutes, if the installation is successful, you get a message stating that you must restart the server to complete the installation. Click the **Close** button, and then click **Yes** to restart your server.

8. When your machine has finished restarting, log on, and the Hyper-V installation finishes (you may have to wait a few moments before Server Manager and the Resume Configuration wizard screens appear). Click **Close** in the Installation Results window.

9. In Server Manager's left pane, click **Roles**. Under Roles Summary on the right, Hyper-V is listed.

10. Close all open windows.

Creating Virtual Machines in Hyper-V

With Hyper-V installed, a new MMC called Hyper-V Manager is added to your Administrative Tools folder. You use Hyper-V Manager to create and manage virtual machines. The first time you run Hyper-V Manager, you may have to accept the end user license agreement. After you accept the EULA, the Hyper-V Manager console shown earlier in Figure 9-2 is displayed. To begin using Hyper-V, click the name of your server in the left pane.

To use virtualization, you must first create a virtual machine. In Hyper-V Manager, all the tasks related to virtual machine creation and management are listed in the right pane under Actions. The process of creating a VM involves just a few general steps:

1. Start the New Virtual Machine wizard from Hyper-V Manager.

2. Give the new VM a descriptive name, such as "Read Only Domain Controller 1."

3. Choose a location for the VM. Storing virtual machines on a hard drive that's separate from your Windows Server 2008 installation is usually best. In datacenter applications, VMs are frequently stored on SANs to provide enhanced reliability and management. By doing so, if a host server goes down or is taken out of service for maintenance, another Hyper-V host can easily be assigned to run its VMs without having to physically move VM files.

4. Assign the amount of memory this VM requires. Memory requirements for virtual machines are the same as the requirements for installing the OS on a physical computer.

5. Configure networking. You have the choice of connecting through one of the host network adapters, creating a private network, an internal network, or leaving the VM disconnected from a network. This option can be changed later.

6. Create a virtual hard disk. You can give the virtual disk a name or accept the default, and you can choose the virtual disk's size and location. Putting virtual disk files on a drive separate from your Windows Server 2008 host's boot drive provides the best performance. You also have the option to use an existing virtual hard disk or attach a hard disk later.

7. Install an OS. In this step, you can choose to install an OS from media inserted in the physical CD/DVD drive of the host machine, a CD/DVD image file (an .iso file), a boot floppy disk image, or the network using PXE boot. You can also choose to install an OS later.

Activity 9-2: Create a Virtual Machine

Time Required: 10 minutes
Objective: Create a new virtual machine

Description: You have installed the Hyper-V role on your server and are ready to create a virtual machine. You have the installation DVD for Windows Server 2008.

1. Log on to your server as Administrator, if necessary.

2. Click **Start**, point to **Administrative Tools**, and click **Hyper-V Manager**.

3. If necessary, click your server name in the left pane of Hyper-V Manager. In the Actions pane, click **New**, and click **Virtual Machine**.

4. Read the information in the Before You Begin window. Note that you can create a default virtual machine simply by clicking Finish in this window. For this activity, click **Next**.

5. In the Name text box, type **VMTest**. You can select the default location or a different location for your virtual machine. To use the default location of C:\ProgramData\ Microsoft\Windows\Hyper-V, just click **Next**.

6. In the Assign Memory window, verify that the value in the Memory text box is **512 MB** (the minimum requirement for Windows Server 2008), and then click **Next**.

7. In the Configure Networking window, click the **Connection** list arrow, and click your network connection in the drop-down list. This action connects your VM to the physical NIC on your host computer.

8. In the Connect Virtual Hard Disk window, you can enter the virtual hard disk's name, size, and location. By default, Hyper-V names the hard drive the same as the VM with the extension of .vhd. You can also use an existing virtual disk or attach one later. Write down the location where Hyper-V stores the virtual hard disk by default in case you want to access the virtual disk later. Click **Next** to accept the default settings.

_____

9. In the Installation Options window, click the **Install an operating system from a boot CD/DVD-ROM** option button. This option causes your VM to boot from an installation DVD inserted into the host machines DVD drive. You can also choose to boot the VM from an image file (.iso) of the installation DVD. Check with your instructor whether you should use the physical DVD drive or an image file. Click **Next**.

10. The Completing the New Virtual Machine Wizard window displays a summary of your virtual machine configuration. Note that you can select to have the VM start after the wizard is finished. For now, click **Finish**. After the virtual machine is created, you're returned to Hyper-V Manager.

11. Close all open windows, or leave Hyper-V Manager open if you're going on to the next activity.

Activity 9-3: Install Windows Server 2008 on a Virtual Machine

Time Required: 30 to 60 minutes, depending on your server's speed
Objective: Install Windows Server 2008 Enterprise Edition on your new virtual machine

Description: You have created a new virtual machine and are ready to install Windows Server 2008. You have the installation DVD for Windows Server 2008.

 This activity covers only the initial steps to get the installation started. The actual installation on a virtual machine is identical to installing Windows Server 2008 on a physical server.

1. Log on to your server as Administrator, if necessary.

2. Insert your Windows Server 2008 installation DVD. (If Autorun is enabled on your DVD drive, the Windows Server 2008 Setup program runs. If it does, exit it.)

3. If necessary, click **Start**, point to **Administrative Tools**, and click **Hyper-V Manager**.

4. In the center pane, right-click the virtual machine you created in Activity 9-2 and click **Connect**. You see a window similar to the one shown in Figure 9-3.

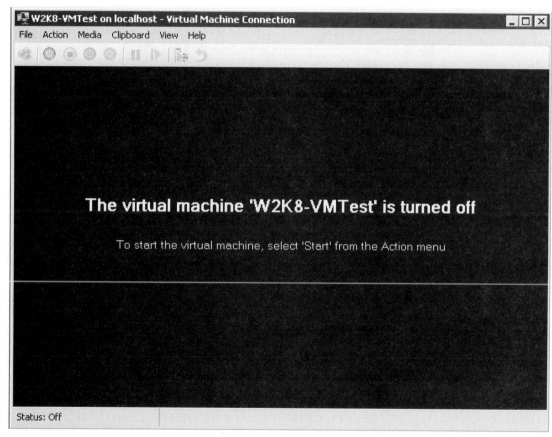

Figure 9-3 A virtual machine before it's started
© Cengage Learning 2012

5. The virtual machine isn't started yet, so click **Action, Start** from the menu. (You can also start the VM by clicking the blue Start icon on the toolbar.)

6. From this point, the installation is identical to the Windows Server 2008 installation steps in Chapter 1, Activity 1-1, until you need to press Ctrl-Alt-Delete to log on. For a Hyper-V virtual machine, you use Ctrl-Alt-End instead. You can also click the Ctrl-Alt-Delete icon on the toolbar or click Action, Ctrl-Alt-Delete from the menu, and Hyper-V sends the keystroke combination to the virtual machine.

7. After you're logged on to the VM, shut it down by clicking **Start, Shutdown**.

8. Close all open windows.

Basic Virtual Machine Management with Hyper-V Manager

With Hyper-V, a virtual machine runs in the background until you connect to it with Hyper-V Manager. A running VM doesn't require using Hyper-V Manager, nor does it require anybody to be logged on to the server. Furthermore, you can configure a VM to start and shut down automatically when the host server starts and shuts down. In addition, like any OS, you can manage a VM remotely by using tools such as Remote Desktop and MMCs if the VM is configured to communicate with the host network.

When you want to configure and manage a VM's properties or access it locally, you do need to run Hyper-V Manager. The middle pane of Hyper-V Manager shows all installed virtual machines at the top; in Figure 9-4, one VM is running and the others are powered off. This pane also displays name, state, CPU usage, uptime, and current operations for each VM. Normally, the Operations column doesn't display anything unless you perform a task such as exporting a VM or creating a snapshot of it. When you select a VM, the Snapshots section shows a list of snapshots created for it. If you click the VM's name in the Snapshots section, you see a screen shot of the VM at the time the snapshot was taken along with the time and date it was taken. The bottom section shows a real-time screen shot of a running VM. When a running VM's screen changes, the screen shot in Hyper-V Manager reflects the change almost immediately.

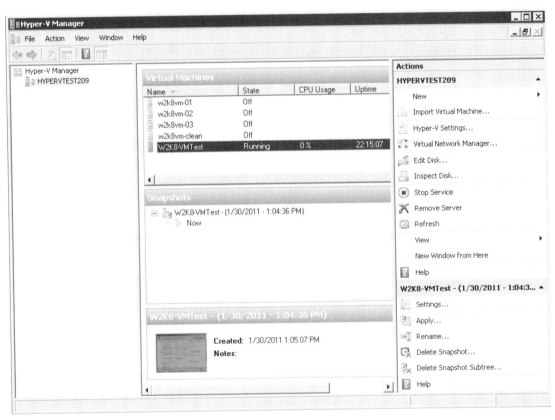

Figure 9-4 Hyper-V Manager showing five virtual machines
© Cengage Learning 2012

Connecting to a virtual machine opens a window that serves as the user interface to the VM and looks similar to a remote desktop connection. You can connect to a VM by using any of the following methods:

- Right-click the VM and click Connect.
- Double-click the VM.
- Select the VM and double-click its screen shot in the bottom section.
- Select the VM and click Connect in the Actions pane.

After you're connected, you see the Virtual Machine Connection console shown in Figure 9-5. The toolbar icons from left to right are as follows:

- Ctrl-Alt-Delete (sends a Ctrl-Alt-Delete keystroke to the VM)
- Start (starts the VM)
- Turn Off (turns off the VM)
- Shut Down (sends a signal to the OS to perform a shutdown)
- Save (saves the VM's state, similar to Windows hibernation mode)
- Pause (pauses the VM, similar to Windows sleep mode)
- Reset (resets the VM)
- Snapshot (creates a snapshot of a VM)
- Revert (reverts to a snapshot of a VM)

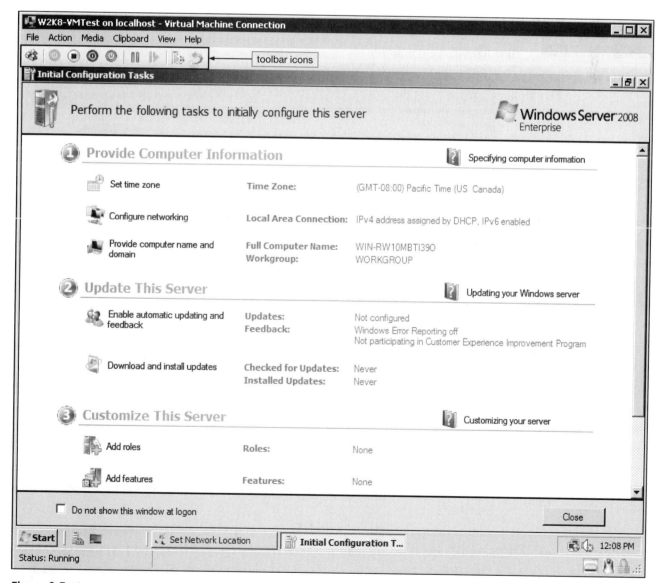

Figure 9-5 The Virtual Machine Connection console

© Cengage Learning 2012

You can access all these toolbar operations from the Action menu, too. The following list summarizes some tasks you can perform with other menus:

- *File.* Access the VM's settings and exit the VM.
- *Media.* Specify a CD/DVD drive the VM should connect to, specify an .iso file the VM mounts as a virtual CD/DVD drive, or specify a floppy disk image that can be mounted as a virtual floppy disk.
- *Clipboard.* Copy a screen shot of the VM to the Clipboard or paste Clipboard text into the VM. You can also copy and paste between the host computer and virtual machines or between virtual machines.
- *View.* Toggle the display of the toolbar and switch to full-screen mode.

If you want to disconnect from a virtual machine, thereby closing the connection console but not shutting down the VM, simply click File, Exit from the menu or close the window.

Activity 9-4: Work with Virtual Machines in Hyper-V Manager

Time Required: 30 minutes
Objective: Explore Hyper-V Manager

Description: You have installed a test VM that you can use to become familiar with managing virtual machines in Windows Server 2008.

1. Log on to your host server as Administrator, if necessary.
2. Click **Start**, point to **Administrative Tools**, and click **Hyper-V Manager**.
3. Right-click the virtual machine you created in Activity 9-2 and click **Connect**.
4. If the VM was powered down, power it on by clicking the **Start** toolbar icon in the connection console or clicking **Action, Start** from the menu. Go immediately to the next step.
5. While Windows is booting, close the connection console by clicking the **X** at the upper right or clicking **File, Exit** from the menu. Notice that in Hyper-V Manager, the VM's CPU usage changes as Windows boots, and the VM's screen shot in the bottom pane changes periodically.
6. Double-click the VM's screen shot at the bottom of Hyper-V Manager to open the connection console to your VM.
7. After Windows finishes booting, click the **Ctrl-Alt-Delete** toolbar icon (the icon that looks like three keyboard keys at the far left) to send a Ctrl-Alt-Delete keystroke to the VM.

 To see a description of any toolbar icon, hover your mouse pointer over it.

8. In the logon window, enter the password you created for the Administrator account and log on.
9. Close any open windows in the VM until only the desktop is displayed.
10. Click **Start**, type **notepad** in the Start Search text box, and press **Enter** to start Notepad.
11. Type your name in a new text document, and then click the **Save** toolbar icon or click **Action, Save** from the menu.

12. Close the virtual machine console. In Hyper-V Manager, note that the State column for the VM shows Saved. Open the VM by double-clicking it. Start the VM by clicking the **Start** toolbar icon, which takes you right where you left off in Notepad.

13. Save the Notepad file to your desktop by clicking **File, Save As** from the menu. In the Save As dialog box, click the **Browse Folders** button. Click **Desktop** under Favorite Links, type **File1.txt** in the File Name text box, and then click **Save**. Exit Notepad.

14. Click the **Snapshot** toolbar icon or click **Action, Snapshot** from the menu. When you're prompted to enter a name, type **BeforeDeletingFile1**, and then click **Yes**.

15. Minimize your VM, and note that the snapshot is listed in Hyper-V Manager in the Snapshots section. Maximize your VM, and delete the Notepad file you created. Empty the Recycle Bin so you know the file is really gone.

16. Click the **Revert** toolbar icon or click **Action, Revert** from the menu.

17. Click **Revert** when prompted. The VM displays a message that it's restoring. When the desktop is displayed again, you should see the Notepad file back on the desktop. Close the virtual machine console.

18. In Hyper-V Manager, right-click the VM and click **Shutdown**. When prompted, click the **Shutdown** button. The Operations column displays "Shutting Down Virtual Machine."

19. Close Hyper-V Manager.

Advanced VM Creation

Virtual machines can be created using other methods besides the New Virtual Machine wizard. Other methods include:

- Importing an exported VM
- Copying the virtual disk
- Converting a physical machine to a virtual machine

Importing an Exported VM

Virtual machines can be exported and then imported again to create one or more new virtual machines. To export a VM, the VM must be turned off. Once exported, the VM can be imported on another server running Hyper-V or on the same server after renaming the original VM. When you choose the Export option for a VM, you are prompted to enter a path where you want the exported VM stored. If you only want the VM configuration exported, you can choose that option and the content of the VM's hard drive is not exported.

Exporting a VM does not change the original VM in any way. You can continue to use the original VM as always.

Activity 9-5: Export and Import a VM

Time Required: 30 minutes
Objective: Export the W2k8-VMTest VM you created earlier and import it

Description: You want to have two VMs with which to work, so you make a copy of a VM. You make the copy by exporting your current VM, renaming it, and then importing it as a new VM.

1. Log on to your host server as Administrator, if necessary.

2. Click **Start**, point to **Administrative Tools**, and click **Hyper-V Manager**.

3. Click to select **VMTest** that you created earlier. In the Actions pane, under VMTest, click **Export**. In the Export Virtual Machine dialog, click **Browse** to select the Export Path.

4. In the Select Folder screen, click **New Folder** and name it **VMExport**. Click **Select Folder**.

5. In the Export Virtual Machine dialog, notice the checkbox labeled "Export only the virtual machine configuration." If you check that box, the VMs hard drive data is not exported so leave it unchecked. Click **Export**.

6. In Hyper-V Manager, notice in the Operations column, you see the word Exporting and the percentage completed. Wait until the export operation completes before continuing to the next step.

7. Right-click **VMTest** and click **Rename**. Type **VMTest1** for the new name.

8. Click **Import Virtual Machine** in the Actions pane. Click **Browse**. Double-click **VMExport** and then click **VMTest**. Click **Select Folder**.

9. If you were performing an export to move this VM to a new machine (rather than copying it), you would probably want to select the *Reuse old virtual machine IDs* option (see Figure 9-6), but since this VM is being imported as a new instance to the same machine the original VM is on, leave that option unchecked. Note the warning at the bottom of the dialog box that states that the folder cannot be imported again. If you wanted to import this VM more than once, you would have to copy the folder before each import. Click **Import**.

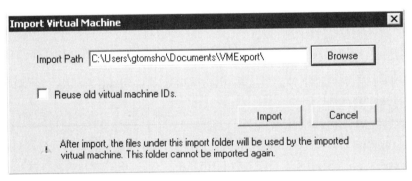

Figure 9-6 Importing a VM
© Cengage Learning 2012

10. Once the import is complete, another VM named VMTest will be listed in Hyper-V Manager. Rename the new VM to **VMTest2**.

11. Close Hyper-V Manager.

Copying a Virtual Disk

Copying a virtual disk doesn't actually create a new VM, but it avoids having to install a guest OS on a newly created VM. The result is not much different than an export/import operation but the procedure is different. The steps are as follows:

1. Copy the virtual hard disk from an existing VM to a new folder or rename the copied file and you can leave it in the same folder as the original virtual disk. Hyper-V virtual hard disks have an extension of .vhd and are usually placed in the location you select when you create a new virtual hard disk in the New Virtual Machine wizard (Step 8 from Activity 9-2). The VM that is currently using the virtual disk should be shut down before you copy it.

2. Create a new virtual machine using the New Virtual Machine wizard but on the Connect Virtual Hard Disk screen, choose the Use an existing virtual hard disk option and browse to the copied virtual hard disk.

3. Finish the New Virtual Machine wizard.

Since the guest OS resides on the virtual hard disk, you will have a new VM with the same guest OS as the virtual hard disk. The only real difference between this method and the export/import method is that you must create the new virtual machine and can change the VM name and configuration when running the New Virtual Machine wizard.

Convert a Physical Machine to a Virtual Machine

Hyper-V does not have any built-in tools to create a virtual machine from a physical computer, but there are tools available to do so. One such tool comes with Microsoft's System Center Virtual Machine Manager (SCVMM) product which is an environment for managing multiple Hyper-V hosts. SCVMM has a Convert physical server wizard that walks you through the conversion process. SCVMM has many other advanced options that are beyond the scope of this book.

A less expensive and less complex option is to download the free disk2vhd utility from *http://technet.microsoft.com/sysinternals/*. Disk2vhd runs on the physical server and creates a virtual hard disk file from the physical disk or disks on the physical server. You can then create a new VM in Hyper-V and choose the option to use an existing virtual hard disk and your physical computer is now a virtual machine. Of course, the original physical computer is unaltered and can be used as always.

Hyper-V has the option to create a new virtual disk by copying the contents of one of the host machine's physical disks. If you remove a computer's OS disk and attach it to the Hyper-V host machine, you can essentially create a new VM from a physical disk. Be aware that the operating system on the physical disk was originally configured for a particular set of hardware; you may have some additional configurations that you will have to carry out. Using the disk2vhd program is probably an easier solution in most cases.

Hyper-V Virtual Networks

Virtual machines are used for a variety of reasons and how a particular VM is used will likely dictate how you want to configure the VM's network connection. A Hyper-V VM's network connection can be connected to one of three types of Hyper-V virtual network:

- External
- Internal
- Private

A fourth option is to not connect your VM to a virtual network at all. You create, delete, and modify virtual networks in Hyper-V by clicking Virtual Network Manager in the Actions pane. The following sections describe the types of virtual networks you can create.

External Virtual Network

An **external virtual network** binds a virtual network to one of the host's physical network adapters, allowing virtual machines to access a LAN connected to the host. During the installation of the Hyper-V role, you have the option of creating an external virtual network by binding one or more of the host's physical adapters to a virtual network (Step 6 of Activity 9-1). Only one external network can be created per physical network adapter. When a VM is connected to an external network, the VM acts like any other device on the LAN. For example, the VM can get an IP address using DHCP from a DHCP server on the external network or you can assign it a static address.

You use an external virtual network when external computers must access the VM or when the VM must have access to external network resources such as when your VM is configured as a Web server, DNS server, or domain controller for example.

 You cannot use a wireless NIC as the target of an external virtual network.

If you are using external virtual networks, it is highly recommended to have more than one physical NIC installed on the host computer. This way, you can dedicate one of the NICs to host communication and the other NIC or NICs can be used by VMs that need an external virtual network connection.

 Other virtualization products call an external network a bridged network.

When a NIC is designated for use in an external virtual network, Windows binds the Microsoft Virtual Network Switch Protocol to the physical NIC and unbinds all other protocols. This process creates a virtual switch through which VMs and the host can communicate with the physical network and each other. A new virtual network adapter (virtual NIC) is created that has all the usual protocol bindings enabled. The VMs that are configured to use the external virtual network are bound to the virtual NIC which communicates through the virtual switch.

To better understand virtual networks, Figure 9-7 shows a host computer without any virtual networks configured and Figure 9-8 shows the host and virtual machines connected to an external virtual network. In Figure 9-8, the host's physical NIC is bound only to the Microsoft Virtual Network Switch protocol and has the physical connection to the external network. The host's physical NIC has a virtual connection to the virtual switch and facilitates communication between VMs and the external network. The new virtual NIC created on the host has all the usual network protocol bindings (Client for Microsoft Networks, File and Printers Sharing for Microsoft Networks, TCP/IP, and so forth) allowing host applications and protocols to communicate through the virtual switch to the external network and the VMs.

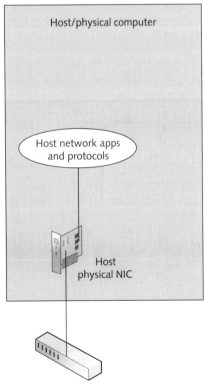

Figure 9-7 A host computer with no virtual networks configured

© Cengage Learning 2012

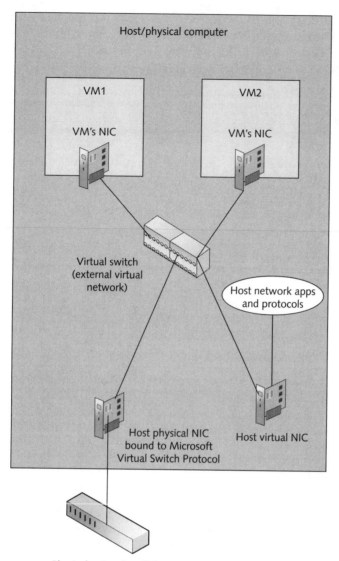

Figure 9-8 A host and VM connected through an external virtual network

© Cengage Learning 2012

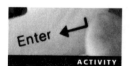

Activity 9-6: Work with External Virtual Networks

Time Required: 20 minutes

Objective: Delete the external virtual network that was created during the installation of Hyper-V, then recreate it.

Description: You want to see how external virtual networks affect the settings of the host computer's network connections. You will delete the current external virtual network and view your network connection's properties. Next, you recreate the virtual network and see how the host network connections are changed.

If you are connected to the host computer via Remote Desktop when you perform this activity, you will lose your connection and will have to reconnect.

1. Log on to your host server as Administrator, if necessary.

2. Click **Start**, point to **Administrative Tools**, and click **Hyper-V Manager.**

3. Click **Virtual Network Manager** in the Actions pane. Click on the virtual network that is listed under New virtual network (it is probably named Local Area Connection - Virtual Network). See Figure 9-9.

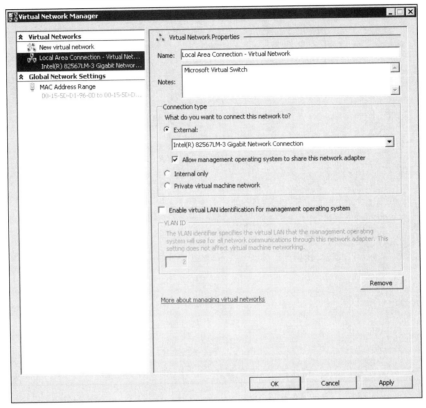

Figure 9-9 Virtual Network Manager
© Cengage Learning 2012

4. Click **Remove** to delete the virtual network, then click **OK**. You are warned that you will lose your network connection temporarily. Click **Yes** to apply the network changes. (If you are connected to the Hyper-V host remotely, you will lose your connection and may have to reconnect to the host.)

5. Open **Network and Sharing Center** and click **Manage Network Connections**. View the properties of **Local Area Connection**. Notice that the Microsoft Virtual Network Switch Protocol is installed but it is not checked which means that it is not bound to the adapter. Close **Local Area Connection Properties**.

6. In Hyper-V Manager, click **Virtual Network Manager**. Click **New virtual network** if necessary, and click **External** if necessary, and then click **Add** to create a new external virtual network (see Figure 9-10).

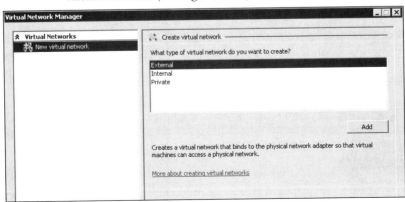

Figure 9-10 New virtual network
© Cengage Learning 2012

7. Under New Virtual Network give the virtual network a name. Type **ExternalNet1** in the Name box and click **OK**. Click **Yes**.

8. If you closed the Network Connections screen, open it again. You will see a new connection (probably named Local Area Connection 2). View the properties of **Local Area Connection**. Notice that only Microsoft Virtual Network Switch Protocol is checked. This is the physical NIC that creates the virtual switch for the external network. Open the properties of **Local Area Connection 2** and you will see that all the protocols are checked except Microsoft Virtual Network Switch Protocol. This is a virtual NIC that your VMs and host computer will use to communicate with the virtual switch and therefore the physical network. Figure 9-11 shows both network connections side by side.

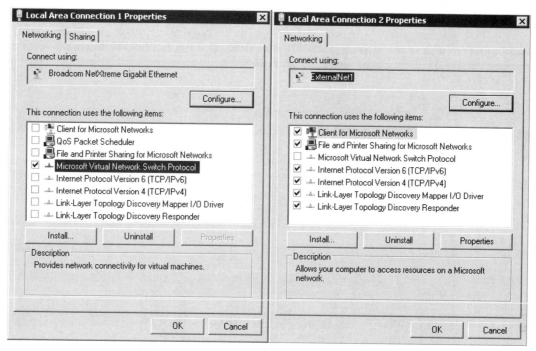

Figure 9-11 The physical NIC bound to the virtual switch protocol (left) and the new virtual NIC
© Cengage Learning 2012

9. Since you deleted the original virtual network, you must re-assign your VM's network connections to the new virtual network. In Hyper-V Manager, right-click **VMTest1** and click **Settings**.

10. In Settings for VMTest1, click **Network Adapter** in the left pane under **Hardware**. In the right pane click the selection arrow for network (it currently should read Configuration Error) and click **ExternalNet1**. Click **OK**. Follow the same procedure for VMTest2.

11. Start both **VMTest1** and **VMTest2**. Try to ping the default gateway or some other device located on the physical network. You should be successful. If you get an error starting one of the VMs due to a conflict, you may need to change the settings on the VM so that the DVD drive is not connected to the physical drive.

12. Turn off the firewall on both VMs: On each VM, open **Network and Sharing Center**, click **Windows Firewall**, click **Turn Windows Firewall on or off**, and then click **Off**. Click **OK**.

13. Verify that you can ping from VMTest1 to VMTest2 and vice versa.

14. Close all open windows (including the VM windows) but stay logged on to the Windows host if you are going on to the next Activity; otherwise shut down your VMs and host machine.

Internal Virtual Network

An **internal virtual network** allows virtual machines and the host computer to communicate with one another but does not provide access by VMs to the physical network. An internal network is not bound to any of the host's physical NICs. When an internal virtual network is created, a new virtual NIC is created on the host computer that is bound to the name of the new internal virtual network. The new virtual NIC allows the host computer to communicate with the VMs on that internal network. A virtual switch is created but it is internal to Hyper-V and therefore cannot be seen on the host computer. The new virtual NIC will, by default, attempt to get an address via DHCP but since it does not have a connection to the physical network, it will be assigned an APIPA address. Any VMs connected to the internal network will also be assigned an APIPA address if you do not assign a static IP address. Figure 9-12 shows a diagram of how an internal virtual network works. Note that the difference between an external and internal virtual network is that the host virtual NIC does not have a connection to the virtual switch, thereby not allowing the VMs to communicate with the physical network. In addition, both the host physical NIC and the host virtual NIC have all the normal bindings, allowing network applications and protocols to communicate with both NICs.

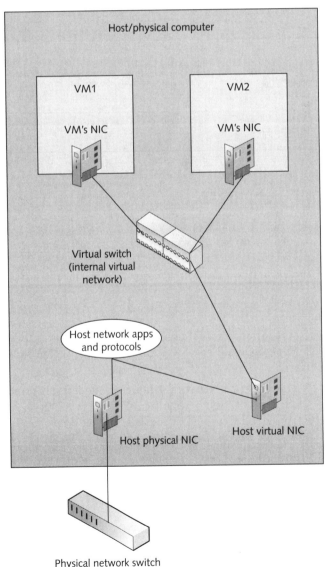

Figure 9-12 An internal virtual network — only the host can communicate with the virtual machines

© Cengage Learning 2012

An internal network is used in scenarios where it is not necessary for devices on the physical network to have direct access to the VMs and vice versa. Examples include test and lab environments in which you want the VMs to be isolated from the physical network but still want to communicate with VMs from the host.

Activity 9-7: Work with Internal Virtual Networks

Time Required: 20 minutes
Objective: Create a new internal virtual network and connect a VM to this network

Description: You want to see how internal virtual networks affect communication among the VMs and the host computer. You create a new internal virtual network and connect one of the VMs to this network.

1. Log on to your host server as Administrator, if necessary.

2. Click **Start**, point to **Administrative Tools**, and click **Hyper-V Manager**.

3. Click **Virtual Network Manager** in the Actions pane. Click **Internal** in the What type of virtual network do you want to create box. Click **Add**.

4. Type **InternalNet1** in the **Name** box. Click **OK**.

5. Open **Network and Sharing Center** and click **Change adapter settings**. You will see a new connection, (probably named Local Area Connection 3). Open the Properties of **Local Area Connection 3** and you will see InternalNet1 in the Connect using box indicating that this network connection is connected to the internal virtual network you created in the previous step. All the standard protocols are bound to this virtual NIC. Close **Local Area Connection 3Properties**.

6. Right-click **Local Area Connection 3** and click **Status** and then **Details**. You will see that the value of the IPv4 IP Address property is an APIPA address. Write the IP address below. Close all open Windows except Network and Sharing Center and Hyper-V Manager.

_____

7. You want to turn off the Windows firewall on Local Area Connection 3 to allow ping messages. In Network and Sharing Center, click **Windows Firewall**. Click **Turn Windows Firewall on or off** and click **Turn off Windows Firewall** for each network location. Click **OK**. Close **Windows Firewall**.

8. In Hyper-V Manager, right-click **VMTest1** and click **Settings**. Under Hardware, click **Network Adapter**. In the **Network** selection box, click **InternalNet1**. Click **OK**. Close Windows Firewall and Network and Sharing Center.

9. Double-click **VMTest1** to connect to it. If the VM is not running start it now. Log on to **VMTest1**.

10. Open a command prompt on VMTest1 and type **ipconfig** and press **Enter**. Notice that the IP address is an APIPA address.

11. Type **ping** *host-address* where *host-address* is the IP address you wrote down in Step 6. The ping should be successful. Start and connect to VMTest2 and determine its IP address. From VMTest1, try to ping VMTest2. Your ping will not be successful since they are no longer connected to the same virtual network.

12. Follow Step 8 to connect VMTest2 to InternalNet1 (replacing VMTest1 with VMTest2). Verify that you can ping VMTest2 from VMTest1 and vice versa.

Private Virtual Network

A **private virtual network** is not much different than an internal virtual network except that the VMs connected to the private virtual network cannot communicate with the host computer. Creating a private virtual network does not create a new network connection on the host computer

9

since there is no connection between the host computer and the VMs. Figure 9-13 shows this configuration. Note that there is no virtual NIC on the host in this configuration as there is no communication between the host and the VMs.

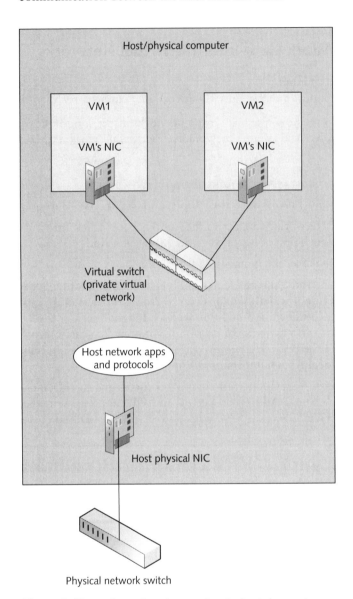

Figure 9-13 A private virtual network—the host does not communicate with the virtual machines
© Cengage Learning 2012

A private virtual network is used when you want to completely isolate the VMs connected to the network from all outside communication. You might use this scenario as a domain test bed or a development network in which you need to isolate the virtual network traffic.

Communicating Between Hyper-V Networks

What if you want to isolate your VMs in their own private network but you want them to be able to access other private networks or an external network? With a physical network, you would do this by creating subnets and using a router to route traffic between them. Hyper-V networks are no different. You can do this in two different ways:

- Create an external and private virtual network. Configure one VM with two NICs and have one NIC connected to each virtual network. Since you can configure a Windows Server 2008 server as a network router, install RRAS on the VM and enable routing. This VM can route packets between the private network and the external network. Figure 9-14 depicts this scenario.

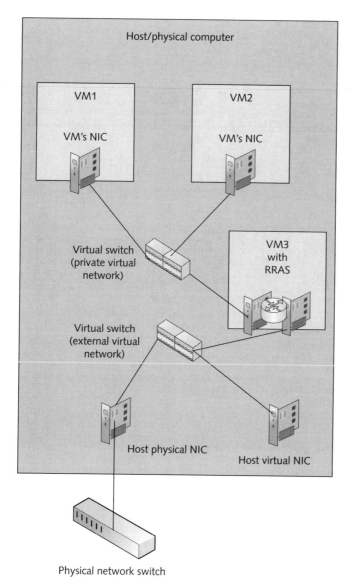

Figure 9-14 Routing between a private and external virtual network
© Cengage Learning 2012

- Create an internal virtual network and enable routing on the host machine so that it routes between the internal and physical networks. Figure 9-15 depicts this scenario.

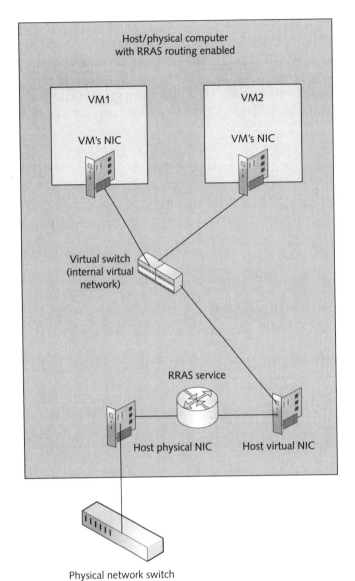

Figure 9-15 Routing between an internal network and the physical network
© Cengage Learning 2012

Using Virtual LAN IDs

Virtual LANs (VLANs) allow you to create subnets, or broadcast domains, on a single external or internal virtual network. To enable VLANs for a virtual network, you click the Enable virtual LAN identification for parent partition checkbox on the Virtual Network Manager (see Figure 9-16). The physical NIC on the host must support VLANs (also called VLAN tagging) for this option to work.

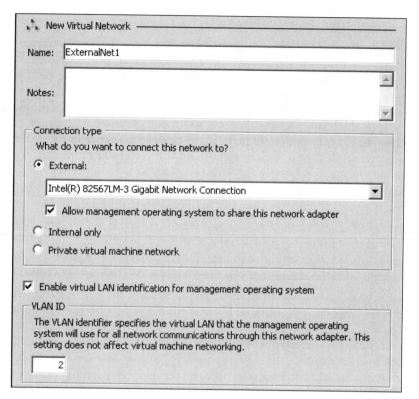

Figure 9-16 Enabling VLAN identification on a virtual network
© Cengage Learning 2012

When you enable **VLAN identification**, you choose an ID number in Virtual Network Manager (the number 2, shown in Figure 9-16). This ID is the VLAN identifier for the host network. When you connect a VM's network interface to a virtual network, you specify the VLAN ID for that VM. All machines (VMs and hosts) that share a common VLAN ID can communicate with one another as if they were on the same subnet. The machines that share a common VLAN ID must be configured with IP addresses that share a common network ID. Machines that have different VLAN IDs cannot communicate directly with one another but can only communicate if a router is configured to route between the VLANs. You would configure a router to route between VLANs just as you would configure one to route between separate virtual networks as discussed in the previous section.

Working with Virtual Hard Disks

A virtual hard disk is a file on the host computer that has the .vhd extension. From the VMs standpoint, a virtual hard disk is no different than a physical hard disk. But, from the perspective of an IT manager using Hyper-V, virtual hard disks are much more flexible than physical disks.

Virtual hard disks can be one of three types:

- *Dynamically expanding.* The virtual hard disk file grows as data is written to it up to the size you specify when the disk is created. The dynamic aspect of this type of disk goes only one way; the file will not shrink when data is deleted from the virtual disk. This option saves host disk space until the disk grows to its maximum size, but at the expense of performance (the system will run slower whenever the virtual hard disk file grows, and its placement on the host's physical storage device may be more fragmented). **Dynamically expanding disks** are typically about 10 to 15 percent slower than fixed size disks, and if the host disk becomes fragmented, the performance could suffer more. But, dynamically expanding disks are a good way to go when evaluating or testing VMs or when performance is not paramount. Additionally, the VMs that use dynamic disks can be backed up faster since the size of the .vhd files is usually smaller than that of a fixed disk.

- *Fixed size.* The full amount of space required for a fixed size disk, as the name applies, is allocated on the host's storage when the virtual disk is created. **Fixed size disks** provide better performance than dynamically expanding disks and are less likely to cause host disk fragmentation. For production virtual machines, fixed size disks are recommended.

- *Differencing.* A **differencing disk** uses a parent/child relationship. A parent disk is a dynamically expanding or fixed size disk with an OS installed, possibly with some applications and data. The parent disk becomes the baseline for one or more child, or differencing disks. A VM that uses a differencing disk operates normally but any changes that are made to the VM's hard disk are made only to the differencing disk, leaving the child disk unaltered. Note that the parent disk should not be connected to a VM since the parent disk must not be changed in any way. Using differencing disks, several VMs can be created using the parent disk as the baseline while only using the additional host disk space of the differencing disk. Differencing disks are an ideal way to quickly provision several VMs without having to install an OS and applications or copy an entire virtual disk. Differencing disks work like dynamically expanding disks in that they start very small and grow as data is written to them.

Creating and Modifying Virtual Disks

Virtual disks can be created when a new VM is created, or they can be created using the New Virtual Hard Disk wizard. When you create a virtual disk during VM creation, the disk is created as a dynamically expanding disk, but you can change it to a fixed size disk later. When you create a disk using the New Virtual Hard Disk wizard, you choose the type of disk you want to create (see Figure 9-17).

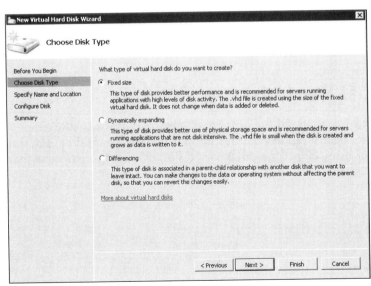

Figure 9-17 New Virtual Hard Disk Wizard

© Cengage Learning 2012

Virtual disks are created in a default location (C:\Users\Public\Documents\Hyper-V\Virtual Hard Disks) unless you specify a different path. You can view and change the default location by clicking Hyper-V Settings in the Actions pane in Hyper-V Manager. Once a virtual disk is created, you can attach it to a new or existing VM.

One thing that makes virtual disks so flexible is your ability to modify certain aspects of the disk, using the Edit Virtual Hard Disk wizard. To start this wizard, you click Edit Disk from the Actions menu in Hyper-V. After you select the virtual hard disk you want to edit, you have a choice of actions you can perform. The options available vary depending upon the type of disk you select. Figure 9-18 shows the options for a dynamically expanding disk.

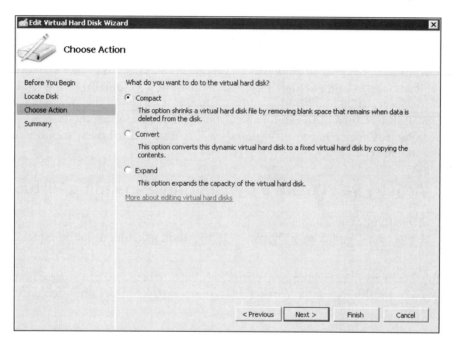

Figure 9-18 Edit Virtual Hard Disk Wizard
© Cengage Learning 2012

The following list describes the disk editing options available:

- *Compact*—Reduces the size of a dynamically expanding disk by eliminating the space used by deleted files.

- *Convert*—Converts a dynamically expanding disk to a fixed size disk and vice versa.

- *Expand*—Allows you to make a fixed size disk or a dynamically expanding disk larger.

- *Merge*—This option is only available for differencing disks. There are two options: You can merge the contents of a differencing disk into its parent disk or merge the differencing disk with the parent disk to create a new disk while leaving the original parent disk unchanged.

- *Reconnect*—Reconnects a differencing disk with its parent disk.

 Before performing any of the disk editing tasks, you must shut down the VM that is connected to the target disk, if any.

A little explanation is needed for a few of the disk editing tasks. When you convert a dynamic disk to a fixed size disk, a new fixed size virtual disk is created, for which you provide a new name. After the conversion is complete, you disconnect the original dynamic disk from the VM and connect the new fixed size disk. Alternatively, you can rename the dynamic disk (or delete it) and then rename the new fixed size disk to the same as the original dynamic disk. Using this method, the VM will connect to the new fixed disk automatically when you restart it. For example, if the original dynamically expanding disk is named VMTest1.vhd, you can name the new fixed size disk VMTest1fixed.vhd when you do the conversion. When the conversion is finished, rename VMTest1.vhd to VMTest1dyn.vhd and rename VMTest1fixed.vhd to VMTest1.vhd.

 If you rename the fixed disk rather than connecting the new fixed disk from the VM's settings, you must ensure that the VM has at least Modify permissions to the new virtual hard disk. In most cases, the Authenticated Users group is automatically assigned the Modify permission which is sufficient, but if the VM fails to start with an "access denied" error, check the permissions of the .vhd file.

Expanding a disk has a few caveats. First, there must not be any snapshots associated with the VM that is attached to the virtual disk you will be expanding. Second, the new space on the hard disk will appear in Windows as unallocated space. You must extend the adjacent volume to make the existing volume larger or create a new volume from the unallocated space. In Windows Server 2008 and Windows Vista/7, you can easily use the Disk Management MMC or the DISKPART command to extend an existing volume, including the system partition, or create a new volume. Older versions of Windows will require a third-party tool if you want to extend the system partition.

Activity 9-8: Create a Dynamically Expanding Virtual Disk

Time Required: 20 minutes
Objective: Create a new Dynamically Expanding virtual disk and attach the disk to a VM

Description: Your VM needs a new virtual hard disk where you can store data files. You create a new Dynamically Expanding virtual disk, attach it to VMTest1 and then create a new volume on the disk.

1. Log on to your host server as Administrator, if necessary.

2. Open **Hyper-V Manager**, if necessary.

3. In the Actions pane, click **New** and click **Hard Disk**. On the Before You Begin screen, click **Next**.

4. On the Choose Disk Type screen accept the default of **Dynamically expanding** and click **Next**.

5. On the Specify Name and Location screen, type **VMTest1-2.vhd** (you will be attaching VMTest1 to this new virtual disk and the -2 in the name indicates it is the second disk, but the name doesn't really matter). Click **Next**.

6. On the Configure Disk screen, type **2** in the **Size** box (see Figure 9-19). We will create a small 2 GB virtual disk since we will be converting it to a fixed size disk later; the larger the disk, the longer it takes to convert and the more storage on the host it takes. Notice that we can copy the contents of an existing physical disk into our new disk if desired. Click **Next**.

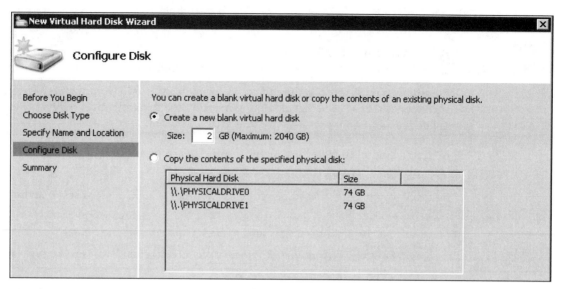

Figure 9-19 Configure Disk screen
© Cengage Learning 2012

7. On the Completing the New Virtual Hard Disk Wizard screen, review the options for the new disk and click **Finish**.

8. Next, you connect VMTest1 to the new virtual disk. Make certain that VMTest1 is powered off. If it isn't, shut down the VM now. In Hyper-V Manager right-click **VMTest1** and click **Settings**.

9. On the Settings for VMTest1 screen, click **IDE Controller 0** (or the name of the controller to which the first virtual disk is connected).

10. Click **Add** to add a hard drive. Notice that you can create a new virtual disk at this time but since the disk we want is already created, click **Browse**. Notice the size of VMTest1-2.vhd; it should only be about 20KB. Click **VMTest1-2.vhd** and click **Open**. Click **OK**.

11. In Hyper-V Manager double-click **VMTest1** and click the **Start** icon. Logon to VMTest1 and click **Start**, and click **Computer**. Notice that the new virtual disk is not listed under Hard Disk Drives. You need to initialize it and create a new volume first.

12. In VMtest1, click **Start** and type **diskmgmt.msc** and press **Enter** in the Start Search box. The Initialize Disk screen prompts you to initialize Disk 1. Click **OK**.

13. Right-click the box next to Disk 1 and click **New Simple Volume**. Finish the New Simple Volume Wizard by accepting the default options. After the disk is finished formatting, close **Disk Management**.

14. In Computer, under Hard Disk Drives, you should see the new volume with drive letter E: assigned. Create a new folder on the E: drive and create a new text file in the new folder.

15. Shut down **VMTest1**. Stay logged on to your server if you are going on to the next activity; otherwise shut down your host machine.

Activity 9-9: Convert a Dynamic Disk to a Fixed Disk

Time Required: 20 minutes
Objective: Convert a dynamically expanding disk to a fixed size disk

Description: You want to get the most performance possible from the new virtual disk you created for VMTest1. You decide that converting the dynamic disk to a fixed size disk will provide the additional performance you are looking for.

1. Log on to your host server as Administrator, if necessary.

2. Open **Hyper-V Manager**, if necessary.

3. Right-click **VMTest1** and click **Settings**. Click the **VMTest1-2.vhd** Hard Drive and click **Edit**.

4. On the Choose Action screen, click **Convert** and click **Next**.

5. On the Convert Virtual Hard Disk screen, click **Browse** and type **VMTest1-2Fixed. vhd** and click **Save**. Click **Next**.

6. On the Completing the Edit Virtual Hard Disk Wizard screen, click **Finish**. It will take a few minutes to complete the conversion.

7. When the conversion is finished, click **Browse**. You will see that the fixed disk is shown with a size of 1 GB. Click **VMTest1-2Fixed.vhd** and click **Open** to attach the fixed disk to VMTest1. Click **OK**.

8. In Hyper-V Manager double-click **VMTest1** and click the **Start** icon. Logon to VMTest1 and click **Start** and click **Computer**. Explore the E: drive to verify that the files you created in the last activity are still there.

9. It is now safe to delete the old dynamic disk (named VMTest1-2.vhd) if desired. Shut down **VMTest1**. Stay logged on to your server if you are going on to the next activity; otherwise shut down your host machine.

Activity 9-10: Create a New VM and Attach a Differencing Disk

Time Required: 20 minutes
Objective: Create a new VM and attach a differencing disk

Description: You have a baseline VM with Windows Server 2008 installed. You want to create a new VM and attach a differencing disk using the original VM's disk as a baseline.

1. Log on to your host server as Administrator, if necessary.

2. Open **Hyper-V Manager**, if necessary.

3. Right-click **VMTest2** and click **Settings**. Note the name and location of the virtual hard drive attached to VMTest2 and write the path and name down below. Click **Remove** to detach the virtual hard disk from VMTest2. Click **OK**.

4. Open an Explorer window and browse to the location of the virtual hard disk you wrote down in the previous step. Rename the virtual hard disk to **VMParent.vhd**.

5. In Hyper-V Manager click **New** and click **Hard Disk** and click **Next**.

6. On the Choose Disk Type screen, click **Differencing** and click **Next**.

7. This differencing disk will be used for VMTest2. On the Specify Name and Location screen, type **VMTest2Diff.vhd** and click **Next**.

8. On the Configure Disk screen, click **Browse** and click **VMParent.vhd**. Click **Open**. Click **Next**. Click **Finish**.

9. Follow Steps 5 through 8 again but this time, in Step 7, type the name **VMTest3Diff.vhd**.

10. In Hyper-V Manager right-click **VMTest2** and click **Settings**. Click **IDE Controller 0** and click **Add**.

11. Click **Browse** and click **VMTest2Diff.vhd** and click **Open**. Click **OK**.

12. Create a new virtual machine by clicking **New** and **Virtual Machine**. Click **Next**.

13. Type **VMTest3** in the Name box and click **Next**. Click **Next** to accept the default amount of memory. Choose InternalNet1 for the network connection and click **Next**.

14. On the Connect Virtual Hard Disk screen, click **Use an existing virtual hard disk** and click **Browse**. Click **VMTest3Diff.vhd** and click **Open**. Click **Next**. Click **Finish**.

15. Start VMTest2 to be sure that everything works okay. Start VMTest3 to be sure it works okay. You now have two VMs that share the same parent virtual disk while each VM uses a separate and much smaller differencing disk. To verify the size of the differencing disk, browse to the location of the virtual hard disks and note that the size of the differencing disks is only about 30 MB while the parent disk is around 10 GB. By using a differencing disk for two VMs, you just saved 10 GB of disk space on your host. If you configured four VMs to use the same parent disk, you would save 30 GB of host disk space!

16. Shut down your VMs, but stay logged on to the host machine if you are going on to the next activity.

Pass-through Disks

A **pass-through disk** is not a virtual disk but a physical disk attached to the host that is in the offline state. A pass-through disk can only be connected to a VM if it has been initialized and has been set to offline status. If you have a physical disk on the host that is offline, you can attach it to a VM from the VM's settings page (see Figure 9-20). Note that if the disk has not been initialized, you must first initialize it and then set it to offline. If the disk already has data on it, the data will be retained and is available to the VM.

From the VM's standpoint, a pass-through disk works just like a virtual disk except that you cannot use any of the disk editing options on a pass-through disk. Furthermore, you cannot take snapshots or use a differencing disk with a pass-through disk. A pass-through disk has modest performance advantages over virtual disks but unless you really need the extra bit of performance, the lack of flexibility with a pass-through disk detracts from its attractiveness as a VM storage option. Some applications that may benefit from the VM using a pass-through disk include SQL servers and high-performance cluster servers.

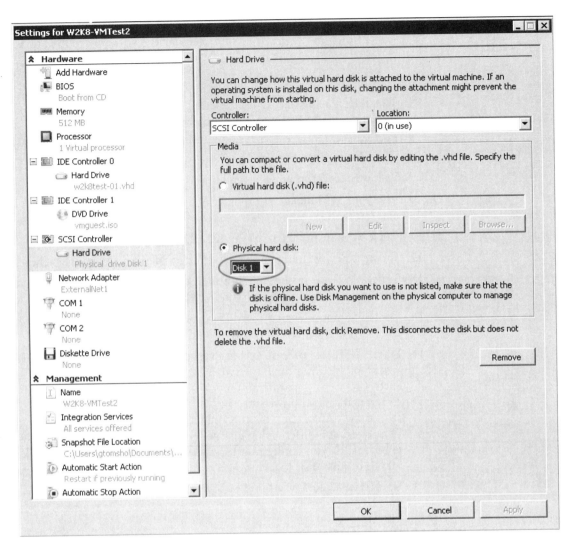

Figure 9-20 Adding a pass-through (physical) disk to a VM

© Cengage Learning 2012

Managing Virtual Machines

Now that you have a general understanding of how Hyper-V works and how to configure virtual networks and virtual hard disks, let's look at additional features you can use to manage and configure the virtual environment. In particular, we will look at the following:

- Virtual machine hardware settings
- Integration services
- Automatic start and stop actions
- Managing snapshots

Virtual Machine Hardware Settings

Virtual machines have a number of hardware settings that can be configured. We have already looked at how to configure the network and hard disk settings. In this section, we'll look at options for changing BIOS settings, modifying the amount of memory allocated to a VM, and the virtual processor settings. Note that most settings cannot be changed unless the VM is powered off.

BIOS Settings

The BIOS settings for a VM have two options you can change: the Num Lock status on startup and the boot order (see Figure 9-21). If you want the Num Lock key turned on when the VM boots, check the box next to Num Lock, otherwise leave it unchecked. To change the order in which the VM's BIOS searches for boot devices, click a device in the Startup order box and click the up or down arrows to change the order of the device. For example, if you already have an OS installed on the VM's hard disk, you might want to set the boot order so that the hard disk (IDE or SCSI) is listed first so that the VM does not attempt to boot from CD.

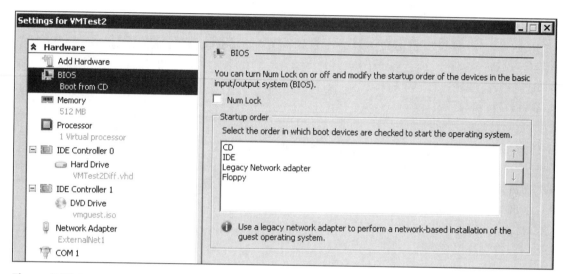

Figure 9-21 BIOS settings

© Cengage Learning 2012

Memory Allocation

You can configure the amount of memory a VM is allocated from the host computer when you create the VM and you can change that amount after the VM is created. The amount of memory you allocate must take into account other VMs that will be running simultaneously and sufficient memory left over for the host server. The host computer needs at least 512 MB of RAM plus 32 MB for each running VM with a memory allocation up to 1 GB. For example, if you will be running three virtual machines, each with 1 GB of memory, you will need 3 × 1 GB for the VMs, plus 32 MB × 3 plus 512 MB for the host; for a total of about 3.6 GB. Since the RAM on most computers is configured in multiples of 2, you will need 4 GB of RAM on your host computer. If your VMs are allocated more than 1 GB, add 8 MB to the host for each additional GB.

A new feature available with Windows Server 2008 R2 Service Pack 1 is dynamic memory allocation. With dynamic memory allocation, you can specify the amount of RAM the VM needs at startup and a maximum amount of RAM it can use. Hyper-V will adjust the memory allocation to that VM up or down based on its actual memory needs between the startup and maximum value you specify.

Virtual Processor Settings

You can adjust how many **virtual processors** (see Figure 9-22) are assigned to the virtual machine up to the total number of physical processors or processor cores installed on the host computer. For example, if you are running your Hyper-V server on a quad-core Xeon, you can assign up to four virtual processors to each of your VMs. However, if your VMs will handle substantial processing workloads it is recommended that you assign virtual processors using a strategy that assigns one or more virtual processors per VM while reserving one physical processor (or processor core) to the host computer. For example, if your host computer runs a quad-core processor, and you will be running three VMs on the host, allocate each VM one virtual processor, thereby reserving one for the host computer. If your VMs are not carrying substantial processing workloads, you can use more virtual processors than there are physical processors (for example, running six VMs, each with one virtual processor allocated on host with only four physical processor cores).

Remember that Windows Server 2008 is a symmetric multiprocessing (SMP) OS, and when more than one physical CPU is installed, they must be identical. For example, you cannot use one dual core CPU and one quad core CPU in the same system. You must use two dual-cores or two quad-cores of the same type.

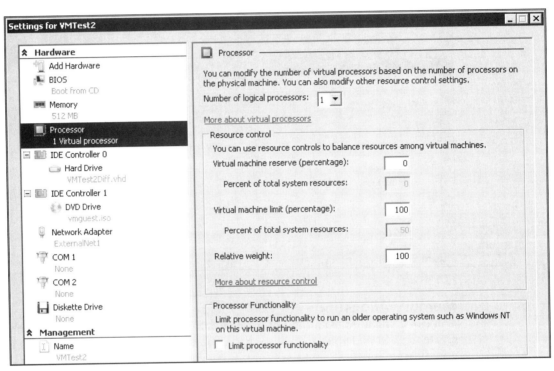

Figure 9-22 Virtual processor settings
© Cengage Learning 2012

The Resource Control section of Figure 9-22 specifies how host resources are allocated to the VM:

- *Virtual machine reserve (percentage).* Of the total processing resources allocated to the VM, this setting specifies what percentage is guaranteed to be available to the VM. The default setting is 0. If you change this setting, the *Percentage of total system resources* value changes to reflect what percentage of the total host processing power is in reserve for the VM. For example, if the VM has been assigned one virtual CPU in a two physical-CPU system, and you reserve 100 percent, then 50 percent of the total system resources will be held in reserve for the VM.

- *Virtual machine limit (percentage).* This value specifies what percentage of the assigned processing power may be used by this VM. If you assign a single virtual CPU to the VM in a two-CPU system, then the VM may use 100 percent of the processing power of one CPU, leaving 50 percent of the total processing power available for other workloads.

- *Relative weight.* Essentially this figure assigns a priority to this VM's access to processing resources when more than one VM is competing for the same processing resource. The value can be from 1 to 10000 with the higher number assigning a higher priority to the VM. If multiple VMs have the same Relative weight value, they will get an equal share of the available resources.

Integration Services

The Integration Services section of a VM's settings (see Figure 9-23) indicates whether Integration Services are installed in a VM. Integration Services is installed on a VM after the OS is installed, by clicking Action and Insert Integration Services Setup Disk. Windows Server 2008, Windows Vista, and Windows 7 automatically install Integration Services when they are installed in a Hyper-V virtual machine. However, you will need to manually install them on older Windows OSs and non-Windows OSs.

You may want to re-install Integration Services on an OS that automatically installs them in case the built-in Integration Services of the guest OS are not the most recent version.

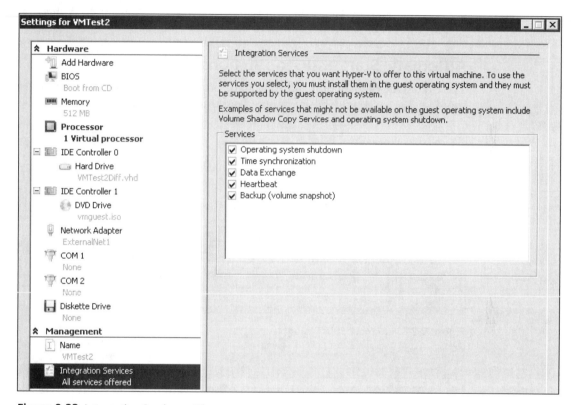

Figure 9-23 Integration Services settings
© Cengage Learning 2012

Integration Services provides enhanced drivers for the guest OS that bring better performance and functionality to IDE and SCSI storage devices, the network interface, and mouse and video devices. The storage controller and network interface drivers included in Integration Services are called **synthetic drivers** which are optimized for use in the Hyper-V environment. **Emulated drivers,** which are used when Integration Services is not installed, are also referred to as legacy drivers.

Enhanced video and mouse drivers contained in Integration Services provides a better experience using a guest OS's user interface. Without Integration Services installed, the mouse is captured by the VM when you click inside the VM window and you must use the Ctrl-Alt-Left Arrow keyboard sequence to release the mouse back to the host OS. With Integration Services installed, you can freely move the mouse from guest to host. Furthermore, if you access the guest OS through Remote Desktop, the mouse is not functional in the guest OS at all unless Integration Services is installed.

Aside from enhanced drivers, Integration Services provides these additional services which you can enable or disable in the VM's settings:

- *Operating system shutdown.* Lets you shutdown the VM by pressing the Shutdown button without connecting or logging on to the VM.

- *Time synchronization.* Allows you to synchronize the VM's time with the host. If the VM is a Windows domain controller, you should not use this option because domain controllers have their own time synchronization mechanism.

- *Data exchange.* Allows the VM and host to exchange information using registry keys.

- *Heartbeat.* Allows the host machine to detect when the VM has locked up or crashed. The host sends heartbeat messages to the guest VM periodically and the heartbeat service on the guest VM responds. If it fails to respond, the host machine will log an event.

- *Backup (volume snapshot).* Allows host backup programs to use Volume Shadow-Copy Service (VSS) to backup VM hard disk files.

Automatic Start and Stop Actions

The Automatic Start Action and Automatic Stop Action settings allow you to specify how a VM should behave when the host computer starts and shuts down; see Figures 9-24 and 9-25.

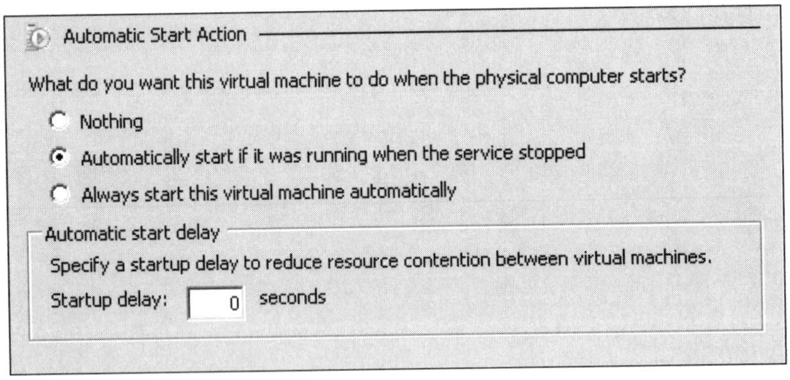

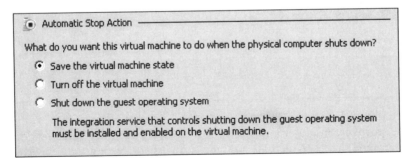

Figure 9-24 Automatic Start Action
© Cengage Learning 2012

Figure 9-25 Automatic Stop Action
© Cengage Learning 2012

The options for Automatic Start Action are:

- *Nothing.* The VM will not be started when the host computer starts.

- *Automatically start if it was running when the service stopped.* If the VM was running when the host machine was last running, the VM will be started when the host starts. If the

VM had not been running then the VM is not started. This is the default start action and should be used with production VMs.

- *Always start the virtual machine automatically.* The VM will always be started when the host starts.

- *Startup delay.* If multiple VMs are set to start automatically, you may want to set a startup delay of varying amounts for each VM to avoid resource contention. Also, if the services of one VM are dependent on another VM, you can set the delay time to ensure that the VMs are started in the proper order.

The options for Automatic Stop Action are:

- *Save the virtual machine state.* The state of the VM is saved when the host is shut down, which is similar to hibernate mode for a desktop computer. When the VM is restarted, it picks up where it left off. This is the default stop action, but it is not recommended for domain controllers.

- *Turn off the virtual machine.* This option powers down the VM, which is like pulling the power cord on a physical machine. This is not a recommended option unless the VM does not support shutdown, but even then, the save option is probably preferable.

- *Shut down the guest operating system.* The VM's OS will undergo a normal graceful shutdown procedure as long as Integration Services are installed and shutdown is supported by the guest OS. This is the recommended option for most situations.

Managing Snapshots

Snapshots are one of the features that make working with VMs so flexible compared to physical machines. Snapshots let you revert your VM to a previous state, allowing you to explore what-if scenarios and recover from installations and configurations that have gone wrong. And you are not limited to a single snapshot. You can create up to 50 snapshots per VM and revert your VM to any one of the saved snapshots. This feature is particularly useful in testing and lab environments because you can reset your test environment to its original state by a click of a button.

While snapshots do not take up a lot of disk space because they work much like a differencing disk, you still need to be aware of some issues regarding snapshot storage:

- By default, snapshots are stored in the C:\ProgramData\Microsoft\Windows\Hyper-V folder. Because this location is on the host's system disk (where the C:\Windows folder is stored), for performance reasons, you may want to relocate your snapshots folder to a different disk if possible. You can change the snapshot storage location for each VM through the VM's settings in Hyper-V Manager.

- Once a snapshot is created for a VM, you cannot change the snapshot location for that VM (but each VM can have a different snapshot location if desired).

- You should always use Hyper-V Manager to delete snapshots; snapshot files should not be deleted manually because the files must be merged with the original hard disk file.

- If you delete a snapshot to free up disk space, the actual snapshot file is not deleted until the VM is shutdown. In fact, what actually occurs is that the snapshot file (snapshot files are named with the .avhd extension) is merged with the original hard disk file (.vhd) and that process cannot occur until the VM is shut down. It may take some time for the merge to occur depending on the size of the snapshot file. Once the files are merged, the snapshot file is deleted by the system. Ideally, you should check that the snapshot file (with .avhd extension) has been deleted before restarting the VM.

- If you create a snapshot while the VM is running, the amount of space required for the snapshot includes the amount of memory allocated to the VM (much like a hibernate file), which increases the total amount of space required for the snapshot substantially. Ideally, create snapshots while the VM is shut down to reduce the disk space used.

A few of the caveats involved in using snapshots have been mentioned earlier in the chapter, but it may be useful to repeat them here:

- Snapshots should not be used in distributed database environments or transactional systems such as with domain controllers or mail servers. In fact, Microsoft does not support the use of snapshots on VMs hosting Active Directory or Active Directory Lightweight Directory Services.

- Snapshots decrease the disk performance of the virtual machine.

- Snapshots must be deleted before expanding a disk.

- Snapshots cannot be used with pass-through or differencing disks.

- If you create a snapshot while the VM is running, the amount of space required for the snapshot includes the amount of memory allocated to the VM (much like a hibernate file), which increases the total amount of space required for the snapshot substantially. Ideally, create snapshots while the VM is shut down to reduce the disk space used.

Reverting to and Applying Snapshots

There are two ways to use a saved snapshot: revert and apply. Reverting to a snapshot returns the VM to the state of the VM when the last snapshot was taken. The Revert option is available in the Actions pane of Hyper-V Manager when a VM is selected and no snapshots are currently selected (see Figure 9-26). In the figure, if you click the Revert option in the Actions pane, VMTest1-Snapshot 3 will be applied to VMTest1.

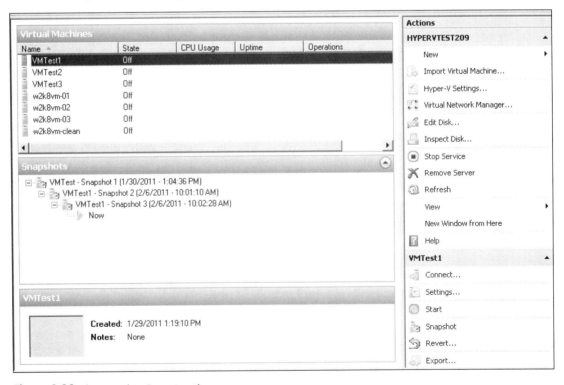

Figure 9-26 The snapshot Revert option
© Cengage Learning 2012

Applying a snapshot allows you to select a particular snapshot and apply it to the VM. The Apply option is available when a particular snapshot is selected in the Snapshots pane. Selecting the most recent snapshot and applying it has the same effect as Revert. However, if you apply an earlier snapshot, a new snapshot subtree is created as in Figure 9-27. In Figure 9-27, VMTest1-Snapshot 2 was applied, and the VM is now in the state of the VM when Snapshot 2 was taken, as indicated by the Now arrow. VMTest1 - Snapshot 3 is still available but if you take another snapshot, a new subtree under the Now arrow is started.

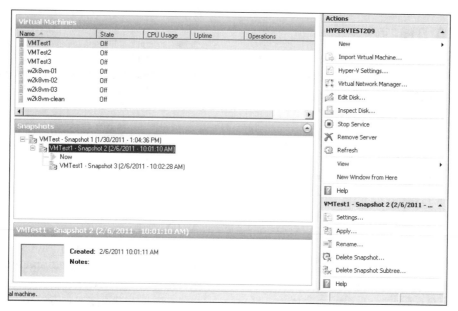

Figure 9-27 The snapshot Apply option
© Cengage Learning 2012

In summary, virtualization has gone from a novelty to a mainstream technology in just a few years. Your understanding of how to use Hyper-V and other virtualization technologies is paramount for a successful career working in an IT datacenter. In fact, it is so important that Microsoft has dedicated certifications for using virtualization technologies. You can read more about these certifications at *http://www.microsoft.com/learning/en/us/certification/cert-virtualization.aspx*.

Best Practices

1. Use virtualization to consolidate servers and to replace old or unreliable hardware.

2. Use the Server Core installation option for single-role servers and Read-only domain controllers because of the smaller footprint and attack surface on Server Core.

3. Make sure you have purchased the appropriate number of licenses for your VMs—keeping in mind the additional licenses for virtual instances you receive for Standard, Enterprise, and Datacenter editions.

4. Don't use physical installation media—install your VMs from the DVD .iso image file rather than using a physical disk.

5. If you will be running several Hyper-V hosts, consider using Microsoft System Center Virtual Machine Manager (SCVMM). SCVMM provides additional management and monitoring tools not found in Hyper-V Manager.

6. Use virtual internal or private networks when using VMs for testing and development, thereby avoiding conflicts with the physical LAN.

7. If you plan to use the VLAN ID feature, your host's NICs must support VLAN tagging.

8. Use differencing disks to quickly provision new, identical VMs, but be sure not to connect the parent disk to a VM.

9. Use fixed size disks or pass-through disks when disk performance is paramount for your VM application.

10. If you update Windows Server 2008 and Hyper-V, you may need to update the integration services on your existing VMs for optimal performance and reliability.

11. Use a startup delay when multiple VMs are set to automatic start, thereby avoiding resource contention and failures caused by VM dependency.

Chapter Summary

- Virtualization creates an emulated computer environment that allows multiple OSs to run on the same physical computer at the same time. Hyper-V is a type 1 hypervisor that creates the necessary virtualization environment. Other virtualization software, such as Virtual PC or VMWare Workstation are type 2 hypervisors.

- Virtualization can be used in labs and test environments but type 1 hypervisors like Hyper-V are targeted for use in production environments. Some of the key applications for virtualization in the datacenter include server consolidation, testing, live migration, and dynamic provisioning.

- Hyper-V is installed as a server role in Windows Server 2008 64-bit versions of Standard, Enterprise, and Datacenter editions. The CPU on the host machine must be 64-bit and support virtualization extensions such as AMD-V or Intel-VT.

- Standard edition includes a license for one virtual instance of Windows Server 2008 while Enterprise edition includes four virtual instances and Datacenter edition includes unlimited virtual instances.

- VMs are created using Hyper-V Manager. As part of the creation process, you can specify the amount of RAM allocated to the VM, the name and type of virtual hard disk, and the type of virtual network the VM should connect to. VMs can also be created by importing an exported VM, copying the virtual disk of another VM and converting a physical machine to a virtual machine.

- There are three types of virtual networks: external, internal, and private. External networks connect the VM to the host's physical network while internal networks only allow VMs to communicate with one another and the host. Private networks allow communication only between the VMs connected to the private network. More than one private and internal network can be created on a host.

- Three types of virtual hard disks can be created: dynamically expanding, fixed size, and differencing. A third type of hard disk can be attached to a VM, called a pass-through disk which is an offline physical disk attached to the host.

- Many aspects of a VM's physical environment can be configured including the BIOS settings, memory allocation, virtual processor settings. A VM's software environment can be enhanced by installing Integration Services which provides enhanced drivers for disk, network, display, and mouse devices. VM start and stop actions can be configured to determine what actions the VM should perform when the host computer is shut down and started. Snapshots allow you to revert a VM to a previous state. Snapshots cannot be used with pass-through or differencing disks and should not be used on domain controllers.

Key Terms

bare-metal virtualization   OS virtualization in which the hypervisor runs directly on the host computer's hardware and controls and monitors guest OSs. Also called a type 1 hypervisor.

differencing disk   A dynamically expanding virtual disk that uses a parent/child relationship in which the parent disk is a dynamically expanding or fixed size disk with an OS installed with possibly some applications and data. The differencing disk is a child of the parent and changes are only made to the differencing disk while the parent disk remains unaltered.

dynamically expanding disk   A virtual hard disk in which the initial size of the .vhd file is very small but can expand to the maximum size specified for the virtual disk.

emulated driver   Legacy driver installed on a VM that is used when synthetic drivers are not available or not installed.

external virtual network   A virtual network whereby one of the host's physical network adapters is bound to the virtual network switch, allowing virtual machines to access a LAN connected to the host.

fixed size disk   A virtual hard disk in which the full size of the disk is allocated on the host system when the virtual disk is created.

guest OS   An operating system installed on a virtual machine.

host computer   The physical computer on which virtual machine software is installed and virtual machines run.

host operating system   The originally installed operating system (if applicable) on the physical computer on which VM software is installed and VMs run.

hosted virtualization   OS virtualization in which the hypervisor is installed in a general-purpose host OS, such as Windows 7 or Linux, and the host OS accesses host hardware on behalf of the guest OS. Also known as a type 2 hypervisor.

hypervisor   The component of virtualization software that creates and monitors the virtual hardware environment, which allows multiple VMs to share physical hardware resources.

Integration Services   A software package installed on a VM's guest OS that provides enhanced drivers for the guest OS, bringing better performance and functionality to IDE and SCSI storage devices, the network interface, and mouse and video devices. Integration Services also better integrates the VM with the host OS providing services such as data exchange, time synchronization, OS shutdown, and others.

internal virtual network   An internal network is not bound to any of the host's physical NICs but a host virtual NIC is bound to the internal virtual switch. This allows virtual machines and the host computer to communicate with one another but VMs cannot access the physical network.

live migration   A process in which a virtual machine is moved to new hardware for performance or reliability improvements while the VM is running, resulting in practically no downtime.

pass-through disk   A physical disk attached to the host system that is placed offline so that it can be used by a VM instead of, or in addition to, a virtual disk.

private virtual network   A virtual network in which there is no host connection to the virtual network thereby allowing VMs to communicate with one another, but there is no communication between the private virtual network and the host.

snapshot   A partial copy of a virtual machine made at a particular moment, used to restore the virtual machine to its state when the snapshot was taken.

synthetic driver   Driver installed on a VM with Integration Services that is optimized for use in the Hyper-V environment.

virtual disk   One or more files stored on the host computer that represent the hard disk of a virtual machine.

virtual instance   An installation of Windows Server 2008 in a Hyper-V virtual machine.

virtual machine (VM)   A virtual environment that emulates a physical computer's hardware and BIOS.

virtual network   A network configuration created by virtualization software and used by virtual machines for network communication.

virtual processor   The virtual representation of a physical processor or processor core residing on the host which can be assigned to a virtual machine.

virtualization   A process that creates a software environment to emulate a computer's hardware and BIOS, allowing multiple OSs to run on the same physical computer at the same time.

VLAN identification   When enabled, subnets, or broadcast domains, can be created on a single external or internal virtual network. Machines that share a common VLAN ID can communicate with one another directly, but those assigned different VLAN IDs must communicate through a router.

Review Questions

1. Which of the following best defines a virtual machine?

   a. Computer hardware that supports virtualization extensions

   b. The environment that emulates a physical computer's hardware and BIOS

   c. The operating system installed on a VM

   d. A computer with the Hyper-V role installed

2. Which of the following is described as a partial copy of a VM made at a particular moment?

   a. virtual disk

   b. differencing disk

   c. hypervisor

   d. snapshot

3. Which Windows Server 2008 Edition includes four virtual instances of Windows Server 2008 in the license?

   a. Enterprise Edition

   b. Standard Edition

   c. Datacenter Edition

   d. Web Edition

4. What type of virtualization environment are you most likely to use for server virtualization in datacenters? (Choose all that apply.)

   a. hosted virtualization

   b. type 2 hypervisor

   c. bare-metal virtualization

   d. type 1 hypervisor

5. You have just purchased a new server with Windows Server 2008 Enterprise 32-bit Edition preinstalled. The server has 4 GB RAM, a 100 GB hard drive, and an Intel Xeon processor with Intel-VT. You plan to install the Hyper-V server role on this server and run one or two Windows Server 2008 VMs, each with a 1 GB RAM allocation. You have found that your server solution does not work for this purpose, what should you do?

   a. Install more RAM

   b. Install a bigger hard disk

   c. Install a 64-bit edition of Windows Server 2008

   d. Upgrade the processor

6. If you want to run two VMs on a Windows Server 2008 Standard Edition server, how many Windows Server 2008 licenses must you purchase in total?

   a. 1

   b. 2

   c. 3

   d. none

7. A virtual network with the host's physical NIC bound to the Microsoft Virtual Network Switch Protocol is called which of the following?

   a. external virtual network

   b. private virtual network

   c. switched virtual network

   d. internal virtual network

8. You've created a VM with Windows Server 2008 installed along with some applications. You want to quickly create a second virtual server that initially has the same configuration options and installed applications as the first one. You want good disk performance from both VMs. What should you do?

   a. Create a new VM. Create a differencing disk for the second VM and assign the first VM's virtual disk as the parent disk; the first VM will continue to use its original virtual disk.

   b. Export the first VM and import it. Use the imported VM as the second virtual server.

   c. Create a new VM. Create a snapshot of the first VM. Copy and rename the snapshot file and use it for the second VM's virtual hard disk.

   d. Create a new VM. Convert the virtual disk of the first VM to a pass-through disk and use the pass-through disk as the second VM's virtual hard disk.

9. You have an old server running Windows Server 2008 that has had several intermittent hardware failures in the past few months causing the server to shut down. You have not been able to isolate the problem, but you suspect the hard drives may be beginning to fail. The server is no longer in warranty. You have been using a Hyper-V server for about a year now with two VMs running on it. The quad-core server has plenty of disk space and ample processing power. Which of the following might be a good solution for the ailing server that requires the least amount of administrative effort?

   a. Purchase a new machine. Remove the hard disk from the old server and install it in the new server.

   b. Create a new VM on your Hyper-V server. Remove the hard disk from the old machine and install it in the Hyper-V server. Set the disk offline and use it as a pass-through disk for the new VM.

   c. Create a new VM on your Hyper-V server. On the old server, run a physical to virtual conversion. Use the resulting .vhd file as the virtual disk for the new VM. Take the old server offline.

   d. Create a new VM on your Hyper-V server. Install Windows Server 2008 as the guest OS. Carefully configure the guest OS to match the configuration of the old server. Take the old server offline.

10. You have three VMs that must communicate with one another and must also be able to communicate with the host computer. The VMs must not be able to access the physical network directly. What type of virtual network should you create?

    a. private

    b. internal

    c. host-based

    d. external

11. You are installing a new VM in Hyper-V that requires excellent disk performance for the installed applications to perform well. The applications require a virtual disk that is about 100 GB. Your host has two drive bays; one is used as the Windows system disk and the other is a data disk. Your host is currently running a VM that uses a virtual disk stored on the host's data drive. The currently running VM requires little disk access and uses only 20 GB of the host's data drive and will max out at 40 GB. The host's data drive is 500 GB. What type of disk should you use for the new VM you are installing?

    a. differencing disk

    b. dynamically expanding disk

    c. pass-through disk

    d. fixed size disk

12. Your Hyper-V server has a single disk of 200 GB that is being used as the system disk and to host a dynamically expanding disk for a Windows Server 2008 VM. Your VM's virtual disk has a maximum size of 200 GB and it is currently 80 GB and growing. You only have about 30 GB free space on the host disk. You are finding that disk contention with the host OS and the constant need for the virtual disk to expand is causing performance problems. You also have plans to install at least one more VM. You have installed a new 500 GB hard drive on the host. You want to ensure that your VM does not contend for the host's system disk and is not hampered in disk performance by the expansion process. What should you do?

    a. Create a new fixed size disk on the new drive. Use disk management on the VM to extend the current disk onto the new fixed size disk.

    b. Shut down the VM. Convert the dynamically expanding disk to a fixed size disk, being sure to place the fixed size disk on the new host drive. Connect the VM to the fixed size disk in place of the dynamically expanding disk. Delete the old virtual disk.

    c. Shut down the VM. Create a new fixed size disk on the new drive. Copy the contents of the dynamically expanding disk to the new fixed size disk. Connect the VM to the fixed size disk in place of the dynamically expanding disk. Delete the old virtual disk.

    d. Create a new fixed size disk on the new drive. Add the fixed size disk to the VM as a new disk. On the VM, create a new volume on the new disk and begin saving files to the new volume.

    e. Set the new host disk offline and use it as a pass-through disk for the VM. Use the Convert Virtual Disk option to convert the current dynamically expanding disk to the pass-through disk. Delete the old virtual disk.

13. Your network has been experiencing long power outages that have caused your Hyper-V servers to shut down once the UPS battery is drained. When power returns, your Hyper-V servers automatically reboot but your VMs are not starting. You have been told to make sure the VMs start when the host starts. What should you do?

    a. Change the VM's BIOS settings

    b. Write a script on the host that automatically starts the VMs when the host starts

    c. Reinstall Integration Services

    d. Change the Automatic Start Action on the VMs

14. You have solved the problem with your VMs not starting when the host restarts, but now you find that your VM's are taking an awful long time to start when the host starts. On some hosts, you have as many as six VMs. You also find that the VM running an application server cannot initialize properly because the VM running DNS is not available immediately. What can you do to improve the startup time of the VMs and solve the application server problem?

    a. Set a Virtual Machine Priority in the Hyper-V settings

    b. Set a Startup delay for each VM, making sure the delay for the DNS server is less than that of the application server

    c. Change the BIOS settings of the DNS server to use the Quick Boot option

    d. Assign more virtual processors to the VMs you want to start faster

15. You have found that snapshots for your test VMs are taking up too much space on the host's system disk. You currently have two test VMs running, each with one snapshot. The snapshots represent your baseline testing environment. You are finished with your current testing and are ready for another round of testing but you want to make sure your snapshots are stored on another volume. What should you do?

    a. In Hyper-V Manager, change the snapshots path in Hyper-V Settings to point to the other volume; the snapshots will be moved automatically.

    b. Use Windows Explorer to move the snapshot files from their current location to the other volume.

    c.   Shut down the VMs. Apply the snapshot to each VM. Delete the snapshots using Hyper-V Manager. Change the path of the snapshot files to the other volume. Create a new snapshot for each VM.

    d.   In each VM's settings, change the snapshot path. Apply the snapshot and then create a new snapshot for each VM. Delete the old snapshots using Windows Explorer.

16.   Which of the following is true about using differencing disks?

    a.   Snapshots can be used with differencing disks but performance is decreased

    b.   The parent disk must not be changed

    c.   The parent disk must always be connected to a running VM

    d.   Differencing disks are a lot like fixed disks

    e.   Snapshots can be used with differencing disks but performance is decreased.

17.   You have four snapshots of a VM. You want to return the VM to the state when the second snapshot was taken. Which snapshot option should you use?

    a.   Apply

    b.   Save

    c.   Select

    d.   Revert

18.   You are working with a Windows Server 2003 VM in Hyper-V. Every time you click your mouse in the VM's window, it is captured and you have to enter Ctrl+Alt+Left Arrow to use the mouse on the host OS. This is getting annoying. What can you do to make using the VM more pleasant?

    a.   Install a new mouse on the host system that supports Hyper-V

    b.   Install Integration Services on the host computer

    c.   Install Integration Services on the VM

    d.   Install emulated mouse drivers on the VM

19.   You want to run four VMs on a Hyper-V server. Two VMs need to be assigned 1 GB RAM and two need to be assigned 1.5 GB RAM for optimal performance. How much RAM should the host computer have installed?

    a.   512 MB

    b.   4 GB

    c.   5 GB

    d.   6 GB

20.   You want to run three VMs on a Hyper-V server. Two of the VMs should be assigned two virtual processors while the other requires only one. The host should have at least one physical processor dedicated to it. What configuration should you use on the host?

    a.   A quad-core CPU

    b.   Two quad-core CPUs

    c.   Two dual-core CPUs

    d.   One quad-core and one dual-core CPU

9

Case Projects

Case Project 9-1: Choosing Virtual Disk Configurations

You have two Windows Server 2008 computers with the Hyper-V role installed. Both computers have two hard drives, one for the system volume and the other can be used for data. One server, named HyperVTest is primarily going to be used for testing and what-if scenarios and its data drive is 250 GB. You estimate that you might have eight or ten VMs configured on HyperVTest with two or three running at the same time. Each test VM will have disk requirements ranging from about 10 GB to 30 GB. The other server, named HyperVApp will run in the datacenter with production applications installed in your datacenter. HyperVApp's data drive is 500 GB. You expect two VMs to run on HyperVApp, with disk space needs of about 150 to 200 GB each. Both VMs will run fairly disk-intensive applications. Given this environment, describe how you would configure the virtual disks for the VMs on both servers. Explain your answer.

Case Project 9-2: Choosing a Virtual Network Configuration

You are setting up a test environment that involves two subnets with three Windows Server 2008 servers on each subnet. The servers will be running network services that are broadcast-based such as DHCP. Your host computer is attached to your production network so you must avoid any conflicts. You want the two subnets to be able to communicate with one another. Your test environment will be a single Windows Server 2008 machine running Hyper-V. How should you configure your virtual network?

Case Project 9-3: Implementing a Hyper-V Solution

In this case project, you will create three Hyper-V VMs named VM1, VM2, and VM3 and configure virtual networks. Figure 9-28 depicts the network (this is the same figure as Figure 9-14) configuration. Create the VMs and configure the virtual networks. There is no need to install an OS on the VMs unless you want to test your configuration. As documentation of your completed configuration, provide your instructor with the following:

- Screenshots of the Hyper-V Virtual Network Manager page; each screenshot should have one of the virtual networks selected so its type can be determined.

- Screenshots of the Settings page of each VM.

- Your IP addressing scheme showing the IP addresses/default gateways of each NIC on the VMs and the host.

- What must be configured on one of the VMs to communicate with the physical network? On what VM does this configuration take place?

Your instructor may add additional requirements to this project.

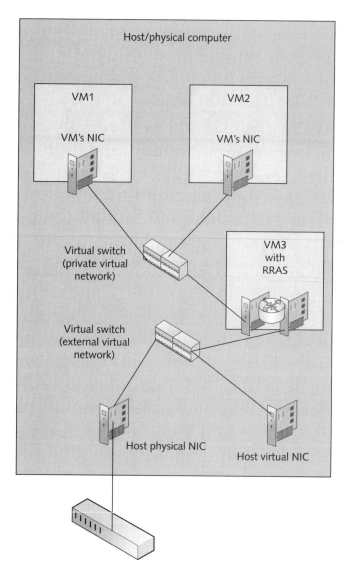

Figure 9-28 Diagram for Case Project 9-3

© Cengage Learning 2012

9

Chapter 10

Configuring Windows Server 2008 for High Availability

After reading this chapter and completing the exercises, you will be able to:

- Discuss Windows Server 2008 high availability technologies
- Configure round-robin DNS
- Configure network load balancing
- Configure a failover cluster

Businesses depend on their networks and network data more than ever before. If the network servers are not available, in many cases, productivity comes to a grinding halt. The importance of server high availability cannot be overstated, so Windows Server 2008 provides a number of high availability server options to ensure that productivity continues even if one server fails.

This chapter discusses the high availability options available in Windows Server 2008, including hardware redundancy, round-robin DNS, network load balancing, and failover clustering.

Windows Server 2008 High Availability Technologies

High availability can be described with terms like mean time between failures (MTBF), mean time to recover (MTTR), recovery point objective (RPO), and recovery time objective (RTO), but, the bottom line is that **high availability** simply means that data and applications are available when you need them, even in the event of a system failure.

You are probably already familiar with some types of high availability such as that which you get with Active Directory when you have at least two domain controllers (DCs) on the network. Active Directory has built-in replication that ensures that if one DC goes down, one or more other DCs have all the data needed to continue to manage the domain. And DNS has similar facilities to ensure name resolution continues even when one DNS server fails.

High availability can also mean fast response time from a service or application such that two or more servers spread the workload when a single server doesn't have the resources or bandwidth to handle the volume of service requests.

While Active Directory and DNS have some high availability features built-in, what about all your other services and applications? Your database or Web site may be a central component of your business operation, and almost every network needs high availability to their shared files and printers. Fortunately, Windows Server 2008 has high availability features that can accommodate almost any service or application to which network users need fast access 24 hours a day, 7 days a week.

Server high availability is usually accomplished with some type of fault tolerance. **Fault tolerance** in this context is the ability of a server to recover from some type of hardware failure. Fault tolerance often involves redundant hardware. **Redundant hardware** is the use of two or more devices that perform the same task so that if one fails or has reached its performance limits, the other device is activated. Or, all devices can share the workload, thereby putting less stress on a single device and often providing better performance.

For server high availability, fault tolerance can be accomplished at the component level or the server level. The focus of this chapter is server-level high availability, but since Windows Server 2008 has a number of component-level high availability features, we'll briefly discuss them here. Besides, if you are willing to incur the costs of server-level high availability, you are more than likely going to use servers that support one or more component-level fault tolerant features.

Component-Level Fault Tolerance

Server hardware differs from desktop hardware in a number of ways, but none is more important than the fault tolerant features that most servers are equipped with. At minimum, most servers have these fault tolerant features:

- *ECC memory*. While more expensive than non-ECC memory, **Error Correction Code (ECC) memory** modules, along with the supporting motherboard hardware, can detect and sometimes correct bit errors caused by electrical disturbances. ECC memory functionality is carried out in hardware so it is not necessary for the OS to support it.

- *RAID disk configurations*. RAID was discussed in Chapter 3 and is likely a part of most server configurations. As a refresher, only RAID levels above RAID 0 provide fault tolerance. RAID 1 and RAID 5 are common server disk configurations, and RAID 6 and RAID 1+0 (RAID 10) are becoming more common. While hardware RAID (RAID functions carried out by the disk controller) are preferable, Windows Server 2008 supports software RAID 0, RAID 1, and RAID 5 if the server hardware doesn't support RAID.

- *Hot-swappable disks.* Even fairly basic servers today support the ability to add and remove disk drives while the system is running. This feature must also be supported by the OS; all Windows Server 2008 editions support hot-swappable disks. If a disk in a RAID array fails, the disk can be replaced while the system continues to run, thereby incurring no downtime.

Some servers use external storage such as SANs rather than locally connected hot-swappable drives.

While the features listed above provide some level of fault tolerance and are available on even basic servers, more expensive servers are available that support the following features:

- *Redundant power supplies.* Two or more power supply units, each with sufficient power to maintain the running server, work in tandem to supply the server with power. Since each unit only has half the work to do, reliability should be better, and if one unit fails, the other can keep the system running.

- *Hot add/replace memory.* Memory can be added and/or replaced while the system is running. Only supported in high-end servers, hot add memory is supported by Windows Server 2008 Enterprise Edition while hot add and hot replace is supported by Datacenter Edition.

- *Hot add/replace CPU.* Only Windows Server 2008 Datacenter Edition supports this high-end server feature.

10

Server-Level High Availability/Fault Tolerance

The presence of a range of fault-tolerant components in the servers can, no doubt, help a server administrator sleep easier, but some failures are beyond the ability of fault-tolerant components to recover from. In addition, sometimes you simply can't help but take down a server for maintenance. This is where server-level high availability technologies come in.

Windows Server 2008 provides three primary high availability technologies, each of which is discussed in the sections that follow:

- *Round-robin load balancing.* Round-robin load balancing is sometimes referred to as a poor man's load balancer, but it has its place in high availability and is the technique used to load balance domain controllers and some Web servers.

- *Network load balancing (NLB) clusters.* NLB distributes client requests among the cluster members and dynamically adjusts the distribution based on changing conditions.

- *Failover clusters.* Two or more servers that function as a single logical unit which are connected by a separate high-speed network link. If one server fails, the others detect this and take on the failed server's workload.

Round-Robin Load Balancing

Round-robin load balancing, also referred to as round-robin distribution, uses multiple DNS records to resolve the same host name to multiple IP addresses. The DNS server cycles through the duplicate host records, returning a different IP address for each subsequent query. For example, if you have a Web site hosted by a server that cannot keep up with the workload, you can host the site on a second server. So you now have two servers, each with the same Web site content. You could add a third server or more if necessary. Web clients access the server using the name www.yourdomain.local. Your DNS records for yourdomain.local may look like Table 10-1 if you had three servers, each with the same content.

Table 10-1 DNS records for www.yourdomain.local in a round-robin load balancing scheme

Record type	Host name	Address
A	www	192.0.2.1
A	www	192.0.2.2
A	www	192.0.2.3

In Table 10-1, each host record in the DNS database has a different IP address associated with it. Now, say that you have three clients requesting pages from www.yourdomain.local as illustrated in Figure 10-1. Client1 queries the DNS server first and receives the IP addresses in this order: 192.0.2.1, 192.0.2.2, 192.0.2.3. Client1 will attempt to access the server using the first IP address in the list (192.0.2.1) returned by the DNS server. Client2 queries the DNS server next and receives the addresses in this order: 192.0.2.2, 192.0.2.3, 192.0.2.1. Client2 accesses the server using 192.0.2.2. Client3 receives the IP addresses in this order: 192.0.2.3, 192.0.2.1, 192.0.2.2. A fourth client would receive them in the original order.

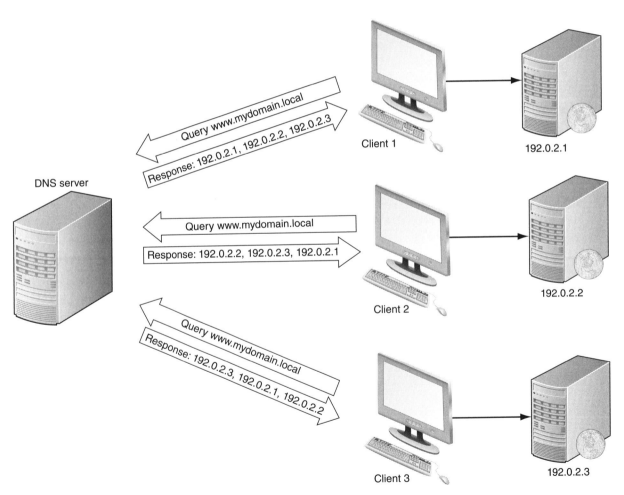

Figure 10-1 Using DNS for round-robin load balancing

© Cengage Learning 2012

In this way, each server receives one of N client requests where N is the number of servers mapped to the same DNS name. This type of load balancing has its flaws as outlined below:

- *No recognition of a down server.* The DNS server has no way of knowing if one of the servers in a round-robin list goes down, resulting in clients attempting to communicate with a server that is no longer responding. The record of the down server must be deleted from the DNS server but it will still take some time before any cached records by downstream servers or clients are updated.

- *Cached client records.* Clients that cache DNS records will continue to use the same IP address for subsequent accesses to the host until the cached records expire.

- *All servers have equal priority.* Round-robin DNS cannot discriminate among servers of unequal performance. If one server has higher performance capabilities than another, you might want the higher-performance server to receive a higher proportion of client requests. DNS round-robin does not let you assign weight or priority to one record over another so each server's IP address will be placed first in the response list an equal number of times.

Activity 10-1: Install DNS and Create a New Zone

Time Required: 15 minutes
Objective: Install the DNS server role and create a new zone

Description: You need to understand how DNS round-robin load balancing works so you can implement it for your Web server. You will install the DNS Server role and create a new zone and then in the next activity, you will create A records for round-robin functionality.

1. Log on to your Windows Server 2008 computer as Administrator, if necessary. If Server Manager doesn't start, click the server icon in the Quick Launch toolbar.

2. In the left pane of Server Manager, click **Roles**.

3. Click **Add Roles** in the Roles Summary pane on the right. In the Before You Begin window, click **Next**.

4. In the Select Server Roles window, click to select the **DNS Server** check box, and then click **Next**.

5. The next window displays information about the DNS Server role. Read this information, and then click **Next**.

6. On the Confirm Installation Selections screen, click **Install**. When the installation is complete, click **Close**.

7. To open DNS Manager, click **Start, Administrative Tools**, and click **DNS**.

8. Click to expand the DNS server node, and click **Forward Lookup Zones**. Right-click **Forward Lookup Zones** and click **New Zone**. The New Zone Wizard starts. Click **Next**.

9. In the Zone Type screen, accept the default zone type of **Primary** and click **Next**.

10. In the Zone Name screen, type **rrtest.local** (for round-robin test) and click **Next**. Accept the default file name for the zone and click **Next**.

11. In the Dynamic Update screen, click **Next** to accept the default. Click **Finish**.

12. Keep DNS Manager open for the next activity.

10

Activity 10-2: Configure DNS for Round-Robin Load Balancing

Time Required: 15 minutes
Objective: Create A records and view round-robin configuration options

Description: Now that you have your zone created, you can configure the DNS server for round-robin load balancing. First, you will check the DNS server options to verify that round-robin is enabled. Then you create A records for your Web server. Finally, you will test round-robin functionality using nslookup.

1. Log on to your Windows Server 2008 computer as Administrator, if necessary. Start DNS Manager if necessary.

2. In the left pane of DNS Manager, right-click the server node and click **Properties**. Click the **Advanced** tab as shown in Figure 10-2.

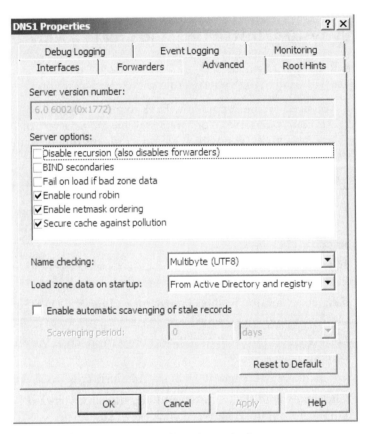

Figure 10-2 DNS server Properties Advanced tab
© Cengage Learning 2012

3. By default, round-robin is enabled. If you want to disable round-robin, you would clear the check box. Click **Cancel**.

4. Click to expand **Forward Lookup Zones**, if necessary and click **rrtest.local**. Right-click **rrtest.local** and click **New Host (A or AAAA)**.

5. In the New Host screen, type **www** in the Name box and type **192.0.2.100** in the IP address box. Click **Add Host**. Click **OK**.

6. Repeat step 5 two more times, using **www** for the name and **192.0.2.101** and **192.0.2.102** respectively for the IP address. Click **Done**. Your zone data should look similar to Figure 10-3.

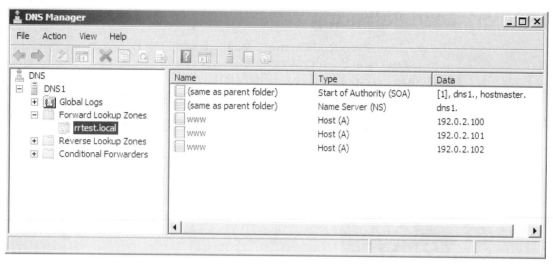

Figure 10-3 Zone data with three A records
© Cengage Learning 2012

7. To test the round-robin configuration, you can use nslookup. Open a command prompt. Type **nslookup** and press **Enter**.

8. Make sure the server nslookup will query is your server by typing **server 127.0.0.1** and pressing **Enter**.

9. Type **www.rrtest.local** and press **Enter**. The DNS server should return all three IP addresses defined for host www. Type **www.rrtest.local** and press **Enter** again. You should see the order of the returned addresses has changed. You should get output similar to Figure 10-4.

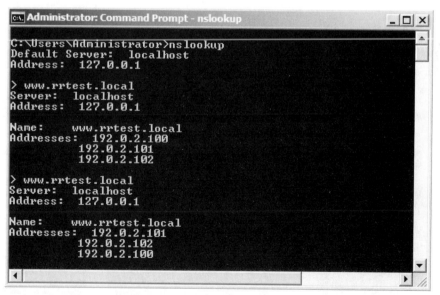

Figure 10-4 Testing round-robin DNS with nslookup
© Cengage Learning 2012

10. If you continue to query for www.rrtest.local you should see the order of the returned addresses change with each query. Close the command prompt.

While round-robin load balancing is useful for basic load balancing requirements, its shortcomings, as mentioned above, might lead you to use a more sophisticated load balancing method that provides a more robust solution. The Windows Server 2008 Network Load Balancing feature, discussed next, may be just what you need.

Network Load Balancing

The Windows Server 2008 **network load balancing** (**NLB**) feature uses server clusters to provide both scalability and fault tolerance. A **server cluster** is a group of two or more servers that are configured to respond to a single virtual IP address. Based on an internal algorithm, the servers decide which server should respond to each incoming client request. To provide scalability, the servers in an NLB cluster share the load of incoming requests based on rules you can define. To provide fault tolerance, a failed server can be removed from the cluster and another server can take its place and begin servicing client requests that were handled by the failed server. While NLB does provide a level of fault tolerance, its primary function is to efficiently handle a large volume of client traffic.

 A server cluster is sometimes referred to as a server farm.

From a client computer's perspective, a server cluster appears on the network as a single device with a single name and IP address. A cluster is assigned a name, much like a server is assigned a host name and the cluster is assigned an IP address. Client computers connect to the cluster rather than to the individual servers that make up the cluster. Figure 10-5 illustrates an NLB cluster where three servers participate in the cluster. The clients in the figure use a single virtual IP address, in this example 10.1.1.1, to access the cluster. The NLB software running on the servers responds to the virtual IP address and decides which of the three servers should respond to each client request.

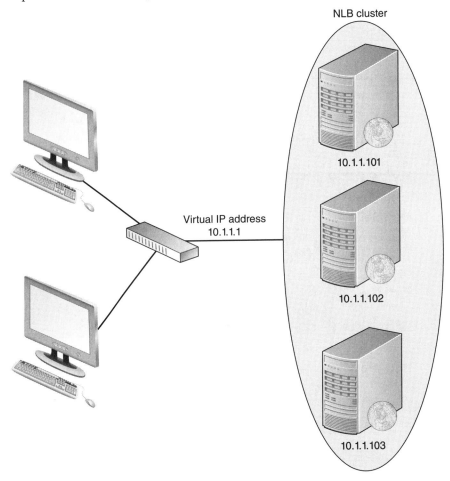

Figure 10-5 A logical depiction of network load balancing
© Cengage Learning 2012

NLB is well suited to TCP/IP-based applications such as Web servers and streaming media servers where the data can be easily replicated among the participating servers and is not changed by users. NLB clusters are also effective in distributing the load among VPN servers and terminal server farms.

NLB is not advisable if the data being accessed on the servers require exclusive access such as with database, file and print, and e-mail applications. Failover clusters, discussed later in this chapter, are a better fit for those types of applications.

Installing Network Load Balancing

NLB is available on all three editions of Windows Server 2008, plus Web edition. While NLB clusters don't have any special hardware requirements, it is important that each server in the cluster is configured with the same OS version and that updates are consistent among all servers. Typically, servers participating in an NLB cluster should not provide services other than the services that the cluster is providing. For example, it is not recommended to use a domain controller as a cluster server.

NLB must be installed on each server in the cluster and the networking services that will be load balanced must be installed and configured identically. NLB does not provide data replication so the cluster administrator must ensure that the data provided by the cluster servers is consistent among all servers.

Ideally, the servers in an NLB cluster should be configured with two NICs. One NIC is used for communication with network clients that request cluster services while the other NIC is dedicated for communication among the cluster members. Figure 10-6 shows this arrangement. The second NIC can be configured to operate on a separate logical IP network as Figure 10-6 shows, or they can be configured for the same IP network as the NLB clients.

10

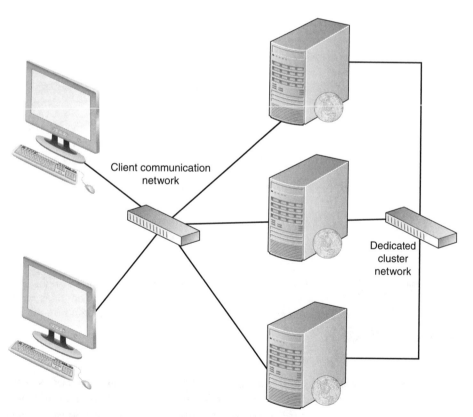

Figure 10-6 NLB cluster – servers have two NICs
© Cengage Learning 2012

NLB is installed as a feature using Server Manager as detailed in Activity 10-3. Once installed, NLB is configured for all participating servers using the Network Load Balancing Manager console. An NLB cluster can be configured from any of the servers running the NLB Manager console.

Activity 10-3: Install the Network Load Balancing Feature

Time Required: 10 minutes
Objective: Install the network load balancing feature on Windows Server 2008

Description: Your Web site is increasingly popular and performance has been degrading steadily over the past few months. You decide to deploy a second server and configure NLB to distribute the load between two Web servers. Your servers should be named NLB1 and NLB2. Figure 10-7 illustrates the topology; however, the network clients shown in the figure are not required to complete the activity.

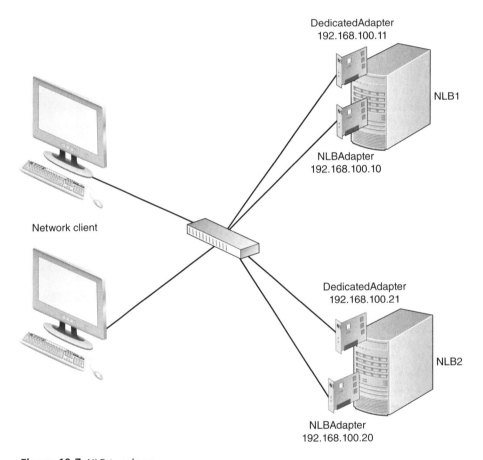

Figure 10-7 NLB topology
© Cengage Learning 2012

   The remaining activities in this chapter require two Windows Server 2008 servers with two NICs. If the available lab equipment does not meet these requirements, these activities can be done as a demonstration.

1. Log on to the NLB1 server as Administrator.
2. Open **Network and Sharing Center** and click **Manage network connections.** Rename Local Area Connection to **NLBAdapter** and Local Area Connection 2 to **Dedicated-Adapter** (see Figure 10-8). You rename the connections so that you can easily identify each connection when setting up load balancing. DedicatedAdapter is used to communicate among the servers in the cluster and to accept direct, non-cluster connections with clients. NLBAdapter is the connection that is used to communicate with clients accessing services provided by the load balanced cluster.

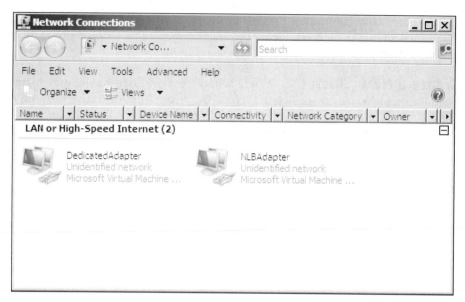

Figure 10-8 Preparing network connections for an NLB cluster
© Cengage Learning 2012

3. Right-click **NLBAdapter** and click **Properties**. Double-click **Internet Protocol Version 4 (TCP/IP)**. Set the IP address to **192.168.100.10** with a subnet mask of **255.255.255.0**. Click **Advanced** and click the **DNS** tab. Click to uncheck the **Register this connection's address in DNS** check box. This is done so that only the Dedicated-Adapter's address is listed in DNS. Click **OK** until you are back to the Network Connections window.

4. On the DedicatedAdapter connection, set the IP address to **192.168.100.11** with a subnet mask of **255.255.255.0**. Close Network Connections and Network and Sharing Center.

5. Open **Server Manager** and click **Features**. Click **Add Features**. In the Select Features screen, click the check box next to **Network Load Balancing** and click **Next**. Click **Install**.

6. On the Installation Results screen, confirm that Network Load Balancing was successfully installed and click **Close** to return to Server Manager.

7. Log on to NLB2 as Administrator and repeat steps 2 through 6. In step 3, use values **20** and **21** respectively in the fourth octet of the IP addresses of NLBAdapter and DedicatedAdapter.

8. Stay logged on to both servers for the next activity.

Creating a Network Load Balancing Cluster

Once NLB is installed on each server you can create a load balancing cluster and configure load balancing options. The creation of an NLB cluster involves the following tasks:

- Create a new cluster
- Select a host and network interface to participate in the cluster
- Configure the host priority/host ID
- Set the cluster IP address
- Set the cluster name and operation mode
- Configure port rules
- Add additional servers to the cluster

Additional configuration of the cluster can be done later if you wish to change how traffic is distributed among the servers. We'll take a closer look at each task before you configure an NLB cluster in Activity 10-4.

Create a New Cluster   To create a new network load balancing cluster, open Network Load Balancing Manager (shown in Figure 10-9) from Administrative tools on one of the servers that has the NLB feature installed. If you right-click Network Load Balancing Clusters, you have the option of creating a new cluster or connecting to an existing cluster.

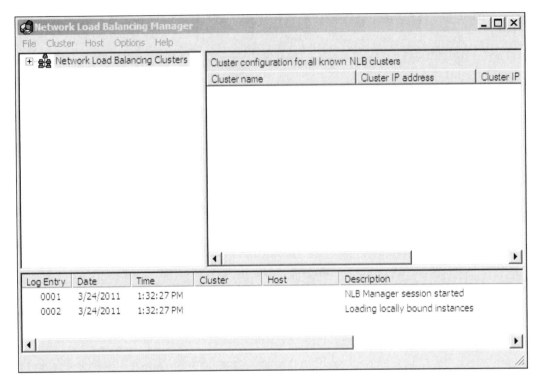

Figure 10-9 Network Load Balancing Manager
© Cengage Learning 2012

Select a Host and Network Interface to Participate in the Cluster   When you create a new cluster, you must specify a host that will participate in the new cluster. You can type the name of the server from which you are running Network Load Balancing Manager or a different server. In most cases, you will type the name of the server from which you are running NLB Manager. Once NLB Manager is connected to the server you specify, you are asked to select the network interface that the server will use in the new cluster. If you have more than one network interface, you should choose the interface that will be used to communicate with client computers accessing the cluster. In our example topology depicted in Figure 10-7, this is the interface named NLBAdapter. In addition, if you are using two NICs, you should remove the dedicated IP address (see Figure 10-14, later in the chapter).

Configure the Host Priority/Host ID   Each host participating in an NLB cluster is assigned a unique host ID which is also the host's priority in the cluster. You can have up to 32 servers in an NLB cluster so you can choose a priority value from 1 to 32. The cluster member that has the lowest priority (ID) handles all cluster traffic that is not associated with a port rule. This behavior can be overridden by defining specific port rules (discussed below). Every server in a cluster must have a unique priority value.

Set the Cluster IP Address The cluster IP address, or **virtual IP address,** is the address by which the networking services provided by the cluster are accessed by network clients. A DNS host record should exist for the cluster name mapped to this address. If you are using a single NIC configuration for your NLB servers, the cluster IP address will be added to the TCP/IP properties of the adapter; although, depending on your NIC, you may have to add this address manually. If you are using two NICs, the cluster address will replace the current address assigned to the NLB adapter, assuming you removed the dedicated IP address on the NLB adapter. You can use either IPv4 or IPv6 addresses.

Set the Cluster Name and Operation Mode The cluster name and operation mode are set in the Cluster Parameters screen shown in Figure 10-10. The cluster name is the fully qualified domain name (FQDN) that clients will use to access the cluster and is specified in the Full Internet name box in the figure. The name should have a corresponding DNS host record entry associated with the cluster IP address. So, referring to Figure 10-10, you would need a DNS zone named mydomain.local with an A record for host nlb with IP address 192.168.100.100.

New Cluster : Cluster Parameters ☒

Cluster IP configuration

IP address: 192.168.100.100 ▼

Subnet mask: 255 . 255 . 255 . 0

Full Internet name: nlb.mydomain.local

Network address: 02-bf-c0-a8-64-64

Cluster operation mode

⊙ Unicast

○ Multicast

○ IGMP multicast

< Back   Next >   Cancel   Help

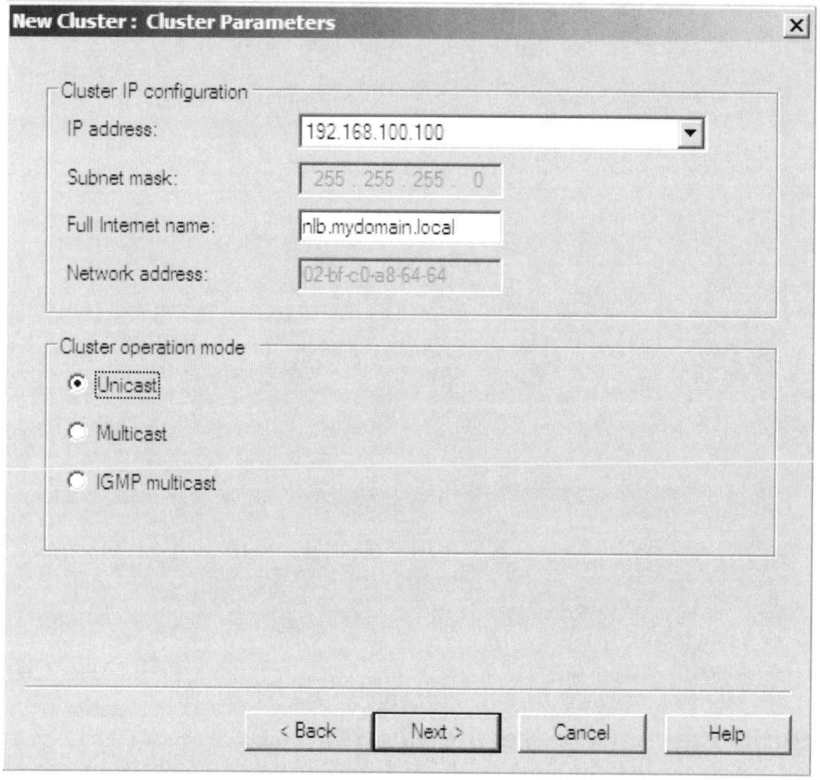

Figure 10-10 Cluster Parameters
© Cengage Learning 2012

You must have DNS set up correctly for NLB to work properly. A zone for the FQDN specified for the cluster name and appropriate A records for each server must be configured. In addition, you must create an A record for the cluster name and cluster IP address (NLB and 192.168.100.100 in Figure 10-10).

The **cluster operation mode** specifies the type of network addressing used to access the cluster: Unicast, Multicast, or IGMP multicast. The default option is Unicast. The multicast options can make network communication more efficient, but multicast support must be available and configured on your routers and switches.

Configure Port Rules The last step in the initial configuration of your NLB cluster is to define port rules. A **port rule** specifies which type of TCP or UDP traffic the cluster should respond to and how that traffic is distributed among the cluster members. The default port rule, shown in Figure 10-11 specifies that all TCP and UDP traffic on all ports are balanced across the members of the cluster according to each member's load weight. Each cluster member can be assigned a load weight whereby the traffic is distributed proportional to the member's load weight with respect to the load weight of the other members. The higher the load weight, the more traffic that member will handle. Port rules can be modified at any time if you wish to change the default behavior of the cluster. Cluster configuration is discussed later under Configuring an NLB Cluster.

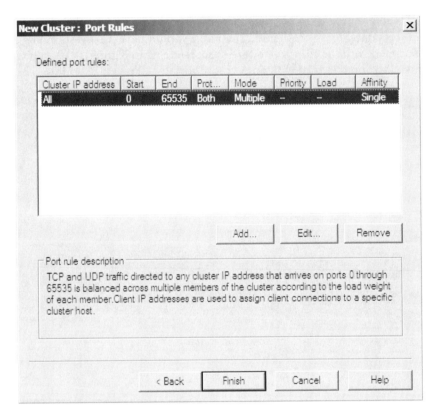

Figure 10-11 Default port rule
© Cengage Learning 2012

Add Additional Servers to the Cluster Once your cluster is created, you can add additional servers to the cluster. You do so from Network Load Balancing Manager by right-clicking the cluster and clicking Add Host to Cluster. However, the Network Load Balancing feature must first be installed on the server that you wish to add to the cluster. Once again, you must select the network interface the server will use for communication with clients. And you must assign a priority. Since the value 1 is already used for the first server in the cluster, the priority value defaults to 2. You have the opportunity to assign port rules for the new server, and if necessary, change the load weight. The load weight value defaults to Equal and valid values are 0 to 100. Once you have at least two servers in the cluster, you can further configure your cluster.

Activity 10-4: Create an NLB Cluster

Time Required: 15 minutes
Objective: Create an NLB Cluster

Description: Now that you have the NLB feature installed on your two servers, you can create the cluster and add the servers to the cluster.

A DNS server should be available with a zone named mydomain.local. Both servers should have their IP address settings configured so that their Preferred DNS Server points to the DNS server that manages that zone. A records for each server's DedicatedAdapter address should be in the zone and an A record for NLB with IP address 192.168.100.100 should also be created. This activity can still be completed without proper DNS configuration but NLB may report errors. Figure 10-12 shows the DNS configuration this activity uses.

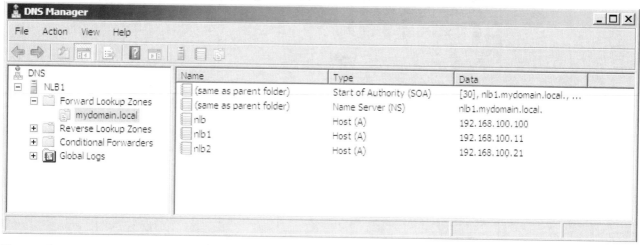

Figure 10-12 DNS configuration for this NLB activity
© Cengage Learning 2012

10

1. Log on to the NLB1 server as Administrator.

2. Open **Network Load Balancing Manager** from Administrative Tools.

3. Right-click **Network Load Balancing Clusters** and click **New Cluster**. In the Host box, type **nlb1** and click **Connect**. Once connected, the New Cluster: Connect screen shows the available interfaces for server nlb1 as shown in Figure 10-13. Click **NLB-Adapter** and click **Next**.

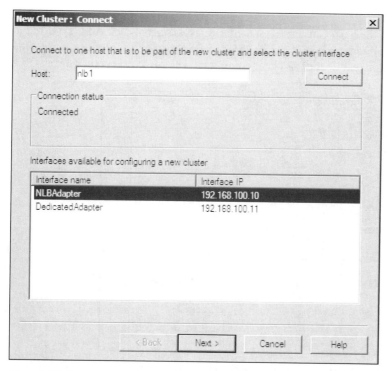

Figure 10-13 New Cluster: Connect screen
© Cengage Learning 2012

4. In the New Cluster: Host Parameters screen (Figure 10-14), you choose the Priority (unique host identifier). Accept the default value of 1. The Dedicated IP addresses section lists the IP address that will be used when an external device communicates directly with the server. The Dedicated IP address is only used if you are using a single adapter configuration. Since you have two adapters, click the listed IP address and click **Remove**. The Default state option specifies how this host should behave when it boots. The default state is Started which means that this host participates in the cluster when the system boots. Click **Next**. Click **Yes** on the No Dedicated IP Addresses message.

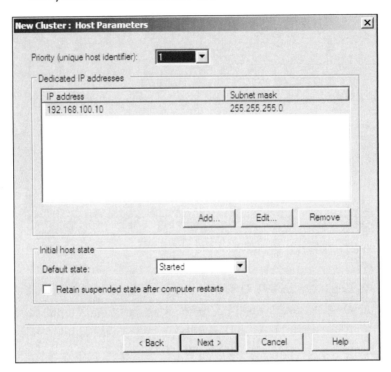

Figure 10-14 New Cluster: Host Parameters screen
© Cengage Learning 2012

5. On the New Cluster: Cluster IP Addresses screen, click **Add**. Type **192.168.100.100** in the IPv4 address box and **255.255.255.0** in the Subnet mask box (see Figure 10-15). This is the virtual IP address client computers will use to access the cluster. Click **OK**. Click **Next**.

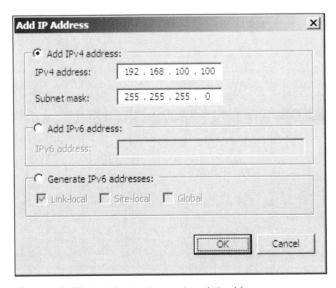

Figure 10-15 Specify the cluster virtual IP address
© Cengage Learning 2012

6. On the New Cluster: Cluster Parameters screen type **nlb.mydomain.local** in the Full Internet name box (see Figure 10-16). This is the name client computers use to access the cluster. Leave the Cluster operation mode set to Unicast, which is the default setting. Click **Next**.

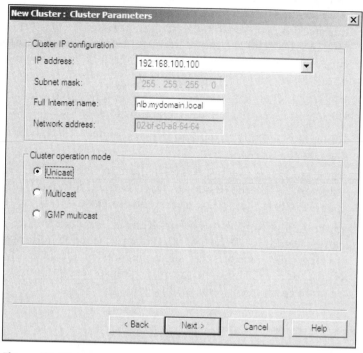

Figure 10-16 New Cluster: Cluster Parameters screen
© Cengage Learning 2012

7. On the New Cluster: Port Rules screen (see Figure 10-17), read the Port rule description for the default port rule. Click **Finish**.

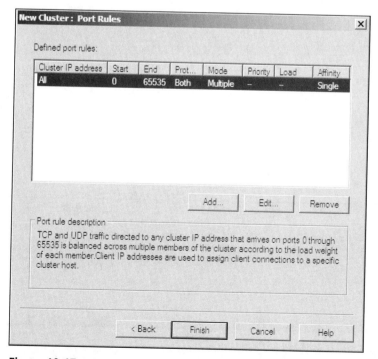

Figure 10-17 New Cluster: Port Rules screen
© Cengage Learning 2012

8. You are brought back to the Network Load Balancing Manager console. You may see some errors in the log screen at the bottom of Network Load Balancing Manager. If you do, check your DNS configuration and network adapter IP address settings. If you see an error stating "The bind operation was successful but NLB is not responding to queries," you will have to manually set the cluster IP address on the network interface. To do so, open the properties page for **NLBAdapter**, double-click **Internet Protocol Version 4**, and click **Advanced**. Click **Add** under IP addresses. Type **192.168.100.100** for the IP address and **255.255.255.0** for the subnet mask and click **Add**. Click **OK** until you see the Network Connections window. Shut down and restart NLB1 and open Network Load Balancing Manager.

9. Next, add NLB2 as a second cluster host. Click to expand **Network Load Balancing Clusters** if necessary. Right-click **nlb.mydomain.local** and click **Add Host to Cluster**.

10. In the Host box, type **nlb2** and click **Connect**. Click **NLBAdapter** if necessary and click **Next**.

11. In the Add Host to Cluster: Host Parameters screen, leave the Priority at the default value of 2. Click the IP address listed in the Dedicated IP addresses section and click **Remove**. Click **Next**. Click **Yes** on the No Dedicated IP Addresses message.

12. In the Add Host to Cluster: Port Rules screen click **Finish**. You may have to add the cluster IP address (192.168.100.100) as a second IP address to NLBAdapter on NLB2 if you get the error message mentioned in step 8. A properly configured and working NLB cluster will show the status of both servers as Converged and both servers will be outlined in green as shown in Figure 10-18.

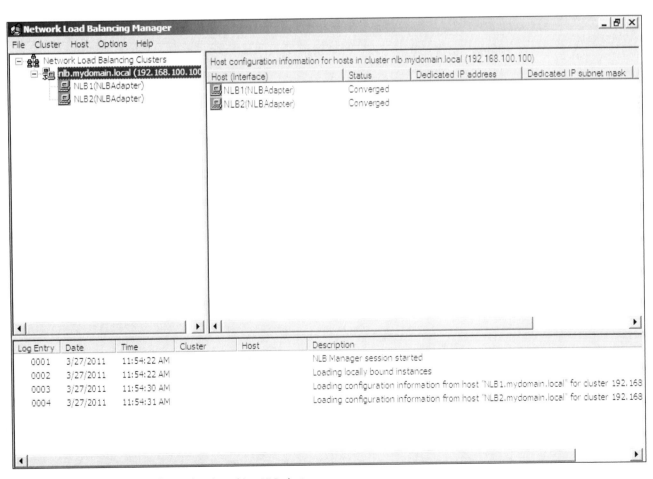

Figure 10-18 A properly configured and working NLB cluster

© Cengage Learning 2012

Configuring an NLB cluster can be a complex undertaking and much can go wrong. DNS must be set up properly, your NICs must be capable of dynamic MAC address changes, and your IP configuration must be correct. If you believe you have everything set correctly but NLB Manager still reports errors, shut down both servers and restart them. Open NLB Manager once both servers have completely restarted to see if the problem is resolved.

Configuring an NLB Cluster

Once you have a running NLB cluster, you can further configure the cluster and host settings. Configuration of the NLB cluster is generally broken into three categories:

- Cluster properties
- Host properties
- Port rules

The sections that follow discuss each of these configuration areas.

Configuring Cluster Properties
To configure cluster properties, in Network Load Balancing Manager, right-click the cluster name and click Cluster Properties. The properties of a cluster include the cluster's IP address and several cluster parameters. These settings affect the cluster as a whole, not any particular cluster server. The cluster IP address is set when you create the cluster and it can be changed on the Cluster IP Addresses tab of the cluster Properties dialog (see Figure 10-19). You can also add or remove IP addresses from this tab. You may want to assign more than one IP address to a cluster when you are running multiple instances of the same service on your cluster such as two Web servers, each responding to a different IP address.

The cluster address is a virtual IP address but it is still configured in the TCP/IP Properties of an adapter on each server that is a cluster member. When you add a host to the cluster and select an adapter, the Add Host to Cluster wizard may configure the adapter for you, but if it is not successful in doing so, you may have to configure the adapter with the cluster address manually.

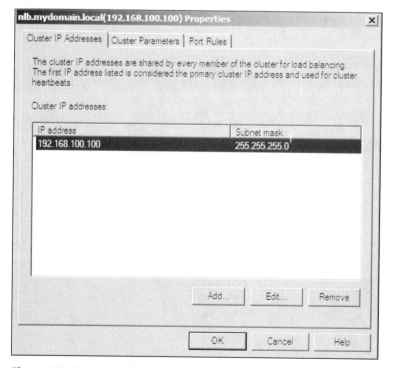

Figure 10-19 Cluster Properties: Cluster IP Addresses tab
© Cengage Learning 2012

Cluster parameters are configured on the Cluster Parameters tab of the Cluster Properties dialog. Figure 10-16, shown previously, shows this tab. The cluster parameters consist of the following items:

- *IP address*. Select the cluster's primary IP address. If more than one IP address is configured for the cluster, you can choose the primary address from the selection box.

- *Subnet mask*. The subnet mask for the specified IP address. If you need to change this, you must do so on the Cluster IP Addresses tab.

- *Full Internet name*. This is the fully qualified domain name (FQDN) assigned to this cluster. This name must have an entry in DNS which must resolve to the cluster's primary IP address.

- *Network address*. This is the MAC address of the cluster. In Unicast operation mode, this address is configured on the cluster adapter on each server in the cluster. The NICs on your servers must support changing the built-in MAC address. The NLB service automatically makes this change to the selected cluster adapter on each host server.

- *Cluster operation mode*. The choices for cluster operation mode are Unicast, Multicast, and IGMP multicast. The default mode is Unicast. If either multicast mode is selected, the cluster MAC address is changed to a multicast MAC address. A multicast MAC address can be identified by the least significant bit of the first octet being set to binary 1. In addition, in multicast mode, the server adapter can also use its built-in MAC address. If IGMP multicast mode is selected, switches that support IGMP will only forward NLB frames out switch ports to which NLB servers are connected. In unicast mode, switches flood NLB traffic out all switch ports.

Configuring Port Rules If you created the cluster leaving the default port rules in place, then the cluster responds to all TCP and UDP communication directed to the cluster's virtual IP address (in our example, the virtual IP address is 192.168.100.100). In most cases, you will want to change the port rules to only accept communication on the cluster address for services that are specifically offered by all cluster members. For example, if the purpose of the cluster is to provide scalable access to a Web site, you would create port rules that allow TCP port 80 and possibly port 443 (for secure HTTP) while disallowing all other ports. Port rules apply to all hosts in a cluster and are configured from the Port Rules tab of the Cluster Properties dialog (see Figure 10-20).

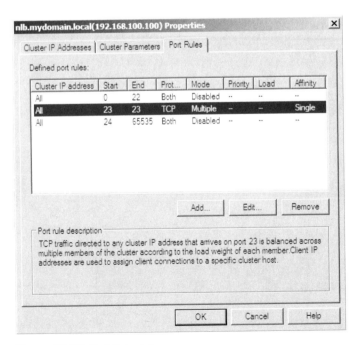

Figure 10-20 Port Rules tab
© Cengage Learning 2012

In Figure 10-20, three port rules were created. The first rule instructs the cluster to discard all traffic directed to the cluster in which the TCP or UDP ports are in the range 0 to 22. The second rule instructs the cluster to accept traffic that arrives on TCP port 23. The third rule instructs the cluster to discard all traffic for all ports greater than 23.

To create or edit a rule, click Edit or Add on the Port Rules tab of the cluster Properties dialog to get the Add/Edit Port Rule dialog shown in Figure 10-21. The port rule properties are as follows:

- *Cluster IP address.* The port rule can apply to all cluster IP addresses (the default) or you can select an address if there is more than one IP address assigned to the cluster.

- *Port range.* You specify the port range from 0 to 65535. To select a single port, make the From and To values the same.

- *Protocols.* You can specify the TCP or UDP protocols or both.

- *Filtering mode.* The options for **filtering mode** are Multiple host or Single host. Multiple host is the default and provides scalability such that network traffic on the specified hosts is load balanced among all cluster hosts according to each cluster host's assigned weight value. If Single host is selected, the host with the highest priority handles all traffic on the specified port(s). If the host with the highest priority does not respond, the host with the next highest priority responds.

The Single host option provides a level of fault tolerance but does not provide scalability. In Multiple host mode, you select a **client affinity value** of one of the following:

- *None.* With this option, any cluster member may respond to any client request, even multiple requests from the same client. For example, if the cluster is serving a Web site, a client may request multiple Web pages or multiple elements of a single Web page. With the None affinity option, one cluster member might handle one of the page requests while another cluster member handles another request. This works well with the TCP protocol only, and only when the content being served is fairly static and stateless.

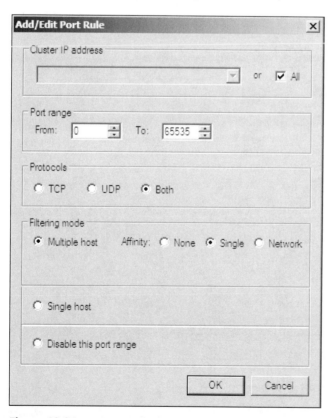

Figure 10-21 Add/Edit Port Rule tab

© Cengage Learning 2012

- *Single.* This is the default affinity setting for port rules and it specifies that multiple requests from the same client are directed to the same cluster host. This setting must be used if the application has some level of dynamic data or if client state must be maintained, for example, if the client must authenticate or establish an encrypted session.

- *Network.* This affinity setting is used to ensure that a single cluster host responds to client connections that come from a specific Class C network. This setting is used when clients access the cluster from behind multiple proxy servers which may cause the client's source address to appear different on subsequent requests. This setting assumes that all the proxy servers are located in the same Class C subnet.

- *Disable this port range.* Choose this option when you want the cluster to discard packets matching the protocol and ports specified.

Configuring Host Properties

To configure host properties, in Network Load Balancing Manager, right-click a host under the cluster name and click Host Properties. You'll see a screen similar to Figure 10-22. The Host Parameters tab consists of the following items:

- *Priority (unique host identifier).* This value, as discussed earlier, serves two purposes. It serves as an identifier for each host whereby no two hosts can be assigned the same value. It also serves as a priority value in which the host with the lowest value will handle all traffic not covered by a port rule that is directed towards the cluster.

- *Dedicated IP addresses.* This is one or more IP addresses configured on the host's cluster adapter that is used for non-cluster (dedicated) communication. If a second NIC is used for non-cluster communication, this list can be empty because the second adapter's IP address is automatically used as the dedicated IP address.

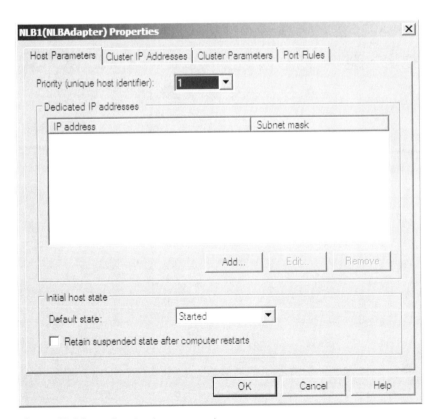

Figure 10-22 Configuring host properties
© Cengage Learning 2012

- *Initial host state.* This property controls how the NLB service behaves when the operating system boots. There are three options for this property: Started, Stopped, and Suspended. The default option is Started, specifying that the host should join the cluster when the OS starts. If Stopped is selected, the host will not join the NLB cluster until it is manually started. If Suspended is selected, the host will not join the cluster when the OS starts and will not respond to remote NLB commands until it is resumed.

- *Retain suspended state after computer restarts.* If this box is checked, the cluster host will remain suspended if the host restarts while in a suspended state regardless of the Default state option that is selected.

The Cluster IP Addresses tab shows the cluster IP address(es). The Cluster Parameters tab shows you the cluster parameters shown in Figure 10-19, above, but you cannot change those parameters from this interface.

The Port Rules tab allows you to edit port rules that are not disabled. Port rules for each host can be configured as follows (see Figure 10-23):

- *Multiple host filtering mode.* If the port rule filtering mode is set to Multiple host, a load weight can be assigned to the host for that port rule. By default, all hosts have equal weight, but if you want certain hosts to handle more traffic than others, you can set the load weight on each host. The load weight should be looked at as a percentage and can be set from 0 to 100. The total weight among all hosts should equal 100.

- *Single host filtering mode.* If the port rule filtering mode is set to Single host, the Handling priority value can be set. The host with the highest handling priority will handle all traffic that meets the port rules criteria. This value overrides the host priority value and allows you to assign different hosts to handle different types of traffic.

10

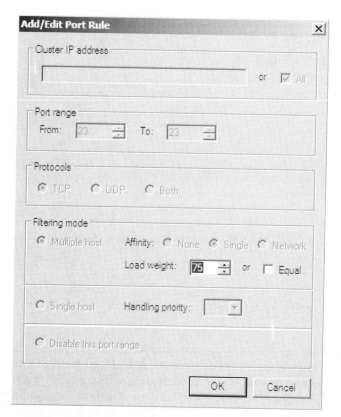

Figure 10-23 Changing the load weight or handling priority for a host

© Cengage Learning 2012

Managing an NLB Cluster

You may need to perform maintenance tasks on your cluster servers like you would with any network server. To that end, you can change the state of individual hosts or the cluster as a whole. Figure 10-24 shows the options available for controlling the hosts that are cluster members. To control all hosts, right-click the cluster node and click Control Hosts. To control a single host, right-click the host and click Control Host.

- *Start*. Starts the NLB service on the host and causes the host to join the cluster and begin handling NLB traffic.

- *Stop*. Stops the NLB service. The host will not handle any NLB traffic.

- *Drainstop*. The host completes any active NLB sessions and stops taking new sessions. Use this option instead of Stop if the host is actively serving clients. After using this option, the host will be in the stop state and must be started when you are ready for it to begin handling NLB traffic again.

- *Suspend*. This places the host in the suspended state which prevents it from handling new NLB traffic as well as NLB control commands except for Resume.

- *Resume*. Resumes a suspended host but places it in the Stop state. The host can take NLB commands and must be started before it will resume handling NLB traffic.

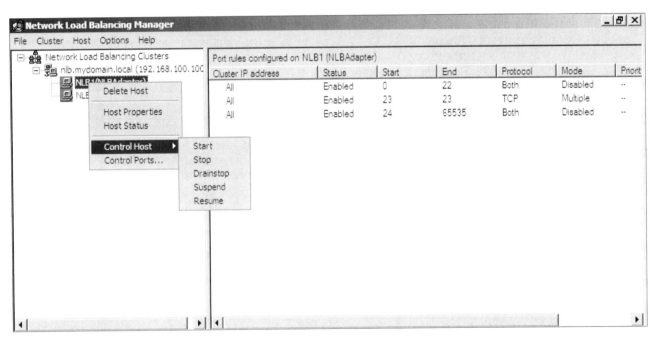

Figure 10-24 Controlling hosts
© Cengage Learning 2012

Failover Clusters

A failover cluster has different objectives compared to an NLB cluster. While an NLB cluster is targeted primarily towards scalability, a failover cluster is deployed for high availability. Whereas an NLB cluster works best with fairly static, read-only data access, a failover cluster is well suited to back-end database applications, file-sharing servers, messaging servers and other applications that are both mission critical and deal with dynamic read/write data.

Before we get too far into discussing failover clusters, now would be a good time to define some terms that will be used in describing failover clusters:

- **Clustered application**—An application or service that is installed on two or more servers that participate in a failover cluster. Also called clustered service.

- **Cluster server**—A Windows Server 2008 server that participates in a failover cluster. A cluster server is also referred to as a cluster node or cluster member.

- **Active node**—A cluster member that is responding to client requests for a network application or service. Also referred to as active server.

- **Passive node**—A cluster member that is not currently responding to client requests for a clustered application but is in standby mode to do so if the active node fails. Also referred to as passive server.

- **Standby mode**—A cluster node that is not active is said to be in standby mode.

- **Quorum**—The cluster configuration data that specifies the status of each node (active or passive) for each of the clustered applications. The quorum is also used to determine, in the event of server or communication failure, if the cluster is to remain online and which servers should continue to participate in the cluster.

- **Cluster heartbeat**—Communication between cluster nodes that provides status of each of the cluster members. The cluster heartbeat, or lack of it, informs the cluster when a server is no longer communicating. The cluster heartbeat information communicates the state of each node to the cluster quorum.

- **Witness disk**—The witness disk is shared storage used to store the cluster configuration data and is used for helping to determine the cluster quorum.

Failover clusters consist of two or more servers, usually of identical configuration, that access common storage media. Typically, storage is in the form of a SAN, a storage technology discussed in Chapter 3. As a refresher, a Storage Area Network (SAN) is external storage that can be shared among several servers and each server sees the SAN volumes as locally attached storage. The servers are connected to the SAN device through a secondary high-speed network connection. One server in a failover cluster is considered the active server while one or more other servers are passive. The active server handles all client requests for the clustered application, while the passive server(s) wait in a type of standby mode. If the active server fails and stops responding, one of the passive servers becomes active and begins handling client requests. Figure 10-25 depicts this arrangement.

You might think that implementing a failover cluster wastes a lot of resources and money, for example, if you have a cluster of four servers and only one is actually doing anything. Keep in mind that when thinking of a failover cluster, you are providing high availability for an application or service. You may have several services for which you need high availability and you can design your clusters so that each server is active for a particular application or service and in standby mode for the services that the other servers are providing. That way, each server is active, just not for the same application.

How a Failover Cluster Works

Failover clusters work by utilizing two or more servers, along with shared storage to provide fault tolerance and high availability. Like an NLB cluster, client computers see the failover cluster as a single entity accessible by a single name or IP address. All servers have access to the application data so that if the active server fails, another server can take over the clustered application. So, the question is, how do the passive servers know when the active server is no longer able to serve client requests? They do so using a process called a *quorum*. A quorum in this context is a consensus among the cluster elements of the status of the cluster. Now, since hardware and software can't really have opinions about things, the quorum is really just a database that contains cluster configuration information. This database defines the role of each cluster member and ultimately specifies which server should be active and which are passive. Each cluster member must have the same configuration information in order for the cluster to operate correctly. If a cluster server cannot access the quorum data, the server cannot participate in the cluster.

A failover cluster can only operate correctly if all cluster members can communicate with one another, so that all members have access to the same quorum data. The cluster network is **partitioned** if communication fails among the cluster servers, resulting in two or more sub-clusters, each with the objective of providing the clustered service. Since only one server can be active, this

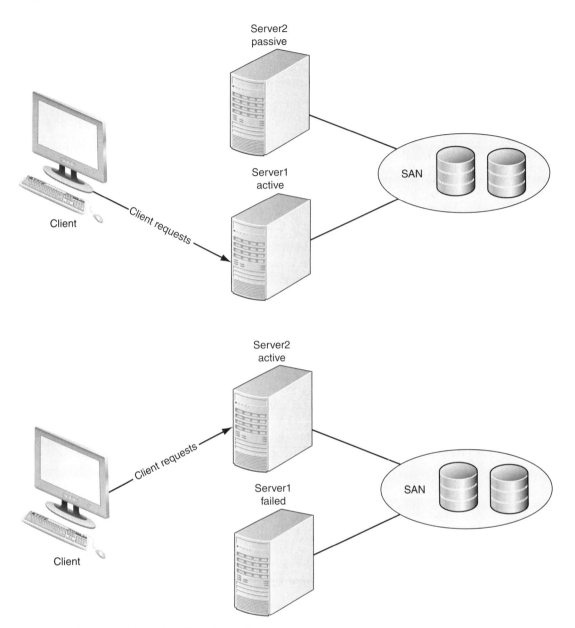

Figure 10-25 Logical depiction of a failover cluster
© Cengage Learning 2012

situation poses a problem. This is where the quorum comes in. The quorum process is designed so that only one partition, or sub-cluster, will be able to continue participating in the cluster.

Quorum Models   Since failover clusters can be designed in a variety of configurations, there are a variety of methods by which quorums are maintained. The best model is usually automatically selected during the cluster installation. There are four quorum models:

- *Node Majority quorum.* This model is used for failover clusters that have an odd number of members. Quite simply, the majority rules. If fewer than half of the nodes fail, the cluster continues to run. If the cluster becomes partitioned, the partition with the majority of nodes (greater than half of the total) owns the quorum and the other nodes are removed from the cluster. For example, in a five-node cluster, if two servers fail or become partitioned, they are removed from the cluster and the cluster continues to run with the remaining three servers.

- *Node and Disk Majority quorum.* This model is used by default on clusters with an even number of cluster nodes and utilizes the witness disk. The cluster quorum data is stored on the witness disk which is shared among all nodes. With this configuration, the cluster is operational as long as at least half of the cluster members are online and can communicate with the witness disk. However, if the witness disk fails, the cluster can continue running only if a majority (at least half plus one) of servers are communicating.

- *Node and File Share Majority quorum.* This model uses a file share to store the quorum data rather than shared storage but is otherwise similar to Node and Disk Majority.

- *No Majority: Disk Only quorum.* This model allows the cluster to remain operational as long as the witness disk is available to at least one server. This model can endure failure of all but one server, but if the witness disk fails, the entire cluster is unavailable.

Requirements for a Failover Cluster

The first requirement for a failover cluster is that all cluster servers must have Windows Server 2008 Enterprise or Datacenter edition installed. Either edition supports up to 16 cluster members in the 64-bit (x64) edition or 8 cluster members in the 32-bit (x86) edition. Also, be aware that the application you wish to cluster may limit the total number of cluster members.

Aside from the Windows Server edition, there are a few other hardware and software requirements that must be met before you can build a failover cluster:

- Identical or nearly identical server components
- Identical CPU architecture (x64 or x86)
- Components should meet the "Certified for Windows Server 2008" logo requirements
- Separate adapters for shared storage communication and network client communication
- A supported cluster-compatible storage technology: Serial Attached SCSI (SAS), Fibre Channel, or iSCSI storage technology should be used. SATA is acceptable, but not recommended. Parallel SCSI for cluster storage is not supported in Windows Server 2008
- For iSCSI, you must use a separate network adapter that is dedicate to cluster storage
- A minimum of two volumes, one of which will serve as the witness disk for the cluster
- Cluster servers must run the same edition of Windows Server 2008
- Cluster servers must be members of a Windows domain. A cluster server can be a domain controller but this configuration is not recommended
- All clustered applications or services must be the same version and all cluster servers should have the same updates and service packs installed

Cluster Storage Requirements   The storage requirements for a failover cluster are unique in that, in most configurations, the clustered application's data must be available to all cluster members, even though only one cluster member at a time will access it. If the currently active cluster server fails, another cluster member must have access to the same data so it can begin serving client requests. Shared storage is required on clusters that use the Disk Majority and No Majority: Disk Only quorum models. Most clustered applications use these models. In addition, all components of the storage system should be Windows Server 2008 certified and use digitally signed device drivers.

Failover Cluster Installation

The failover cluster function on Windows Server 2008 is installed as a feature using Server Manager. The procedure for installing and creating a failover cluster is generally as follows:

- Install the Failover Clustering feature on all servers
- Verify cluster server network and shared storage access

- Run the cluster validation wizard
- Create the cluster

The first step is self-explanatory and simply involves using the Add Features Wizard in Server Manager. You won't even have to restart your server after installing the Failover Clustering feature. Please note that you should not configure failover clustering and network load balancing on the same server. The remaining three steps warrant further explanation.

Verify Cluster Server Network and Shared Storage Access

You can actually perform this step before installing the Failover Clustering feature but just make sure this step is complete before moving on to the next step. The exact procedure you use to do this depends upon the type of shared storage you are using for your cluster and the configuration of your network. In short, verify that all of your servers can communicate with computers on the client network and that your shared storage is visible in Disk Management.

Run the Cluster Validation Wizard

Before you create a new cluster, you should run the Validate a Configuration wizard from the Failover Cluster Management console, shown in Figure 10-26. The Failover Cluster Management console is added to Administrative Tools after you install the Failover Clustering feature. If your server is not in a domain or you are not logged on using a domain account, you will receive a warning message declaring that some management functions will not be available. In fact, your server must be in a domain and the account with which you are logged on must be able to create a cluster object in Active Directory before any useful cluster management tools are available.

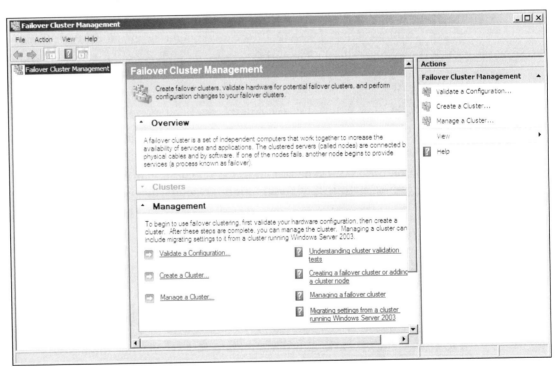

Figure 10-26 Failover Cluster Management console
© Cengage Learning 2012

You can run the Validate a Configuration wizard as many times as you need to until your configuration properly validates. It is even recommended to run this wizard periodically on a running cluster to make sure the configuration is still in good working order. On the first screen of the wizard, you are prompted to enter the names of the servers that will participate in the cluster. If you are running the wizard on an existing cluster, you can enter the cluster name instead.

Next, you choose the testing options you want. The choices are to run all tests or only selected tests. When you are validating a cluster configuration for the first time, you should run all tests.

If you are validating an existing cluster, you can limit the tests to suspected problem areas. The selected tests will run and a summary report is displayed on the screen. If there are errors, they will be listed in the report, hopefully, with sufficient information for you to resolve the problems. If there are no errors, the report indicates the configuration is suitable for clustering.

Setting up a failover cluster is a complex task requiring at least two Windows Server 2008 Enterprise servers and a shared storage server such as an iSCSI target server. If your lab does not have sufficient hardware for all students to do the following activities, they could be done as a demonstration.

Activity 10-5: Install the Failover Clustering Feature

Time Required: 5 minutes
Objective: Install the Failover Clustering feature on two servers

Description: Before you begin, verify the following: You have two Windows Server 2008 Enterprise Edition computers available. NLB Clustering has been uninstalled. Both servers are members of a domain. Two network adapters are installed on each server. Network adapters are configured for different subnets where one of the subnets is used to communicate among the servers and the other with shared storage. Servers in this activity are named Server1 and Server2, but your servers can be named whatever you like. An example topology is shown in Figure 10-27. In this topology, Windows Storage Server was used along with the iSCSI Software Target Management console to create iSCSI shared storage for the cluster servers.

10

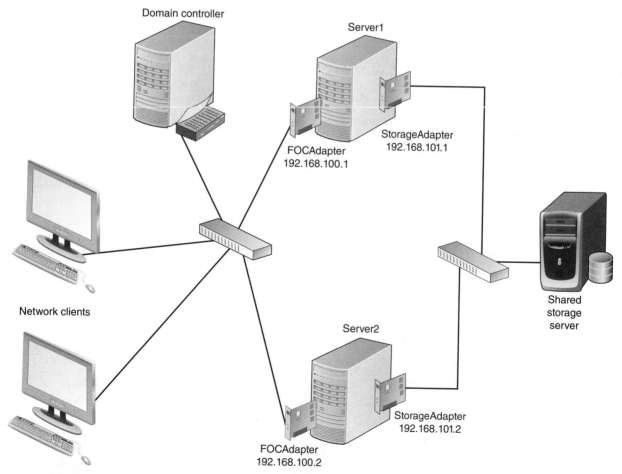

Figure 10-27 Example failover cluster diagram
© Cengage Learning 2012

1. Log on to Server1 as the domain Administrator.
2. Open **Server Manager** if necessary.
3. Install the **Failover Clustering** feature using the Add Features wizard in Server Manager.
4. Repeat steps 1-3 for Server2.

Activity 10-6: Validate a Cluster Configuration

Time Required: 15 minutes
Objective: Run the Validate a Configuration wizard from Failover Cluster Management

Description: You have two servers that are ready to be deployed in a failover cluster configuration. You have installed the Failover Clustering feature and are ready to validate your configuration before creating the cluster.

1. Log on to Server1 as the domain Administrator, if necessary.
2. Open **Failover Cluster Management** from Administrative Tools.
3. Click **Validate a Configuration** in the Actions pane to start the wizard. Read the Before You Begin screen and then click **Next**.
4. In the Select Servers or a Cluster screen, type **Server1** and click **Add**. Then type **Server2** and click **Add** again. See Figure 10-28. Click **Next**.

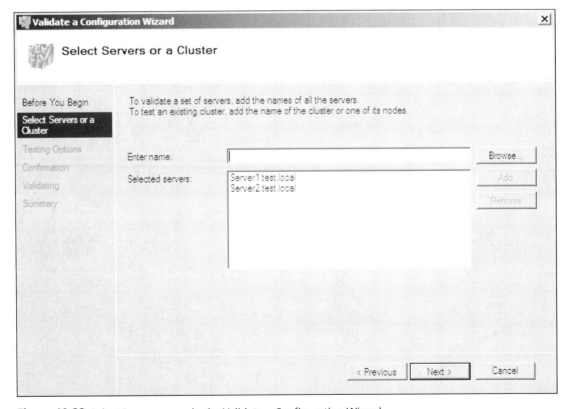

Figure 10-28 Select Servers screen in the Validate a Configuration Wizard
© Cengage Learning 2012

5. In the Testing Options screen, leave the default option of Run all tests (recommended) selected (see Figure 10-29) and click **Next**.

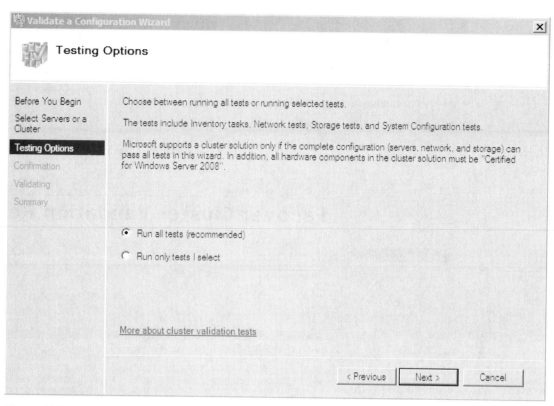

Figure 10-29 Testing Options screen
© Cengage Learning 2012

6. The Confirmation screen reviews your validation settings (see Figure 10-30). Click **Next**.

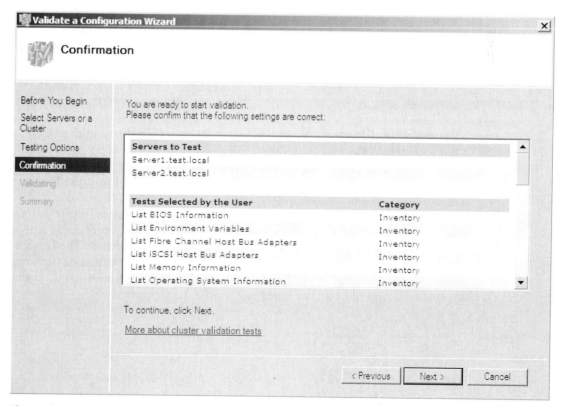

Figure 10-30 Confirmation screen
© Cengage Learning 2012

7. The validation test will run and each test will report results as it runs. The Summary screen has a button that allows you to review the validation report (see Figure 10-31).

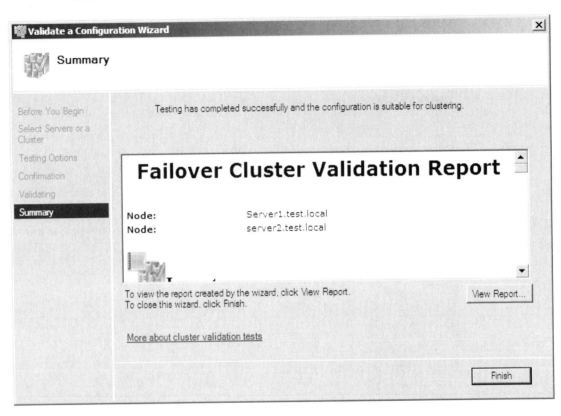

Figure 10-31 Summary screen
© Cengage Learning 2012

8. If errors or warnings are reported in the Summary screen, click on **View Report** to get additional information on the warnings or errors. Click **Finish**. Resolve any problems found and run the validation wizard again if necessary.

9. Leave the Failover Cluster Management console open if you are going on to the next activity.

Create the Cluster Once your network and servers are validated, you can create a new failover cluster. The process is similar to the processes for validating the configuration and for creating an NLB cluster and is detailed in Activity 10-7.

During the process of creating the cluster, you are asked to provide a name for the cluster in the Access Point for Administering the Cluster screen. You are also asked to provide an IP address. This name and address is used for accessing the cluster for the purposes of administering it. The name and IP address are added to DNS as a host record. In addition, a new computer object is created in Active Directory with the name of the cluster. The IP address is assigned to the network adapter that is selected for handling cluster clients on one of the servers (usually the one that you are running the Failover Cluster Management console on). If that server becomes unavailable, the address is assigned to the other cluster server.

Activity 10-7: Create a Failover Cluster

Time Required: 15 minutes
Objective: Create a new failover cluster

Description: Your cluster servers and network environment have been validated, so it's time to create the failover cluster.

1. Log on to Server1 as the domain Administrator, if necessary.

2. Open **Failover Cluster Management** from Administrative Tools, if necessary.

3. Click **Create a Cluster** in the Actions pane to start the wizard. Read the Before You Begin screen and then click **Next**.

4. In the Select Servers screen, type **Server1** and click **Add**. Then type **Server2** and click **Add** again. Click **Next**.

5. In the Access Point for Administering the Cluster screen, type **Failover1** for the Cluster Name. Click where it says **Click here to type an address** and type **192.168.100.200** for the address (see Figure 10-32). This is a virtual address like an NLB cluster uses. A host record with the name and address is added to DNS. Also, an Active Directory computer object is created. Click **Next**.

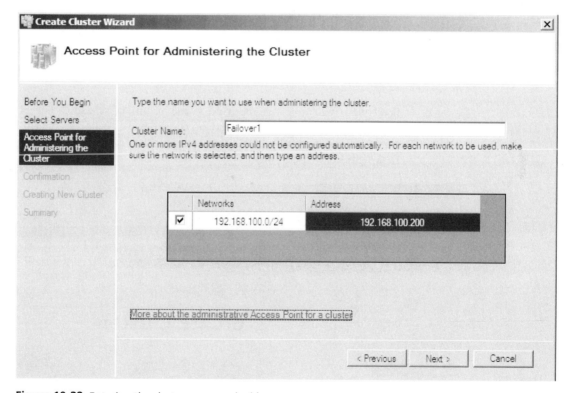

Figure 10-32 Entering the cluster name and address
© Cengage Learning 2012

6. The Confirmation screen shows you the settings that will be used to create the cluster (see Figure 10-33). Click **Next**.

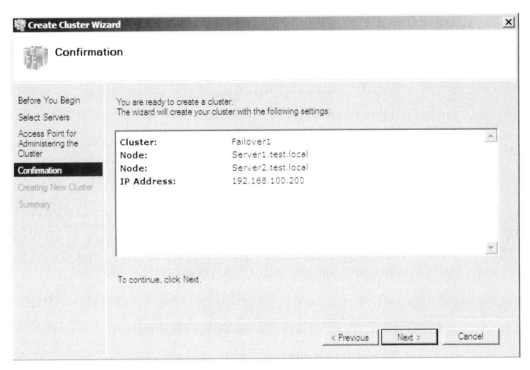

Figure 10-33 Confirmation screen
© Cengage Learning 2012

7. If errors or warnings are reported in the Summary screen (Figure 10-34), click **View Report** to get additional information on the warnings or errors. In Figure 10-34, the cluster was successfully created and the quorum mode that was selected is Node and Disk Majority. Click **Finish**.

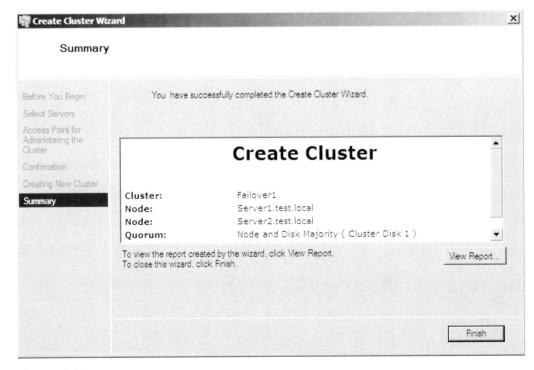

Figure 10-34 Summary screen
© Cengage Learning 2012

8. The next step is to review your cluster configuration in Failover Cluster Management. In the middle pane, review the cluster summary. In the left pane, click to expand **Nodes** to view the servers and their status in the middle pane. You can click any of the servers to get more details about the particular node (see Figure 10-35).

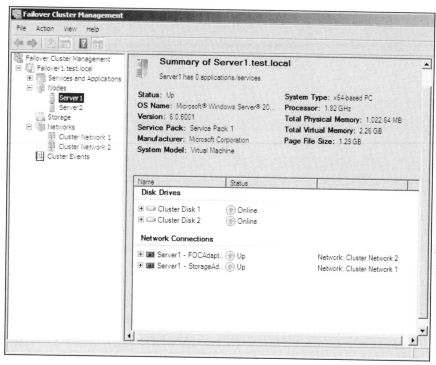

Figure 10-35 Reviewing the cluster: nodes
© Cengage Learning 2012

9. In the left pane, click **Storage** to see a summary of the cluster storage (see Figure 10-36). Notice that one of the disks was assigned as the Witness disk for the quorum.

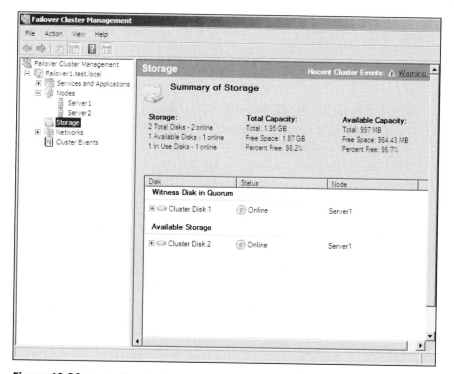

Figure 10-36 Reviewing the cluster: storage
© Cengage Learning 2012

10

10. In the left pane, click **Networks** to review the cluster networks (see Figure 10-37). Notice in Figure 10-37 that one of the networks is listed as Internal and the other is listed as Enabled under Cluster Use. The Internal network is used for cluster communication and access to the shared iSCSI storage.

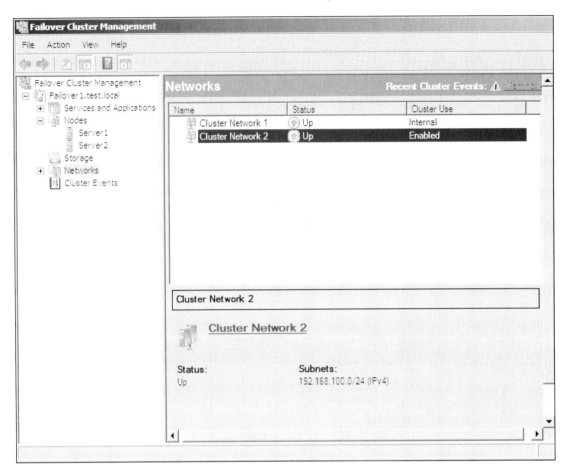

Figure 10-37 Reviewing the cluster: networks
© Cengage Learning 2012

11. Close Failover Cluster Management.

Configuring Failover Clustering

Once a cluster is created, a number of configuration tasks should be performed. These include but are not limited to the following:

- Configuring the cluster networks
- Configuring the quorum model
- Configuring a service or application

Configuring the Cluster Networks
The networks in your cluster are the critical link between clients and your clustered application and between your cluster nodes and their shared storage. Each network adapter on your servers should be connected to a different subnet and ideally, the network adapters should be renamed to reflect the network function. For example, in Figure 10-27, the network adapters were named FOCAdapter (for Failover Cluster Adapter)

and StorageAdapter. In Failover Cluster Management, the networks will simply be named Cluster Network 1 and Cluster Network 2. You should rename these to reflect the purpose of the network. To do so, in Failover Cluster Management, expand the Networks node in the left pane and click Cluster Network 1. In the Actions pane, click Rename. In our example cluster, Cluster Network 1 is the internal network used to access the shared storage, so we could name it StorageNet. With a network selected, you click Properties in the Actions pane to change how the network is used. If the network is used for iSCSI as this one is, you want to choose Do not allow the cluster to use this network (see Figure 10-38).

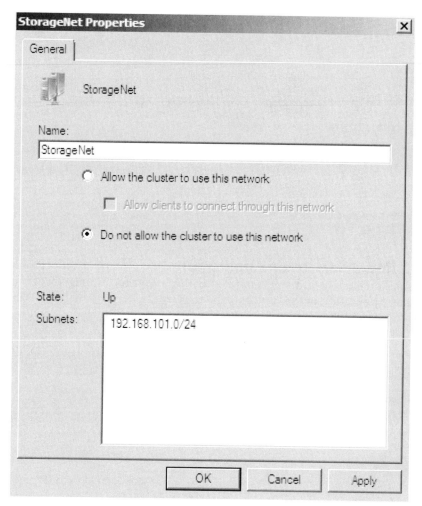

Figure 10-38 Cluster network properties
© Cengage Learning 2012

Configuring the Quorum Model If the quorum model selected by the Create Cluster process is not suitable for your environment, you can change it. In Failover Cluster Management, click the name of the cluster in the left pane and in the Actions pane, click More Actions and then Configure Cluster Quorum Settings. The Configure Cluster Quorum Wizard walks you through the process of changing the model (see Figure 10-39).

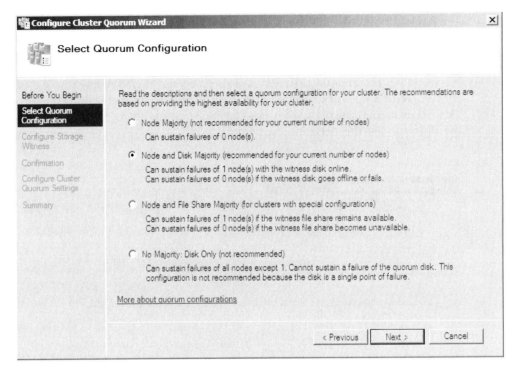

Figure 10-39 Configure Cluster Quorum
© Cengage Learning 2012

Configuring a Service or Application To configure a service or application, click Services or Applications in the left pane of Failover Cluster Management and click Configure a Service or Application in the Actions pane to start the High Availability Wizard. A number of Windows Server 2008 roles and features can be configured for failover clustering as shown in Figure 10-40.

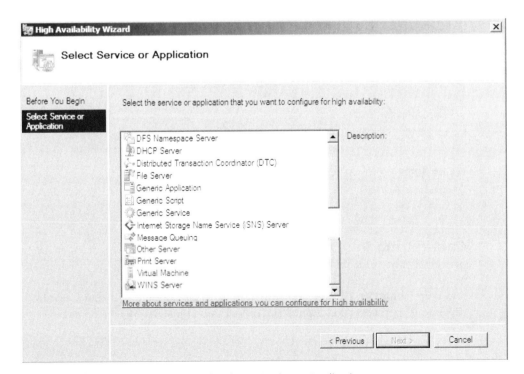

Figure 10-40 High Availability Wizard: Select a Service or Application
© Cengage Learning 2012

Before you run the High Availability Wizard, in most cases you must install the role or feature on each server in the cluster. We will demonstrate the procedure in the next activity using the File Server role. During the configuration of a service, you are prompted to provide a name that clients will use when accessing the service. By default, the High Availability Wizard creates a name for you consisting of the cluster name and an abbreviation of the service. For example, if you install the File Service on cluster Failover1, the suggested name will be Failover1FS.

You will also be prompted for the IP address that clients will use to access this cluster service. Just as with the access point for administering the cluster, a host record is created in DNS and a new computer object is created in Active Directory.

Activity 10-8: Create a File Server Failover Cluster

Time Required: 15 minutes
Objective: Configure the File Server role on the failover cluster

Description: Your cluster is up and running. Now it's time to configure a role for high availability. You will configure the File Server role.

1. Log on to Server1 as the domain Administrator, if necessary.

2. Open **Failover Cluster Management** from Administrative Tools, if necessary.

3. Click to expand the cluster node in the left pane. Click **Services and Applications** to start the High Availability Wizard.

4. Read the information in the Before You Begin screen and click **Next**.

5. In the Select Service or Application screen, click **File Server**. Click **Next**.

6. In the Client Access Point screen, accept the default name assigned (FailoverFS) and then click to add an address. Assign address **192.168.100.201** to this cluster service (see Figure 10-41). Click **Next**.

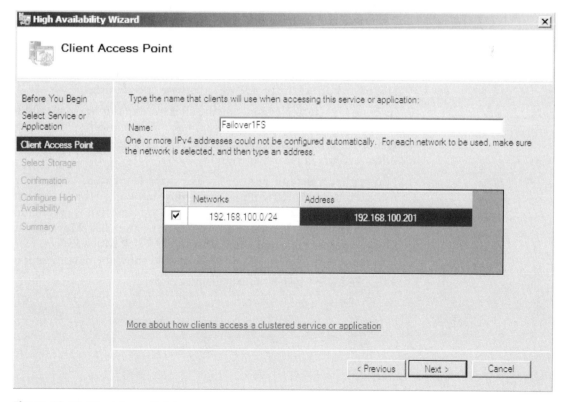

Figure 10-41 Client Access Point screen
© Cengage Learning 2012

7. In the next screen, you select the storage volume you want to use. These servers were set up to share two iSCSI volumes and one of them is used as the witness disk. Click the check box next to **Cluster Disk 2** (see Figure 10-42). Click **Next**.

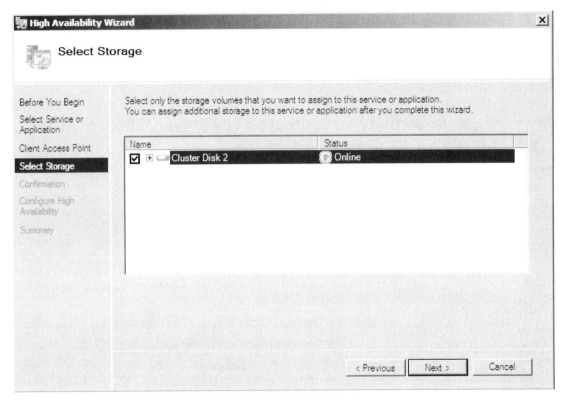

Figure 10-42 Select Storage screen
© Cengage Learning 2012

8. Review the information on the Confirmation screen and click **Next**.

9. If any errors or warnings were generated, click **View Report** on the Summary screen and try to correct the problems; otherwise click **Finish**.

10. In Failover Cluster Management, click to expand **Services and Applications** and click **FailoverFS** to review the summary information for the clustered service (see Figure 10-43). Notice that one of the servers is designated as the Current Owner. The other server is in passive or standby mode.

11. Notice that a default administrative share is created. You can create new shared folders on the shared volume using the Share and Storage Management or Add a shared folder link in the Actions pane. To test your failover configuration, right-click **Failover1FS** under Services and Applications and click **Move this service or application to another node** and choose the server. Click **Move FailoverFS to Server2** to confirm the action. The summary screen should show the new current owner.

12. Close Failover Cluster Management.

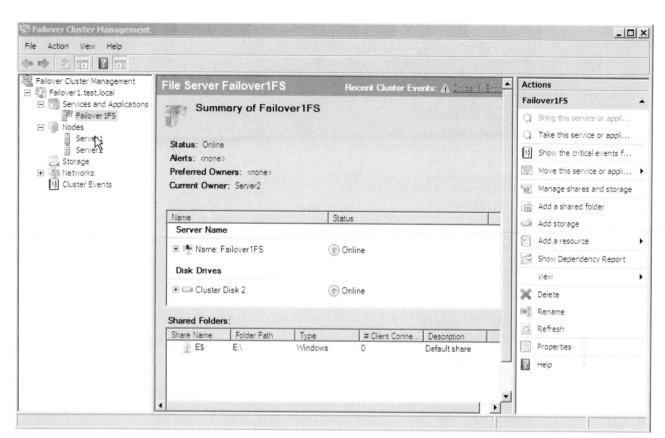

Figure 10-43 Viewing summary information of the new File Server cluster
© Cengage Learning 2012

Once your service is configured, you can further configure high availability options. Some of the options you can configure include:

- **Preferred owner.** The preferred owner is the server that will be selected as the active server for the service or application. To configure the preferred owner, right-click a server node under Services and Applications to display the properties for that service cluster. The available servers are listed and you can check the box next to one or more servers to specify the preferred owner. By default there is no preferred owner. The most preferred server is at the top. See Figure 10-44.

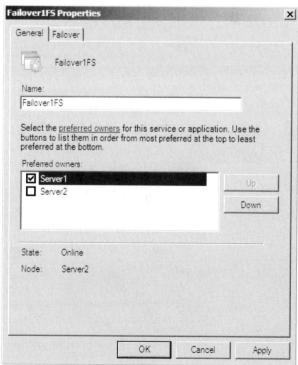

Figure 10-44 Preferred owner selection
© Cengage Learning 2012

- **Failover options.** Set this option from the Failover tab of the clustered service's property screen. The Maximum failures in the specified period value specifies how many times the service will attempt to restart or failover to another server in the specified period. In Figure 10-45, the service will attempt to failover two times within six hours. If the service fails a third time within the six hours, the service will be left in the failed state.

- **Failback options.** If a preferred owner is specified you have the option to revert to the most preferred owner when that server is available again. The failback can occur immediately or between certain hours of the day.

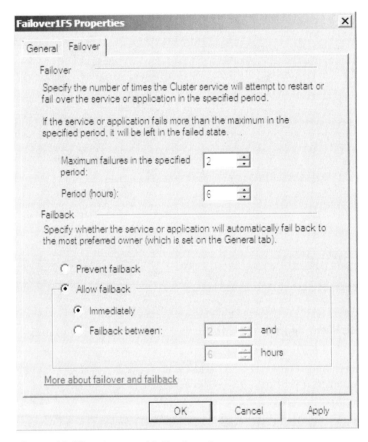

Figure 10-45 Failover and failback options
© Cengage Learning 2012

Best Practices

1. High availability software solutions are augmented by hardware fault tolerance; make sure your server hardware has fault-tolerant features such as hot-swappable RAID disk drives and redundant power supplies.

2. Use round-robin load balancing for an easy and quick load balancing solution but be aware of its limitations: no recognition of a down server, cached client records, and lack of prioritization.

3. Use network load balancing for applications in which the data being accessed is easily replicated among servers and is not changed by users.

4. Before using any clustering solution, make sure your OS version and updates are consistent among all servers.

5. Before creating your NLB cluster, make sure that DNS is set up correctly; a zone for the FQDN of the cluster must exist and A records for each server and the cluster name must exist.

6. It is recommended that you use multiple NICs on your server whereby one NIC is dedicated to non-cluster related communication.

7. Create port rules to ensure the cluster only accepts communication for services that are specifically offered by all cluster members.

8. Use the Multiple host filtering mode option on your NLB cluster to provide scalability; use the Single host filtering mode to provide fault tolerance without scalability.

9. Use failover clusters to provide the highest level of fault tolerance.

10. Be sure to choose the quorum model that best supports your failover cluster configuration.

11. Server components used in a failover cluster should meet the Certified Windows Server 2008 requirements.

12. For best disk performance in your failover cluster, use SAS, Fibre Channel, or iSCSI storage technologies.

13. Run the cluster validation wizard before you create a new cluster and again periodically after your cluster is running to revalidate the configuration.

10

Chapter Summary

- Server high availability is accomplished using fault tolerance. For server high availability, fault tolerance can be accomplished at the component level or the server level. Component level fault tolerance includes ECC memory, RAID configurations, redundant power, and hot add/replace components.

- Server-level high availability includes round-robin load balancing, network load-balancing clusters, and failover clusters.

- Round-robin load balancing uses multiple DNS records to resolve the same host name to multiple IP addresses. DNS returns the IP addresses in a different order each time the name is resolved. Round-robin DNS has flaws: no recognition of a down server, cached client records, and all servers have equal priority.

- NLB uses server clusters to provide scalability and fault tolerance. A server cluster is a group of two or more servers that are configured to respond to a single virtual IP address. To provide scalability, the servers in an NLB cluster share the load of incoming requests based on rules you can define. To provide fault tolerance, a failed server can be removed from the cluster and another server can take its place and begin servicing client requests that were handled by the failed server.

- Configuring an NLB cluster is broken into three categories: cluster properties, host properties, and port rules.

- A failover cluster is deployed for high availability. A failover cluster is well suited to back-end database applications, file sharing servers, messaging servers and other applications that are both mission critical and deal with dynamic read/write data.

- Failover clusters consist of two or more servers, usually of identical configuration, that access common storage media. Typically, storage is in the form of a SAN. One server in a failover cluster is considered the active server while one or more other servers are passive.

- All failover cluster servers have access to the application data so that if the active server fails, another server can take over the clustered application. The passive servers know when the active server is no longer able to serve client requests using a process called a quorum. A quorum is a consensus among the cluster elements of the status of the cluster.

Key Terms

active node   A cluster member that is responding to client requests for a network application or service. Also referred to as active server.

client affinity value   An option that is specified in multiple host filtering mode that determines whether the same or a different host will handle successive requests from the same client.

cluster heartbeat   Communication between cluster nodes that provides status of each of the cluster members. The cluster heartbeat, or lack of it, informs the cluster when a server is no longer communicating. The cluster heartbeat information communicates the state of each node to the cluster quorum.

cluster operation mode   A cluster parameter that specifies the type of network addressing used to access the cluster: unicast, multicast, or IGMP multicast.

cluster server   A Windows Server 2008 server that participates in a failover cluster. A cluster server is also referred to as a cluster node or cluster member.

clustered application   An application or service that is installed on two or more servers that participate in a failover cluster. Also called clustered service.

error correction code (ECC) memory   Memory modules, which, along with the supporting motherboard hardware, can detect and sometimes correct bit errors caused by electrical disturbances.

failback options   If a preferred owner is specified this option specifies that the cluster should revert to the most preferred owner when that server is available again. The failback can occur immediately or between certain hours of the day.

failover cluster   Two or more servers that appear as a single server to clients. One server in a failover cluster is considered the active server while one or more other servers are passive. The active server handles all client requests for the clustered application, while the passive server(s) wait in standby mode until the active server fails.

failover options   Specifies how many times the service will attempt to restart or failover to another server in the specified period.

fault tolerance   The ability of a server to recover from some type of hardware failure. Fault tolerance often involves redundant hardware.

filtering mode   An option in a port rule that specifies whether multiple hosts or a single host will respond to traffic identified by the port rule. Multiple host is the default and provides scalability. Single host specifies that the server with the highest priority value will handle the traffic.

high availability   A network or computer configuration in which data and applications are almost always available, even in the event of a system failure.

hot-swappable disks   A disk system that allows you to replace or add new hard disks while the computer is running. Both the hardware and OS must support this feature.

network load balancing (NLB)   A Windows Server 2008 feature that uses server clusters to provide both scalability and fault tolerance. Based on an internal algorithm, the servers decide which server should respond to each incoming client request.

partitioned   A cluster status that can occur if communication fails among the cluster servers, resulting in two or more sub-clusters, each with the objective of providing the clustered service.

passive node   A cluster member that is not currently responding to client requests for a clustered application but is in standby to do so if the active node fails. Also referred to as passive server.

port rule   Specifies which type of TCP or UDP traffic the NLB cluster should respond to and how that traffic is distributed among the cluster members.

preferred owner   The preferred owner is the server that will be selected as the active server for the service or application.

quorum   The cluster configuration data that specifies the status of each node (active or passive) for each of the clustered applications. The quorum is also used to determine, in the event of server or communication failure, if the cluster is to remain online and which servers should continue to participate in the cluster.

redundant hardware   The use of two or more devices that perform the same task so that if one fails or has reached its performance limits, the other device is activated.

round-robin load balancing   A method of providing server scalability that uses multiple DNS records to resolve the same host name to multiple IP addresses. The DNS server cycles through the duplicate host records, returning a different IP address for each subsequent query.

server cluster   A group of two or more servers that are configured to respond to a single virtual IP address.

standby mode   A cluster node that is not active is said to be in standby mode.

virtual IP address   The IP address by which the networking services provided by an NLB cluster are accessed by network clients. A DNS host record should exist for the cluster name mapped to this address.

witness disk   The witness disk is shared storage used to store the cluster configuration data and is used for helping to determine the cluster quorum.

Review Questions

1. Which of the following describe high availability? (Choose all that apply.)

    a. Applications are available even in the event of a system failure

    b. A server that requires no more than one restart per week

    c. Fast response time from a service or application when two or more servers spread the workload

    d. An OS that detects when a memory error has occurred

2. Which of the following best describes redundant hardware?

    a. The use of two or more devices that perform the same task so that if one fails or has reached its performance limits, the other device is activated

    b. A memory module that detects an error and displays a warning message

    c. The ability to add an additional hardware module while the system is running

    d. A multicore CPU whereby if one core fails, another core takes over its processing duties

3. You have an FTP site that gets heavy use by users who download files from it. You have a second computer that you can use to help with the traffic load. The files rarely change and you want to implement the simplest solution to provide rudimentary load balancing. What solution do you recommend?

    a. a failover cluster

    b. shared SAN storage

    c. round-robin load balancing

    d. distributed file system

4. Which of the following are flaws of round-robin load balancing? (Choose all that apply.)

    a. no recognition of a down server

    b. it works with a maximum of two servers

    c. cached client records

    d. all servers have equal priority

5. How does an NLB cluster provide fault tolerance?

    a. Based on an internal algorithm, the servers decide which server should respond to each incoming client request

    b. A failed server can be removed from the cluster and another server can take its place

    c. DNS records are changed to point clients to a different server if one fails

    d. It uses RAID and multiple NICs

6. You have a Web site that serves primarily static content. Your current server is unable to handle the traffic load. You think you need three servers to adequately handle the traffic load, but you want to be able to prioritize how much traffic is handled by each server. Which high availability solution makes the most sense?

    a. Create a round-robin load balancing configuration in Windows Server 2008

    b. Use the Failover Clustering feature in Windows Server 2008

    c. Use the scalable disk array feature in Windows Server 2008

    d. Use the network load balancing feature in Windows Server 2008

7. Which of the following is NOT a step in creating and configuring an NLB cluster?

    a. Configure the host priority

    b. Set the cluster IP address

    c. Configure port rules

    d. Configure a preferred owner

8. Which of the following is a valid NLB cluster operation mode?

    a. Single host

    b. Network

    c. Multicast

    d. Suspended

9. Which filtering mode should you use when you want to provide scalability among several servers in an NLB cluster?

    a. Multiple host

    b. Failback immediate

    c. IGMP multicast

    d. Node majority

10. Under which circumstances should you use the None option when setting the client affinity value?

    a. When you want multiple requests from the same client to be directed to the same cluster host

    b. When clients access the cluster from behind multiple proxy servers

    c. When the content being served is fairly static and stateless

    d. When you want the cluster to discard packets matching the protocol and ports specified

11. Which of the following serves as an NLB cluster server identifier and determines which server will handle traffic not covered by a port rule?

    a. Dedicated IP address

    b. Port range

    c. Priority

    d. Affinity value

12. You manage an NLB cluster comprised of three servers, Server1, Server2 and Server3. Your maintenance schedule indicates that Server1 is due for cleaning maintenance whereby you vacuum the dust and reseat all components. The NLB cluster is in constant use so you don't want to interrupt any clients currently being served by Server1. Which option should you use to take Server1 temporarily offline while allowing it to complete active client requests?

    a. Stop

    b. Suspend

    c. Resume

    d. Drainstop

13. Which of the following is a failover cluster server that does not respond to client requests but is available to do so if the active server fails?

    a. Passive node

    b. Quorum node

    c. Active node

    d. Suspended node

14. Which of the following describes a cluster that has been broken into two or more sub-clusters due to lack of communication?

    a. Quorum

    b. Partitioned

    c. No majority

    d. Sanctioned

15. Which of the following are valid quorum models? (Choose all that apply.)

    a. Node Majority

    b. No Majority: Disk Only

    c. Node and Disk Majority

    d. File Share and Disk Majority

16. Which of the following are requirements for creating a failover cluster? (Choose all that apply.)

    a. Identical CPU architecture

    b. Two or more quad-core CPUs

    c. Windows Server 2008 Standard edition or higher

    d. Servers must be Active Directory domain members or domain controllers

17. You are configuring a failover cluster. You want to choose a failover cluster quorum configuration that can endure failure of all but one server and remain operational. Which quorum configuration should you choose?

    a. Node Majority

    b. No Majority: Disk Only

    c. Node and File Share Majority

    d. Node and Disk Majority

10

18. What is created in Active Directory during the failover cluster creation process?

    a. A computer object bearing the name of the cluster

    b. A SAN object bearing the name of the witness disk

    c. An A record with the name and IP address of the cluster

    d. A cluster object containing the names of all the cluster servers

19. Which of the following is true about the network configuration of failover cluster?

    a. The shared storage should be on the same subnet as the cluster clients

    b. Cluster servers require a minimum of three NICs

    c. The iSCSI storage server should be on a separate subnet from the cluster clients

    d. All NICs on each server must be configured on the same subnet

20. Which of the following failover cluster options specifies how many times a clustered service can restart or fail to another server in a specific time period before the service is left in the failed state?

    a. Preferred owner

    b. Failover options

    c. Affinity value

    d. Failback options

Case Projects

CASE PROJECTS

Case Project 10-1: Choosing a High Availability Solution

You have been hired to set up the network and servers for a new company that will use Windows Server 2008. The company is investing in an application that all employees will use on a daily basis and that will be critical to the company's business. This application uses a back-end database and is highly transaction-oriented so data is read and written frequently. To simplify the maintenance of the front-end application, users will be running it through remote desktop servers. The owner has explained that the back-end database must be highly available and the remote desktop servers must be highly scalable to handle hundreds of simultaneous sessions. What high availability technologies do you recommend for the back-end database server and the remote desktop servers? Explain your answer.

Case Project 10-2: Server Requirements for a Failover Cluster

You will be implementing the application discussed in the previous case project. This is a new company, so there are currently no servers of any kind—you will be setting everything up from scratch. Describe the minimum requirements needed to implement the solution. Include in your answer the number of servers and what they will be used for, the number and editions of Windows Server 2008, and the basic network configuration along with any other devices you might need. Make a drawing of the network.

70-643 Exam Objectives

Table A-1 maps the Windows Server 2008 Applications Infrastructure, Configuring (70-643) exam objectives to the corresponding chapter and section title where the objectives are covered in this book. Major sections are listed after the chapter number, and applicable subsections are shown in parentheses. After each objective, the percentage of the exam that includes the objective is shown in parentheses.

Table A-1   Objectives-to-chapter mapping

Domain objective	Chapter and section(s)
Deploying Servers (28 percent)	
Deploy images by using Windows Deployment Services	Chapter 2: Deploying Images Using Windows Deployment Service Chapter 2: Installing Windows Deployment Services Chapter 2: Configuring Windows Deployment Services Chapter 2: Capturing and Deploying WDS Services Chapter 2: Other Common Deployment Tasks
Configure Microsoft Windows activation	Chapter 2: Volume Activation
Configure Windows Server Hyper-V and virtual machines	Chapter 3: Manage Virtual Hard Disks Chapter 9: Hyper-V Installation Chapter 9: Creating Virtual Machines in Hyper-V Chapter 9: Hyper-V Virtual Networks Chapter 9: Working with Virtual Hard Disks Chapter 9: Managing Virtual Machines
Configure high availability	Chapter 10: Windows Server 2008 High Availability Technologies Chapter 10: Network Load Balancing Chapter 10: Failover Clusters
Configure storage	Chapter 3: Overview of Disk Management Capabilities Chapter 3: Manage Virtual Hard Disks Chapter 3: Mount Points Chapter 3: Multipath I/O Chapter 3: Microsoft iSCSI Software Initiator Chapter 3: Storage Area Networks
Configuring Remote Desktop Services (26 percent)	
Configure RemoteApp and Remote Desktop Web Access	Chapter 4: Authentication and Single Sign-On Chapter 4: Publishing Remote Applications Chapter 4: Packaging RemoteApp Programs Chapter 4: Remote Desktop Web Access
Configure Remote Desktop Gateway (RD Gateway)	Chapter 4: Authentication and Single Sign-On Chapter 4: Packaging RemoteApp Programs Chapter 4: Remote Desktop Gateway Chapter 5: RD Gateway

(continued)

Configure Remote Desktop Connection Broker	Chapter 4: Device Redirection Chapter 5: Remote Desktop Connection Broker
Configure and monitor Remote Desktop resources	Chapter 5: Managing Remote Desktop Session Host
Configure Remote Desktop licensing	Chapter 5: RD Licensing
Configure Remote Desktop Session Host	Chapter 5: Managing Remote Desktop Session Host
Configuring a Web Services Infrastructure (25 percent)	
Configure Web applications	Chapter 6: Configuring Web Applications Chapter 6: Manage Web Sites
Manage Web sites	Chapter 6: Manage Web sites
Configure a File Transfer Protocol (FTP) server	Chapter 6: Configuring an FTP Server
Configure Simple Mail Transfer Protocol (SMTP)	Chapter 6: Configuring an SMTP Server
Manage the Web Server (IIS) role	Chapter 7: Managing Internet Information Services (IIS)
Configure SSL security	Chapter 7: Configuring SSL Security
Configure Web site authentication and permissions	Chapter 7: Configuring Web Site Permissions and Authentication
Configuring Network Application Services (21 percent)	
Manage the Streaming Media Services role	Chapter 8: Configuring Windows Media Server
Secure streaming media	Chapter 8: Securing Content
Configure SharePoint Foundation options	Chapter 8: Configuring Microsoft Windows SharePoint Services Server Options
Configure SharePoint Foundation integration	Chapter 8: Configuring Microsoft Windows SharePoint Services Server Options (Configuring Windows SharePoint Services E-Mail Integration)

.NET Framework A software framework for Windows operating systems provided by Microsoft that includes a code library and other programming tools for managing programs.

Active Directory Microsoft directory services technology providing various network services.

active node A cluster member that is responding to client requests for a network application or service. Also referred to as active server.

application infrastructure An infrastructure that provides the tools and services for applications to work together and integrate within an enterprise.

Application Pool A list of one or more URLs served by a worker process or group of worker processes that is isolated from other groups of worker processes.

ASP.NET Microsoft Web application framework that enables developers to develop dynamic Web sites, services, and applications.

Asymmetric Logical Unit Access (ALUA) Occurs when the characteristics to access a device differ from one port to another port. For example, SCSI target devices might need to define different access characteristics when the target ports are in separate physical units.

attack surface Code in a Web application that can be run by unauthenticated users.

bare-metal virtualization OS virtualization in which the hypervisor runs directly on the host computer's hardware and controls and monitors guest OSs. Also called a type 1 hypervisor.

basic disk A physical disk that contains partitions (primary and extended) and/or logical drives. A basic disk can contain up to four primary partitions or three primary partitions and an extended partition.

bindings The IP address, port, and sometimes a host name over which a Web object (Web, FTP, SMTP site) will communicate with the client.

boot image Client computers will boot into a boot image in order to install the operating system.

broadcast Content streaming controlled on the server side; the server has control of all aspects of playback.

caching server In relation to Media Services, a server that connects to the Media Services Server retrieves the content and streams it to multiple clients.

capture image A capture image enables you to create custom install images. You can capture the image of an operating system using the Image Capture Wizard and use that image as your install image.

Certificate Authority (CA) A trusted entity that issues digital certificates that can be used by Web sites to establish their identity to users connecting to them.

Certificate Signing Request (CSR) A block of encrypted text that is generated on the server that the certificate will be used on. The CSR contains information that will be included in the certificate plus the public key that will be used. The corresponding private key is created at the same time.

Challenge Handshake Authentication Protocol (CHAP) Provides authentication; Microsoft iSCSI Initiator supports one-way and mutual CHAP.

Client Access License (CAL) Gives a client or device the rights to use or access the services of a server; required for devices or users to connect to a Remote Desktop Session Host server.

client affinity value An option that is specified in multiple host filtering mode that determines whether the same or a different host will handle successive requests from the same client.

cluster The smallest amount of disk space that can be used as an allocation unit for holding a file.

cluster heartbeat Communication between cluster nodes that provides status of each of the cluster members. The cluster heartbeat, or lack of it, informs the cluster when a server is no longer communicating. The cluster heartbeat information communicates the state of each node to the cluster quorum.

cluster operation mode A cluster parameter that specifies the type of network addressing used to access the cluster: unicast, multicast, or IGMP multicast.

cluster server A Windows Server 2008 server that participates in a failover cluster. A cluster server is also referred to as a cluster node or cluster member.

clustered application An application or service that is installed on two or more servers that participate in a failover cluster. Also called clustered service.

Code Access Security (CAS) A security mechanism within the .NET Framework that helps protect computers from malicious code.

cryptographic service provider (CSP) A means of providing hardware or software based encryption and decryption.

Deployment Server Provides complete Windows Deployment Services functionality and when you select the Deployment Server option, both the Deployment Server and Transport Server are installed, which includes the WDS image store.

Desktop Experience Includes features common on Windows client operating systems, such as Windows 7.Common features include Windows Media Player, desktop themes, Video for Windows (AVI support), Windows Defender, Disk Cleanup, Sync Center, Sound Recorder, Snipping Tool, and others.

device redirection A capability that enables a device to be connected to the local device but be accessible through the Remote Desktop Services session.

Device Specific Module (DSM) Contains hardware specific information about the device that is used to optimize connectivity. It is recommended to use the DSM provided by the vendor for optimal connectivity results.

differencing disk A dynamically expanding virtual disk that uses a parent/child relationship in which the parent disk is a dynamically expanding or fixed size disk with an OS installed with possibly some applications and data. The differencing disk is a child of the parent and changes are only made to the differencing disk while the parent disk remains unaltered.

digital rights management (DRM) Tools and methodologies used to control and limit access to and usage of digital content.

discover image A disk image that enables operating system installation on a system that cannot boot from the network using the Pre-Boot Execution Environment (PXE).

Disk Management console Used to manage disks, create volumes, create partitions, and perform other disk management tasks. Disk Management is part of the Server Manager console.

display data prioritization A feature that controls the bandwidth ratio of input versus output prioritization; the default is a 70:30 ratio of input to output.

Domain Name System (DNS) TCP/IP application protocol that translates domain names into IP addresses.

dynamic disk A physical disk that manages its volumes using a database, and supports many features a basic disk does not, such as volumes spanning multiple disks. Dynamic disks do not use partitions or logical drives, and because they use a database to store information, they offer greater flexibility for volume management.

Dynamic Host Configuration Protocol (DHCP) Network protocol used for the dynamic assignment of IP address and other configuration information.

dynamic least queue depth Performs load balancing based on the least queued path. It forwards input/output to the path with the least number of requests.

dynamically expanding disk A virtual hard disk in which the initial size of the .vhd file is very small but can expand to the maximum size specified for the virtual disk.

emulated driver Legacy driver installed on a VM that is used when synthetic drivers are not available or not installed.

encoding The process where digital content is converted into an appropriate format for streaming.

Encrypting File System (EFS) Microsoft file system that provides symmetric encryption to preserve data confidentiality.

error correction code (ECC) memory Memory modules, which, along with the supporting motherboard hardware, can detect and sometimes correct bit errors caused by electrical disturbances.

extended partition A non–bootable partition. An extended partition can be subdivided into logical drives. One extended partition can exist on a hard drive.

external virtual network A virtual network whereby one of the host's physical network adapters is bound to the virtual network switch, allowing virtual machines to access a LAN connected to the host.

failback A load-balancing method similar to failover. The primary difference is that failback will switch back to the primary path when the primary path is restored.

failback options If a preferred owner is specified this option specifies that the cluster should revert to the most preferred owner when that server is available again. The failback can occur immediately or between certain hours of the day.

failover The failover load balancing policy is not an actual load balancing method; instead, it specifies the primary path and standby paths. It is not load balancing, since the primary path is always used unless there is a failure of the primary path. If the primary path fails, a standby path is used.

failover cluster Two or more servers that appear as a single server to clients. One server in a failover cluster is considered the active server while one or more other servers are passive. The active server handles all client requests for the clustered application, while the passive server(s) wait in standby mode until the active server fails.

failover clustering Provides high-availability to services and applications by enabling an application to failover from one server to provide continued service.

failover options Specifies how many times the service will attempt to restart or failover to another server in the specified period.

fault tolerance The ability of a server to recover from some type of hardware failure. Fault tolerance often involves redundant hardware.

Fibre Channel A high-speed network technology that is commonly used in storage area networks for high-speed connections to storage devices.

File Transfer Protocol (FTP) A simple protocol designed specifically to transfer files.

filtering mode An option in a port rule that specifies whether multiple hosts or a single host will respond to traffic identified by the port

rule. Multiple host is the default and provides scalability. Single host specifies that the server with the highest priority value will handle the traffic.

fixed size disk A virtual hard disk in which the full size of the disk is allocated on the host system when the virtual disk is created.

font smoothing A setting that creates anti-aliasing on screen text to make fonts smoother and easier to read. ClearType fonts are supported if ClearType is enabled on the server and Font Smoothing is enabled.

FTPS (FTP over SSL) Encrypting the login to the FTP server and the file transfer using the SSL protocol and a certificate.

Fully Qualified Domain Name (FQDN) A domain name reference that includes the host (e.g., www), the domain (e.g., mydomain), and the top level domain (e.g., .com).

Group Policy Microsoft Group Policy provides centralized management and control of users and groups.

Group Policy Editor (gpedit) Microsoft Windows Server 2008 tool that provides the capability to edit and manage group policies.

group policy management The management and maintenance of group policies.

Group Policy Management Console (GPMC) An MMC (Microsoft Management Console) snap-in for managing group policies.

guest OS An operating system installed in a virtual machine.

GUID Partition Table (GPT) Defines the physical hard disk's partition table layout. The GPT is often used to overcome the 2.2 TB limitation of MBR partition tables. Used on Windows Vista and later.

high availability A network or computer configuration in which data and applications are almost always available, even in the event of a system failure.

High-Performance Computing (HPC) An edition of Windows Server 2008 for enterprise high-performance computing needs.

Host Bus Adapter (HBA) Used to connect a system to other network and storage devices.

host computer The physical computer on which virtual machine software is installed and virtual machines run.

host operating system The originally installed operating system (if applicable) on the physical computer on which VM software is installed and VMs run.

hosted virtualization OS virtualization in which the hypervisor is installed in a general-purpose host OS, such as Windows 7 or Linux, and the host OS accesses host hardware on behalf of the guest OS. Also known as a type 2 hypervisor.

hot-swappable disks A disk system that allows you to replace or add new hard disks while the computer is running. Both the hardware and OS must support this feature.

Hypertext Transfer Protocol (HTTP) A TCP/IP protocol used for retrieving hyperlinked documents and information.

Hyper-V The server virtualization capability provided in Windows Server 2008.

hypervisor The component of virtualization software that creates and monitors the virtual hardware environment, which allows multiple VMs to share physical hardware resources.

install image An operating system image deployed to the client computer.

Integration Services A software package installed on a VM's guest OS that provides enhanced drivers for the guest OS, bringing better performance and functionality to IDE and SCSI storage devices, the network interface, and mouse and video devices. Integration Services also better integrates the VM with the host OS providing services such as data exchange, time synchronization, OS shutdown, and others.

internal virtual network An internal network is not bound to any of the host's physical NICs but a host virtual NIC is bound to the internal virtual switch. This allows virtual machines and the host computer to communicate with one another but VMs cannot access the physical network.

Internet Information Services (IIS) A Microsoft Windows Server component that provides Web server tools, services, and functionality.

Internet Protocol Security (IPSec) A protocol that provides authentication and encryption at the Network layer.

Internet Small Computer System Interface (iSCSI) A storage networking standard for carrying SCSI commands over IP networks.

IPv4 Internet Protocol Version 4, the most commonly used version of IP, which provides a 32-bit IP address.

IPv6 Internet Protocol Version 6, the newest version of IP that provides a 128-bit IP address.

iSCSI driver The Microsoft iSCSI Initiator includes an iSCSI driver, which is used to send iSCSI commands over the network.

iSCSI Naming Service (iSNS) Enables better management by automatically discovering targets on the network.

iSCSI Qualified Name (IQN) Each software initiator is identified by a unique iSCSI Qualified Name, or IQN.

iSCSI Software Initiator A protocol for connecting host computers to an external storage array through the network adapter.

iSCSI target Any device that receives iSCSI commands.

Kerberos A protocol for clients to present network credentials for authentication. Tickets are obtained from a Kerberos Key Distribution Center and presented to the server to authenticate the client.

Key Management Service (KMS) Enables volume activation within an organization's own network.

LDAP (Lightweight Directory Access Protocol) The standard by which directory services software communicates with each other.

live migration A process in which a virtual machine is moved to new hardware for performance or reliability improvements while the VM is running, resulting in practically no downtime.

live streaming Streaming audio or video directly from an encoded source.

logical unit number (LUN) Number that identifies a device being addressed, such as those being addressed by Fibre Channel or iSCSI.

Master Boot Record (MBR) The first sector, which is the boot sector, of a storage device.

Microsoft Point of Sale for .NET device redirection This enhancement enables supported point of sale devices, such as bar code readers, to be used with

Remote Desktop Services. You need to ensure that you have the most recent version of the Microsoft POS for .NET software downloaded from the Microsoft Web site.

mirror volume Copies the data written to one disk to another disk to increase fault tolerance.

monitor spanning The capability of spanning multiple monitors with a total maximum resolution of 4096 × 2048.

mount points Enable you to access a volume from a folder on another disk; a mount point folder can be assigned to a drive.

multicast A method of streaming that sends a single stream to a point that clients connect to and receive the content. Publishing point can only be broadcast.

multipath I/O Provides the capability to read and write data using multiple paths to a storage device. This capability increases fault tolerance against single points of failure within the communication path and the devices on the communication path to the storage device by having redundant paths accessible to a storage device.

Multiple Activation Key (MAK) Enables product activation on a system on a one-time basis. MAK uses Microsoft's hosted activation services.

NCSA Fixed text-based log file format developed by the National Center for Supercomputing Applications at University of Illinois at Urbana-Champaign.

Network Access Protection (NAP) Introduced in Windows Server 2008, enables administrators to define system health policies and monitor network and server resources to ensure that these policies are being followed.

network application services Services that enable network applications, application monitoring, and application performance.

network load balancing (NLB) A clustering technology available in Windows Server 2008 that balances network traffic across multiple devices and is often used for network redundancy.

Network Policy Server (NPS) The Microsoft implementation of a Remote Authentication Dial-in User Service (RADIUS) server and proxy in Windows Server 2008.

NTFS New Technology File System, the standard file system used in Microsoft operating systems.

NTLM NT LAN Manager; an older Windows challenge/response authentication protocol used on networks that include Windows operating systems as well as stand-alone systems.

on-demand Content streaming controlled on the client side. The client has control of all aspects of playback (rewind, fast forward, etc.).

parity A fault-tolerance technique that performs a logical operation on the data and stores the result of the operation on either a dedicated or a main data disk.

partition One physical drive can be partitioned into multiple logical partitions.

partitioned A cluster status that can occur if communication fails among the cluster servers, resulting in two or more sub-clusters, each with the objective of providing the clustered service.

passive node A cluster member that is not currently responding to client requests for a clustered application but is in standby to do so if the active node fails. Also referred to as passive server.

pass-through disk A physical disk attached to the host system that is placed offline so that it can be used by a VM instead of, or in addition to, a virtual disk.

physical drive The physical hard drive. One physical drive can be partitioned into multiple logical drives.

pipelining Microprocessors use pipelining to begin executing multiple instructions simultaneously. The microprocessor will begin executing the next instruction before the current instruction has been completed.

playlist A list of content to be streamed.

Plug and Play (PNP) device redirection PNP devices can be redirected from the local device to the Remote Desktop Services session. This capability is based on the Media Transfer Protocol (MTP) and Picture Transfer Protocol (PTP).

port Number assigned to user sessions and server applications in an IP network.

port rule Specifies which type of TCP or UDP traffic the NLB cluster should respond to and how that traffic is distributed among the cluster members.

PowerShell A powerful Windows Server 2008 command-line interface (CLI) and full scripting language for administrative tasks.

Pre-Boot Execution Environment (PXE) An environment to boot computers over a network connection.

preferred owner The preferred owner is the server that will be selected as the active server for the service or application.

primary partition A primary partition contains one file system and is marked as a bootable partition.

private virtual network A virtual network in which there is no host connection to the virtual network thereby allowing VMs to communicate with one another, but there is no communication between the private virtual network and the host.

proxy server In relation to Media Services, a server that connects to the Media Services Server, retrieves a broadcast stream, and streams it to multiple clients.

publishing point The object Windows Media Services uses to identify the physical path and other characteristics of content to be streamed.

quorum The cluster configuration data that specifies the status of each node (active or passive) for each of the clustered applications. The quorum is also used to determine, in the event of server or communication failure, if the cluster is to remain online and which servers should continue to participate in the cluster.

RD Connection Broker Remote Desktop Connection Broker; a Windows Server 2008 role service that enables a user to reconnect to an existing session in a load-balanced server farm.

RD Licensing A Windows Server 2008 license management system for Remote Desktop Services. This system allows servers to obtain and manage Client Access Licenses (CALs).

Real Time Streaming Protocol (RTSP) Protocol used to transfer streaming media from the server to the client. Best for live streaming.

recycling An operation in IIS 7 that allows you to restart an Application Pool while allowing it to complete requests that are already in progress.

Redundant Array of Independent Disks (RAID) A data storage technology that is used to increase performance and fault tolerance. RAID can be implemented through software or hardware. Windows Server 2008 supports RAID 0, RAID 1, and RAID 5 through software implementation.

redundant hardware The use of two or more devices that perform the same task so that if one fails or has reached its performance limits, the other device is activated.

RemoteApp Enables you to publish applications for client access; with RemoteApp you can publish individual applications instead of having to publish the entire desktop, which was the only option available in previous versions of Remote Desktop Services.

Remote Desktop Connection A Windows Server feature used by clients to remotely connect to a server and remotely run applications.

Remote Desktop Connection Authorization Policies (RD CAPs) Enables you to specify which users can connect to the Remote Desktop Gateway server, specify the requirements that users must meet to connect, and specify whether to enable or disable client device redirection.

Remote Desktop Easy Print This enhancement enables redirection of the default printer without having to match print drivers on the client computer and the Remote Desktop Session Host Server.

Remote Desktop Gateway (RD Gateway) A role service in the Remote Desktop Session Host server role that allows authorized remote users to connect to resources on an internal corporate or private network from any Internet-connected device.

Remote Desktop Licensing (RD Licensing) A license management system for Windows Server 2008 Remote Desktop Services that allows Remote Desktop Session Host servers to obtain and manage client access licenses (RD CALs) for devices and users that are connecting to a server.

Remote Desktop Resource Authorization Policies (RD RAPs) Enables you to specify the network resources that users can connect to, specify the user groups and computer groups, and specify whether to use the default TCP port 3389 or allow a connection through another port.

Remote Desktop Services Windows feature that enables users to access programs installed on a terminal server or to access the Windows desktop; one of the server roles available in Windows Server 2008 R2. In Server 2008 and earlier, this feature was called Terminal Services.

Remote Desktop Session Host One of the server roles available in Windows Server 2008 R2.

Remote Desktop Web Access (RD Web Access) A role service in the Remote Desktop Services role that lets you make RemoteApp programs, and a connection to the Remote Desktop Session Host server desktop, available to users from a Web browser.

Remote Installation Services (RIS) Provides a remote deployment capability available in Windows Server 2003; replaced by WDS in Windows Server 2008.

reverse DNS lookup Resolves a host's IP address to its name.

rights account certificates (RACs) Used by AD RMS to identify trusted users and groups that can generate rights-protected content.

Rights Policy template Where access permissions and file expirations are designated for particular media controlled by AD RMS.

round-robin load balancing A method of providing server scalability and load balancing that uses multiple DNS records to resolve the same host name to multiple IP addresses. The DNS server cycles through the duplicate host records, returning a different IP address for each subsequent query.

round-robin with a subset of paths A load balancing policy similar to round-robin, but with standby paths ready for use if the primary paths fail. For normal operations, it uses a subset of paths for input/output. The standby paths are then used in the event that a primary path fails or is otherwise unavailable.

role Defines the services and functionality that will be provided by the server operating system.

Secure Sockets Layer (SSL) A cryptographic protocol that provides secure communication over the Internet.

Serial Attached SCSI (SAS) A data transfer technology for moving data between storage devices.

Serial Attached Storage (SAS) A bus technology for transferring data between storage devices and disk drives.

server cluster The virtual combination of multiple servers that appear as one server; a group of two or more servers that are configured to respond to a single virtual IP address. In relation to AD RMS, a group of servers administering rights policies.

Server Core A minimal, command-line installation of Windows Server 2008 that is designed to provide a hardened, secure system.

Server Manager Console that centralizes the server management tools including roles, features, diagnostics, configuration, and storage.

Server Message Block 2.0 (SMB2) Protocol that improves the efficiency and speed of transferring files between computers.

simple volume A simple volume includes space from only one disk.

single sign-on (SSO) A feature that enables users to enter their credentials once and be able to access other systems and services, based on their rights and permissions, without having to reenter their credentials each time.

site bindings Site configuration information that defines what protocols are connected to a particular port number, IP address, and optional host header.

SMTP (Simple Mail Transfer Protocol) A protocol that defines how e-mail is sent across a network.

snapshot A partial copy of a virtual machine made at a particular moment, used to restore the virtual machine to its state when the snapshot was taken.

Software License Manager (Slmgr.vbs) A Visual Basic (VB) script that is used to configure Volume Activation.

spanned volume A spanned volume has a single address with hard disk sections logically combined and referred to as a single element. You can use up to 32 disks in a spanned volume.

spoofing A way hackers can try to gain access to a system by masquerading as someone or something trusted by the system (e.g., using an email address of someone within the domain).

SSL (Secure Sockets Layer) A protocol that allows identification of a site, and encryption of data passed between the client and the site.

standby mode A cluster node that is not active is said to be in standby mode.

Storage Area Network (SAN) A group of remote storage devices that are accessible to servers and appear to be locally attached to the server.

Storage Manager for SANs Windows Server 2008 console used to manage the physical storage arrays and the Storage Explorer enables you to manage available connections, such as Fibre Channel connections and iSCSI connections.

Storage Services Windows Server 2008 storage technologies for providing fault-tolerant storage.

streaming Serving audio and video directly to a player versus requiring the content to be completely downloaded first.

striped volume A striped volume writes data across multiple disks to increase performance.

subnet address The address that specifies a logical IP network.

subnet mask Used to determine which of the bits in an IP address are part of the subnet address and which bits are part of the host address.

synthetic driver Driver installed on a VM with Integration Services that is optimized for use in the Hyper-V environment.

TLS (Transport Layer Security) The successor to SSL.

Transport Server Provides the core networking components to transmit data, such as operating system images, from a standalone server, but it does not include the WDS image store. It is used for booting from the network using PXE and TFTP and is often used in environments without AD DS, DNS, or DHCP.

Trivial File Transfer Protocol (TFTP) A file transfer protocol that is similar to a basic form of FTP and is used to transfer files; uses User Datagram Protocol (UDP).

unicast A method of streaming where each client connects and has its own dedicated stream of content. Publishing point can be on-demand or broadcast.

Universal Description, Discover, and Integration (UDDI) Windows Server feature that provides the capability to publish and locate Web services information.

virtual directories Allow a Web site or Web application to access content outside of the default file structure, allowing you to create common areas.

virtual disk One or more files stored on the host computer that represent the hard disk of a virtual machine.

Virtual Hard Disk (VHD) format A format specification commonly used with the Hyper-V functionality for supporting a virtual machine hard disk and file systems. A virtual machine hard disk is seen as a hard disk but is implemented as a single file on the native host file system.

virtual instance An installation of Windows Server 2008 in a Hyper-V virtual machine.

virtual IP address The IP address by which the networking services provided by an NLB cluster are accessed by network clients. A DNS host record should exist for the cluster name mapped to this address.

virtual machine (VM) A virtual environment that emulates a physical computer's hardware and BIOS.

virtual network A network configuration created by virtualization software and used by virtual machines for network communication.

virtual private network (VPN) A private network that is like a tunnel through a larger network that enables secure communications between networks.

virtual processor The virtual representation of a physical processor or processor core residing on the host which can be assigned to a virtual machine.

virtualization A process that creates a software environment to emulate a computer's hardware and BIOS, allowing multiple OSs to run on the same physical computer at the same time.

VLAN identification When enabled, subnets, or broadcast domains, can be created on a single external or internal virtual network. Machines that share a common VLAN ID can communicate with one another directly, but those assigned different VLAN IDs must communicate through a router.

volume A logical interface referring to data from sections of multiple disks.

Volume Activation (VA) Provides the capability for volume licensing; automates the activation process and makes the management of the activation process much more efficient.

Volume License Key (VLK) A term that refers to the product key used for volume licensing, allowing one product key to be used for multiple installations.

W3C log file format A customizable text-based format that is the default log file format for IIS. W3C is an organization that develops Web standards based on feedback from member organizations and the public.

Web parts Predefined SharePoint components or modules.

Web Services Windows Server 2008 feature that provides Web server and application platform tools.

weighted path A load balancing policy that assigns weights to determine the path chosen. A path with a higher number, or weight, has less priority. When performing input/output, the path with the least weight is selected.

Windows Deployment Services (WDS) A Windows Server 2008 role that provides the capability to install supported Windows operating systems and applications remotely using a network-based installation.

Windows Management Instrumentation (WMI) A Windows Server 2008 feature that provides Web-based management tools and capabilities.

Windows Remote Management (WinRM) A new feature in Windows Server 2008 that enables remote administration of the server; administrators can remotely run management scripts and manage data on remote machines.

Windows SharePoint Services (WSS) Windows Server 2008 service that provides a collaboration and document management capability.

witness disk The witness disk is shared storage used to store the cluster configuration data and is used for helping to determine the cluster quorum.

XML (Extensible Markup Language) A format for representing, describing, and classifying Web-delivered information.